COMPANION TO RUSSIAN STUDIES
VOLUME 2

AN INTRODUCTION TO
RUSSIAN LANGUAGE AND LITERATURE
edited by Robert Auty and Dimitri Obolensky

COMPANION TO RUSSIAN STUDIES

COMPANION TO RUSSIAN STUDIES 2

AN INTRODUCTION TO

RUSSIAN LANGUAGE AND LITERATURE

EDITED BY
ROBERT AUTY
PROFESSOR OF COMPARATIVE SLAVONIC PHILOLOGY
IN THE UNIVERSITY OF OXFORD

AND

DIMITRI OBOLENSKY
PROFESSOR OF RUSSIAN AND BALKAN HISTORY
IN THE UNIVERSITY OF OXFORD

WITH THE EDITORIAL ASSISTANCE OF
ANTHONY KINGSFORD

CAMBRIDGE UNIVERSITY PRESS
CAMBRIDGE
LONDON · NEW YORK · MELBOURNE

Published by the Syndics of the Cambridge University Press
The Pitt Building, Trumpington Street, Cambridge CB2 1RP
Bentley House, 200 Euston Road, London NW1 2DB
32 East 57th Street, New York, NY 10022, USA
296 Beaconsfield Parade, Middle Park, Melbourne 3206, Australia

First published 1977

Printed in Great Britain by
Western Printing Services Limited, Bristol

Library of Congress Cataloguing in Publication Data

Main entry under title:

An introduction to Russian language and literature.

(Companion to Russian studies, 2)

Includes bibliographies and index.

1. Russian philology – History. I. Auty, Robert.
II. Obolensky, Dimitri, 1918– III. Series.
PG2051.15   891.7   75–10689
ISBN 0 521 20894 7

CONTENTS

CONTENTS

CONTENTS

10

The Soviet Theatre

MICHAEL GLENNY

Lecturer in Russian,
University of Birmingham
page 271

ILLUSTRATIONS

PREFACE

The *Companion to Russian Studies* aims at providing a first orientation for those embarking on the study of Russian civilization, past or present, in its most important aspects. It lays no claim to cover them all. While we hope that it will be of use to university students of Russian language and literature, Russian history, or Soviet affairs, it is equally directed to the general reader interested in these subjects. Each chapter seeks to offer a self-contained introduction to a particular topic; but the editors have not wished to impose a uniform pattern, and each author has been free to approach and present his subject in his own way. Particular care has been taken to provide up-to-date bibliographies, which are intended as a guide to further study.

As is the way with collective works of this kind, the *Companion* has been some years in the making. We should like to express our gratitude to the contributors for their forbearance – sometimes sorely tried – in the face of difficulties and delays which have held up the completion of the enterprise. Economic considerations beyond our control have made it necessary to divide the contents of what had originally been planned as a single book into three volumes. The first is mainly concerned with the history of Russia and the Soviet Union; the second with Russian language and literature; the third with art and architecture. However, the three volumes, for which we share the editorial responsibility, should be regarded as complementary parts of a single whole.

We are grateful to all those at the Cambridge University Press who, over the years, have been involved in this project. Above all we wish to record our debt to Mr Anthony Kingsford, whose great experience in book production, unflagging energy, and expert knowledge of many aspects of Russian studies have been of the greatest value at every stage.

R.A.
D.O.

Oxford
1975

TRANSLITERATION TABLE

		1	2
А	а	a	a
Б	б	b	b
В	в	v	v
Г	г	g	g
Д	д	d	d
Е	е	ye/e	je/e
Ё	ё	yo/o	jo/o
Ж	ж	zh	ž
З	з	z	z
И	и	i	i
Й	й	y	j
К	к	k	k
Л	л	l	l
М	м	m	m
Н	н	n	n
О	о	o	o
П	п	p	p
Р	р	r	r
С	с	s	s
Т	т	t	t
У	у	u	u
Ф	ф	f	f
Х	х	kh	ch
Ц	ц	ts	c
Ч	ч	ch	č
Ш	ш	sh	š
Щ	щ	shch	šč
	ъ	—	—
	ы	y	y
	ь	'	'
Э	э	e	e

Ю ю	yu	ju
Я я	ya	ja
(I i)	i	i
(Ѣ ѣ)	ě	ě
(Ѳ ѳ)	f	f
(V v)	i	i

The transliteration system given in column 1 is used in
all sections of the *Companion* except chapter 1 of this volume,
The Russian Language, where the 'philological' system
given in column 2 is employed. The bracketed letters at
the end of the alphabet were discontinued by the
spelling reform of 1917–18.

ye (*je*) is written for Cyrillic e initially, after vowels,
and after ъ and ь. *o* appears for ё after ж, ч, ш, щ. In
proper names final -ый, -ий is simplified to -*y*.

Proper names or titles which have a generally accepted
anglicized form are usually given in that form, e.g.
Archangel, Dimitri, Gogol, Khrushchev, Likhachev, Lvov,
Maly Theatre, Meyerhold, Moscow, *Novy Mir*, Potemkin,
Vilna.

1

THE RUSSIAN LANGUAGE*

ROBERT AUTY

ORIGINS

Russian is today the native language of more than 150,000,000 persons in the Soviet Union. It is spoken from the borders of White Russia and the Ukraine to the Pacific Ocean, and from the Arctic Circle to the Black and Caspian Seas and the approaches to the Caucasus. In the Soviet border-lands – the Baltic republics, White Russia, the Ukraine, the Caucasus, and central Asia – as well as in the various non-Russian enclaves of Siberia it is the second language of the great majority of the inhabitants.

The present extent and importance of the Russian language are the result of a long and gradual historical process which is discussed elsewhere in this work. It is closely related to the ten other Slavonic languages spoken in Europe today. Together with Ukrainian and White Russian it forms part of the East Slavonic sub-group; slightly farther afield lie the West Slavonic languages – Czech, Slovak, Polish, Sorbian – and the South Slavonic languages – Slovene, Serbo-Croat, Macedonian and Bulgarian. All these languages may be traced back to a single common ancestor which we call Common Slavonic. This was the language spoken by the Slavs when they were still a relatively unitary group of tribes living in a territory which, while we cannot identify it with precision, seems likely to have covered considerable parts of the present-day Ukraine and Poland. Until the sixth and seventh centuries, when the migrations of the Slavonic tribes into the territories which they now occupy were intensified, the Common Slavonic language must have known few dialectal differences. Indeed, even as late as AD 900 it is clear that the regional varieties of Slavonic were

*Russian words are stressed if they are part of the present-day language and the stress is therefore identifiable. Old Russian words are not stressed.

Square brackets enclose phonetic transcriptions according to the system of the International Phonetic Association. Oblique brackets / . . . / are occasionally used to indicate a phoneme as opposed to its various phonetic realizations.

I have used the 'philological' variant of the transliteration system except for names of persons and places, where I have used the normal system employed elsewhere in the book.

The following abbreviations are used: R Russian; OR Old Russian; WR White Russian; OCS Old Church Slavonic.

1

mutually comprehensible to the extent that they were still regarded as a single language. The end of the Common Slavonic period, linguistically speaking, comes with the consolidation of Slavonic national states in the ninth and tenth centuries – Moravia, Bulgaria, Rus', Poland, Croatia, and the Serbian principalities of the Balkans. With the doubtful exception of certain inscriptions, the oldest written records of the Russian language date from the eleventh century. Nevertheless, it is possible, by employing the methods of comparative and historical linguistics, to gain a fairly clear impression of what the Russian language was like in the ninth and tenth centuries, when it was first emerging as a separate entity. No doubt it would be more correct to speak here not of 'Russian' but of 'East Slavonic'. The language spoken in the East Slavonic area from the beginning to the thirteenth or fourteenth century was the common ancestor of the three languages we know today as Russian, White Russian and Ukrainian. Nevertheless, it is convenient to use the familiar and conventionally accepted term 'Old Russian' rather than the neutral but cumbersome 'Old East Slavonic'.

Some other matters of terminology may be touched on here. Russian is still sometimes referred to as 'Great Russian', though 'Little Russian', a term used in tsarist times for Ukrainian, has now rightly fallen into disuse. These appellations, like that of 'West Russian' which was sometimes applied to White Russian, were an attempt to claim the speakers of all three languages for the Russian nation. Similarly, the use of the term 'Ruthenian' for the nationality and language of the Ukrainians of the former Austro-Hungarian Empire was designed to conceal their kinship with the Ukrainians or 'Little Russians' of Russia. 'White Russian' is the term that will be used in this book to translate R белорусский WR беларускі. It is more natural in English than the various hybrids such as Belorussian, Byelorussian, Bielorussian, which are preferred by some writers.

The Slavonic languages are one of the groups of languages which form the Indo-European family. Common Slavonic may be regarded as a sister-language of Greek, Latin, Sanskrit, Hittite, and other ancient Indo-European languages. A particularly close relationship links the Slavonic with the Baltic languages, of which Lithuanian and Latvian are still spoken. One of the characteristic features of Indo-European was a complex system of inflections – nominal and verbal – which can be seen reflected in classical Greek and Latin, in Sanskrit, and in some other ancient Indo-European languages. It is noteworthy that Russian, like most of the other Slavonic languages, has preserved much of this grammatical structure to this day, whereas such languages as English, French or modern Greek have considerably simplified the inflectional system attested for their ancestor-languages a millennium or so ago. Russian, like most of the Slavonic and Baltic languages, has preserved a complex system of nominal declensions

2

which still shows six of the eight Indo-European cases. The verbal conjugations have, it is true, been considerably simplified if we compare them with the system of the classical Greek or Latin verb: the complex system of forms expressing tenses, moods and voice has been greatly reduced. Here, however, the Slavonic languages have developed and systematized the category of aspect: in every verbal form the nature or duration of the action is specified by appropriate morphemes. In Russian the category of aspect has become more important than that of tense.

The Russian vocabulary has been greatly augmented and diversified in the course of the centuries. Alongside the basic Common Slavonic words which Russian shares with its sister-languages we find many strata of loan-words, reflecting the various cultural influences and historical vicissitudes that have affected the life of the Russian nation in different periods: in particular Greek, Norse, Turkic, Polish, French, German and English words have been assimilated. The purism which has caused some languages to reject foreign loans has found little or no expression in the formation of modern Russian.

A special factor in the development of the written and standard spoken forms of the Russian language is the influence of Old Church Slavonic, the earliest written form of Slavonic which came to Russia together with Christianity in the tenth century. This language, based on a Macedonian Slavonic dialect, was close to Russian but differed in many details of phonology, morphology, syntax and lexicon. It was the earliest written language used by the Russians and came to be regarded as a higher, more solemn or 'literary' form of the vernacular. The Russian standard language of today results from the complex interplay of vernacular and Church Slavonic elements.

SOURCES

To study the history of the Russian language we must supplement the language of today, in its standard and dialectal variants, with the written records of the language which now extend over nearly a thousand years. The earliest preserved manuscript is the *Ostromir Codex*, a Russian Church Slavonic translation of the gospels copied in Novgorod in 1056–7. A number of other religious or learned texts are only a little younger. The spoken vernacular is more faithfully reflected in a number of secular texts, mostly legal documents, of which we have examples from the twelfth century onwards. Particularly numerous and linguistically interesting are the texts scratched on birch-bark which have been discovered during the excavations of medieval Novgorod by Soviet archaeologists since 1951. A full list of the manuscript sources up to the end of the fourteenth century is given by

Kiparsky (1963).[1] The dualism of vernacular and Church Slavonic texts continued until the early nineteenth century when the Russian literary language became stabilized as a compromise between the two elements. Even in earlier periods the two variants of the language were not always clearly distinguished. Mutual influences were always at work, even at times when the functional differences between the two 'styles' were deliberately observed. This problem will be discussed at greater length below.

PHONOLOGY

In the eleventh century, the period from which we have the earliest Russian texts, the language must have possessed a system of vowel phonemes which may be tabulated as follows:

$$i \quad y \quad u$$
$$ь \qquad ъ$$
$$ě$$
$$e \quad o$$
$$a$$

Of the phonetic realization of these phonemes in speech we can of course have no certain knowledge, but certain probabilities can be established. *y* was no doubt already very similar to the modern Russian sound represented by the letter ы. ъ and ь, conventionally known as the hard and soft jers, were very short vowels, the first no doubt to some extent labialized (with *u* quality), the second a non-labialized front vowel (with *i* quality). The quality of ě, the sound represented in the old Cyrillic alphabet by the letter ѣ and commonly known by the name of that letter *jat'*, cannot be established with certainty for the earliest period. The evidence of Finnish loan-words from proto-Russian (probably borrowed in the period between the seventh and ninth centuries) points to a very open front vowel: e.g. Finnish *määra* 'measure' < R *měra*. It must in the course of time have become more closed, for it merged, in the different East Slavonic dialects, with either *e* or *i*. In the eleventh century it was no doubt still distinct from both these vowels.

Old Church Slavonic, the language of the religious texts introduced to Russia with Christianity, reflects a sound system which was in certain respects more archaic, closer to Common Slavonic, than that of Old Russian. This included two vowels additional to those listed above, the nasal vowels ę and ǫ. These two sounds, no doubt pronounced in late Common Slavonic times rather similarly to the vowels in French *fin* and *bon*, were represented in the Cyrillic alphabet by the letters ѧ (ę) and

---

[1] See the Guide to further reading, p. 39.

Ѫ (ǫ). Eleventh-century texts written in Russia frequently confuse ǫ and u, ę and ja, so that it is clear that these vowels had by then become denasalized. That the nasal vowels had existed in an earlier phase of Russian is attested by Finnish loan-words such as *kuontalo* 'tow' < *kǫdělъ*, cf. R кудéль, and *suntio* 'sexton' < *sǫdьja*, cf. R судья 'judge'. It is generally supposed that the process of denasalization was complete by the mid-tenth century. The chief evidence for this is provided by the Slavonic names of the Dnieper rapids which are listed in the treatise *De administrando imperio* composed in about 950 by the Byzantine Emperor Constantine Porphyrogenitus. One of these rapids is given as βερούτζη which the author says has the meaning 'the boiling of the water'. There is little doubt that the East Slavonic word in question is the present participle *vьručьjь* 'boiling, seething', which is a development of the Common Slavonic *vьrǫtj-*. Another rapid is named by the Emperor as νεασήτ which must be an East Slavonic *nejasyt'*, deriving from Common Slavonic *nejęsytъ* 'the insatiable one'. Thus, it is clear that the nasal vowels were not present in the Russian phonological system even in the tenth century. With the introduction of Old Church Slavonic to Rus' at the end of that century the two letters indicating the nasals were brought in but were regarded by Russian speakers as no more than orthographical variants for the phonemes *u* and *'a*. The letter for the back nasal Ѫ was used to a certain extent in the middle ages but was ultimately abandoned. Ѧ, the letter for the front nasal, eventually became the most frequent representation of *'a*, and lives on in a modified form in the new Cyrillic letter я.

The jers, also known as reduced vowels and (especially in grammars written in Russia) as surds (*глухие*), underwent various changes in all the Slavonic languages. Their development in Russian will be discussed below. It seems probable that they survived in Russian longer than they did in most other Slavonic languages. In the Russian of the eleventh century they were still present as individual phonemes, as they were in the earliest Old Church Slavonic.

The phonetic value of *jat'* in late Common Slavonic and in Old Russian cannot be established with certainty. It had developed from Indo-European *ē* and from the Indo-European diphthongs *ai̯* and *oi̯* (probably with an intervening monophthongal stage). It seems probable that in the late Common Slavonic stage it had become some kind of diphthong, perhaps *eä*. In Old Church Slavonic *ě* and *'a* coalesced in a sound which was probably *ä*, the vowel heard in English *man*. In eleventh-century Old Russian the pronunciation of *jat'* probably varied regionally; some texts already show a tendency for this sound to merge with *e*.

In the course of the historical period the vowel system that has been described above was simplified by the disappearance of the phonemes *ь*, *ъ* and *ě*. All the other vowels remained, though various phonetic processes

5

brought about changes in their frequency and distribution. A further development of the greatest importance was a reduction or change in quality which affected all unstressed vowels, with the result that modern Russian has two different vowel systems, one for stressed and one for unstressed vowels.

A development which took place in the period before the appearance of the first texts, and which distinguished the East Slavonic languages from all other varieties of Slavonic, affected the Common Slavonic groups *ăr*, *ăl* when they were preceded and followed by consonants. These groups are conventionally designated *tărt*, *tălt*, where *t* represents any consonant. Common Slavonic short *ă* changed to *o* at the end of the prehistoric period; some scholars assume that this change had already taken place at an earlier stage of Common Slavonic and designate the groups in question as *tort* and *tolt*. In Russian these groups changed into *torot, tolot*. This treatment, with the development of an additional syllable, is known as pleophony (R полногла́сие). Other Slavonic languages, notably Old Church Slavonic, treated these groups in a different way, lengthening the vowel and reversing the order of vowel and liquid, to produce *trat* and *tlat*. Common Slavonic long *ā* remained in the Slavonic languages as *a*; quantity disappeared as a phonemically relevant feature. Thus Common Slavonic *gărdŭ, vărnŭ, gălvā, băltă* became R го́род 'town', во́рон 'raven', голова́ 'head', боло́то 'swamp' as against OCS *gradŭ, vranŭ, glava, blato*. Common to both treatments is the tendency to abolish closed syllables: in the period before the disappearance of the weak jers all syllables in Slavonic languages ended with a vowel.

Analogous changes affected the Common Slavonic groups *tert, telt*. Common Slavonic *bergŭ, merti, melkă, šelmŭ* (borrowed from Germanic *helm*) became R бе́рег 'bank', (у)мере́ть 'to die', молоко́ 'milk', OR шеломъ 'helmet' as against OCS *brĕgŭ, mrĕti, mlĕko, šlĕmŭ*. The slightly aberrant treatment of the *telt* groups in Russian is no doubt due to the influence of the velar (back) *l* which, in the case of молоко́, induced the velarization of both the surrounding vowels. In the case of шеломъ *š*, still palatalized in Old Russian, no doubt caused the retention of the front vowel in the first syllable.

Phonetic changes of a similar character affected the Common Slavonic initial groups *ărt-, ălt-*, again giving rise to differences between Russian and Old Church Slavonic. While Common Slavonic *ărdlă, ălnŭ* become R ра́ло 'plough', лань 'doe' and similarly OCS *ralo*, Church Slavonic *lani*, Common Slavonic *ărbŭ, ălkŭtĭ* become OR роб 'slave', R ло́коть 'elbow', but OCS *rabŭ, lakŭtĭ*. The different treatment of the two sets of words in Russian (which is paralleled in the West Slavonic languages) is generally explained as the result of differences of intonation in Common Slavonic times. *ărdlă, ălnŭ* are assumed to have had rising (acute) intonation against falling (circumflex) intonation in *ărbŭ, ălkŭtĭ*. In Russian, as in the West

Slavonic languages, these intonational differences were transmuted into differences of vowel quality. While there is some evidence in the intonational and quantitative characteristics of certain West and South Slavonic languages to make this theory a plausible one, the matter is complicated and other explanations are possible.

A very early change, but one which seems still to have been in progress in the early historical period, was that of an initial e- (je-) to o-. Thus a Common Slavonic *jezero*, preserved as such in Old Church Slavonic, becomes R óзеро 'lake'. Norse and Greek names borrowed in the ninth and tenth centuries show this change: Old Norse *Helga* > R Óльга, Old Norse *Helgi* > OR Ольгъ > R Олéг, Greek Εὐδοκία > OR Овьдотья > R Авдóтья. This change is peculiar to the East Slavonic languages.

Important changes affected the jers in the period from the tenth to the twelfth centuries. In late Common Slavonic times these vowels must have been pronounced rather differently according to their position in the word. Those in 'weak' position disappeared in all the Slavonic languages, those in 'strong' position became full vowels. In Russian, as in the other East Slavonic languages, strong ь became e and strong ъ became o. To determine whether a jer was strong or weak it is necessary to count the jers in successive syllables beginning with the end of the word. The odd jers are in weak position and disappear, while the even ones are in strong position and become 'vocalized'. Thus Common Slavonic *kъto*, *dǫbъ* become R кто 'who', дуб 'oak'; Common Slavonic *sъnъ*, *dьnь* become R сон 'sleep', день 'day'; and Common Slavonic *dьnьsь* becomes R (archaic and poetic) днесь 'today'. The oldest preserved Old Church Slavonic texts, written in the tenth and early eleventh centuries, preserve the jers in their original positions to a very large extent, and so represent the Common Slavonic situation with relatively little change. In Russian, too, the eleventh-century texts, such as the Ostromir Gospels, write the jers in the great majority of cases. It seems likely that isolated jers were the first to disappear, perhaps first of all in final position, as we may deduce from the example, already quoted, of νεασήτ ~ неясыть, where the Greek spelling indicates the loss of the final vowel but is unable to represent the palatalization of the consonant -t'. Medial jers followed, and the Ostromir Codex shows examples such as кто and книга. The 'vocalization' of the strong jers seems to have been a slightly later process. Early thirteenth-century manuscripts confuse the letters ь and e, ъ and o, which indicates that the jers had already merged with the appropriate full vowels by this date. This confusion is particularly characteristic of thirteenth-century texts from certain northern areas, in which we find, for example, берьго (= берегъ) and отидето (= отидетъ) (Treaty between Smolensk and Riga, 1229). Thus it is reasonable to assume that the process of change extended over the greater part of the twelfth century.

In certain cases the treatment of the jers seems not to have followed the regular pattern. These exceptions can for the most part be explained by analogy, by the desire to avoid difficult consonant groups, or by the influence of Church Slavonic, in which (especially in singing) the jers continued to be pronounced, though probably as *e* and *o*. It is sometimes claimed that a jer under the stress was more likely to be vocalized, even though isolated, than one in unstressed position. However, the majority of cases of this kind can be explained in other ways. Analogy affected in particular certain noun-paradigms where the regular treatment of the jers brought about discrepancies. Thus съньмъ (nom. sing.) regularly gave OR снемъ 'assembly' but съньма (gen. sing.) became сонма. The regularity of the paradigm was restored by the acceptance of сонм as the nominative form. чьсть develops regularly to честь 'honour' but the genitive чьсти appears in Old Russian as чти. The modern language has brought in the analogical form чести. It must be assumed that the 'regular' and 'irregular' forms existed side by side for a certain period before the paradigm became fixed; and there are many examples of such doublets in Old Russian, e.g. жерца/жреца < жьрьца ~ жьрьць > жрец 'priest'.

The tendency to avoid complex consonant groups is apparent in such forms as пёстрый < пьстрый 'variegated', стекло́ < стькло 'glass' (we still find the alternative скло in Pushkin) and the place-name Псков, where Old Russian still has the alternative Плесковъ (cf. the German form of the name *Pleskau*) from Пльсковъ.

Church Slavonic influence is responsible for such forms as собо́р 'cathedral' side by side with сбор 'collection' < съборъ, восто́к 'east' < въстокъ and for all instances of the prefix воз-, where the jer was invariably isolated.

Cases where stress has been adduced as the influence preventing the disappearance of a jer are доска́ 'board' < дъска and тёща 'mother-in-law' < тьща. In the former case however it is more likely that the form is analogical, influenced by the genitive plural досок < дъскъ; and in the latter case it was no doubt the analogy with тесть 'father-in-law' < тьсть that was decisive.

Despite the workings of analogy that have been illustrated above many paradigms still show the results of the changes in the jers in the varying forms of their stem. Alternations of the type сон/сна and день/дня came to be regarded as regular, to such an extent that some other nouns in which there had never been a jer were assimilated to the same pattern. This is the case with ров gen. рва 'ditch' formerly рова and лёд gen. льда 'ice' formerly леда.

In a number of words a jer was followed by *j* + vowel, as in the nom. sing. masc. of adjectives such as Common Slavonic *novъjь* 'new' or in words such as *mъjǫ* 'I wash', *pьjǫ* 'I drink', *šьja* 'neck'. Here the jers generally developed regularly, so that we find OR новои 'new', пью 'I drink'. When an isolated jer of this kind was under the stress it was vocalized, so that we have R мóю 'I wash', шéя 'neck'. In its treatment of these 'tense' jers, as they are generally called, Russian differs both from Old Church Slavonic and from the other East Slavonic languages. In Old Church Slavonic tense ъ develops to *y* and tense ь to *i*, so that we have OCS *novyjь, myjǫ, pijǫ, šija*. A similar development took place in Ukrainian and White Russian, producing Ukrainian новий, мию, п'ю, шия and White Russian новы, мыю, п'ю, шыя. One consequence of the different development of these groups in Old Church Slavonic and Russian is that a number of verbal nouns in -*ьje* have alternative forms, sometimes leading to semantic distinction. The vernacular Russian житьё 'life', бытьё 'existence' stand in the modern language side by side with the Church Slavonic житиé 'life of a saint', бытиé 'being', 'the Book of Genesis'.

As has been noted above, the phonemes /e/ and /ě/ must have been still distinct in the earliest Russian. It may well be that the original distinction was simply one of quantity /æ/∼/æ:/; but it seems probable that this was reinterpreted as a qualitative difference /æ/∼/e/. The phonetic realization of the closed variant may have differed in different dialectal areas. This would explain the fact that *ě* changed in some North Russian dialects and in Ukrainian to *i*, while in the South Russian dialects and in White Russian it coalesced with *e*. In the standard language of today, based on the dialect of Moscow, the reflex of original *ě* is *e*. A few apparent exceptions can be explained by sporadic causes.

Another change which probably took place in the eleventh and twelfth centuries was the transformation of *e* to *o*. This occurred when *e* was stressed and was either in final position or followed by a hard consonant. This change is not expressed in normal Russian orthographical practice; though occasionally the ′*o* pronunciation is indicated by adding a diaeresis to the e, thus весёлый 'gay', сёла 'villages'. The change affected not only original *e* but also *e* < ь, e.g. осёл 'ass'. In twelfth- and thirteenth-century texts there are a number of examples of orthographic o for ё in unstressed syllables, e.g. съкажомъ 'we shall say'. The fact that Ukrainian still shows many cases of this kind has led some scholars to believe that the change originally affected *e* in all syllables but was later restricted, in Russian and White Russian, to stressed syllables. Moreover, the great majority of the early Russian examples, and all the Ukrainian ones, are of *e* preceded by *š, ž, č, šč* or *j*. It is therefore assumed that the change took place initially after these sounds and was later extended, in Russian and White Russian but not in Ukrainian, to every stressed *e*. Nevertheless, the Russian language today shows numerous examples of stressed *e*. They can be explained in various ways. The change *e* > *o* seems to have been completed at a time when *e* and *ě* were still separate phonemes: words containing stressed *ě* remained unaffected by the change. Thus we have лес < лѣсъ 'forest' and пе́на < пѣна 'foam'. Church Slavonic words were unaffected by the change and retained their original pronunciation, e.g. крест 'cross', же́ртва 'sacrifice'. This situation gave rise to some doublets, e.g. не́бо 'heaven' but нёбо 'palate'. In some cases an originally soft consonant following the stressed *e* was later hardened, after completion of the change of *e* to *o*. Thus the stressed vowel in коне́ц 'end', вене́ц 'garland' reminds us that *c* was soft until the sixteenth century. The *e* of пе́рвый 'first', верх 'summit' was retained because the originally soft *r* was only hardened in the eighteenth century. Stressed *e* is also found in a number of foreign loan-words, e.g. склеп 'vault' from Polish, биле́т 'ticket' from German, etc., and in the prefixes не- and без-.

Analogy has further modified the state of affairs that has just been outlined. The plural of звезда́ < звѣзда 'star' is звёзды by analogy with such words as сестра́ ∼ сёстры. In verbal forms such as несёте 'you bear', идёте 'you go' the change to *o* has taken place despite the following soft consonant, by analogy with other forms, in the paradigm such as несёт 'he bears', идём 'we go'.

The most far-reaching changes in the Russian vowel system were the result of the reductions of unstressed syllables which are collectively known as *akan'je* ('a pronunciation'). In modern standard Russian the system of vowels in stressed syllables is as follows:

$$i \quad (y) \quad u$$
$$e \quad o$$
$$a$$

In unstressed syllables however only the following vowel system appears:

$$i \quad u$$
$$a$$

That is to say, unstressed *a* and *o* appear as [a] or its allophones [ʌ] and [ə], while unstressed *e* appears as [i]. This state of affairs is the result of modifications of unstressed syllables which took place, in all probability, between the thirteenth and fifteenth centuries in the dialects of south and central Russia. The North Russian dialects were not affected by these changes and are to this day characterized by *okan'je* ('o pronunciation'). White Russian also shows *akan'je*, but not Ukrainian. In modern standard Russian unstressed *o* appears as [a] or [ʌ] in immediately pretonic position and in initial position but as [ə] in all other positions. Thus we have [gəra'da] 'towns', ['gorət] 'town', [atxa'dit] 'to go away', [gərəda'voj] 'urban'. Unstressed *e* appears as [i] in standard Muscovite pronunciation, and this pronunciation is now the most widespread, though at one time [e] or [eⁱ] were also common. Thus we have [şi'stra] 'sister', [şi'lo] 'village'. Unstressed /'a/ or /ja/ are also generally pronounced [i] in an immediately pretonic syllable. In other unstressed syllables *e* and *'a, ja* are pronounced ['ə] or ['ı].

The first certain indications of *akan'je* in the texts are found in the fourteenth century, in the form of sporadic confusion of *a* and *o* in unstressed syllables. Despite this a number of scholars have strongly argued the thesis that this phenomenon represents a continuation of the Common Slavonic state of affairs. In Balto-Slavonic and in early Common Slavonic, Indo-European short *a* and *o* coalesced as *a* (though it may well in the later stages have developed a certain degree of rounding and may then have been similar to the vowel in American English *hot* or Hungarian *van*). In the late Common Slavonic period this *a* changed to *o*. Those who argue that *akan'je* was not a late development believe that in the later White Russian and south Russian areas the change to *o* took place only under the stress. The chief weakness of this theory is the absence of support in the early texts. It is sometimes argued that this is due to the fact that most of the early texts come from areas (the Ukraine and north Russia) which developed *okan'je* and that we therefore cannot expect to find confusion of *a/o* in them. The influence of Old Church Slavonic is also sometimes mentioned as a factor which obscured the presence of *akan'je* in the spoken language of the period of the early texts. However, even in texts that come from areas which now show *akan'je* we find no traces of it before the fourteenth century. For instance, in the treaty between Smolensk and Riga of 1229, which shows a number of vernacular features and must to some extent reflect the speech of Smolensk (now in the area of *akan'je*), *a* and *o* are not confused. Late origin is therefore likely; though the problem cannot be regarded as finally solved. It is difficult, moreover, to explain the geographical distribution of the phenomenon, with *akan'je* in the south-east (south Russia) and north-west (White Russia) and *okan'je* in the south-west (the Ukraine) and north-east (north Russia). It has plausibly been argued that *akan'je* arose through the influence on Russian of Mordvinian, a Uralic language spoken in a wide area between the Oka and the Volga. In the Moksha variety of Mordvinian every unstressed *o* is pronounced [a] or [ə]. If this theory is correct the phenomenon may have originated in the thirteenth century, perhaps in the region of Ryazan', and then have spread to the north-west and south.

The consonantal system inherited by the earliest Russian from late Common Slavonic was as follows:

p	b	t	d			k	g
	v	s	z	š	ž	ch	
		c		č			
	m		n		ň		
			l		l'		
			r		r'		

11

At this period the palatalization of consonants was not phonemically relevant, though it is fairly certain that all consonants were palatalized when they were followed by a front vowel (*e, ě, ь, i, ę*). *k, g, ch* were always followed by back vowels. *c* (properly *c'*), *č, š, ž* were always soft and had no hard counterparts. It is noteworthy that at this stage the phoneme /f/ did not exist in Russian. Foreign *f* appears in early loan-words as *p*, e.g. па́рус 'sail' from Greek φάρος, О́сип 'Joseph' from Greek Ἰωσήφ. When the jers in weak position disappeared /v/ often came to stand immediately before a voiceless consonant and became assimilated to it as [f], e.g. въторъи > второ́й 'second' (phonetically [fta'roj]). The same change affected a /v/ which after the fall of the weak jers came to be in final position, where all consonants were unvoiced, e.g. домовъ > домо́в 'houses (gen. pl.)', phonetically [da'mof]. Thus the sound [f] became frequent as an allophone of /v/ and it became easier to accept foreign loan-words containing *f* without modification of the sound. Thus modern Russian has words such as факт 'fact', февра́ль 'February'. Moreover, the dental spirant [θ], occurring in Greek, was taken over in loan-words as [f], e.g. the personal names Фёдор < Greek Θεόδωρος, Фёкла < Greek Θέκλα.

The disappearance of the weak jers also exercised an important influence on the consonant system of Russian in that it created a situation in which the 'hardness' or 'softness' of consonants became phonemically relevant. Thus, as long as the jers were still pronounced цѣпъ 'flail' was distinguished from цѣпь 'chain' by the quality of the final vowel; but after the disappearance of these vowels the words were distinguished only by the presence or absence of palatalization in the final consonant. This development was also encouraged by the change *e > o*, after the completion of which pairs such as нос 'nose' ~ нёс 'he carried' and вол 'ox' ~ вёл 'he led' were distinguished only by the softness or hardness of the initial consonant.

In the course of the Old Russian period certain changes also affected those consonants which in the earliest phase had been invariably soft: *c, č, š, ž*. Of these only *č* has remained soft in the contemporary language. *š* and *ž* probably became hard in the course of the thirteenth or early fourteenth century, as we deduce from such fourteenth-century spellings as жывите 'you live', держыть 'to hold', both attested in 1389. The traditional spelling with и has, however, prevailed in the modern language, thus masking the hard character of these sounds. *c* lost its palatalization rather later: the earliest orthographical indications of the hardening occur in the sixteenth century, e.g. отецъ 'father', концы 'end (loc. sing.)' in the late sixteenth-century *Domostroj*.

In Common Slavonic and in the earliest Russian the velar consonants *k, g, ch* could only appear before back vowels. Already in the eleventh century, however, we find examples of these sounds before *e* and *ě* both in loan-words and in native inflectional endings, and by the fourteenth century it seems that the groups *ky, gy, chy* had been universally replaced by *ki, gi, chi*. Thus OR Кыевъ > R Ки́ев, OR ногы > R но́ги 'legs', OR хытрыи > R хи́трый 'clever'.

ACCENTUATION

From the comparison of the attested Slavonic languages among themselves and with the Baltic languages we know that early Common Slavonic had a number of phonemically relevant prosodic characteristics. The stress could be on any syllable of a word; vowels might be distinguished by quantity (long or short); and, at any rate in long stressed syllables, intonation played a distinguishing role: we speak of acute (probably rising) or circumflex (probably falling or falling-rising) intonation. The closest approach to this system that has survived in the spoken vernaculars of today is found in certain archaic Serbo-Croatian dialects spoken in the northern Adriatic region. All other Slavonic dialects, and all the standard Slavonic languages, show considerable modifications of the Common Slavonic state of affairs. Russian, in common with the other East Slavonic languages, has lost the distinctive features of quantity and intonation but has retained free word-stress. In a number of cases we can, by comparing Russian with other languages that have retained free stress, establish the position of the word-stress in Common Slavonic. It is however certain that many changes have taken place in the stress of Russian words since the earliest period, many of them due to morphological analogy, i.e. the influence of paradigmatic patterns. Moreover, accentual changes are constantly taking place, if only to a limited extent, and even in the present-day language we can often distinguish obsolescent, 'old-fashioned', from more modern accentuations in individual words or paradigms. Thus, for example, the pronunciation of the plural oblique cases of язы́к 'tongue, language' with stem-stress as язы́кам, язы́ках etc. has now almost entirely been replaced by ending-stress: языка́м, языка́х; and the loanwords библио́тека, доку́мент are now generally pronounced библиоте́ка, докуме́нт. The study of these accentual changes is however difficult in view of the limited sources available. In the Kievan period texts were in general not stressed. In the fourteenth and fifteenth centuries it became the custom, under the influence of Serbian and Bulgarian scribal habits, to indicate the word-stress by diacritic signs. But many of the texts concerned were Church Slavonic rather than vernacular Russian; and Church Slavonic had often retained or developed different accentuations from those of the popular language. Moreover, the accentuation of secular texts

was abandoned with the orthographic reform of Peter I (1710). Nevertheless, the study of the texts available, together with other evidence, such
as the dictionaries and grammars of the eighteenth and nineteenth centuries, enables certain conclusions to be reached about the changes that
have taken place, though research on this subject has not long been
systematically pursued. The most important results have been obtained
by V. Kiparsky (1962).[1]

MORPHOLOGY: THE NOUN

Common Slavonic inherited from Indo-European a system of nominal
inflection (declension) similar to that which we find in Greek, Latin or
Sanskrit. Of the eight Indo-European cases seven were retained: the
ablative seems to have coalesced with the genitive. Modern Russian retains
six of these: the vocative has disappeared except for a few stereotyped
archaisms. In general, the declensional system of the modern Russian noun
is very close to the medieval state of affairs: such changes as have taken
place are changes of detail and have not greatly modified the essential
pattern.

In Common Slavonic the following nominal declension-classes were
distinguished, according to the vowel or consonant which characterized
the stem-suffix (the word-forming suffix which originally linked the root,
which expressed the basic meaning of a noun, with the case endings):
feminine *a*-stems (*ryba*), feminine *ja*-stems (*zemlja*), masculine and neuter
o-stems (*rabъ*, *město*), masculine and neuter *jo*-stems (*konь*, *polje*),
masculine *u*-stems (*domъ*), feminine *y(ъv)*-stems (*kry*, gen. *krъve*),
masculine and feminine *i*-stems (*pǫtь*, *kostь*), neuter *n*-stems (*sěmę*),
masculine *t*-stems (*lokъtь*), neuter *nt*-stems (*telę*, gen. *telęte*), feminine
r-stems (*mati*, gen. *matere*), neuter *s*-stems (*slovo*, gen. *slovese*).

In Old Russian all these classes are identifiable except the *t*-stems which
early coalesced with the *jo*-stems. Examples of the paradigms that existed
in the earliest stage of Russian are shown in the tables below. Many of
the consonantal stems had ceased to be productive even in the Common
Slavonic period; and the development of the Russian language has seen
a continuing process of assimilation of these anomalous classes to more
productive ones. In Old Church Slavonic, which reflects the late Common
Slavonic stage, the degree of reciprocal influence between the *o*-stems and
u-stems was so great that it is difficult to speak of them any longer as
separate classes; and in Russian the same process of fusion was completed in the historical period. The most productive classes were the
a/ja-stems, *o/jo*-stems, and to a lesser extent the *i*-stems.

[1] See Guide to further reading on p. 39.

MORPHOLOGY: THE NOUN

NOUNS: VOCALIC STEMS

		-a-	-ja-	-o- m.	-jo- m.
Singular	N.	рыба	земля	рабъ	конь
	A.	рыбу	землю	рабъ	конь
	G.	рыбы	землѣ	раба	коня
	D.	рыбѣ	земли	рабу	коню
	L.	рыбѣ	земли	рабѣ	кони
	I.	рыбою	землею	рабомь	конемь
	V.	рыбо	земле	рабе	коню
Plural	N.	рыбы	землѣ	раби	кони
	A.	рыбы	землѣ	рабы	конѣ
	G.	рыбъ	земль	рабъ	конь
	D.	рыбамъ	землямъ	рабомъ	конемъ
	L.	рыбахъ	земляхъ	рабѣхъ	конихъ
	I.	рыбами	землями	рабы	кони
Dual	N.A.	рыбѣ	земли	раба	коня
	G.L.	рыбу	землю	рабу	коню
	D.I.	рыбама	земляма	рабома	конема

		-o-	-jo- n.	-u-	-i- m.	-i- f.
Singular	N.	мѣсто	поле	домъ	путь	кость
	A.	мѣсто	поле	домъ	путь	кость
	G.	мѣста	поля	дому	пути	кости
	D.	мѣсту	полю	домови	пути	кости
	L.	мѣстѣ	поли	дому	пути	кости
	I.	мѣстомь	полемь	домъмь	путьмь	костью
	V.	мѣсто	поле	дому	пути	кости
Plural	N.	мѣста	поля	домове	путье	кости
	A.	мѣста	поля	домы	пути	кости
	G.	мѣстъ	поль	домовъ	путьи	костьи
	D.	мѣстомъ	полемъ	домъмъ	путьмъ	костьмъ
	L.	мѣстѣхъ	полихъ	домъхъ	путьхъ	костьхъ
	I.	мѣсты	поли	домъми	путьми	костьми
Dual	N.A.	мѣстѣ	поли	домы	пути	кости
	G.L.	мѣсту	полю	домову	путью	костью
	D.I.	мѣстома	полема	домъма	путьма	костьма

NOUNS: CONSONANTAL STEMS

		-es- n.	-men- n.	-ent- n.
Singular	N.	слово	имя	теля
	A.	слово	имя	теля
	G.	словесе, -и	имене, -и	теляте, -и
	D.	словеси	имени	теляти
	L.	словесе, -и	имене, -и	теляте, -и
	I.	словесьмь	именьмь	телятьмь

15

N.	словеса	имена	телята
A.	словеса	имена	телята
G.	словесъ	именъ	телятъ
D.	словесьмъ	именьмъ	телятьмъ
L.	словесьхъ	именьхъ	телятьхъ
I.	словесы	имены	теляты

Dual N.A.	словесѣ	именѣ	телятѣ
G.L.	словесу	имену	теляту
D.I.	словесьма	именьма	телятьма

	-n- m.	-jan- m.	-ъv- (-ū-) f.	-er- f.
Singular N.	дьнь	(горожанинъ	цьркы	мати
A.	дьнь	горожанинъ	цьркъвь	матерь
G.	дьне, -и	горожанина	цьркъве, -и	матере, -и
D.	дьни	горожанину	цьркъви	матери
L.	дьне, -и	горожанинѣ	цьркъве, -и	матере, -и
I.	дьньмь	горожаниномь)	цьркъвью	матерью
Plural N.	дьне, -ье	горожане	цьркъви	матери
A.	дьни	горожаны	цьркъви	матери
G.	дьнъ, -ьи	горожанъ	цьркъвъ	матеръ
D.	дьньмъ	горожаньмъ	цьркъвамъ	матерьмъ
L.	дьньхъ	горожаньхъ	цьркъвахъ	матерьхъ
I.	дьньми	горожаны	цьркъвами	матерьми
Dual N.A.	дьни	(горожанина	цьркъви	матери
S.L.	дьну, -ью	горожанину	цьркъву	матеру
D.I.	дьньма	горожанинома)	цьркъвама	матерьма

The seven cases of the Common Slavonic noun were the nominative, genitive, dative, accusative, instrumental, locative, and vocative. There were three numbers, singular, dual and plural, as in other early Indo-European languages. Of these categories the dual number and the vocative case soon disappeared from the language, though they left behind them residual traces which are still present in the language of today.

It is probable that the dual number was obsolescent already at the time of the earliest recorded texts. Its declension was a restricted one, containing three forms which expressed nominative–accusative–vocative, genitive–locative, and dative–instrumental functions respectively. Examples of the use of plural forms when the dual would be expected, and also incorrect uses of the dual forms, are found from the early thirteenth century; and although fourteenth-century texts still provide many instances of the regular use of the dual forms there is little doubt that these are due to the conserving influence of Church Slavonic.

In the modern language we may regard óчи 'eyes' and ýши 'ears' as dual forms. Despite certain difficulties in explaining the -i ending in these cases it is clearly not a plural ending; plural forms would be *ока, *уха (or possibly очеса, *ушеса – the former actually attested as a Church

Slavonicism – for both these nouns were originally *s*-stems). Глазá, the normal word for 'eyes' in the modern language, is also no doubt an unchanged dual form, though this fact is obscured by the spread of -*a* as a nominative plural ending, as will be noted below.

Descriptive grammars state that the genitive singular is used after the numbers 2, 3, and 4. The source of this usage is no doubt in dual phrases such as два столá 'two tables', два коня 'two horses'. In certain instances a difference of accentuation between the nominative dual and the genitive singular has survived into the modern language: два часá 'two o'clock', but gen. sing. чáса, два шагá 'two steps', but gen. sing. шáга. Once these forms ceased to be felt as dual they were reinterpreted as genitives and the usage spread to other classes of noun, e.g. две жéнщины 'two women', and to the other numerals, 3 and 4, which had originally been followed by the nominative plural, unlike the numerals from 5 upwards which were followed by the genitive plural. Thus in the modern language we have три сестры́ 'three sisters', четы́ре гóда 'four years'.

Like the dual forms, those of the vocative case had a limited inventory even in Common Slavonic times. No vocative forms are recorded for the consonantal stems and the vocative is primarily, if not exclusively, associated with nouns denoting living beings. The earliest texts (e.g. the Ostromir Codex of 1056–7) show examples of the nominative being used for an expected vocative; and it is certain that the vocative had disappeared as a living category by the fourteenth century, and very likely a good deal earlier. The situation in the spoken vernacular is obscured in this, as in so many other instances, by the influence of Church Slavonic where the vocative lived on. Certain stereotyped forms, e.g. княже 'prince', господине 'lord', сыну 'son', lived on into the seventeenth century. In the modern language we find Бóже 'God', and Гóсподи 'Lord', either in their proper religious sense or as expletives; and on occasion other vocatives occur in high style, or sometimes with humorous connotations, e.g. óтче 'father', человéче 'man'. Early confusion between the vocative and the nominative no doubt explains the use of vocative forms in medieval northern texts (chiefly from Novgorod) of the type: 'Заложи церковь Съмьюне' 'Symeon founded a church' (Novgorod Chronicle, 1377) or even: 'Въдале Варламе . . .,' 'Varlam gave . . .' (late twelfth-century deed of gift), where the vocative ending has even spread to the participial form as a totally redundant suffix.

An important change in the functional employment of the case-endings was brought about by the development of the genitive–accusative, that is to say the use, in respect of nouns denoting living beings, of the genitive in accusative function. This usage, already attested though not universal in Old Church Slavonic, first affected masculine nouns, where the nominative and accusative forms had become identical in Common Slavonic times:

17

rabъ, конь, sуnъ, gostь could all be either nominative or accusative. Thus subject and object were not formally distinguished, and the urge to restore such a distinction no doubt led to use of genitive forms with accusative function. There are examples of the genitive–accusative in the earliest Russian texts, but the old and the new accusative forms lived side by side for centuries. By the sixteenth century the genitive–accusative was usual for persons but not yet for animals, but this distinction had ceased to be made by the end of the seventeenth century. The usage never spread to the singular of feminine nouns, where the distinction between nominative and accusative had never disappeared (жена́ nom., жену́ acc.; the feminine *i*-stems included no words denoting animate beings). In the plural the genitive–accusative established itself more slowly. Originally nominative and accusative were distinguished in the masculine *o*-stems (раби nom., рабы, acc.), but this distinction began to be lost from the thirteenth century: the first examples of genitive plural forms with accusative function are found in the fourteenth century. These are masculine nouns; but in the sixteenth century we also find this usage with feminine nouns, where it is normal by the end of the following century. A few set phrases in the modern language retain stereotyped old accusatives: вы́йти за́муж 'to marry [of a woman]'; на́ конь! 'to horse!'; произвести́ в офице́ры 'to commission as an officer', приня́ть в чле́ны па́ртии 'to receive into the party' etc.

The most important changes of case-endings affect the forms of the nominative plural of masculine nouns and the streamlining of the oblique cases of the plural. In the earliest Old Russian the nominative plural of masculine *o*-stems ended in -*i* which, owing to sound-changes of the Common Slavonic period, palatalized a preceding velar consonant: thus we have вълкъ 'wolf' ∼ вълци, другъ 'friend' ∼ друзи, монахъ 'monk' ∼ монаси. This -*i* contrasted with the -*y* of the accusative plural. Already in the thirteenth century however there are instances of -*y* in the nominative. After a period of confusion between -*i* and -*y* the latter ending seems to have become almost universal by the late fifteenth century. After the change of *ky, gy, chy* to *ki, gi, chi* the accusatives волки etc. replaced the anomalous nominatives mentioned above. In the modern language two *o*-stems retain the ending -*i*: сосе́ди 'neighbours' and че́рти 'devils'. The reason for this is not clear; but the 'soft' nominative ending has caused the entire plural paradigm to enter the *jo*-stem class, so that the oblique cases appear as сосе́дей, сосе́дям . . ., чертей, чертя́м . . . In general we must see the spread of the -*y* ending in the nominative plural as part of the tendency to introduce greater uniformity into the multiplicity of forms presented by the Common Slavonic declensional system. The generalization of -*y* as a nominative plural ending meant that this case had the same ending in both the masculine *o*-stems and the feminine *a*-stems: the *jo*-stems and *ja*-stems already shared an identical ending in the nominative and accusative plural: кони ∼ души.

However, another change affecting the nominative plural of masculine *o*/*jo*-stem nouns tended in the opposite direction. Through the introduction and widespread application of the nominative plural ending -*á*/-*já* Russian set itself apart from all other Slavonic languages. Forms such as городá which cannot be interpreted as duals occur from the late fifteenth century onwards with increasing frequency until in the early eighteenth century they are extremely common. This form has continued to spread until the present day, so that a great number of common nouns show this ending, e.g. век 'age' ∼ векá, вéчер 'evening' ∼ вечерá, дом 'house' ∼ домá, жéмчуг 'pearl' ∼ жемчугá, край 'region' ∼ края́, нóмер '[hotel] room' ∼ номерá, пóезд 'train' ∼ поездá, учи́тель 'teacher' ∼ учителя́. The spread of the -*a* ending has gone even further in the colloquial language, and normative grammars tend to discourage the use in writing of such forms as библиотекаря́ 'librarians', инжинерá 'engineers', пароходá 'steamships'. The reasons for the origin and spread of this ending are not entirely clear. Certainly the confusion of the dual with the plural must have had some influence on the process; but it also seems probable that the influence of neuter plural *o*-stem endings such as местá 'places' played some part. This hypothesis is supported by the fact that in late medieval texts there are tendencies towards a fusion of the masculine and neuter *o*-stems, expressed in the appearance of the nom. pl. ending -*y* even in neuter nouns, e.g. блюды for блю́да 'dishes'. The adoption of -*a* for the masculines may have been a further expression of this tendency towards unification of the two paradigms. In the anomalous forms сыновья́ 'sons', кумовья́ 'godfathers' we find a contamination of the old *u*-stem ending -*ove* (OR сынове) and the new -*já* ending. In the case of other plurals in -*ja* or -*já* such as брáтья 'brothers', друзья́ 'friends' we have either a survival or the influence of what were originally collective nouns (OR братья 'brotherhood').

In the early Old Russian period the endings of the dative, instrumental and locative plural varied considerably according to the various stem-classes (cf. the tables on pp. 15–16). In the modern language all classes have taken on the endings originally proper to the -*a*/-*ja*-stems, thus зубáм, зубáми, зубáх from зуб 'tooth', зверя́м, зверя́ми, зверя́х from зверь 'wild beast', именáм, именáми, именáх from и́мя 'name' etc. parallel with the unchanged женáм, женáми, женáх from женá 'wife'. The process seems to have been a slow one; while the earliest examples of the new forms are found in the thirteenth century they do not seem to have attained universal acceptance until the late seventeenth century. Here again however we do not know to what extent the written texts reflect Church Slavonic influence.

19

The process of simplification of the declensional system of Common Slavonic has resulted in a situation which allows descriptive grammarians to speak of only three declension classes in modern standard Russian, corresponding in essence to the *a*-stem, *o*-stem, and *i*-stem classes. Certain minor anomalies do not invalidate this scheme. Essentially the *u*-stems have coalesced with the *o*-stems, the masculine *i*-stems with the *jo*-stems; and the consonantal stems have all coalesced with other classes: the *s*-stems and *ent*-stems with the *o*-stems and all the others (including the *ъv*-stems) with the *i*-stems. Certain anomalous forms, e.g. the nominatives время 'time', дочь 'daughter' as against genitives времени, дочери, the nom. acc. pl. небеса from небо 'heaven' (clearly a Church Slavonic form), remind us of the earlier history of the classes concerned. The *ent*-stems have developed a totally new singular paradigm based on what was originally a diminutive suffix, so that we have телёнок 'calf', nom. pl. телята as against or теля телята. Only the anomalous дитя 'child' retains the old nominative and the original stem-suffix in the oblique cases of the singular which, however, have taken on *i*-stem endings, gen., dat., loc. дитяти, instr. дитятею. This word is obsolescent in the modern language: only the nom. and acc. are in normal use, and then usually in metaphorical senses. The plural дети is however current: the forms are those of the *i*-stems.

The number of *u*-stem nouns must have been very restricted already in Common Slavonic times; and even in Old Church Slavonic it is difficult systematically to keep apart the *o*-stem and *u*-stem paradigms. In Russian the coalescence is complete. While the predominant pattern is that of the *o*-stem paradigm the influence of the *u*-stems is shown in the genitive plural in *-ov* and in the alternative genitive and locative singular forms in *-u*.

The Common Slavonic genitive plural ending was for the *o*-stems *-ъ* and for the *u*-stems *-ovъ*. With the disappearance of weak jers the *o*-stems had a zero suffix, and this is still that of the neuters, e.g. сёл, мест. In the masculines this form was generally replaced by the *u*-stem ending by the fifteenth century, so that in the modern language we have слонов 'elephants', городов 'towns', together with the originally *u*-stem домов 'houses'. Nevertheless a number of words still show the zero ending, e.g. сапог 'boots', чулок 'stockings' (both identical with the nom. sing.) but волос from волос 'hair' with change of stress. It is difficult to know what has preserved the old form in these cases; but in many other instances it has become characteristic of particular formal or semantic classes. Thus граждан from гражданин 'citizen', телят from телёнок are survivals of the old consonant-stem genitive plural and corresponding forms are found in all words of the two classes in question. The zero ending is frequent in units of measurement appearing after numerals (пять раз 'five times', сто грамм 'a hundred grammes'), with the word человек 'person', also after numerals (шесть челове́к 'six people') etc., and generally in certain words designating soldiers (солда́т 'soldiers', гуса́р 'hussars', партиза́н 'partisans'), and nationalities (грузи́н 'Georgians', мордви́н 'Mordvinians', цыга́н 'gipsies') etc.

In the Old Russian period we find both -*a* and -*u* more or less indiscriminately as endings of the genitive singular of hard masculine inanimate nouns, whatever their origin. From the sixteenth century onwards the use of these endings becomes more systematized. Lomonosov in his grammar of 1755 regards -*u* as characteristic of low style or popular speech. In the modern language -*u* has become a kind of partitive ending in the case of nouns denoting material substances, collective entities or abstract concepts, e.g. стака́н ча́ю 'a glass of tea', кусо́к са́хару 'a piece of sugar', ма́ло наро́ду 'few people', мно́го шу́му 'much noise'. It also occurs in a number of stereotyped adverbial phrases, e.g. со стра́ху 'for fear', и́з дому 'from home'. The spread of genitives in -*u* to a wide range of *o*-stem nouns is a phenomenon which Russian shares not only with White Russian and Ukrainian but also with Polish, Czech and Slovak. In all these languages there are today far more -*u* forms than in Russian, though the degree of systematization varies. The discrepancy between present-day literary Russian and these cognate languages is such that B. O. Unbegaun preferred to regard the situation in this, as in various other phenomena, as a direct continuation of the written Church Slavonic language, with the surviving -*u* forms representing a limited degree of vernacular influence on the Church Slavonic system.

Endings in -*u*/-*ju* also occur in the locative singular of certain (usually monosyllabic) -*o*/-*jo*-stem nouns. In this case they are always stressed. Here too we have to do with the influence of the original *u*-stems. The earliest certain examples are from the thirteenth century; at first they are very commonly from words whose root ended in a velar, *k*, *g* or *ch*, e.g. на снѣгу́ 'in the snow', на воску́ 'on wax', but the form spreads widely up to the eighteenth century. In many cases there was wavering between -*ú*/-*jú* and -*ě*. It is difficult to speak of semantic differentiation between the two forms, but the use of *u* forms seems to have been on the increase in the past century or so. The modern language shows, for instance, на берегу́ 'on the bank', в бою́ 'in battle', в кругу́ 'in a circle', на посту́ 'at one's post', в саду́ 'in the garden'. Here too it is possible to regard the spread of *u* forms as a gradual encroachment of the East Slavonic vernacular on an essentially Church Slavonic literary language.

Modern standard Russian contains a large number of nouns which are not declinable; Unbegaun states that there are more than 300, excluding proper names. With the exception of certain surnames all were originally foreign loan-words. Certain other Slavonic languages, e.g. Czech, Slovak and Serbo-Croat, assimilate foreign loans as far as possible to the native declension classes, according to their ending; Russian however rarely does this in the case of words ending in a vowel. The indeclinable nouns may be roughly classified as follows: (a) nouns in *-i, -u,* e.g. такси́ 'taxi', Тбили́си 'Tiflis', кенгуру́ 'kangaroo', Баку́ 'Baku'; (b) nouns in *-o, -e,* e.g. бордо́ 'claret', кино́ 'cinema', Ó́сло 'Oslo', ко́фе 'coffee', шоссе́ 'highway'; (c) some nouns in *-a* (all foreign proper names in *-á* are indeclinable), e.g. бра 'lamp-bracket', буржуа́ 'bourgeois', Дюма́ 'Dumas', Йошка́р-Ола́ 'Yoshkar-Ola [capital of the Mari (Cheremis) ASSR]'; (d) Ukrainian surnames in *-enko, -ko,* e.g. Иса́ченко 'Isachenko', Франко́ '[the Ukrainian poet Ivan] Franko'; (e) Russian surnames which were originally genitives, e.g. Жива́го 'Zhivago', Дурново́ 'Durnovo', Кручёных 'Kruchonykh'.

MORPHOLOGY: THE PRONOUN AND ADJECTIVE

Few changes have affected the system of personal pronouns which Russian inherited from Common Slavonic. The pronoun of the first person was originally язъ, and this is frequent throughout the middle ages, side by side with the abbreviated form я which is universal by the end of the seventeenth century. The Old Church Slavonic (originally Bulgarian) form азъ is also commonly found in high-style texts until the eighteenth century. Certain minor changes of form in the oblique cases of the first and second person pronouns need not be mentioned here; but we may note the disappearance of the short forms of the accusative мя, тя and dative ми, ти which lived on as enclitic forms until the seventeenth century. The short accusative of the reflexive pronoun ся has indeed survived into the modern language but only as a kind of suffix denoting passive or middle voice, e.g. разуме́ется 'it goes without saying [lit. it is understood]', мо́ется 'he is washing [himself]'.

The original nominative singular of the third person pronoun *jь* (in origin a demonstrative pronoun) has disappeared in Russian as in all other Slavonic languages, though the oblique cases have remained with little change, e.g. его́, ему́. The substitution of another demonstrative form онъ must have taken place in Common Slavonic times. The influence of Church Slavonic was apparent in the form ея which was the normal written form of the gen. sing. feminine until the orthographical reform of 1917. This was the direct descendant of OCS *jeję* and was pronounced as written in high style, at least until the early nineteenth century. In normal speech it was replaced by the vernacular form её which is attested in medieval texts; the vowel of the second syllable must early have become assimilated to *-e* and underwent the change of *e* to *o*. The modern form is её.

Of the Old Russian demonstrative pronouns тъ, та, то 'that' and сь, си, се 'this', the former has lived on with a reinforced nominative masculine form тот <тътъ which owes its origin to the desire to counteract the reduction of тъ > т which resulted from the disappearance of the weak jers. сь, си, се also developed modified forms, most frequently сеи (сесь), сия, сие, but this pronoun has become obsolete except for a few compounds and set phrases, e.g. сегóдня 'today', до сих пор 'so far', сию́ минýту 'this minute'. It has been replaced by the form э́тот which is first attested in the seventeenth century.

In Common Slavonic the adjectives were originally declined like nouns; but a new adjectival declension developed through the fusion of adjectival forms with the postposed demonstrative pronoun *jь*. Thus there arose such forms as masc. sing. nom.* *novъ-jь*, gen. *nova-jego*, dat.* *novu-jemu*, fem. sing. nom.* *nova-ja*, gen.* *novy-jeję*, dat. *nově-jeji* etc. These forms underwent contractions, but some of them still survived unchanged into OCS, e.g. *novajego*, masc. sing. neut. *novoje* etc. The compound forms were semantically distinguished from the simple ones in that they indicated definiteness: thus OCS *novyjь domъ* 'the new house', *novъ domъ* 'a new house'. The compound forms underwent further and sometimes variant contractions in vernacular Russian: the vernacular forms sometimes show the influence of the *o*-stem pronominal endings such as *togo, tomu*. Thus Old Russian texts show a variety of forms, Church Slavonic gen. sing. masc. новаго alternating, for example, with vernacular нового, and Church Slavonic gen. sing. fem. новыя with vernacular новоѣ. As has been seen above (p. 9) the modern nom. sing. masc. ending -ый in нóвый etc. is of Church Slavonic origin. Until the early part of the present century it was however pronounced as if it were the vernacular form новой ['novəj]. The influence of the orthography has restored a 'Church Slavonic' pronunciation in normal current usage, i.e. [novɨj]. The orthography of certain other forms continued to reflect Church Slavonic influence until the spelling reform of 1917: the gen. sing. masc. was spelt in -аго, e.g. нóваго, чужáго (the latter word being pronounced [tʃu'ʒovə]); and the nom. acc. pl. fem. and neut. were written in -ыя, thus нóвыя, pronounced identically with the masc. нóвые.

The nominal forms of the adjective live on for the most part only in predicative function: он бóлен 'he is ill', бýдьте добры́ 'be so kind'. The possessive adjectives of the type отцóв 'the father's', сéстрин 'the sister's' have however retained a certain number of nominal case endings, e.g. отцóва gen. sing. masc., отцóву dat. sing. masc.

MORPHOLOGY: THE VERB

The Russian verbs can be conveniently classified according to the suffix which characterizes the stem of the present tense, with subdivisions to take account of variations of the infinitive stem. The resulting classes are as follows. (The forms are those of Old Russian.)

1. Verbs in -*e*-, (a) with no infinitive stem-suffix, e.g. third person sing. ведеть inf. вести 'carry', живеть, жити < *živ-ti 'live', можеть, мочи 'be able'; (b) with infinitive suffix -*a*-, e.g. береть, брати 'take', зоветь, звати 'call'.
2. Verbs in -*ne*-, infinitive in -*nu*- (Common Slavonic -*nǫ*-), e.g. крикнеть, крикнути 'shout'.
3. Verbs in -*je*-, (a) with no infinitive stem-suffix, e.g. дѣлаеть, дѣлати 'do', умѣеть, умѣти 'know how to'; (b) with infinitive in -*a*-, e.g. таеть, таяти 'thaw', пишеть, писати 'write', плачеть, плакати 'weep'.
4. Verbs in -*i*-, (a) with infinitive in -*i*-, e.g. ходить, ходити 'go'; (b) with infinitive in -*ě*-, e.g. видить, видѣти 'see'; (c) with infinitive in -*a*-, e.g. держить, держати 'hold'.
5. Athematic verbs (i.e. verbs with no stem-suffix and which also show some different personal endings from the verbs of the previous four 'thematic' classes). Five such verbs are attested in Old Russian: есть, быти 'be', дасть, дати 'give' ѣсть ѣсти 'eat' вѣсть, вѣдѣти 'know', имать, имати, имѣти 'have'.

Old Russian shows three simple tenses, the present, the aorist and the imperfect, of which only the first has survived into the modern language. In addition there were a number of compound tenses which combined participial forms with forms of the auxiliary verb быти: perfect, pluperfect, conditional and future perfect. Of these only the perfect and conditional survive, the former as an all-purpose preterite. Three persons were expressed and three numbers (singular, plural and dual). As with the noun, the dual number has disappeared. The dual forms were clearly obsolescent already in the thirteenth century, if not earlier. The presence of such forms can often be ascribed to Church Slavonic influence.

Apart from changes due to the phonetic evolution that has been described earlier, the system of personal endings in the present tense has remained very stable. Significant changes have however affected the second and third persons singular and several of the athematic present-tense endings. In the second person singular Old Russian showed ведеши, пишеши etc. while the modern language has ведёшь, пишешь. The

24

earliest examples of -шь are attested in the thirteenth century; the change is generally ascribed to simple phonetic erosion, influenced no doubt by the tendency towards a parallelism of two-syllable forms in the singular paradigm after the disappearance of weak jers had brought about a two-syllable form ведет, пишет in the third person.

The third person singular ending in OCS was -tъ; Old Russian texts from the beginning show -tь. The modern literary language has -т in common with northern and central dialects, as against the -ть which the southern dialects (and Ukrainian) share with Old Russian. White Russian also shows the corresponding ending -ць. The same alternation is observable in the forms of the third person plural: -т in modern standard Russian and in the northern and central dialects, -ть in South Russian dialects and Ukrainian, -ць in White Russian. -ть is what we should expect by comparison with corresponding forms in other Indo-European languages: cf. Greek, ἔστι, Sanskrit *ásti* 'is'. However, Old Church Slavonic regularly shows -тъ. It is difficult to explain the origin of the forms in -тъ. It may be that the two endings reflect a dialectal difference in Common Slavonic, of unknown origin. We may be fairly certain that the presence of -тъ in the modern standard language reflects the influence of Church Slavonic as well as that of the northern dialects. -ть is preserved in есть 'is, there is' and суть 'are, there are': the other forms of the present tense of быти having fallen into disuse, these two words were isolated from the general system of verbal paradigms.

Of the five 'athematic' verbs listed above two have disappeared from the language: вѣсть вѣдѣти has been replaced by знать (the old root is still discernible in the obsolescent ведать); and имамь имати has been replaced by another derivative from the same root, the regular class III verb имѣю имѣть. быти has survived as быть but with a much reduced inventory of present-tense forms. есть is used in the sense of 'there is, there are' or in the sense of 'exists', and its usage is not restricted to the third person. суть is virtually obsolete in the language of today. The forms of the first and second persons must have disappeared early from the spoken language. When they occur in the texts they are due to Church Slavonic influence and the forms are sometimes incorrect or used incorrectly.

The two remaining verbs of the athematic class have survived, as дать and есть; their present-tense forms are дам, дашь, даст, дадим, дадите, дадут and ем, ешь, ест, едим, едите, едят. The first person singular preserves the old ending which has however been hardened (like all examples of -мь except the numerals семь, восемь). In the second person singular the OR forms даси, ѣси have been replaced by forms influenced perhaps by the corresponding forms of the thematic verbs or possibly by the imperative forms дажь, ѣжь, with unvoicing of the final consonant. The

-d- of the plural forms is a survival from the earliest phase of Slavonic: ѣмь < *ědmi, дасть < *dad-ti etc.

Modern Russian has a single preterite tense: дал 'gave', дѣлал 'did', жил 'lived', шёл 'went'. The form in *-l* was originally a past active participle which came to be used in Common Slavonic together with the present tense of быти to form a compound perfect. This lived on into Russian, so that in the texts of the early period we have such forms as далъ есмь 'I have given', умерлъ есть 'he has died' etc. Old Russian also possessed two other preterite tenses, the aorist and imperfect. Typical paradigms were as follows:

Aorist

Singular	1	знахъ	идохъ
	2	зна	иде
	3	зна	иде
Plural	1	знахомъ	идохомъ
	2	знасте	идосте
	3	знаша	идоша
Dual	1	знаховѣ	идоховѣ
	2	знаста	идоста
	3	знасте	идосте

Imperfect

Singular	1	знахъ	несяхъ
	2	знаше	несяше
	3	знаше	несяше
Plural	1	знахомъ	несяхомъ
	2	знашете	несяшете (несясте)
	3	знаху	несяху
Dual	1	знаховѣ	несяховѣ
	2	знашета	несяшета (несяста)
	3	знашете	несяшете (несясте)

It is difficult to know how far these two tenses formed part of the system of the spoken language in the early Old Russian period. It is noteworthy that in the earliest secular texts we find examples of the perfect but none of the simple preterite tenses. Thus the Tmutorakan' inscription of 1068 states: 'глѣбъ кнѧзь мѣрилъ м(оре) по ледоу (Prince Gleb measured the sea across the ice)'. Some of these early instances of the perfect are ambiguous, in that they may be interpreted either as genuine perfects or as pure preterites. There is however no ambiguity about certain passages in the treaty between Smolensk and Riga of 1229 which give a simple narrative of past events without ever using aorist or imperfect forms. Learned texts regularly use the aorist and, to a very limited extent, the imperfect right up to the seventeenth century. Thereafter these forms are not used in the vernacular. It would seem that the aorist and the imperfect were almost exclusively Church Slavonic elements in the language even in the period of the earliest attested documents. V. Kiparsky has aptly compared their status in the medieval language to that of the imperfect subjunctive and past definite in modern French: they were known to all speakers but used almost exclusively in writing.

The forms of the original perfect have survived in modern Russian as a simple preterite. Unlike certain other Slavonic languages (e.g. Czech, Serbo-Croat) Russian has abandoned the use of the auxiliary verb in these forms, so that we have я дал, ты дал, он дал 'I, you, he gave'. It is clear from the texts of the eleventh and twelfth centuries that already then the auxiliary was optional. It is probable that it first disappeared in the third person forms. Vestiges of the use of the auxiliary lived on into the seventeenth century.

Of the other compound tenses of Old Russian only the conditional survives in the modern language (дал бы 'would give'). The particle бы formally perpetuates the third person singular aorist of быти.

Old Russian had no future tense; future time was expressed by various different verbal forms. Sometimes the present tense (of either the perfective or the imperfective aspect) was used. The forms of the 'future perfect' (the perfective present of быти, i.e. буду etc., + the -l participle) were most frequently used in the protasis of conditional sentences referring to the future or without a precise temporal definition, e.g. 'ѹже боудеть оубилъ ... тъ тако ѥмоу платіти (If he kills . . . then he must pay.)' (*Russkaja Pravda*, 1282). The simple future could also be expressed by means of various auxiliary verbs, especially начну (почну), имамь, хочу, with the infinitive. It is not until the sixteenth century that we find unambiguous examples of the modern imperfective future in буду + infinitive, and it is not until the seventeenth century that it becomes common, alternating even then with стану + infinitive. From the evidence of the texts it is clear that this construction came to Muscovy from the west: it is very probably an imitation of the corresponding Polish construction (*będę robić* 'I shall do') which first penetrated into White Russian and thence into the language of Muscovy.

The system of verbal nouns and adjectives which existed in Common Slavonic has been considerably modified in Russian. The infinitive has, it is true, changed little. Old Russian still had -*i* as the ending of all infinitives, e.g. дѣлати 'do', вести 'lead', мочи 'be able'. During the medieval period however the final -*i* was lost when not stressed, so that we now have дѣлать, вести, мóчь. Early texts show a few examples of the supine, a form indicating purpose after verbs of motion, e.g. идеть . . . искатъ кунъ (1350) 'he goes to seek marten-furs'. Its presence in the texts may well be due to Church Slavonic influence.

Old Russian in its earliest phase had an elaborate system of participles (verbal adjectives). Typical nominative singular forms may be tabulated as follows:

Present	*Past*
Active I masc. neut. неса, fem. несучи	masc. несъ, fem. несъши, neut. несъше
III masc. neut. пиша, fem. пишучи	masc. писавъ, fem. писавъши, neut. писавъше
IV masc. neut. прося, fem. просячи	masc. просивъ, fem. просивъши, neut. просивъше
Passive несомъ -а -о	несенъ -а -о

Even in the earliest period few forms of the oblique cases are found. In common with the adjectives, the participles showed compound forms with the originally pronominal suffixes (see above p. 23), e.g. несаи, несыи. By analogy new nominative masculine forms such as видячи came into existence. In the later development the simple and compound forms of the present active participle go different ways. The masculine nominative singular remains as an uninflected 'gerund' with adverbial function, and the anomalous ending -*a* is replaced by -*ja* through analogy with the forms of class IV verbs. Thus the modern language shows such forms as кла́дя 'putting', слепя́ 'blinding', дава́я 'giving'. The compound forms in -*čij* have become adjectives devoid of verbal function: the most frequent examples are in -*jačij*, originally from class IV verbs, e.g. горя́чий 'hot', вися́чий 'hanging', бродя́чий 'nomadic', but also летýчий 'flying, volatile'. The function of the verbal adjective in present active meaning has been taken over by Church Slavonic forms in -*ščij*, e.g. чита́ющий 'reading', говоря́щий 'speaking'.

Since at least the seventeenth century the past active participle, too, has survived only as an indeclinable 'gerund' in -*v* or -*vši*. In the modern language these forms are found only with verbs of perfective aspect. The forms in -*v* are now more common in the literary language than those in -*vši* which have a slightly popular stylistic nuance, except in reflexive verbs, where they are the only possible alternative. Thus we find откры́в 'having discovered', устрани́вши 'having removed', призна́вшись 'having confessed'.

The passive participles, present and past, are still present in the modern language. The present passive forms in -*m*- belong to the literary language and are no doubt Church Slavonic rather than vernacular in origin. Apart from genuinely participial forms such as ожида́емый '(being) expected', ликвиди́руемый '(being) liquidated', some words of this class have become simple adjectives, e.g. люби́мый 'favourite', непобеди́мый 'invincible', or even nouns, e.g. сказу́емое '[grammatical] predicate', насеко́мое 'insect'.

The past passive participle is formed in -*n*- or -*t*- and there has been some wavering in the past between the two forms. Long and short forms of these participles are fully in use in the modern language, e.g. откры́т(ый) 'opened', испечён(ный) 'baked'. The -*nn*- of the long form is not original, having been introduced to these participial forms by analogy with adjectives in *-nьn-* such as пи́сьменный 'written', госуда́рственный '(of the) state': the original form is preserved in some adjectives such as солёные (огурцы́) 'salt (gherkins)'.

VOCABULARY

The lexical stock inherited by the Russians when their language began its independent life was shared with the speakers of other Slavonic languages; and many words were of course ultimately of common Indo-European origin. Thus три, сестра́, гусь immediately betray their connection with 'three', 'sister', 'goose'; and the common origin of дом, ле́вый, есть with Latin *domus, laevus, est* is immediately clear even to the non-philologist. Another, more considerable, group of words is common to all or many of the other Slavonic languages, e.g. рука́ 'hand', нога́ 'leg, foot', оте́ц 'father', хлеб 'bread', вода́ 'water', идти́/ходи́ть 'go', ста́рый 'old' and a host of others. A number of words of this group are shared with the Baltic languages, or with one of them (particularly Lithuanian) and thus provide evidence for a Balto-Slavonic cultural community at an early period. Examples are Lithuanian *rankà* 'hand', *galvà* 'head', *širdìs* 'heart' (cf. R рука́, голова́, се́рдце).

This basic lexical stock has been expanded and modified over the centuries in response to the developing needs of the Russian language-community. New words have been created not merely by the exploitation of the word-forming potentialities of the Russian language system itself but also, and to a very considerable extent, by the acceptance of foreign words or the fashioning of Russian words on the basis of foreign models. Such extensions of vocabulary reflect the multifarious cultural influences to which the Russian people have, voluntarily or involuntarily, been exposed in the course of their history.

With the acceptance of Christianity and its concomitant, literacy, from Bulgarian sources the Old Church Slavonic language became the vehicle of religious, learned and literary texts. Thus the Russian abstract vocabulary reflected the phonological and morphological characteristics of the Bulgaro-Macedonian dialect on which St Cyril has based his liturgical language. The modern language shows благослови́ть 'bless', вре́мя 'time', страна́ 'country' (cf. OR бологого 'good', OR веремя 'time', R сторона́ 'side'). Some of the words borrowed were not Slavonic but Greek in form, e.g. ева́нгелие 'gospel', иере́й 'priest' from Greek εὐαγγέλιον, ἱερεύς. A few other words had been borrowed from Greek at an earlier date, e.g. па́рус 'sail' < Greek φάρος, гра́мота 'document' < Greek γράμματα, крова́ть 'bed' < Greek κραββάτιον.

The Norsemen (Varangians) who played such a significant part in the foundation and early development of the Kievan state might have been expected to leave a decisive imprint on the language; but in fact there are very few words indeed in modern Russian that can be traced to this source. Examples are я́корь 'anchor' < Old Norse ankari, я́бедник 'slanderer, tale-teller' (cf. OR ябетьникъ 'official, judge') < Old Norse embætti. A few others are found in medieval texts, referring to the social organization of the Kievan state, e.g. OR тиунъ 'steward' < Old Norse þiónn. A number of personal names which at first sight look typically Slavonic are in fact inherited from the Norse ruling élite of Kiev: Игорь < Ingvarr, Ольга < Helga, Глеб < *Гълѣбъ < Guðleifr. The overwhelming probability that the name of Russia itself is of Scandinavian origin is discussed in Vol. 1, p. 53.

The conquest of the principalities of Rus' by the Mongols in the thirteenth century and their subjection to the local sovereignty of the Golden Horde, with its administrative centre on the lower Volga, have left important traces in the Russian language. The majority of the conquering troops and of the administrators of the occupying power with whom the Russians came into contact were speakers of Turkic languages (collectively and imprecisely known as Tatars); and from these languages a series of words were adopted in the fourteenth century and later. Most of them are concerned with military, administrative and financial concepts. It is not always possible to identify the particular language or dialect which gave rise to a given word; some may indeed have been borrowed in slightly differing forms before becoming stabilized in the Russian vernacular. Such words are де́ньги 'money', казначе́й 'treasurer', карау́л 'guard, sentry', же́мчуг 'pearl', OR тамга 'seal' (and its derivative тамо́жня 'custom-house'), OR ямъ 'post-station' and its derivative ямщи́к 'coachman', and several others.

Even after the throwing off of the 'Mongol-Tatar yoke' Russian speakers continued to be in contact with Turkic languages; and such contacts were further encouraged by the Russian penetration and colonization of Siberia from the sixteenth century onwards, which also led to contacts with Uralic and Palaeo-Asiatic languages. Turkic loans which may belong to this period include башма́к 'shoe' and сунду́к 'chest, trunk'.

Medieval Russian shows relatively few traces of western influences. The contacts between the northern cities (Novgorod, Pskov, Smolensk) and the Germans of the Hansa or the Teutonic Order caused a few Germanisms to appear in legal and administrative documents, e.g. OR пробстъ 'provost', мастеръ 'master', ратманъ 'magistrate'. Such words were short-lived, however: OR рытарь 'knight' is a medieval German borrowing but has survived in the modern language only in the form ры́царь which shows the subsequent influence of the Polish form rycerz.

The intensification of contacts, hostile or friendly, with Poland–Lithuania from the fifteenth century onwards led to the absorption of many words from Polish, some of them ultimately deriving from languages further west. This aspect of Russian lexical history is still inadequately studied, but recent researches, especially those of Gerta H. Worth, have shown that many such westernisms which had previously been assigned to the Petrine or post-Petrine period are attested in west Russian or Ukrainian sources of the seventeenth or even the sixteenth centuries. Such words are библиотéка 'library', аптéка 'pharmacy', орáтор 'orator'.

The process of westernization of Russian economic, social and intellectual life, which was deliberately and energetically set in train by Peter I, brought with it a whole mass of foreign loan-words. Though many of these were short-lived a very large number still exist in the modern language. They may be roughly classified as follows: (a) administrative terms, e.g. бухгáлтер 'accountant' < German *Buchhalter*, контóра 'office' < German *Kontor*, комúссия 'commission' < Polish *komisja*; (b) naval and military terms, e.g. бак 'forecastle' < Dutch *bak(boord)* or German *Back(bord)*, киль 'keel' < Dutch *kiel* or German *Kiel* (or possibly even from the English word), гренадéр 'grenadier' < French *grenadier*, цейхгáуз 'magazine' < German *Zeughaus*; (c) terms denoting abstract concepts, e.g. клúмат < French *climat*, университéт 'university' < German *Universität*, метáлл 'metal' < German *Metall* or French *métal*; (d) terms denoting new concrete objects, e.g. гáлстук 'cravat, tie' < German *Halstuch* + Dutch *halsdoek* (both галздук and галстух are attested in the eighteenth century), парúк 'wig' < eighteenth-century German *Parücke* + French *perruque* (possibly with influence of Dutch *paruik*), портрéт < German *Porträt* or French *portrait*. It is characteristic of many of these words that the precise foreign source cannot be identified. In view of the presence in Russia at the time of numbers of Dutch, German, French and English technicians, scholars, teachers, traders, etc. we must in several cases assume multiple borrowing; and this is also made probable by the variant forms of some of the early attestations of the words in question.

Since the early eighteenth century Russian has continued to absorb foreign loan-words; the influence of particular languages has ebbed and flowed according to the dominant streams of cultural influence. French influence was strong in the eighteenth century; and in addition to loan-words such as those noted above this influence expressed itself in the form of semantic calques, where existing Russian words were given a new semantic content. For example трóгать 'touch' and its derivative трóгательный took on the emotional connotations of French *toucher*, *touchant*; and French *prendre part* gave rise to a new Russian idiom принять учáстие 'take part'. In the course of the nineteenth century the influence of German abstract thought gave rise to many calques that have become fully domesticated, such as мировоззрéние 'world-view,

31

philosophy of life' < German *Weltanschauung*, образова́ние 'culture, education' < German *Bildung*.

Even in the Soviet period Russian has remained hospitable to foreign words. комба́йн 'combine harvester', диспе́тчер 'controller (of movement of transport etc.)', джаз 'jazz' are characteristic examples. The revolutionary changes in social and economic life since 1917 have naturally had a profound influence on the vocabulary. In addition to foreign loans and to words formed in accordance with traditional patterns, post-revolutionary Russian shows a remarkable proliferation of words formed from combinations of initial letters or syllables. СССР 'ussr', МГУ (= Моско́вский Госуда́рственный Университе́т) 'Moscow State University' and the like may perhaps only marginally be considered as 'words'; but in the case of ВУЗ (= высо́кое уче́бное заведе́ние) 'institution of higher education', НЭП (= но́вая экономи́ческая поли́тика) 'New Economic Policy' or МХАТ (= Моско́вский Худо́жественный Академи́ческий Теа́тр) 'Moscow Art Theatre' the base-words are only potentially present in the speaker's consciousness. Equally numerous are words formed from syllables, e.g. госизда́т (= госуда́рственное изда́тельство) 'State publishing house', колхо́з (= коллекти́вное хозя́йство) 'collective farm', райко́м (= райо́нный комите́т) 'district party committee'. Rather rarer, but still apparently a productive class, are combinations of syllables and initials in the same word, e.g. райфо́ (= райо́нный фина́нсовый отде́л) 'district department of finance'.

DIALECTS

Originally spoken in a relatively limited area of Eastern Europe, Russian has spread in the past four or five centuries over vast regions of the Eurasian land-mass and is now spoken from the Baltic to the Pacific and from the White Sea to the borders of China. Nevertheless, dialectal differences are relatively small compared with those found in, say, German, Italian or English, or in territorially much less extensive Slavonic languages such as Slovene or Slovak. This homogeneity is no doubt largely due to the relative lack of geographical obstacles, in particular of mountains, which might have encouraged the development of marked local dialects. Three basic dialect-areas are distinguished: North, South and Central Russian.

The North Russian dialects are spoken in the northern and some eastern parts of European Russia; the southern boundary of their territory runs north of Novgorod, south of Yaroslavl' and Kostroma, north of Gor'ky (Nizhny Novgorod), and swings south-east to include much of the Volga basin and the towns of Ufa, Saratov and Chkalov (Orenburg). The

Fig. 1. Dialect map of western USSR

area of the South Russian dialects is bounded by a line running east from the White Russian border well to the north of Smolensk, south of Moscow and Vladimir, and south-westwards to the Caucasus, including the towns of Voronezh and Tambov. The Central Russian dialects are spoken in the narrow band that lies between the other two regions and includes the towns of Moscow, Vladimir and Gor'ky. The dialects brought to Siberia by the Russian colonists were for the most part of the North Russian type. Detailed and up-to-date studies of the Siberian dialects are lacking; but there is little doubt that the original North Russian dialect-basis has been strongly influenced, in the last half-century, by the standard language.

The most characteristic features of the North Russian dialects are *okan'je* (distinction of unstressed *o* and *a*), the presence of plosive [g] as in the standard language, omission of intervocalic [j], i.e. the pronunciation of красная, знáет as ['krasnaa, 'znaet], the pronunciation of hard -*t* in third-person verbal forms, e.g. несёт, несýт, as in the standard language. Two other characteristic northern features occur only in some of the dialects. *Cokan'je*, the failure to distinguish the sounds *c* and *č*, is widely found in medieval texts from northern centres such as Pskov and Novgorod. It most frequently expresses itself in the pronunciation of *c* for *č*, e.g. [tsas, 'tsistɪj] alongside [ko'lɛts]; in some dialects however *c* is replaced by *č*, so that we have [tʃas, 'tʃistɪj, ko'lɛtʃ]. Some northern dialects also show the syntactical phenomenon of a postpositive definite article, e.g. дóмот 'the house', женáта, 'the woman', селóто 'the village'. This phenomenon too is found in Old Russian literary texts, as for instance in the seventeenth-century autobiography of the Archpriest Avvakum.

The southern dialects are especially characterized by *akan'je* (failure to distinguish unstressed *a* and *o*), pronunciation of original *g* as a voiced velar fricative [γ], and soft *t* in third-person verbal forms (несéть, несýть). All the southern dialects show *jakan'je* (failure to distinguish between unstressed *'a*, *'e* and *'o*), but this feature expresses itself in different ways and thus forms one of the criteria for classifying the dialects. It may appear as 'strong' *jakan'je*, i.e. the three sounds when unstressed always appear as *'a* (ṛaṭ'i, ṛaḵ'i, ṇaṣ'i for standard пятú, рекú, несú); as 'moderate' *jakan'je*, i.e. *a* before following hard consonant but *i* before following soft consonant [ṇa'su] but [ṇi'ṣi]; or as 'dissimilative' *jakan'je*, i.e. [ṇa'su, ṇa'ṣi] but [ṇi'sla, ɣi'la] for standard несу, неси, несла, вела.

The Central Russian dialects are of secondary origin, combining some northern with some southern features. They show the northern plosive *g* and hard -*t* of third-person verb-forms, together with the southern feature of *akan'je*. The formation of the central dialects must be associated with the rise of the Muscovite state and with movements of population into the central region from both north and south. The speech of Moscow provided the dialect-basis for the standard language and as such it continues to exercise a powerful influence on all the regional dialects.

THE RUSSIAN LITERARY LANGUAGE

All the reliable evidence points to the fact that writing came to be regularly practised in Kievan Rus' only after the conversion of Vladimir in *c*. 988, and that the language then used was Old Church Slavonic, imported from Bulgaria and written in the Cyrillic alphabet which had been devised in that country in about A.D. 900.[1]

The earliest preserved text written in Russia is the *Ostromir Codex* written in Novgorod in 1056–7 by the Deacon Grigory for Ostromir, *posadnik* of Novgorod. It is a version of the gospels in Old Church Slavonic, clearly transcribed from a Bulgarian original but nevertheless containing a number of systematic Russian features, especially in the phonology. This Russianized form of Church Slavonic became the literary language of Kievan Rus'. The differences between Old Church Slavonic of the Bulgarian variety and the East Slavonic vernacular of Rus' must at that period have been very slight, particularly as the language will certainly have from the outset been pronounced by the Russians in accordance with the phonological system of their own language. It cannot have been long before the new literary language came to be regarded by its users as simply a higher form of their own vernacular. Nevertheless, its usage was functionally restricted. Church Slavonic was used for religious and learned texts, with varying admixtures of vernacular elements. However, for legal and administrative purposes something approaching a pure vernacular language was used. Documents of this kind begin with the *Mstislavova gramota* of *c*. 1130 and, although they are much less numerous than the Church Slavonic texts, they are of course of immense value for our knowledge of the history of the language. Of particular interest are a large number of texts scratched on birch-bark and found in Novgorod by archaeologists from 1951 onwards. They consist for the most part of personal and business correspondence and date from the twelfth and thirteenth centuries.

Tendencies towards a fusion of the learned and popular varieties of the language were checked by conservative scholars of the fourteenth and fifteenth centuries who, partly under the influence of the practice of Serbian and Bulgarian refugees from the Turkish-occupied Balkans, attempted to restore in orthography and style a 'purer' Church Slavonic language.

Thus functional dualism continued to characterize Russian writings until the eighteenth century. The language of legal and administrative

[1] See Chapter 2A.

texts became relatively stabilized in the sixteenth century in the chancery language (прика́зный язы́к) which was used not only for official purposes but also in texts of more general interest such as the treatise on domestic economy *Domostroj*. The variety of expression provided by the two linguistic models or styles came to be exploited for literary purposes – to very great effect in the late seventeenth-century autobiography of the Archpriest Avvakum.

The reforms of Peter I did not stop short of the language. In 1710 he approved a reform of the alphabet: for secular printed texts a new 'civil alphabet' (гражда́нская а́збука) was to be used, the forms of whose letters were simplified and assimilated to those of the Roman alphabet used in western Europe. This reform tended still further to restrict the sphere of influence of Church Slavonic, for which the old alphabet continued to be used. The relationship between the vernacular and Church Slavonic formed the subject of much discussion and argument in the course of the eighteenth century. M. V. Lomonosov in his work О по́льзе книг церко́вных в росси́йском языке́ (1757) advanced the theory of three styles, in fact a codification of the types of functional variant which had already for some time existed in the language. At the same time the modernization and stabilization of educated usage under the influence of western languages continued apace. Here the writings of N. M. Karamzin were of considerable influence. By the early nineteenth century the Russian literary language began to take on its modern form, as a fusion of Church Slavonic and vernacular elements. The emergence of the new literary language is generally associated with the work of A. S. Pushkin, who at once gathered together the varied elements of the Russian linguistic heritage and provided an unsurpassed exemplar of what now became one of the great literary languages of the world.

RUSSIAN AND CHURCH SLAVONIC

As has been seen above, the development of the Russian literary language has been the history of the interpenetration and ultimate fusion of what were originally two separate linguistic systems, Russian and (Old) Church Slavonic. Moreover, it is not merely the written language that has undergone this process: the spoken form of the standard language too reflects the fusion of the two elements which have in the course of the last two centuries become so indissolubly combined that only the linguistic analyst can distinguish them from one another. Some of the original Church Slavonic features have been mentioned earlier. The most important are the following:

(i) the representation of original *tărt, tălt, tert, telt* as *trat, tlat, tret*

(< *trĕt*), *tlet* (< *tlĕt*), e.g. Ленингра́д ~ го́род 'city', хлади́ть 'chill' ~ хо́лод 'cold', преступа́ть 'transgress' ~ переступа́ть 'cross over', Мле́чный путь 'Milky Way' ~ молоко́ 'milk';

(ii) the representation of original *ărt, ălt* as *rat, lat* as against the East Slavonic *rot-, lot-,* e.g. во́зраст 'age' ~ рост 'growth', ладья́ 'boat [in poetical style]', 'rook [in chess]' ~ ло́дка 'boat';

(iii) the representation of original *dį* as *žd,* as against the East Slavonic *ž,* e.g. наде́жда 'hope' ~ надёжный 'reliable';

(iv) the representation of original *tį* (*ktį*) as *šč,* as against the East Slavonic *č,* e.g. по́мощь 'help [noun]' ~ помо́чь 'help [verb]';

(v) the retention of *e* under stress, e.g. не́бо 'sky, heaven' ~ нёбо 'palate';

(vi) prothetic *j-* in *ju-,* e.g. юг 'south' ~ у́тро 'morning';

(vii) the vocalization of weak jers, particularly in prefixes, e.g. вопро́с 'question', воспита́ть 'educate', собо́р 'cathedral';

(viii) the change of 'tense' *ь* to *i,* e.g. ору́жие 'weapon' ~ ружьё 'rifle'.

Most of these features are stylistically neutral and have entered the general inventory of Russian linguistic means of expression, so that -*ašč-,* -*ušč-* are simply Russian morphemes like any other: their Church Slavonic origin has no significance in the synchronic language-system. The case of the variant treatments of the *tărt, tălt, tert, telt* groups is different: here the alternative forms to some extent signal semantic or stylistic differentiation. зла́то 'gold', брег 'shore' are used only in poetry or styles influenced by Church Slavonic, as against the unmarked зо́лото, бе́рег.

In the case of глава́ ~ голова́, however, the distinction is semantic: the former means 'chapter, head [of a department, undertaking etc.]' while the latter means 'head' in the purely anatomical sense. Church Slavonic morphemes are very widely used for the creation of technical terms. Thus 'mammal' is млекопита́ющее, preserving the Church Slavonic form of the word for 'milk'; 'goalkeeper' is врата́рь, the Church Slavonic word for 'gatekeeper' (cf. воро́та 'gate'). The presence of two alternative morphemes adds to the expressive possibilities of the language, as can be seen from the pair хладнокро́вный 'possessing *sang-froid*', холоднокро́вный 'cold-blooded [in the zoological sense]'. Thus the originally Church Slavonic elements in the language play a part comparable to the Latin elements in modern English.

Some Church Slavonic elements in the orthographical system were removed by the orthographic reform of 1917. The letter ѣ, long identical in pronunciation with e, was abolished, as was the equally redundant **v,** used for the *i* sound in some Greek loan-words. The 'hard sign' ъ was retained only medially, to indicate the hardness of a consonant when followed by *j,* e.g. объявля́ть 'declare', объём 'content'. The Church Slavonic genitive singular feminine of the third-person pronoun ея́ was replaced by its vernacular equivalent её in accordance with the actual pronunciation; the nominative plural feminine of the same pronoun онѣ gave way to они; the Church Slavonic masculine and neuter genitive singular of adjectives -aro was replaced by the vernacular -oro in accordance with the actual pronunciation; and the artificial distinction in the nominative plural forms of adjectives between the masculine нóвые, сúние and the feminine and neuter нóвыя, сúния (< the Church Slavonic feminine form -yję) was also abolished.

RUSSIAN AND ITS NEIGHBOURS

As was stated on p. 2 it would be strictly correct to speak, in the ninth and tenth centuries, of 'Old East Slavonic' rather than of Old Russian, for the dialects in question were still relatively undifferentiated and formed the common ancestor of the three modern languages Russian, White Russian, and Ukrainian. Given a different historical development, a single modern vernacular might have evolved; but the result of the Mongol subjection of the central Russian principalities and the consequent absorption of the White Russian and much of the Ukrainian areas by the Grand Duchy of Lithuania was an accentuation of dialectal differences that already existed, so that in the fourteenth and fifteenth centuries we find texts that can already be claimed as White Russian or Ukrainian or, at least, as some separate variety of East Slavonic distinct from the language of Muscovy. The Chancery language of the Grand Duchy of Lithuania in the fifteenth and sixteenth centuries was an amalgam of many elements, but the White Russian component was strong. Galician documents from the fourteenth century onwards are full of Ukrainianisms. Numerous later texts testify to the growing independence of the two western members of the East Slavonic language-group; though it was not until the nineteenth century that the two languages took on anything like a generally accepted literary form. Despite the attempts to conceal the separate existence of Ukrainian and White Russian under the names 'Little Russian' and 'West Russian' in the late nineteenth and early twentieth centuries the languages continued to be cultivated and their existence and status were at last recognized in the Soviet Union as languages of separate constituent republics. Subject though they are to the constant pressure of Russian, as the language of the dominant nationality of the Union, these two languages continue to maintain their separate life.

GUIDE TO FURTHER READING

DICTIONARIES

The best available dictionary of the standard language of today is that prepared by the Institute of Linguistics of the Soviet Academy of Sciences: M. P. Alekseyev, S. G. Barkhudarov *et al.*, *Slovar' russkogo jazyka*, 4 vols. (Moscow, 1957–61). More compendious, and with a certain amount of historical information, is the dictionary issued by the Academy's Institute of the Russian Language: V. I. Chernyshov, S. G. Barkhudarov, V. V. Vinogradov, F. P. Filin *et al.*, *Slovar' sovremennogo russkogo literaturnogo jazyka*, 17 vols. (Moscow–Leningrad, 1950–65). The most complete and up-to-date Russian–English dictionary is the *Oxford Russian–English Dictionary*, ed. Marcus Wheeler *et al.* (Oxford, 1972). The standard etymological dictionary is that of Max Vasmer, *Russisches etymologisches Wörterbuch*, 3 vols. (Heidelberg, 1953–8), Russian translation M. Fasmer, *Etimologičeskij slovar' russkogo jazyka*, 4 vols. (Moscow, 1964–73). For the study of the medieval language the work by I. I. Sreznevsky, *Materialy dlja slovarja drevnerusskogo jazyka*, 3 vols. (St Petersburg, 1893–1912; photomechanic reprints, Graz, 1957 and Moscow, 1958), is still indispensable. A useful short differential Old Russian–Russian dictionary is that by Horace G. Lunt, *Concise Dictionary of Old Russian (11th–17th Centuries)* (Munich, 1970).

DESCRIPTIVE GRAMMARS

An excellent concise reference grammar is that of B. O. Unbegaun, trans. D. P. Costello, *Russian Grammar* (Oxford, 1957). N. Forbes, *Russian Grammar*, 3rd edn revised and enlarged by J. C. Dumbreck (Oxford, 1964), is another useful handbook with a more practical orientation. The standard normative grammar, useful for its compendious examples but lagging some way behind present-day written and spoken usage, is V. V. Vinogradov *et al.*, *Grammatika russkogo jazyka*, 3 vols. (Moscow, 1953–4). More up to date and compact is N. Yu. Shvedova *et al.*, *Grammatika sovremennogo russkogo literaturnogo jazyka* (Moscow, 1970). The contrastive grammars of A. V. Isačenko, *Die russische Sprache der Gegenwart, Teil I. Formenlehre* (Halle (Saale), 1962), where the language of comparison is German, and *Grammatičeskij stroj russkogo jazyka v sopostavlenii s slovackim. Morfologija*, 2 vols. (Bratislava, 1954 and 1960), are also valuable. A stimulating survey of the present-day language is D. Ward, *The Russian Language Today* (London, 1965).

HISTORICAL GRAMMARS

The best is that by V. Kiparsky, *Russische historische Grammatik*, I: *Die Entwicklung des Lautsystems* (Heidelberg, 1963); II: *Die Entwicklung des Formensystems* (Heidelberg, 1967); III: *Entwicklung des Wortschatzes* (Heidelberg, 1975). Valuable are also two Soviet works: V. I. Borkovsky and P. S. Kuznetsov, *Istoričeskaja grammatika russkogo jazyka* (Moscow, 1963), and V. V. Ivanov, *Istoričeskaja grammatika russkogo jazyka* (Moscow, 1964). Rather less satisfactory, but nevertheless useful, is W. K. Matthews, *Russian Historical Grammar* (London, 1960). A. I. Sobolevsky, *Lekcii po istorii russkago jazyka*, 4th edn (Moscow, 1907; photomechanic reprint, The Hague, 1962), can still be read with great profit: later historical grammars owe a great debt to Sobolevsky's work. The history of Russian accentuation is well treated by V. Kiparsky, *Der Wortakzent der russischen Schriftsprache* (Heidelberg, 1962).

TEXTS

An excellent collection of texts to illustrate the history of the language is contained in

S. P. Obnorsky and S. G. Barkhudarov, *Chrestomatija po istorii russkogo jazyka*, vol. I, 2nd edn (Moscow, 1952; photomechanic reprint, London, 1971), vol. II i (Moscow, 1949), vol. II ii (Moscow, 1948).

DIALECTS
A succinct but useful survey is given in chapter v, pp. 86–106, of W. K. Matthews, *The Structure and Development of Russian* (Cambridge, 1953). More extensive and up to date is the work edited by R. I. Avanesov and V. G. Orlova, *Russkaja dialektologija*, 2nd edn (Moscow, 1965).

THE LITERARY LANGUAGE
There is no really satisfactory historical account of the whole history of the literary language. The essential facts are usefully presented by G. O. Vinokur, trans. M. A. Forsyth, ed. J. Forsyth, *The Russian Language – a Brief History* (Cambridge, 1971). A helpful guide is L. A. Bulakhovsky, *Istoričeskij kommentarij k russkomu literaturnomu jazyku*, 5th edn (Kiev, 1958). Of great importance for the problems of the literary language are the studies of B. O. Unbegaun, some of the more important of which are contained in his *Selected Papers on Russian and Slavonic Philology* (Oxford, 1969). The same author's *La Langue russe au XVIᵉ siècle 1500–1550*, I: *La flexion des noms* (Paris, 1935) has an importance that transcends the limits of its title. Of fundamental importance for the development of the vocabulary of the literary language are two works by Gerta Hüttl-Worth, *Die Bereicherung des russischen Wortschatzes im XVIII. Jahrhundert* (Vienna, 1956), and *Foreign Words in Russian. A Historical Sketch, 1550–1580*, University of California Publications in Linguistics, vol. 28 (Berkeley and Los Angeles, 1963).

OLD CHURCH SLAVONIC
Old Church Slavonic, a knowledge of which is indispensable for an understanding of the history of the Russian literary language, may be studied in the manual by G. Nandriş and R. Auty, *Handbook of Old Church Slavonic*, 2 vols. (London, 1959 and 1968).

EAST SLAVONIC LANGUAGES
Useful sketches of the grammar of Ukrainian and White Russian can be found in R. G. A. de Bray, *Guide to the Slavonic Languages*, 2nd edn (London and New York, 1969).

For further orientation in the literature of the subject students should consult B. O. Unbegaun and J. S. G. Simmons, *A Bibliographical Guide to the Russian Language* (Oxford, 1953), and, for publications after 1953, the annual commented bibliographies contributed by B. O. Unbegaun to the *Revue des Études slaves* (Paris) under the heading 'Chronique: russe'.

2

RUSSIAN WRITING AND PRINTING

A. WRITING

ROBERT AUTY

There is no direct or certain evidence of written documents among the eastern Slavs before the official conversion of Rus′ under Vladimir in c. 988. It is no doubt likely that attempts were made, either by Slavs or foreigners, to write down Russian words by means of foreign alphabets, especially Greek, for limited practical purposes. But no texts of this kind have survived and speculation about them is unprofitable. Certain pieces of evidence have been interpreted as testifying to the existence of a system of vernacular writing before 988, but none is entirely convincing. In the Church Slavonic *Life of St Cyril*, certainly composed in the ninth century but only preserved in later manuscripts, there is a passage (ch. VIII) describing how Constantine–Cyril, sojourning in the Crimea on the way to the Khazar realm, found 'a gospel and psalter written in Russian letters' ('rusьskymi pismeny pisano') and that he promptly learned the language in question. The passage has been interpreted in various ways. Some have taken it at its face value as evidence of the existence of a written Russian language in c. 860. The letters in question have been supposed by some to be a kind of proto-Cyrillic, by others to be the prototype of the Glagolitic alphabet (of which the great majority of scholars believe St Cyril to have been the originator). Yet the inherent unlikelihood of the existence at the date in question of Russian translations of the gospel and psalter have led most scholars to seek for other interpretations. There has been an ingenious suggestion that the books were Gothic; but there is nothing to support this conjecture other than the undoubted fact that a community of Gothic Christians did exist in the Crimea at the time of St Cyril's visit. Much more probable is the suggestion that *rusьskymi* is a medieval Russian scribe's alteration of an original *surьskymi* 'Syriac'. This metathesis has been found in other medieval manuscripts and there is little doubt that we have here a further example of it.

More tangible is the evidence of an earthenware vessel, excavated by archaeologists in 1949 at Gnyozdovo near Smolensk, which is ascribed to the early ninth century and bears an apparently Cyrillic inscription:

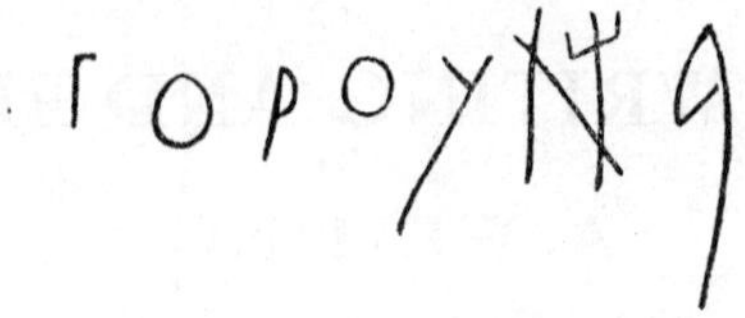

Fig. 2. The Gnyozdovo inscription

The obscurity of the final letters make the inscription difficult to interpret: it may be read as гороуна (i.e. '[the property] of Gorun'), or, less probably, as гороушьна ('mustard-seeds', i.e. the contents of the jar). In either case there can be no certainty that the vessel was made and inscribed in Russia. It may well have come from the Balkans with a Byzantine trader and cannot, in any case, serve as firm evidence for writing in the Smolensk region in the early ninth century.

The Russian Primary Chronicle contains the text of treaties made between Rus′ and the East Roman Empire in 911 and 944, after Oleg's and Igor's expeditions against Byzantium; and it is often asserted that these must have been drawn up in the Russian vernacular as well as in Greek, and indeed that the text of the Primary Chronicle preserves the original or something close to it. This too, however, is no more than conjecture. The extant text of the Chronicle was written down some centuries after the events recorded in these passages, albeit on the basis of earlier records; and it is in any case not clear from the text in what language the treaties were drawn up. The nature of the evidence does not enable us either to accept or reject these texts as proof of the existence of systematic vernacular writing in pre-Christian Kievan Rus′.

Prince Vladimir accepted Christianity for himself and his people in c. 988. Within a few decades literacy must have made great strides in Rus′, for we have a number of manuscripts from the second half of the eleventh century, beautifully executed and written, in some cases certainly, in others probably, by Russian scribes. The originals came for the most part from Bulgaria and were written in the Bulgarian form of Old Church Slavonic. Copied in Rus′, they took on local linguistic characteristics. The script was the uncial Cyrillic that had been devised in Bulgaria in the late ninth century. It is possible that the first Slavonic alphabet, the Glagolitic, was also to some extent in use in Rus′. No Glagolitic manuscript is preserved from the East Slavonic area; but there are instances of occasional Glagolitic letters being used in Russian Cyrillic manuscripts, as well as marginal annotations in Glagolitic. Moreover, the scribe Upyr′ Likhoy, writing in 1047, stated that he had transcribed the manuscript he was writing ис коуриловицѣ. It is probable that to this writer 'Cyrillic' still meant Glagolitic, and that the attribution to St Cyril of the alphabet that now bears his name arose later, when the Glagolitic alphabet had fallen out of use in the East Slavonic and East Balkan areas.

It was in any case the Cyrillic alphabet that became the normal medium of writing in eleventh-century Russia. The earliest dated manuscript is the Gospel-book (lectionary) written in 1056–7 by the Deacon Grigory for Ostromir, *posadnik* of Novgorod. The language is regular Old Church Slavonic with certain modifications in accordance with Russian usage; the text was certainly copied from an original made in Bulgaria. The script resembles that of contemporary Bulgarian manuscripts. It is the uncial type (*ustav*) which is based on ninth- and tenth-century Greek majuscule letters and which had become formalized in the scriptoria of the Bulgarian Empire. This is the style of writing which was universal in the East Slavonic area until the late fourteenth century and was used even after that for ceremonial purposes. The letters are written separately, with few or no ligatures and often without word-divisions; and they are of an almost geometrical regularity and symmetry, although from the twelfth century onwards there is a gradual but marked falling-off from the calligraphic perfection of the earliest manuscripts.

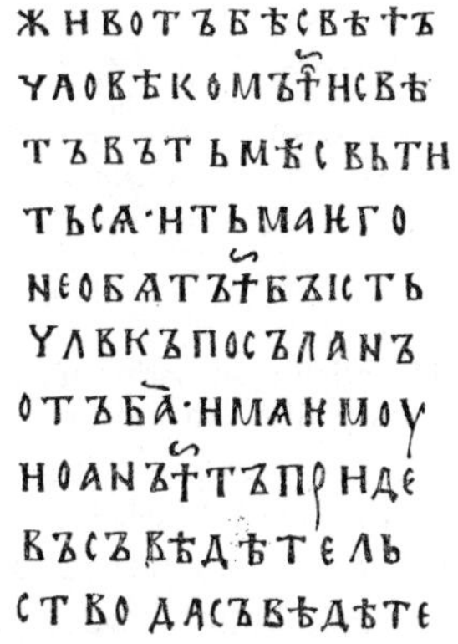

ЖИВОТ Ъ БѢСВѢТѢ
ҮЛОВѢКОМЪТӤНСВѢ
ТЪВЪТ ЬМѢСВЬТИ
ТЬСА·НТЬМАКГО
NЕОБАТЪТЕЗЮ ТЬ
ҮЛВКЗПОСЗЛАНЗ
ОТЪБА·НМАНЮҮ
НОАНЪТТЗПРНДЕ
ВЗСЗВѢДѢТЕЛЬ
СТВО ДАСЪВѢДѢТЕ

Fig. 3. Part of a page of the Ostromir Gospel Codex of 1056–7 (*ustav*)

A less careful style of writing, the semi-uncial (*poluustav*), which had arisen in the Balkans in the thirteenth century, became common in Russia towards the end of the fourteenth century (Fig. 4). The letters are smaller, the strokes forming them are thinner, and the harmonious regularity of the letter forms is to some extent lost, though the style still shows considerable aesthetic qualities compared with later cursive styles.

At about the same time, in the chancery of the Grand Duchy of Lithuania in Vilna, a cursive form of Cyrillic developed (*skoropis'*), partly under the influence of scribes from the Balkans but with some influence of Latin-alphabet cursive styles current in Poland. *Skoropis'*

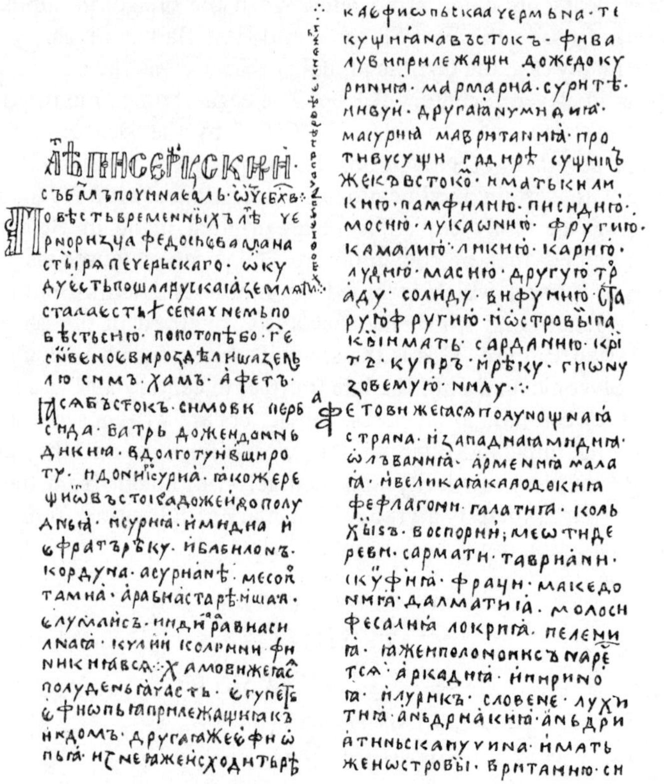

Fig. 4. A page from the Hypatian manuscript of the Chronicle (*poluustav*), early fifteenth century

was used for diplomatic and legal documents; for religious or other more ambitious texts *ustav* and *poluustav* continued to be used. From Lithuania the *skoropis'* spread to Moscow, though here from the beginning this style developed its own idiosyncratic forms (Fig. 5).

All the types of writing so far mentioned were produced by (quill) pen and ink. Until the fourteenth century all preserved Russian manuscripts were on parchment; in the course of that century paper began increasingly to come into use, and by the sixteenth century parchment was used only for documents of particular importance or for codices. There is, however, one further group of documents which is of particular interest for the history of Russian culture and to some extent also for the history of the language. This is represented by the texts written on birch bark between the eleventh and fifteenth centuries which have been unearthed by archaeologists in Novgorod and, to a very limited extent, in other medieval Russian sites.

44

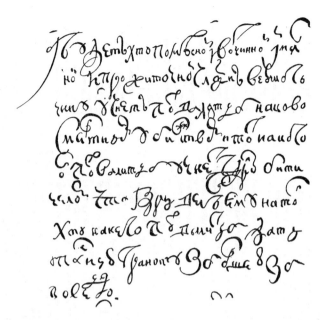

Fig. 5. A passage from the *Ulozheniye* of 1649 (*skoropis'*)

The texts are scratched by means of a bone stylus (a specimen of this instrument has been found) on the smooth inside surface of the bark. We know this means of writing to have been used by the Golden Horde in the thirteenth century and in Russia itself in later times (seventeenth–eighteenth century). Clearly birch bark provided a cheap and conveniently available alternative to parchment or paper for documents of an ephemeral kind. The texts are indeed mostly of a private character, concerned with commercial and personal matters.

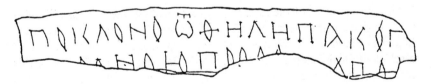

Fig. 6. Thirteenth-century birch-bark text from Novgorod

The ornamentation of medieval manuscripts does not fall within the subject of this chapter; but an exception must be made for that type of decoration which is itself formed from the letters of the text and is known in Russian as *vyaz'* (Fig. 7). This was a Byzantine development from the custom of writing the first line (sometimes the title) of a text in larger

Fig. 7. Examples of *vyaz'*: (a) Muscovy 1587. (b) Muscovy (1689).
(c) Lithuania, sixteenth century.

letters than the rest of the text. Sometimes this first line was also illuminated, and from the eleventh and twelfth centuries the letters were often
joined and intertwined, by means of extensions and ligatures, so as to form
a self-contained decorative pattern. South Slavonic manuscripts show this
type of decoration from the thirteenth century, and in the late fourteenth
century we find the first Russian examples. Two types of *vyaz'* were
developed in the Balkans – the 'natural' manner, in which the letters to
some extent retained their rounded shapes and were embellished by
stylized leaf and flower ornaments, and the 'geometrical' manner, where
the harmony and proportions of the letters were emphasized without any
extraneous features. A compromise manner also developed, in which the
'geometrical' forms of the letters were combined with scrolls and floral

elements. All these types found their way to the East Slavonic area; in the Grand Duchy of Lithuania the 'natural' type was adopted, while in Muscovy the 'geometrical' type was preferred and indeed developed in a highly individual way.

GUIDE TO FURTHER READING

An admirably clear and succinct introduction to the study of Russian palaeography is V. N. Shchepkin, *Uchebnik russkoy paleografii* (Moscow, 1918), reprinted as *Russkaya paleografiya* (Moscow, 1967). A more detailed manual is E. F. Karsky, *Slavyanskaya kirillovskaya paleografiya* (Leningrad, 1928). Useful is also L. V. Cherepnin, *Russkaya paleografiya* (Moscow, 1956). Although it concentrates almost exclusively on manuscripts written in the Grand Duchy of Lithuania, B. Horodyski, *Podręcznik paleografii ruskiej* (Cracow, 1951), is one of the most useful introductory manuals of the subject. A very good study of the Novgorod birch-bark texts (covering all those found up to 1953) is that of W. Kuraszkiewicz, *Gramoty nowogrodzkie na brzozowej korze*, 2 vols. (Warsaw, 1957). The texts discovered since 1953 must be studied in A. V. Artsikhovsky and V. I. Borkovsky, *Novgorodskiye gramoty na beryoste (iz raskopok 1953–1954 gg.)* (Moscow, 1958); *Novgorodskiye gramoty na beryoste (iz raskopok 1955 g.)* (Moscow, 1958); *Novgorodskiye gramoty na beryoste (iz raskopok 1956–1957 gg.)* Moscow, 1963); *Novgorodskiye gramoty na beryoste (iz raskopok 1958–1961 gg.)* (Moscow, 1963).

B. PRINTING

J. S. G. SIMMONS

The first surviving book with a dated Moscow imprint is the Liturgical Epistle-book (*Apostol*) which Ivan Fyodorov and Pyotr Timofeyev Mstislavets began printing on 19 April 1563 and completed on 1 March 1564. By then books had been printed in Cyrillic type for over seventy years, and in Moscow itself several unsigned ('anonymous') books had preceded or been printed much at the same time as the *Apostol*. These were all liturgical works and in their external features they resemble – though they do not rival – the splendid *Apostol* itself. The early Moscow books are all folios and they closely follow the local manuscript tradition in their general layout, in their use of red printing, in the large size and calligraphic styles of their types, in their ornament (especially the characteristic and beautiful interlace or foliage *zastavki* or headpieces), in their use of ornamental letter-ligature (*vyaz'*), and in their lack of title-pages.

The relationship between the 'Anonymous Press' and the two *pervopechatniki* is uncertain, but the latter were at first explicitly sponsored by Tsar Ivan IV and Metropolitan Makary. None the less, after printing two editions of an octavo Book of Hours (*Chasovnik*) from August to October 1565, the two men left Muscovy taking at least a part of their typographical materials with them. They printed at Zabludov in White Russia in 1569–70 but later parted company, Pyotr Mstislavets going to Vilna and Ivan Fyodorov to Lvov where he printed a second edition of the *Apostol* and the first Church Slavonic primer (both in 1574). By 1578 he was at Ostrog in Volhynia where he gave evidence of his learning (he was possibly a graduate of Cracow University) by printing a little Greek–Church Slavonic chrestomathy; the great Ostrog folio *editio princeps* of the Church Slavonic Bible followed three years later (1581), and Fyodorov died in Lvov on 6 December 1583.

Official printing revived at Moscow within four years of the departure of the *pervopechatniki*. A Psalter was published in 1568, and in 1577 another Psalter (and probably a Book of Hours a little later) came from the press at Tsar Ivan's Aleksandrovskaya Sloboda. In Moscow itself printing began again in 1589, but the total number of known Moscow-printed books from the beginnings to 1612 does not exceed thirty.

After the chaos of the Time of Troubles the official Moscow Printing House (*Pechatnyy dvor*) began to function in the summer of 1614. By 1620 it had its own buildings just north of the Kremlin, where it was divided for production purposes into 'huts' (*izby*) for each of which a master printer was responsible. Some of its more noteworthy products were the primers (1634 and 1637) issued by the most enterprising of its master printers, Vasily Fyodorovich Burtsov, which preserve the tradition of Ivan Fyodorov's 1574 Lvov original; the *Ucheniye i khitrost' ratnago stroyeniya pekhotnykh lyudey* (1647–9, a translated treatise on infantry tactics and the first purely secular Moscow-printed book); and the first civil law code to be printed in Moscow, the *Ulozheniye* of 1649.

As regards design, seventeenth-century Moscow books continued to follow the style of the earliest Moscow products. A few new types were cut, but all were in the Ivan Fyodorov tradition; a small letter made its appearance in 1648 and was later used in the 1663 Bible – the *chef-d'œuvre* of seventeenth-century Moscow typography. Cast ornaments are found from the 1640s but the woodcut remained the normal decorative medium: such woodcuts copied and developed motifs which are traceable to the earliest Moscow printing. Headpieces, however, tend to become more symmetrical and architectural in design and from 1677 include a small cross as a signal that the texts they accompany incorporate the Niconian corrections. The first Moscow title-page did not appear until 1641 (in a *Kanonnik* printed by Burtsov) but title-pages are rare until the

1660s. Some of them, e.g. that of the 1663 Bible, and some of the woodcut frontispieces and frames are not without merit. Engraved plates of Dutch origin had appeared in the *Ucheniye i khitrost'* of 1647–9, but the earliest evidence for the use of the rolling-press in Muscovy dates from 1677.

By the end of the seventeenth century only about 500 books had been printed in Moscow, almost all of which were religious in content. During the century similar works were printed outside Moscow, on territory which became (or was eventually to become) part of the Russian Empire, at – among other places – Vilna (to 1644) and Kuteyno (1637–54) and, in the Ukraine, at Kiev (from 1616), Lvov, and Chernigov (from 1679). The Ukrainian publications in particular are already notable for the excellence of their woodcut decoration and illustration.

The end of the seventeenth century marks a turning point in the history of Russian printing. Peter the Great wished to encourage the spread of secular knowledge and arranged for Jan Tessing and Il'ya Kopiyevsky to commission books, and for Heinrich Wetstein to print to order in Amsterdam (1699–1705). The dozen or so books which they produced were printed in types which, though of Dutch make, differed little in design from those used by the *pervopechatniki*. Peter evidently thought that both the Dutch and the contemporary Moscow types were unsuitably complex, and commissioned more streamlined alphabets from Moscow and Amsterdam punch-cutters. The resultant 'secular face' (*grazhdanskiy shrift*), which omitted some letters (others were dropped in 1735, 1738, 1758 and 1917) stood in the same general relationship to the old 'ecclesiastical face' (*tserkovnyy shrift*) as roman type does to black-letter. The first secular-face book (a work on geometry) appeared in Moscow in 1708, and as the new types became available the use of the ecclesiastical face was restricted to religious and liturgical works.

The first Russian newspaper was established in 1702, and the new capital, St Petersburg, with its face set firmly towards the West, was soon to break the near-monopoly of Moscow printing. Five presses were established in the city between 1711 and 1727, including the important secular presses of the Senate (1724) and the Academy of Sciences (1727). The balance was somewhat restored by the setting up in Moscow of a press at the first Russian university in 1756, but although its average output (quantitative and qualitative) was to surpass that of any other Russian press, of the approximately 10,000 books printed in secular types in Russia during the eighteenth century (as against 1,500 or so ecclesiastical editions), considerably more than half came from St Petersburg presses. Printing in ecclesiastical types continued both at Moscow and St Petersburg and also at Kiev and in half-a-dozen other provincial centres, but secular printing in the provinces did not develop until after the decree of 1783 which authorized the establishment of presses on private initiative. Between 1784 and the end of the century some 250 titles had been printed in a score of Russian provincial towns, including Tobol'sk in Siberia and Perm' in the Urals – at the latter improbable place the first Russian printing manual was published in 1796. Presses were even established on a couple of private estates – Ruzayevka and Kazinka – where their owners printed their own lucubrations and Voltairiana respectively. The second half of the century also saw the rise of the Russian periodical press; over one hundred journals made their appearance between 1755 and the end of the century, some of them satirical and influential, most of them short lived and with relatively small circulations.

During the eighteenth century the physical features of the Russian book developed along lines which were to make it (*mutatis mutandis*) indistinguishable from the contemporary western European product: type-design, layout, the use of engraved plates no longer surprise by their unfamiliarity. Type-design indeed follows Western trends in that towards the end of the century the two main foundries (the Academy of Sciences at St Petersburg and the University Press at Moscow) were producing types which, though based on the Petrine design, show quasi-Didot features.

The last decade of the eighteenth century was marked by increasing repression, starting with the confiscation of A. N. Radishchev's privately-printed and bitter *Puteshestviye* in 1790. The previous decade, during which N. I. Novikov, the enlightened lessee of the Moscow University Press, had produced nearly 900 titles (over one-third of the national output), was only a memory when in 1796 all independent presses were closed down. With the turn of the century, however, came the wind of change. In 1801 the new emperor, Alexander I, abolished the censorship and permitted the setting-up of independent presses once again. By 1811 there were 106 printing houses in Russia. A well-equipped State Paper Printing House (*Ekspeditsiya zagotovleniya gosudarstvennykh bumag*), which incorporated a paper-mill, was established at St Petersburg in 1818 and was soon employing 500 hands. Stereotyping (1814) and the first printing machine (1816) were imported into Russia from Britain by the Russian Bible Society. Such technical advances encouraged the development of the newspaper press, and it is significant that it was the *Severnaya pchela* (1825–64) – the first privately-owned Russian newspaper to give political news – that installed the first Russian-made printing machine in 1829. In general, however, the mechanization of printing processes was slow to develop in Russia.

The circulation of literature in manuscript in Russia well into the nineteenth century is only partly explicable in terms of censorship: it was also in part due to the limited output of the available presses. One way in which the demand for 'reading-matter' had been met ever since the seventeenth century was by means of the mass-production of chapbooks and broadsheets (*lubki, lubochnye izdaniya*) in which both illustrations and text were printed – and could be almost indefinitely reprinted – from the same woodblock, or copper or lithographic plate. Largely owing to the introduction of the last technique into Russia in 1816 the circulation of *lubki* reached vast proportions during the second half of the nineteenth century and continued until the early years of the twentieth. At the other end of the scale, the lithographic technique was used in fine books, e.g. for the plates and title-pages of some of the historical works splendidly printed for Count N. P. Rumyantsev by Vsevolozhsky and Selivanovsky in Moscow between 1813 and 1829. Chromolithography was first practised in Russia by K. Ya. Tromonin in 1833.

The second quarter of the nineteenth century was an unpropitious time for printing. Censorship had tightened after the honeymoon at the beginning of Alexander I's reign, and as a result of the unsuccessful Decembrist revolt in 1825 the screw was turned with a vengeance. As a consequence, in the thirty years between 1825 and 1855 the annual output of books rose from 583 to no more than 1,012. The shake-up in Russian society produced by the Crimean war and the death of Nicholas I in 1855 marked yet another turning point: censorship underwent some relaxation in the 1860s, and in the fourteen years between 1855 and 1868 annual book production rose from 1,012 to 3,366 titles; in 1865 twenty-eight independent newspapers were being published; between 1855 and 1861 the number of journals more than doubled (104 to 230); and between 1861 and 1868 the number of printing houses in the Empire increased from 164 to over 500 (nearly half of them lithographic). Relatively few of the presses were in the provinces – in 1860 Russian books were printed in no more than twenty-seven provincial towns throughout the Empire. Most of the printing houses were small: the development of large commercial undertakings, e.g. A. S. Suvorin in St Petersburg and I. P. Sytin in Moscow, dates from the 1870s. Their items of heavy equipment were mainly imported (the first rotary by Suvorin in 1878), though a native machine-building industry had begun to be of some importance in the 1860s. Its products, however, could not compete with the imported article, and the last Russian machine-building plant had closed down some time before 1917. Mechanical composition was both a late development and a characteristic feature of newspaper houses, e.g. Suvorin and Sytin; linotype and monotype machines were first imported in 1905; and it is significant that in 1913, when 2.7 million copies of 856 newspapers (including, incidentally, some Bolshevik ones) were being issued, there were only some 200 linotypes in operation in the Empire.

In its design, the nineteenth-century Russian book followed a path which ran parallel to its western European counterparts. As regards illustration techniques lithography (which reached a high standard in the 1840s) yielded to steel-engravings, and steel-engravings to the line-block and the half-tone; high-quality photogravure and collotype were later developments. There was no Russian equivalent to the 'private press movement', but at the turn of the century the artists of the 'World of Art' (*Mir iskusstva*) school, e.g. L. S. Bakst, A. N. Benois, I. Ya. Bilibin, and Ye. Ye. Lansere, applied their refined taste and brilliant technical skills to book illustration and design. They found their inspiration for the most part in the Russian past, in folk art, in eighteenth-century Russian rococo, and in Russian neo-classicism of the early nineteenth century – plus a dash of Aubrey Beardsley. Much of their work went into handsomely-produced journals and limited editions (often printed by the State Paper Printing Office or by Golike and Vil'borg in St Petersburg), but their influence was felt at all levels and many average Russian books published during the first three decades of the twentieth century owe their distinction directly or indirectly to the artists of *Mir iskusstva*. Their influence was also felt in the field of type-design and led to the cutting of faces which looked back to eighteenth-century Russian exemplars, having broken away from the 'Russianized romans' – ultimately of German origin – which had earlier predominated.

By the beginning of the First World War Russia had a printing industry which was generally under-equipped by western European standards but which included a number of very large undertakings and many presses, e.g. that of the Academy of Sciences, capable of producing complex work of the highest quality. Improvements in design, the relative innocuousness of the censorship (undermined by the revolutionary events of 1905), and the growth in readership augured well for the future: in 1914 over 32,000 titles were published. All changed with the war and revolution: the war-time collapse of the economy, the nationalization of plants after 1917, and the catastrophes of the period of war communism and intervention at first placed printing on a hand-to-mouth basis. But the ideological importance of the industry was clear, and during the 1920s the situation was gradually restored. The diversity which followed on the New Economic Policy in 1921 led to a revival, and some of the books produced by the 'World of Art' designers who remained in Russia, e.g. S. V. Chekhonin, B. M. Kustodiyev, and D. I. Mitrokhin, and – at the other end of the spectrum – by Lissitzky and his school, are outstanding for their harmony and impact respectively. V. A. Favorsky, too, brilliantly developed the delicate art of the wood-engraver along lines which combined tradition and innovation.

The avowed aim of the new regime in Russia was to build a printing industry capable of satisfying the demands of the newly literate masses, including the populations of the non-Russian nationalities. Type design was consequently more concerned with extra sorts than with new faces, and the earliest of the original post-Revolutionary faces date from the mid-1930s which, incidentally, is also the period when a Soviet machine-building and composing-machine-building industry at last came into production. The second world war dealt another body blow to Soviet printing, but during the thirty years which have elapsed since its end the industry has been re-established on a more productive scale than ever, with large printing combines in many parts of the USSR catering for the immense runs which are such a characteristic feature of the largest publishing industry in the world. General design improved noticeably during the second half of the period and a few original text and display faces of merit have been produced by Soviet designers. The advantages that compulsory standardization brings with it seem, however, to have been accompanied by a relative absence of experimentation, and the average mass-produced Soviet book is sometimes gratuitously undistinguished. But here the fault often lies with poor paper, poor casing, and the emphasis on quantity imposed by the need to meet the demands of a vast and avid reading public.

GUIDE TO FURTHER READING

BIBLIOGRAPHY
E. L. Nemirovsky, *Problemy knigovedeniya, istoriya knizhnogo dela: obzor litera-tury, 1964–1969 gg.* (Moscow, 1970). For the literature to 1963 and from 1970 onwards see the lists in the first and third items in the following paragraph and also *ABHB: Annual Bibliography of the History of the Printed Book and Libraries*, I, 1970 (The Hague, 1973) onwards.

GENERAL
400 let russkogo knigopechataniya, 2 vols., ed. A. A. Sidorov (Moscow, 1964); E. I. Katsprzhak, *Istoriya knigi*, 2nd edn (Moscow, 1964); *Kniga: issledovaniya i materialy*, I– (Moscow, 1959–).

BY PERIOD (see also under Lithuania, Ukraine and White Russia below)
E. L. Nemirovsky, *Vozniknoveniye knigopechataniya v Moskve: Ivan Fyodorov* (Moscow, 1964); A. S. Zyornova, *Nachalo knigopechataniya v Moskve i na Ukraine* (Moscow, 1947); K. Appel, 'Die Anfänge des Buchdrucks im Moskauer Russland', *Archiv für Geschichte des Buchwesens*, X (1969–70), cols. 1355–98; S. P. Luppov, *Kniga v Rossii v XVII veke* (Leningrad, 1970); *idem, Kniga v Rossii v pervoy chetverti XVIII veka* (Leningrad, 1973); M. N. Kufayev, *Istoriya russkoy knigi v XIX veke* (Leningrad, 1927).

DESIGN, ILLUSTRATION
A. A. Sidorov, *Istoriya oformleniya russkoy knigi*, 2nd edn (Moscow, 1964); *idem, Drevnerusskaya knizhnaya gravyura* (Moscow, 1951); Ya. P. Zapasko, *Mistets'ka spadshchyna Ivana Fyodorova* (Lvov, 1974); A. S. Zyornova, *Ornamentika knig*

moskovskoy pechati XVI–XVII vv.: al'bom (Moscow, 1952); *idem, Ornamentika knig moskovskoy pechati kirillovskogo shrifta, 1677–1750,* 2 vols., limited edition (Moscow, 1963); A. A. Sidorov, *Russkaya grafika nachala XX veka: ocherki istorii i teorii* (Moscow, 1969); V. P. Bogdanov *et al., Ot azbuki Ivana Fyodorova do sovremennogo bukvarya,* ed. A. I. Markushevich (Moscow, 1974).

CHAPBOOKS, POPULAR PRINTS, ENGRAVED BOOKS

D. A. Rovinsky, *Russkiye narodnyye kartinki,* 5 vols. text, 4 vols. plates (St Petersburg, 1881–93); Yu. Ovsyannikov, *Lubok: russkiye narodnyye kartinki XVII–XVIII vv.* (Moscow, 1968; text in Russian and English); S. A. Klepikov, 'Russian block books of the seventeenth and eighteenth centuries', *Papers of the Bibliographical Society of America,* LXV (1971), 213–24; *idem,* 'Russkiye graviro-vannyye knigi XVII–XVIII vekov', *Kniga: issledovaniya i materialy,* IX (1964), 141–77.

TECHNICAL ASPECTS

V. P. Orlov, *Poligraficheskaya promyshlennost' Moskvy: ocherki razvitiya do 1917 goda* (Moscow, 1953); E. L. Nemirovsky, Articles in *Poligrafiya,* 1963, no. 10, pp. 33–6; no. 11, pp. 27–30; no. 12, pp. 24–7; 1964 no. 1, pp. 32–6.

TYPE DESIGN

A. G. Shitsgal, *Russkiy grazhdanskiy shrift, 1708–1958* (Moscow, 1959); *idem, Russkiy tipografskiy shrift: voprosy istorii i praktika primeneniya* (Moscow, 1974); I. L. Kaldor, 'The genesis of Russian grazhdanskiy shrift or civil type', *Journal of typographic research* (Cleveland, USA), III (1969), 315–44; IV (1970), 111–37.

MISCELLANEOUS

Censorship

L. M. Dobrovol'sky, *Zapreshchonnaya kniga v Rossii, 1825–1904* (Moscow, 1962).

Journals, newspapers

V. G. Beryozina *et al., Istoriya russkoy zhurnalistiki XVIII–XIX vekov,* ed. A. Zapadov, 3rd edn (Moscow, 1973); B. I. Yesin, *Russkaya dorevolyutsionnaya gazeta* (Moscow, 1971).

Reading public

E. V. Bank, *Izucheniye chitateley v Rossii v XIX v.* (Moscow, 1969).

Revolutionary press

I. G. Levitas *et al., Revolyutsionnyye podpol'nyye tipografii Rossii, 1860–1917 gg.* (Moscow, 1962).

LITHUANIA

A. Anushkin, *Na zare knigopechataniya v Litve* (Vilna, 1970); L. Vladimirovas, *Frantsisk Skorina – pervopechatnik vil'nyusskiy* (Vilna, 1975).

UKRAINE

O. I. Dey *et al., Knyha i drukarstvo na Ukrayini,* ed. P. M. Popov (Kiev, 1964); Ya. D. Isayevych *et al., Pershodrukar Ivan Fyodorov ta yoho poslidovnyky na Ukrayini (XVI–persha polovyna XVII st.): zbirnyk dokumentiv* (Kiev, 1975); E. L. Nemirovsky, *Nachalo knigopechataniya na Ukraine: Ivan Fyodorov*

(Moscow, 1974): Ya. D. Isayevych, *Pershodrukar Ivan Fyodorov i vynyknennya drukarstva na Ukrayini* (Lvov, 1975); Ya. P. Zapasko, *Mystetstvo knyhy na Ukrayini v XVI–XVIII st.* (Lvov, 1971).

WHITE RUSSIA (see also under Lithuania)

K. K. Atrakhovich *et al.*, *450 hod belaruskaha kniha-drukavannya* (Minsk, 1968).

3

EARLY RUSSIAN LITERATURE

(1000–1300)

DIMITRI OBOLENSKY

The earliest datable works of Russian literature were written in the first half of the eleventh century. The view, advanced by some literary historians, that this literature has a 'prehistory' going back to the tenth century rests on two plausible though unproven hypotheses: that certain passages extant in later works were composed before the year 1000; and that the existence of literacy in tenth-century Russia led to the rise, in this period, of an embryonic literary tradition. The latter hypothesis deserves brief consideration here.

There is no doubt that literature appeared in Russia as a result of the country's conversion to Christianity. Officially this conversion took place in 988 or 989, when Prince Vladimir of Kiev accepted Byzantine Christianity and began to impose it on his subjects. But missionaries from Constantinople are known to have been active in Russia as early as the 860s; and despite the avowed paganism of the greater part of the country's ruling classes between 880 and 980, there is reason to believe that a Christian community existed at least in Kiev, the capital of the realm, continuously, or with brief interruptions, for 125 years before Vladimir's baptism. It seems unlikely that the clergy which ministered to this community was exclusively Byzantine, and that the Christian scriptures and the liturgy were available to Russian Christians in the tenth century solely in the Greek language, with which the great majority of them were unfamiliar. If it is further remembered that the beginnings of Christianity in Russia coincide in time with the mission of Cyril and Methodius to Moravia and with the conversion of Bulgaria to the Christian faith, and that close political relations existed in the tenth century between the Eastern Slavs on the one hand and the Western and Southern Slavs on the other, it will appear highly probable that elements of the Cyrillo–Methodian tradition – the Slavonic liturgy and Slavonic translations of parts of the scriptures – were brought to Russia well before the time of St Vladimir. Though direct evidence on this point is lacking, we may assume that they came either from Moravia and

Bohemia, or from Bulgaria, or even from Constantinople, where the Byzantine authorities in the second half of the ninth century stockpiled Slavonic books for the needs of their missionary enterprises in Slav countries. On these foundations, laid by the Cyrillo–Methodian translations of the Greek liturgy and scriptures into the newly created Old Church Slavonic language, medieval Russian literature was built. The schools founded by Vladimir shortly after his baptism, in which instruction 'in book learning' was imparted (undoubtedly in Slavonic) to children of noble families, were probably the original training ground for the educated *élite* which, in the reign of his son Yaroslav (1019–54), produced the earliest works of this literature.

TRANSLATED LITERATURE

If Christianity provided the initial stimulus for the growth of literacy in Russia, the development of a native literary tradition was facilitated by the importation of an extensive corpus of translated Old Church Slavonic literature. Much of it undoubtedly came from Bulgaria, where at the turn of the ninth century, and especially in the reign of the Tsar Symeon (893–927), the disciples of Cyril and Methodius produced Slavonic versions of many Greek religious and secular writings. To this work of adapting Byzantine civilization to the religious and cultural needs of the empire's Slav converts, the Russians soon made their own contribution. According to the Russian Primary Chronicle, Prince Yaroslav, whom it repeatedly describes as 'a lover of books', 'assembled many scribes and had them translate from Greek into the Slavonic language. And they wrote many books.' This statement, which refers to the year 1037, is followed by another passage in which the chronicler tells us that Yaroslav deposited these books in the newly built church of St Sophia in Kiev, the principal cathedral of the land. The extent of the contribution made by the Russians to this body of translated literature cannot be determined exactly: most of its products are extant in later manuscripts; while the homogeneity of the common Slavonic literary tradition until the end of the eleventh century was such that it is often difficult to distinguish on linguistic grounds an Old Church Slavonic text written in Russia from one composed in Bulgaria or Bohemia. It is safer to accept the view of A. I. Sobolevsky that nearly all the extant translations made in Bulgaria in the ninth and tenth centuries circulated in Russia during the first centuries after the country's conversion, to recognize that a number of other translations were made in this period by Russians, and to list the more important works known to have been available in the Kievan period.

It may be assumed that the earliest translated writings to reach the

Russians were those needed for Christian instruction and worship. The New Testament, translated into Slavonic by Cyril and Methodius for the needs of their mission to Moravia, was available in two different forms: in the full text, intended for private reading, and in selected passages appointed to be read liturgically on Sundays and feast days. An outstanding example of the latter type, known as *aprakos*, is the Ostromir Gospel copied in 1056–7 by the Deacon Grigory, the earliest dated Slavonic manuscript of the Russian redaction. Of the books of the Old Testament, the complete Slavonic version of which was unknown in Russia until the late fifteenth century, the most popular was the Book of Psalms: it was frequently quoted by writers of the Kievan period; it was used as a basic manual for instruction in reading; and its poetic qualities made it an invaluable source of literary inspiration. The literary tastes and techniques of medieval Russian writers were also greatly influenced by Byzantine liturgical poetry, which they learned to appreciate in the Slavonic versions of the liturgies of St John Chrysostom, of St Basil of Caesarea, and of the Presanctified, and of the other Byzantine service books, such as the *Euchologion*, the *Horologion*, the *Triodion*, the *Pentekostarion*, the *Heirmologion* and the *Oktoechos*.

The Slavonic translations of the scriptures and of the liturgical books were the first prerequisites for establishing Christianity in Russia. The next step was to provide the young Russian Church with a means of consolidating and spreading the new faith. The Byzantine missionaries and their Slav converts found this instrument in Greek patristic literature. The most popular were the writings of Basil of Caesarea, Gregory of Nazianzus, John Chrysostom and Ephraim Syrus. Slavonic versions of their works were available separately, but more often in extracts collected in miscellanies. Of these the most notable are the two *Izborniki* copied in 1073 and 1076 for Prince Svyatoslav of Kiev (the first of these, in addition to theological and historical material, contains the treatise 'on tropes and figures of speech in poetry' by the Byzantine grammarian George Choeroboscus), *Zlatostruy* (a collection of John Chrysostom's sermons) and *Pchela* ('Melissa' – 'The Bee') which comprises scriptural and patristic quotations, as well as aphorisms and didactic anecdotes attributed to ancient writers and philosophers, including Plato and Aristotle. It is noteworthy that the great majority of the Greek Fathers whose works were available in Slavonic translations in this period belonged to the golden age of Patristics – the fourth and fifth centuries. Apart from the unrivalled authority enjoyed by these writings in eastern Christendom, this preference can be explained by the fact that they provided theoretical and practical guidance to Russian churchmen who, like their early Byzantine predecessors, strove to impose Christianity upon a still semi-pagan environment.

Another type of religious writing for which the Russians showed a special fondness were the lives of the saints. Most of them were grouped in various collections. The *Prolog*, containing brief notices concerning saints' lives, arranged according to the calendar of the ecclesiastical year, is a translation of the Byzantine *Synaxarion*, with the addition of South Slavonic and Russian material; it was probably translated in Constantinople in the twelfth century by an international group which included Bulgarian and Russian scholars, and it soon became one of the most popular books in medieval Russia. The *Chet'i Minei*, a translation of the Greek *Menaea*, probably known in Russia by the early eleventh century, contain more extensive *Vitae*, arranged by months of the liturgical calendar. Both these collections were mainly intended for public reading in church on the day of the saint's festival. A third kind of hagiographical miscellany were the *Pateriki* ('Books of the Fathers'), which included short stories from the recorded lives of east Christian monks and hermits. Their material was derived from Greek ascetical treatises compiled between the fifth and the seventh centuries, such as *The Book of the Holy Men*, the *Lausiac History* of Palladius and the *Pratum Spirituale* of John Moschus. These translated *Pateriki* did much to stimulate and shape the development of monasticism in Kievan Russia. Some of these *Vitae* circulated as separate works; among the most popular were the *Lives* of St Andrew Salos (*Yurodivyy*) who lived – probably in the tenth century – as a beggar in Constantinople, and of St Alexius, a young Roman nobleman who left his wife on his wedding night and, after many years spent in prayer and fasting in distant lands, returned to die in his parents' home, unrecognized by anyone. Although the considerable majority of the saints' *Lives* current in Kievan Russia were translations from the Greek, a few were imported in the eleventh century from Central Europe: among them were the martyrdom of St Vitus and of St Apollinarius of Ravenna, and the Slavonic *Vitae* of SS Cyril, Methodius and Wenceslas. Apart from their religious significance, some at least of these hagiographical works were, by their literary qualities, capable of bringing enjoyment to the Russian reader and of satisfying his craving for the wonderful and the miraculous.

A special position among the translated religious writings was held by the so-called 'apocrypha'. These were works of Biblical, hagiographical and eschatological content which were not recognized by the Church. Some were openly condemned (Svyatoslav's *Izbornik* of 1073 contains a list of twenty-five 'secret' books on the Church's index), others, which did not explicitly contradict official doctrine, seem to have been tolerated. Among writings regarded as heretical were tales about the creation of man, which ascribe an active role to the devil and contain elements of Bogomilism, a dualist, neo-Manichaean, movement which appeared in

Bulgaria in the tenth century. Of the more harmless 'apocrypha' one of the most popular was 'The Mother of God's Journey through Torments'. It describes in some detail the Virgin's descent into hell, her pity for the damned and her intercession, partly successful, before her Son aimed at relieving their sufferings. The reference, in a twelfth-century Russian manuscript of this work, to a category of sinners, damned for having worshipped a number of East Slavonic pagan divinities, shows that a Byzantine work could be adapted to a local cultural environment. These apocryphal writings, often moving in content and vivid in form, came to Russia mostly via Bulgaria, sometimes, it would seem, through oral channels. Some of them, in the later middle ages, influenced the authors of the *dukhovnyye stikhi*, the native oral religious poems.

A study of these translated works is of interest to the literary historian because it shows that many of them appealed to the Russians not only on account of their religious content, but also for their poetic qualities or narrative interest. Sometimes indeed the edifying and the picturesque were scarcely distinguishable: this is the case of *Barlaam and Josaphat*, a Christian version of an Indian story of the Buddha. Other writings, more explicitly secular in character, were clearly selected for their literary qualities or informative nature. Among them were Josephus' *History of the Jewish War* (translated in Russia in the Kievan period), the *Romance of Alexander* by the Pseudo-Callisthenes, which introduced the Russian reader to the world of antiquity, the *Physiologus*, the *Christian Topography* of Cosmas Indicopleustes, which provided them with a smattering of natural history and geography, and the *Devgeniyevo deyaniye*, generally regarded as a fragmentary Russian prose translation of an early version of the Byzantine epic poem *Digenis Akritas*. All these works were translated from Greek into Slavonic not later than the twelfth century.

Of all the writings of Byzantine secular literature it was the chronicles which had the greatest impact on the educated Russians of the early middle ages. From them they acquired some knowledge of world history and a capacity for independent historical thought. The choice which they made in the corpus of Byzantine historiography was a significant one. This historiography was of two kinds: on the one hand there were the ordered and pragmatic accounts of the recent past by writers who strove to imitate the ideas and style of Herodotus and Thucydides and to discover the causal relations between events; these writings were generally known as histories. On the other hand there were the chronicles, popular works with a conception of history less sophisticated and more explicitly Christian. They were usually written by monks, in homely language, and were intended for a less educated reader. Their theme was world history, from Adam to the writer's time, and they aimed to illustrate the role played by human societies – notably those of the Jews, the Greeks, the

Romans and the Byzantines – in the unfolding story of man's salvation. It is a remarkable fact that, whereas not one of the Byzantine histories seems to have been translated into Slavonic during the middle ages, Slav versions were made of most of the chronicles. Two of them, the Chronicles of John Malalas and of George the Monk (or Hamartolos), had a notable influence on the development of early Russian literature. The former, written in the sixth century, ranges from the Creation to the last years of the reign of Justinian I. It was translated in Bulgaria in the tenth century, and was known in Russia by the late eleventh. The translation of Hamartolos' Chronicle – generally thought to have been done in eleventh-century Russia – combined the original version, a universal history from Adam to 842, with a sequel which carried the history of Byzantium to the year 948. These two chronicles greatly enlarged the geographical horizons of the Russians and, by giving them an outline of world history down to the middle of the tenth century, provided a framework for their own independent historical research. The universalist scope and religious content of the chronicles no doubt explain the fact that the Russians, as well as the other Orthodox Slavs, preferred them to the Byzantine secular histories. The belief that the destiny of nations is a stake in the age-long struggle between the forces of good and evil and that God's plan in history is furthered by the conversion of these nations to the Christian faith – these ideas, which the chronicles expound with special force, could be put to practical use by those Slavs who sought to understand and explain the events of their countries' recent past. This interpretation of history had the further advantage of being incomplete: the common-wealth of Christian nations was ever capable of expansion, and the story left unfinished in the Byzantine chronicles could now be continued by the Russians themselves. As we shall see, the historical writers of Kievan Russia were not slow to draw this conclusion.

The preceding survey of the main types of literature available to the Russians in the early middle ages in translation (mostly from the Greek) may help to illustrate the process of diffusion of Byzantine civilization to the Slav world. Two features of this process are worth noting here. In the first place, it is probable that many of these writings, when they were not translated by the Russians themselves, were chosen and imported either by them or at their request, some indeed, particularly the religious ones, in response to urgent practical needs. Secondly, a number of these works, especially those with a secular content, underwent a gradual change in their adopted home, acquiring new features or developing local variants. By continuing to live and develop on their new soil, in a society which was itself in a state of rapid change, these transplanted works stimulated, by a kind of cultural osmosis, the growth of 'original' literature.

ORIGINAL LITERATURE

The historian of early Russian literature faces at the outset a difficult problem of chronological classification. The 'medieval' period of this literature, which begins in the first half of the eleventh century, is generally held to have come to an end in the second half of the seventeenth. There is far less agreement, however, on the internal divisions within this period of six and a half centuries. On stylistic grounds, perhaps the only clear dividing line can be drawn in the second half of the fourteenth century, when Russian writers, particularly in the field of hagiography, begin to display a new outlook and taste. This new movement, distinguished by linguistic archaism, a somewhat antiquarian outlook, an ornateness of style, a liking for rhetorical turns of phrase and an indebtedness to the mystical tradition of Hesychasm, stemmed in large measure from the Balkans, and is known to Russian literary historians as the 'Second South Slavonic influence' (a term intended to suggest a distinction between it and the Bulgarian literary influence exerted on Russia in the early middle ages). This concept, however, is not wholly appropriate, for it fails to do full justice both to the cosmopolitan nature of this literary movement and to its native Russian antecedents.

In the absence of any wholly satisfactory periodization of Russian medieval literature on literary grounds, it is preferable to seek for other criteria of classification. By combining geographical, linguistic, ethnic and political data, we may draw a more acceptable contrast between two distinct phases of this literature: in broad outline they correspond to the periods between the years 1000 and 1300, and between 1400 and 1700. In the first of these periods Russian literature developed within an area which was still relatively unified. Kiev, at least until the Mongol invasion of 1237–40, enjoyed a real, if gradually diminishing, cultural supremacy; despite the growing political fragmentation, a sense of national unity, rooted in the cultural and political achievements of the eleventh century, was still maintained; and the Russian literary idiom had not yet reached a sufficient degree of differentiation to enable its local variants to achieve the status of independent dialects or languages. By the early fifteenth century the country's cultural, political and linguistic unity was a thing of the past. The heritage of Kievan Russia had to a large extent been taken over by the Principality of Moscow, whose rulers had embarked on the work of 'gathering' the central and northern districts of the country under their sway; communications between Muscovy and the south Russian lands had been greatly weakened by the Mongol invasion; and much of western and southern Russia had been annexed by the Grand

Duchy of Lithuania, now united to the Polish kingdom. The literature of Muscovy and of other areas of central and northern Russia had now scarcely any contact with the literary tradition fostered by Russian writers on Lithuanian territory; and in place of the former linguistic unity, three separate East Slavonic languages – the Great Russian, the Ukrainian and the White Russian (or Belorussian) – were gradually taking shape on the territory which had once been ruled by the princes of Kiev.

In this chronological classification the fourteenth century occupies an intermediate position. Its second half, marked, as we have seen, by the beginnings of the 'Second South Slavonic influence', may properly be recognized as part of Muscovite literature. The relatively few works that have come down to us from the first half of the fourteenth century, written mainly in Moscow, Vladimir, Tver', Novgorod and Pskov, are harder to classify. In some respects, particularly in the field of hagiography, they anticipate political and religious themes and literary preoccupations characteristic of the later middle ages. When due allowance has been made for the imprecision involved in all attempts to classify literary history by periods, it seems most satisfactory to trace the dividing line between the first and the second phases of medieval Russian literature somewhere around the year 1300.

SERMONS

The outstanding work of medieval Russian homiletic art is *The Sermon on Law and Grace*, probably composed about 1050, and ascribed on strong circumstantial and internal evidence to Hilarion, a priest of Prince Yaroslav's private church at Berestovo. In 1051, on the initiative of his sovereign, Hilarion was appointed metropolitan of Kiev. Probably delivered on some festive occasion in the presence of Yaroslav and his court, his sermon is concerned with three main topics which are developed with considerable skill. He first expounds the theme, traditional in Christian apologetics, of the superiority of divine grace, bestowed by Christ on his followers, over the Old Testament concept of Judaic law. The theme is illustrated by a series of allegorical antitheses, e.g. by the contrast between Hagar, the bondswoman, and Sarah, Abraham's free wife. The triumph of Christianity over the Law of Moses is given cosmic significance: 'As the light of the moon gives way to the rising sun, so did the Law pass away when Grace appeared, and the cold of the night vanished when the earth was warmed by the heat of the sun . . . The grace of Christ embraced the whole earth and covered it like the waters of the sea.' From these universal perspectives Hilarion passes to his second theme, the recent conversion of his own country. The land of Russia has now in its turn been visited by God's grace, and the arid soil of its former paganism has been watered by the springs of eternal life. Every Christian country, he states, is indebted for its salvation to a particular missionary or enlightened ruler: Peter and Paul evangelized Rome, John the Evangelist – 'Asia and Ephesus and Patmos', Thomas – India, and Mark – Egypt; the Roman Empire was subjected to Christ by Constantine the Great. Russia owes her conversion to Prince Vladimir, whose good sense and sharpness of mind impelled him to become a Christian and to command his subjects to be baptized. In glowing terms he praises Vladimir for establishing Christianity and building churches and monasteries in his realm. This panegyric leads Hilarion to his third and final theme, the state of Christian Russia in his own time. As Solomon continued David's work, so has Vladimir's achievement been brought to fruition by his son Yaroslav, who has splendidly adorned his capital of Kiev with churches, of which the cathedral of St Sophia holds pride of place. He urges Vladimir to rise from his grave and rejoice at the sight of the Christian faith growing in the lifetime of his descendants, and concludes with a prayer to God for the 'whole Russian land'.

The purpose which led Hilarion to deliver his sermon has been the subject of much scholarly debate. The view that, in contrasting the Old and the New Testaments, he was fighting against Jewish proselytism in Russia (for the existence of which there is no evidence in this period) is wholly unwarranted. Equally untenable is the theory that, in glorifying the spiritual achievements of Vladimir and Yaroslav, Hilarion was trying to support hypothetical claims to ecclesiastical independence from Byzantium. His work, it is true, displays a strong patriotic fervour. Even Vladimir's pagan ancestors are extolled for having reigned 'not in a poor and unknown country, but in the land of Russia, which is known and famed at the four ends of the earth'. Yet there is no trace in his sermon of any anti-Byzantine feeling. On the contrary, he admits that Vladimir's decision to accept Christianity from Byzantium was influenced by reports of 'the Orthodox Greek land, Christ-loving and strong in the faith', and that he imported the true faith to Russia from Constantinople, 'the New Jerusalem'. It is important to realize that Hilarion's devotion to his native land is combined with a keen sense of the universality of Christendom of which the Russians now form a part. 'Together with all Christians', he states, 'we now glorify the Holy Trinity ... To all countries has our God showed mercy, and us too He has not neglected.' It may be that one of the purposes of Hilarion's work was to secure the canonization of Prince Vladimir, which in the event was not achieved before the thirteenth century. But the principal aims of *The Sermon on Law and Grace* were surely to express, in theological and patriotic terms, a sense of triumph at the progress of Christianity in Russia and to extol, in the style of Byzantine imperial panegyrics with which its author was evidently familiar, the contribution made to this progress by his patrons, the ruling family of Kiev.

Hilarion was the greatest, though not the only known, preacher of Kievan Russia. Some reputation in this field was enjoyed by another native primate of the Russian Church, Clement Smolyatich, who was appointed metropolitan of Kiev in 1147. The only extant work which can with certainty be attributed to him is an epistle full of allegorical exegesis of scriptural texts, in which he defends himself against the charge of relying less on the writings of the Christian Fathers than on the works of Homer, Aristotle and Plato. We cannot be certain whether Clement read Greek classical writers in the original, or in translated miscellanies. There are stronger grounds for attributing a knowledge of Greek to Cyril, Bishop of Turov (d. c. 1183), of whom we have eight sermons, delivered on consecutive Sundays beginning with Palm Sunday, several other didactic works, and a number of prayers and hymns. The subject matter of his sermons is wholly derivative: his best known one, written for the Sunday after Easter, in which a poetic description of spring is used to symbolize Christ's resurrection, is modelled on a sermon by St Gregory of Nazianzus. But the patristic material, derived from Gregory, Chrysostom, Ephraim Syrus and other Christian Fathers, is elaborated in his sermons by rhetorical devices, lengthy dialogues and the abundant use of allegory. No less than Hilarion's sermon, Cyril's writings show how rapidly and thoroughly the traditions of Byzantine homiletic and patristic writing were assimilated by the first generations of Russian churchmen. For centuries the works of Hilarion and Cyril remained influential and popular models for their successors.

HAGIOGRAPHY

The abundant hagiographical literature of Byzantine and Central European origin, which circulated in Russia in the eleventh century, soon enabled the Russians to compose, with the help of these models, *Lives* of their own national saints. In 1015, soon after the death of St Vladimir, two of his sons, Boris and Gleb, fell victims of a political murder. The contemporary sources state that this act was instigated by their elder brother Svyatopolk. During the next two decades the belief that the two princely brothers, by the manner in which they met their death, were numbered among the saints began to spread in Russia. Miracles were recorded at their graves; and sometime before 1039 the authorities of the Russian Church endorsed this popular cult by a solemn act of canonization. Russia thus acquired its first formally acknowledged saints.

During the hundred years that followed their death, several hagiographical works devoted to Boris and Gleb were composed in Russia in

Church Slavonic. Three of them are extant: an account of their death, accompanied by a brief liturgical panegyric, which was inserted into the Russian Primary Chronicle under the year 1015; a longer description of the event, interlaced with lyrical passages and popular laments, entitled *The Tale and Passion and Eulogy of the Holy Martyrs Boris and Gleb*; and a full-length *Vita* of the two princes, patterned in form on the conventions of contemporary Byzantine hagiography, written by the Russian monk Nestor of the Kiev Monastery of the Caves. The relationship between these three texts is a complex and much debated problem, and there is still no consensus of opinion on the subject. The present writer believes, with Ludolf Müller, that the chronicle version is the earliest of the three, that *The Tale* (*Skazaniye*) is in part dependent upon it, and that both are probably based on two non-extant sources, the one narrative, the other hagiographical, composed before 1039. It is probably unwise at the present time to attempt to date the *Skazaniye* precisely; on internal evidence it is unlikely to have been written before 1061 or much after 1115. As for the *Vita* (*Chteniye*, 'Legend'), its author, Nestor, is known to have lived in the second half of the eleventh and the early twelfth centuries.

The three works offer the same explanation of the sanctity of Boris and Gleb and of the spiritual significance of their death: they are regarded as martyrs – and described as *strastoterptsy*, 'passion-sufferers' – not in the sense that they were killed for the Christian faith, but because, by their act of non-resistance, they chose to die as innocent and voluntary victims in imitation of Christ. This interpretation of martyrdom seems to owe nothing to Byzantine models; but it was not unknown in the middle ages in Scandinavia and in other Slavonic countries. One of the best known instances is the cult of St Wenceslas of Bohemia, who was put to death (probably in 929) by order of his brother who coveted his throne. The cult of this Czech saint spread to Russia in the eleventh century at the latest, in the wake of the fairly close cultural relations which then existed between Bohemia and Kiev; and the similarity between his death and that of Boris and Gleb is clearly pointed out both in the anonymous *Skazaniye* and in Nestor's *Chteniye*.

The *Skazaniye*, to judge from the numerous manuscripts of it that have survived, was the most popular of the three in medieval Russia. This preference is endorsed by most modern readers. Its literary merits are considerable: the story of the two murders is told with a fine command of dramatic tension and with a pathos enhanced by the author's repeated stress on the pitiful helplessness of the young princes. Both are afraid to die and cling desperately to their last moments on earth. Gleb, confronted with his assassins, pleads for mercy in terms reminiscent of folk laments: 'Have mercy on my youth, have mercy, my lords! . . . Do not reap me from my life that has not ripened, do not reap the unripe ear of corn. Do not cut down the vine that has not grown to maturity . . . This is no murder, but a cutting of unseasoned wood.' Eschewing the conventional heroics of so much of medieval hagiography, the author nevertheless makes it clear that the two brothers, faced with a decision between resistance and death, chose the latter deliberately, in conscious imitation of Christ and his martyred disciples. The terror and the pity which he instilled into his narrative have still today not lost the power to move his readers.

The cult of Boris and Gleb, fostered by the Russian rulers of the eleventh and twelfth centuries, enhanced the prestige of the ruling dynasty and, to that extent at least, acquired political significance. But it is worth remembering, too, that it had a powerful impact upon their compatriots at large; that men and women of all classes and stations of life believed themselves to be the recipients of the two saints' posthumous favours; and that in this cult the Russian people, almost at the dawn of their Christian life, expressed their admiration of, and pity for, innocent suffering.

The popular, and in part secular, nature of the cult of Boris and Gleb differed markedly from another hagiographical tradition which was to leave a more permanent mark on medieval Russian literature. This tradition, purely monastic in character, originated in the Kiev Monastery of the Caves (Pechersky), the leading monastic house of the pre-Mongol period. Several works, devoted to its history and to the lives of its saintly founders, were written within its walls in the eleventh and twelfth centuries. Some time between 1214 and 1226 a number of stories about the lives of its monks were written down by Simon, Bishop of Vladimir and Suzdal', who had been a member of the community, and by Polycarp, one of its resident monks. These various writings were later collected and edited, and in 1462 one of the medieval editors, a monk of the same monastery, gave to this miscellany the title *Pechersky Paterik*. From this is derived the name *Kievo-Pechersky Paterik* (the *Paterikon* of the Kiev Monastery of the Caves) by which it is known today.

The longest – and the earliest datable – item in the *Paterikon* is the *Vita* of St Theodosius, its abbot from c. 1062 to 1074. Its author was the same monk Nestor who wrote the *Chteniye* and played a leading role in the compilation of the Russian Primary Chronicle. He was received into the community in the year in which Theodosius died. Writing as a near contemporary of the events he described, in the very place where they occurred, Nestor, in addition to his considerable gifts as a historian, was in a position to supply much first-hand information on the monastery's early history. Its beginnings were linked with the ascetical life of Antony, a Russian who travelled to Mount Athos in the early eleventh century and there became a monk. According to Nestor, the abbot who professed him said: 'Go back to Russia . . . and may the blessing of the Holy Mountain be with you, for many will become monks because of you.' Antony returned to Kiev and there, on the outskirts of the city, settled in a cave which soon became the nucleus of a community of hermits. The next important stage in the history of the monastery was associated with Theodosius. Nestor describes his two most noteworthy acts as abbot: he moved the main part of the monastery above ground and framed its constitution on the model of the Byzantine Studite Rule; this enabled the principles of an organized community, living, praying and working together under the supervision of an abbot, to supplant, without wholly eliminating, the more individualistic, eremitical ideal of St Antony.

The personality of St Theodosius emerges vividly from Nestor's biography. The critical reader, it is true, faces here the difficulty which is familiar to every student of medieval hagiography: he must endeavour to sift historical fact from pious fiction, to distinguish the authentic detail from the hagiographical cliché and the literary borrowing. The sources of the *Life* of St Theodosius, and of the *Paterikon* as a whole, have been uncovered by Russian and western scholars. It is clear that Nestor borrowed extensively from Byzantine hagiographical and ascetic literature –, which, we have seen, had already been translated into Slavonic – and especially from the sixth-century writings of Cyril of Scythopolis. But it should also be borne in mind that if an episode in a saint's *Life* occurs in an earlier *Vita*, this does not necessarily mean that the episode has simply been lifted from the earlier work and factitiously applied to the next saint: for the traditions of the spiritual life are often of general application, and even the saints have been known to imitate each other. Theodosius' *Vita* comes out well from such a critical examination. The impression we gain is of a man of deep and unassuming humility, moderation in the practice of asceticism, and considerable moral authority, evident in his relations with the princes and nobles of the land, as well as with his own monks.

Attempts have been made to contrast Theodosius' gentleness, humaneness and voluntary self-humiliation with the more sombre and heroic kind of asceticism practised by Antony and his hermits. The latter type is illustrated in a series of portraits of hermits, drawn in the *Paterikon*, who appear as awesome recluses who mortified their passions by superhuman efforts. There is some truth in this antithesis, which reflected the tension, never fully resolved in the history of Byzantine asceticism, between the contemplative calling and the life in a monastic community. Yet the fact that neither Antony nor Theodosius was exclusively committed to his respective ideals of asceticism, and the evidence that in Kiev as in Byzantium the cenobitic and the eremitical life had points of contact, suggest that these two types of monasticism, portrayed in the *Paterikon*, were not so much opposed as complementary. In the last resort this document reveals, in the early phase of Russian monasticism, the same capacity for adapting Byzantine models to local needs and conditions which we find in other fields of medieval Russian culture.

THE PRIMARY CHRONICLE

Chronicles were composed in the pre-Mongol period in several Russian cities, including Novgorod. It was in Kiev, however, that the art of historical writing was, in this period, cultivated most assiduously and with the greatest success. There it enjoyed the patronage of princes and probably of prelates as well; the chroniclers had access to the archives of the royal chancellery and of important monastic houses; and one of these, the Kiev Monastery of the Caves, provided the stimulus, encouragement and historical information necessary for the rise of a continuous tradition of chronicle writing.

The masterpiece of this writing is the *Povest' vremennykh let*, generally known in English as the Russian Primary Chronicle. In its final form it dates from the second decade of the twelfth century. It has survived in several late medieval manuscripts of Russian chronicles, of which it forms the introductory section. The earliest of these redactions are the Laurentian, copied in 1377, and the Hypatian, dating from the first half of the fifteenth century. Internal evidence strongly suggests that the Primary Chronicle was written by a succession of authors, each of whom added to, and probably revised the work of his predecessors. The composite nature of the chronicle was demonstrated in the early years of this century by one of the greatest Russian philologists, A. A. Shakhmatov. His method involved a fourfold aim: to collate all existing chronicle texts; to determine their mutual relations and origin; to reconstruct the prototypes from which they are derived; and to discover the genetic processes by which the extant texts reached their present form. Some of Shakhmatov's conclusions were challenged by several Russian scholars, notably by V. M. Istrin and N. K. Nikol'sky; but his unrivalled knowledge of medieval Russian chronicles, the acuteness of his textual criticism, and the fact that none of the alternative explanations of the history of the text of the Primary Chronicle carry sufficient conviction, have during the past few decades led most philologists and literary historians to accept Shakhmatov's scheme in broad outline, at least as far as his reconstruction of the twelfth-century redactions is concerned. This is roughly the position held by the foremost living authority on medieval Russian chronicles, Professor D. S. Likhachev.

According to this view, the basic version of the *Povest' vremennykh let* was compiled about 1113 in the Kiev Monastery of the Caves by the monk Nestor. This version was based on at least two earlier chronicle texts, compiled in that monastery c. 1073 and between 1093 and 1095. Nestor's version, however, most scholars believe, has not survived in its original form: Shakhmatov held that it was twice revised, first in 1116 in the Monastery of St Michael in Vydubichi in Kiev by its abbot Silvester, the second time in 1118–19, in the Monastery of the Caves.

This reconstruction of the complicated genealogy of the Primary Chronicle remains hypothetical; yet, in the absence of more authoritative and convincing alternative theories, it may command at least tentative assent. Equally conjectural are the attempts of Shakhmatov and his followers to show what each of the successive compilers of the chronicle contributed to its final text. We may accept as probable, however, that the earliest version, which appeared in the reign of Prince Yaroslav of Kiev, was mainly concerned with the history of Russia's conversion to Christianity; and there can be little doubt that the tendency, particularly marked in its opening section, to view the story of the Russian nation against the background of world history owes most to Nestor.

The subject of the chronicle is the history of the Russian state, from its beginnings in the mid-ninth century to the early twelfth. Special prominence is given to the following themes: the coming of the Varangians from Scandinavia; the foundation, under a Viking dynasty and on territory inhabited mainly by Slavs, of the Russian state whose capital, in the second half of the ninth century, was fixed in Kiev; the periodic wars with Byzantium in the tenth century; the country's conversion to Christianity, in the latter part of the century, in the reign of Vladimir; its cultural and religious achievements under Vladimir's son Yaroslav; the growing political disunity after the latter's death in 1054, enhanced by inter-princely strife and invasions of the steppe nomads; and the attempts, applauded by the chroniclers, of some rulers and churchmen to arrest the dismemberment of the realm by joint political and military action. The material is patently derived from a wide variety of sources. For the early period, for which documentary evidence was probably unavailable, the chroniclers seem to have relied in part on oral sagas, some of which may have been of Varangian origin; some of these sagas, which describe the feats and adventures of the pagan rulers of Kiev, show signs of considerable artistic sophistication. In places whole documents are incorporated without change into the narrative, such as the texts of the treaties concluded between Russia and the Empire. Byzantine chronicles, notably those of John Malalas and George the Monk, are summarized or cited; and material obtained from the southern and the western Slavs is made use of. Increasingly, as the narrative progresses and the chroniclers are able to rely on contemporary sources or first-hand knowledge, events are dated with greater precision and the main emphasis is laid on the facts of Russia's internal history.

This disparate material, despite obvious editorial efforts, has not always been successfully unified. The chroniclers' efforts to make their narrative as edifying as possible, as well as their personal bias and at times, no doubt, genuine ignorance, have combined to produce in places puzzling discrepancies and contradictions. Yet, despite the patchwork effect produced by some of the material, and occasional editorial clumsiness, the chronicle impresses the reader by the strength and coherence of its compilers' outlook. In no other work of early Russian literature do we find, so closely combined and felicitously expressed, the belief that divine providence watches over the life of individuals and nations, a moral sense outraged by cruelty and injustice, the recognition of the social benefits conferred by the Christian religion, a high regard for education, the admiration of courage and military achievement, and the realization that the Russian people, through their acceptance of Christianity, have become members of the family of mankind. This last feature, which the chronicle shares with Hilarion's *Sermon on Law and Grace*, and which is particularly marked in its opening section, shows that the writers of Kievan Russia were able to combine a strong attachment to their national heritage with a sense of belonging to the wider community of Christian peoples. Not the least of the chronicle's merits is the richness and variety of its style, which combines the solemn and monumental language of religious instruction, a delicate lyricism derived partly from the Christian liturgy and partly from folk poetry, the art of an accomplished storyteller, and the use of dramatic dialogue and of the pungent aphorism. In its grasp of disparate material, in its sense of the importance of central events, in its desire to discover the meaning of history as a whole, and in the vividness of its language – a combination of Church Slavonic with elements of the spoken vernacular – the Primary Chronicle is superior in many respects to the Byzantine chronicles on which it was partly modelled. The numerous chronicles composed in Russia in the later middle ages sought to imitate the first of the country's historical works; they never equalled it in quality.

THE WRITINGS OF VLADIMIR MONOMAKH

Inserted in the Laurentian version of the Primary Chronicle, under the year 1096, are three works which may well have originally formed a separate collection. They are the *Instruction* (*Poucheniye*) of Prince Vladimir Monomakh, his letter to his first cousin, Prince Oleg of Chernigov, and a prayer usually ascribed to the same author.

Vladimir Monomakh is a notable figure in Russian history. Born in

1053, he was the son of Prince Vsevolod (and thus the grandson of Yaroslav of Kiev) and of a Byzantine princess, who was almost certainly the daughter of the Byzantine Emperor Constantine IX Monomachus. From the latter he probably inherited the nickname Monomakh. Successively prince of Smolensk, Chernigov and Pereyaslavl', he played a leading part in the political affairs of his country during the last quarter of the eleventh century and the early years of the twelfth, and in 1113 was called to the throne of Kiev. Henceforth and until his death in 1125, he was the most powerful prince in Russia. During his reign in Kiev, Russia, virtually for the last time before the Mongol invasion, achieved a considerable degree of political unity and was able to withstand the attacks of the nomadic Polovtsians of the steppe. His family tree is evidence of the matrimonial ties which, in this period, bound the Russian ruling house to the reigning dynasties of Europe: his mother was a Byzantine princess; one of his uncles married the daughter of the king of Poland; his three aunts became queens of Norway, France and Hungary. Vladimir's own wife was Gytha, the daughter of King Harold of England; his eldest son married the daughter of the king of Sweden, his daughter the king of Hungary, and his granddaughter a member of the Byzantine imperial family of the Comneni.

The writings of this cosmopolitan figure, outstanding as a statesman, a general, a writer and a man, cannot fail to have considerable historical importance. Above all this is true of his *Instruction*, probably written in 1117, and addressed in the first place to his sons but also to a wider circle of readers. It consists of a didactic part, in which the author speaks of man's duties to God, his fellow-men, and himself, and of an autobiographical section, in which he relates a number of episodes of his eventful life. Although the didactic passages are based in part on Christian scripture and Byzantine literary models, the author's beliefs and character emerge from them with some clarity. His experience as a Christian, and particularly his meditations on the Psalms, convinced him that man's surest refuge is to trust in God, who will protect him in the hour of trial, when danger threatens him or his principles are put to the test. The life of the Christian active in the world need not involve lengthy prayers or harsh ascetic exercises: 'repentance, tears and works of mercy' are sufficient to gain the kingdom of heaven. His social duties, if he is called to the high office of government, are to dispense justice, to protect the weak, to cooperate with the church, to be efficient in the conduct of war, to control his troops, to preside with love and authority over his family, and to seek good repute abroad by hospitality shown to strangers. Towards himself the ruler must be strict, counting all his actions, both secular and religious, as a 'labour' (*trud*) which requires discipline and training. Some of this advice reveals Vladimir's personal leanings – the value he sets on education (he writes with approval of his father who, without leaving Russia, learnt five languages), his liking for a well-ordered life of daily routine, and his ability to pause in wonder before the manifold beauties of nature and the animal world. In the brief autobiography that follows the didactic section, Monomakh writes mainly of his numerous 'expeditions' (administrative tours of his lands, diplomatic missions and military campaigns against the Polovtsians) and of his hunting exploits. His victories he records laconically: 'God helped us'. His achievements in the chase he also attributes to divine care:

> In Chernigov I captured with my own hands ten and twenty wild horses . . . Two bisons tossed me and my horse on their horns, a stag gored me, an elk trampled me underfoot, another gored me with his horns, a wild boar tore off my sword from my thigh, a bear bit my saddle-cloth next to my knee, and another wild beast jumped on my flank and threw my horse with me. And God preserved me unharmed. I often fell from my horse, fractured my skull twice, and in my youth injured my arms and legs, not sparing my head or my life.

When all allowances have been made for the didactic aims of the *Instruction* and for its author's manifest intention to cut a figure in the eyes of his sons and perhaps of posterity as well, the picture of Monomakh that emerges from his autobiography is living and convincing: manly, warm-hearted, with deep religious conviction and, at times, highly articulate. The sincerity of his convictions, and his moral calibre, are perhaps even more evident in his letter to Oleg. The circumstances in which it was written were tragic and testing. In 1096 one of the chronic bouts of inter-princely warfare broke out in Russia. In this war, in which Vladimir Monomakh and his cousin Oleg were enemies, Vladimir's younger son Izyaslav was killed in battle against Oleg's forces. Vladimir's elder son Mstislav, having secured a cease-fire, persuaded his father to offer Oleg the hand of reconciliation. Vladimir's letter draws its quiet dignity from the strength of Christian forgiveness, from the knowledge of his spiritual bond with Oleg, the godfather of his dead son, and from the need to subordinate his personal feelings to the overriding cause of national unity:

> Oh, long-suffering and wretched man that I am! . . . Look, brother, at our fathers. What did they carry away with them into the grave, except what they did to their souls? You, my brother, should first have written these words to me. When my child – and yours – was killed before your eyes, and when you saw his blood and his body, as he lay like a newly-blossomed and withered flower or a slaughtered lamb, you should have said, standing over him and reading the thoughts of your

soul: 'Alas, what have I done?' . . . You should have repented before
God, sent me a letter of consolation, and let my daughter-in-law come
to me – for in her there is neither evil nor good – that I might embrace
her and mourn her husband and her marriage, in the place of wedding
songs: for I did not behold her joy of former times, nor her wedding,
because of my sins. For God's sake, send her to me with your first
envoy, that I might weep with her, and give her a home, and she might
sit like a turtle-dove upon a dried-up tree, and I may be comforted in
God . . . Is it strange that a man should have perished in war? The best
of our forefathers died in this way . . . Send me your envoy or bishop,
and write me a letter in truth: then you will turn our heart towards you,
and we shall live better than before.

Better than conventional hagiographical eulogies, such words show the
capacities of human character and the impact which the teaching of
Christianity could have upon the society of early medieval Russia.

PILGRIMAGES

Russian pilgrimages to the holy places of the Eastern Church began soon
after the country's conversion to Christianity. Pre-eminent were Mount
Athos, Palestine and Constantinople. St Antony's visit to Mount Athos,
which resulted in the rise of the Kiev Monastery of the Caves, has already
been noted. The earliest account of a Russian pilgrimage to survive from
the pre-Mongol period is that of the Abbot Daniel, who spent sixteen
months in the Holy Land in 1106–7. His travelogue, interspersed with
lengthier description of the more memorable places and with Biblical
reminiscences partly derived from Christian apocrypha, was highly
popular in medieval Russia, to judge from the fact that some hundred
manuscripts of it have survived. Its value to the historian lies partly in
the topographical description of early twelfth-century Palestine, and
partly in its author's response to the situations in which he found himself.
The greater part of the country was then held, albeit precariously, by the
crusaders, whose leader, King Baldwin I, gave Daniel help and protection. Daniel responded to this friendly treatment by a warm appreciation
of Palestine's Frankish overlords. His attitude shows that, despite the
growing rift between the Latin and the Greek Churches, the two traditions could still, at least in the Holy Land, coexist and co-operate on an
amicable footing, and that Russians in the early twelfth century were
capable of genuine tolerance towards Christians of the West. Yet on
occasion Daniel did not conceal his belief in the superiority of his own
Orthodox Christianity. Thus in his account – the most detailed of his
Pilgrimage – of the ceremonies in the Church of the Holy Sepulchre on

Easter eve, he records with evident satisfaction that the Greek and Russian lamps were miraculously kindled by the sacred fire, while the Frankish lamps remained unlit. His patriotism was as strong as loyalty to his church: he tells us that he placed his own Easter lamp before the sepulchre 'on behalf of the whole Russian land', whose representative he felt himself to be. The vividness of some of his descriptions, and the controlled but genuine emotion with which he records his impressions of Christendom's holy places, have secured for Daniel's *Pilgrimage* an honourable place in the history of early Russian literature.

Less interesting from the literary standpoint, but of equal historical importance, is the description of the sanctuaries of Constantinople by Antony, the future archbishop of Novgorod. He visited the city in 1200. His account is mainly of value to archaeologists and art historians, since he describes its churches as they were four years before the destruction wrought by the armies of the Fourth Crusade; but it also provides evidence of the spell cast on the minds of the Russians of the middle ages by the shrines and world-famous relics of Constantinople and by the splendour of the liturgy celebrated in its churches.

HEROIC POETRY

As far as we can judge from very inadequate evidence, a tradition of heroic poetry, glorifying the exploits of men who, by accepting ordeals and overcoming dangers, seek honour and demonstrate their valour in the eyes of their fellow-men, developed in Kievan Russia in the eleventh and twelfth centuries. Historical circumstances must have contributed to the rise of this tradition. The constant struggle to keep at bay the nomadic enemies in the southern steppe, and thus to preserve their Christian heritage and the urban civilization largely derived from Byzantium, fostered the belief among Russians of this period that they were living in a heroic age, in which man can gain honour for himself by showing courage and enterprise. This heroic tradition found an artistic expression in oral and written poetry.

The earliest known oral poems of medieval Russia are the *byliny*, popularly and more accurately known as *stariny*. Recited in recent times by peasant bards, mainly in northern Russia, they have been recorded by scholars during the last two centuries. Their origin, and the history of their transmission, have been much debated and are still far from clear. This is particularly the case of the oldest cycle of *byliny*, in which action is laid in 'glorious and royal Kiev town': most of them are grouped round the figure of Prince Vladimir, who seems to combine the features of Vladimir I (d. 1015) and of Vladimir Monomakh (d. 1125). His court is the focus for the adventures of a group of knightly heroes, the *bogatyri*, who fight in his service against the country's pagan enemies – usually, and anachronistically, called Tatars – for 'Holy Russia' and the Christian faith. Scholars have been puzzled by the fact that these *byliny*, whose setting is Kiev and the open plains of southern Russia, have not been recorded in this area and have mostly been preserved in the far north of the country. Various explanations of this phenomenon have been offered: the remoteness of the area, which enabled this largely secular heroic tradition to escape the later efforts of the Church authorities to suppress it; the illiteracy which helped the bards to memorize these sometimes lengthy poems; the long periods of leisure imposed by the northern climate; and the absence of serfdom which, in the view of some scholars, fostered among the local peasants an independence of mind and an appreciation of the individual qualities of the *bogatyri*.

A continuous existence of the *bylina* tradition from the Kievan period to the present day cannot be proved. Nor has the vexed problem of the relationship between fact and fiction in these poems been satisfactorily solved. None of the existing versions can be attributed with any certainty to a period earlier than the sixteenth century. However, there can be little doubt that some of the popular heroes of the Kievan cycle – notably Il'ya of Murom, Dobrynya Nikitich and Alyosha Popovich – were originally historical persons, that some of the historical and geographical material of these *byliny* reflects an authentically medieval situation, and that their basic stratum goes back in some cases at least as far as the eleventh and twelfth centuries. It is equally undeniable that the heroic outlook and the courtly ideals which they once expressed have been diluted, and to some extent modified, by the peasant environment in which these poems have been preserved in recent centuries.

Another group of medieval *byliny* centres on Novgorod, the great trading centre of north-western Russia. Here the open steppe of the Kievan poems and the chivalrous deeds of their military heroes give way to civic and commercial preoccupations. The heroes of Novgorod seem to belong to a time when the city was at the height of its power and prosperity – the fourteenth century and the first half of the fifteenth. They move in a society that is turbulent, mercantile and in many respects post-heroic. However, in one of the finest of the Novgorod poems – the *bylina* of Sadko, the minstrel who became a rich merchant – the theme of far-flung commerce and worldly success is combined with a much older story of the hero's ability to charm the natural elements by his music, his descent into the depths of the sea, and his encounter with the Sea King.

In view of the later linguistic revisions undergone by the *byliny*, it is hazardous to make any definite assertions about the form and style of the original poems. Yet the highly conservative oral tradition through which they have come down to us, as well as the similarity of many of their stylistic conventions and devices to those of heroic poems of other countries, make it probable that their form has preserved a number of authentic and archaic features. They abound in formulaic phrases, repetitions of words and passages, negative similes, fixed noun–epithet combinations, and hyperbolic descriptions. In the middle ages the *byliny* were chanted, in what was probably a monotonous recitative, to the accompaniment of the *gusli*, a species of harp, played resting on the knees. The unit of composition is the line, not the stanza. Each line has a number of main stresses (usually three), the final one falling on the third syllable from the end, giving the line a dactylic ending. No regular system of rhyming exists, though terminal assonance is common. The average length of *byliny* recorded in modern times is between 200 and 350 lines.

The art of the *byliny*, which relies on repetition and improvisation, is, and probably already was in the middle ages, an essentially oral art. But, as the history of the Homeric poems shows, the growth of literacy in a society which has practised this art for some time makes it possible for a poet familiar with the heroic tradition to enlist the help of writing and thus to enrich the resources of his craft. Such a poet may continue to use many of the conventions of oral recitation, such as repetitions, refrains, fixed epithets and formulaic phrases. Yet, by committing his work to writing, he is able to rearrange his material with more time at his disposal and to compose with far greater care and effectiveness. The result may be a poem of richer texture and greater complexity and sophistication.

Some such process, in the present writer's belief, led to the creation of the *Lay of Igor''s Campaign* (*Slovo o polku Igoreve*). Few works of Russian literature have been the subject of so much study and controversy as this short anonymous text of some 2,500 words. The time and circumstances of its discovery, the fate of its sole manuscript, the obscurity of some of its passages, and the fact that in the whole of Russian pre-Mongol literature no work of a similar genre has been discovered, have endowed the *Slovo* with an aura of mystery and have attracted the intense curiosity of generations of scholars. The only known manuscript, discovered *c.* 1791, perished in 1812 in the fire of Moscow, after an edition had been published in 1800, and a second copy made. This copy as well as the published edition are faulty in places, which accounts for many of the obscurities in the extant text. The view that the *Slovo* is a forgery perpetrated in the late eighteenth century by a person or persons unknown, occasionally expressed in the nineteenth century, has recently been revived by several scholars. The discussion is too complex to be summarized here; and it would be doing both the sceptics and the supporters of the work's authenticity an injustice to discuss any of their arguments in isolation. The present writer can but express his opinion that none of the arguments put forward by the sceptics is sufficiently weighty or convincing to impugn the *Slovo*'s authenticity, and that the linguistic, literary and historical evidence strongly supports the view that it was composed in the twelfth century, most probably about the year 1185.

The subject matter of the *Slovo* is relatively simple. It is the story of a campaign led in 1185 by Igor', Prince of Novgorod-Seversky in south Russia, against the Polovtsians of the steppe. After an initial success, the Russian army was defeated and Igor' was taken prisoner. Soon afterwards he escaped from the Polovtsian camp and returned home to his rejoicing compatriots. These events, which are also described in the Laurentian and Hypatian versions of the chronicle, are treated in the *Slovo* with a large measure of historical accuracy, though the author occasionally, and probably deliberately, altered their sequence, and in accordance with the conventions of heroic poetry seems to take his readers' knowledge of them for granted.

The simplicity of the poem's subject matter is in striking contrast with the complexity of its structure. The narrative thread is frequently interrupted by historical digressions, lyrical invocations, panegyrics and laments. The story of Igor''s campaign is related to the events, glorious or tragic, of the previous century, and the imagery used by the author in these digressions into the past serves to link and harmonize different layers of time. Contemporary princes of Russia, who remained aloof from the campaign of 1185, are praised for their valour and military exploits – above all Prince Svyatoslav of Kiev, Igor''s overlord. In the most celebrated lament of the *Slovo*, Igor''s wife, Yaroslavna, invokes the elements of nature in finely orchestrated stanzas – the wind, the river Dnieper and the sun – begging them to help her husband to return from captivity. The mood of the poem is ambivalent throughout, with panegyrics and laments, joy and sorrow, interwoven: the triumphant confidence of the Russian army's departure gives way to the calamity of defeat, when Igor''s slaughtered soldiers are mourned by men and nature, and lamentation is followed in its turn by the happiness of Igor''s return.

A similar ambivalence is evident in the two basic themes which serve as the foci of the poem: the first is narrative and heroic; the second didactic and political. The courage of Igor' and his companions, their delight in the business of war, their prowess on the field of battle, and the tragic dignity of their defeat are held up for admiration in order to move and exalt the audience, in the true tradition of heroic poetry. Even Prince Oleg of Chernigov, whom the author holds responsible for the internecine warfare that brought great suffering to the Russian land in the late eleventh century, and who 'forged strife with his sword', is shown as a tragic and heroic figure, a restless knight-errant seeking to avenge the wrong done to himself and his family. But from another standpoint the

Russian defeat was a national disaster and Igor' himself, the author points out, was gravely at fault: his campaign was a foolhardy adventure, undertaken for personal glory, without the approval of his sovereign, the prince of Kiev. The latter's rebuke to Igor' (not unmixed with pity) underlines this fact and serves to bring out the author's second basic theme: that the victories of the pagans over the Christians are a direct result of the disunity among the princes of the land. To them the author addresses, in words charged with deep emotion, his appeals to unite in defence of Kiev, for the sake of the land of Russia. These two themes, the heroic and the patriotic, are balanced and at times blended with considerable artistry.

Though some literary historians have held the *Slovo* to be a work of prose, many, probably the majority, regard it – rightly in the present writer's opinion – as a poem. However, on this point controversy has been long and heated, and it must be admitted that the attempts to reduce it to a precise metrical pattern have not so far been successful. The highly musical texture of the poem, the use of repetitions, refrains, formulaic phrases, fixed epithets and negative similes, characteristic of heroic poetry, leave little doubt that the *Slovo* was intended for oral recitation; and the author himself describes his work not only as a lay (*slovo*) and a tale (*povest'*), but also as a song (*pesn'*). He seems, moreover, to have known and sought inspiration in an earlier, oral, tradition: the figure of the eleventh-century bard Boyan, the 'nightingale of olden times', whom he holds in great esteem and whose flights of imagination he professes himself unable to emulate, probably stems from this pre-literary stage. It is equally clear, however, that the *Slovo* was composed in writing: the terseness of its style, the richness and complexity of its imagery, the subtlety of its euphonic devices, make it impossible to believe that it was improvised orally.

A number of problems raised by the literary study of the *Slovo* still await detailed investigation. In particular we need to know more about its precise relationship to non-Russian, especially Byzantine, literature, to native folklore, to the literary conventions of panegyrics and laments, and more generally to the cultural tradition of Kievan Russia. The work's historical significance is more firmly established. It remains a memorial of the last decades of Kievan Russia, on the eve of the Mongol invasions, and of her struggle to survive in an age of chivalry and disaster, of heroism and political folly, of civil strife and barbarian invasions. It may fairly be described as one of the great heroic poems of the world.

THE 'SUPPLICATION OF DANIEL THE PRISONER'

This work of obscure origin and uncertain authorship has survived in two versions, entitled in the manuscripts (none of them earlier than the sixteenth century) *Slovo* ('The Address') and *Moleniye* ('The Supplication'). Their mutual relationship is far from clear: present scholarship inclines to the view that the *Slovo* was written in the mid-twelfth century and was addressed to a prince of Pereyaslavl' (in southern Russia) by one of his retainers, and that the *Moleniye*, written for a prince of another city of Pereyaslavl' (in central Russia), was later, probably in the 1220s or 1230s, adapted to altered conditions. The author's identity is quite uncertain, nor do we know why the manuscripts called him a 'prisoner'. The work is full of lachrymose complaints at his poverty and other unspecified misfortunes. His view of society is decidedly jaundiced: boyars, shrewish wives and dissolute monks are objects of his scorn. The prince alone, to whom he addresses sycophantic eulogies, could ensure for him a happy and prosperous life by taking him into his service. In order to advertise himself he parades his learning, interlaced with witticisms and larded with aphorisms mostly derived from scriptural texts and translated collections of gnomic wisdom. Unconvincing attempts have been made to depict this unattractive character as a misunderstood intellectual or as a member of the under-privileged classes seeking to rise above the limitations of his social status. The literary importance of his work lies in the elements of satire it contains, in the evidence it provides of solid, if eclectic, learning, and in the fact that it is one of the rare pieces of writing of purely secular content to have survived from the pre-Mongol period.

WORKS CONCERNED WITH THE TATAR INVASION

The Mongol invasion of Russia (1237–40), with its consequent destruction of cities and immense loss of life, could hardly fail to result in a decline in the country's literary production. Its shattering effect upon the society and the minds of its victims is depicted, sometimes vividly, in the few works of Russian literature that have survived from the second half of the thirteenth century and from the early fourteenth. Notable among these are the accounts of the first encounters of the Russians with the Tatars, and of the terrible invasion. These stories, however, have survived only in the text of later chronicles, and their original content and form can hence be reconstructed only approximately. In 1223 (or, according to some sources, in 1224) the Russians, allied with the Polovtsians, were overwhelmingly defeated by the Tatars deep in the southern steppe, on the river Kalka, near the Sea of Azov. The Tatars after driving the Russian armies to the Dnieper were recalled to Mongolia by their ruler Genghis Khan. The story of this encounter is briefly told in *The Tale of the Battle on the River Kalka*, probably written soon after the event. It ascribes the defeat to God's punishment for the sins of the Russian people, and sees in the sudden appearance and equally mysterious departure of the Tatars a sign of the impending end of the world: 'We do not know where they came from and whither they went: only God knows.' *The Tale of the Ruin of Ryazan'* is a longer and more sophisticated work. It describes the opening episode in the Tatar invasion of north-eastern Russia in 1237, the capture and sack of Ryazan' by Genghis Khan's grandson, Batu. In the battles before and after the fall of the city, the Russians are shown fighting heroically against overwhelming odds. Even the Tatar khan, though he is depicted as a blood-thirsty lecher, pays tribute to the fearlessness of these 'winged men'. The feats of one of their generals, Yevpaty Kolovrat, who defeats a Tatar leader in single combat, are described in a manner reminiscent of the *byliny*. This work, probably written in approximately its present form in the first half of the fourteenth century (though a thirteenth-century narrative core has been postulated), is remarkable for its combination of the epic style with religious and didactic phraseology, its powerful though restrained lyricism, the conciseness of the battle scenes, its closeness to the conventions of panegyrics and laments, and the use of imagery probably derived from heroic poetry.

The horrors of the Tatar invasion and the indignity of Russia's political enslavement form the background to the sermons of Serapion, Bishop of Vladimir in 1274–5. More explicitly than the authors of the two previous works, he seeks for a moral explanation of the national calamity, and finds it in the evils of Russian society – envy, pride, covetousness and addiction to pagan customs – which have provoked the wrath of the Lord. But the moralizing tone of his sermons is softened by pity for the sufferings of his people:

> The churches of God are destroyed, the holy places are desecrated, bishops have fallen prey to the sword, the flesh of holy monks is delivered as food to the birds, the blood of our fathers and brothers has watered the earth, the valour of our princes and generals is no more, our soldiers, filled with fear, have run away, a multitude of our brethren and children has been led away into captivity . . . our land has become the property of foreigners, we have become an object of shame to the neighbouring lands, and a laughing-stock to our enemies.

PRINCELY BIOGRAPHIES

The tradition of secular biography began to develop in different parts of Russia in the second half of the thirteenth century. Its roots lay mainly in the chroniclers' custom of writing brief obituary notices about the outstanding rulers of the land, as well as in Kievan hagiography. It probably owed something as well to Byzantine secular biography and to the thirteenth-century *Lives* of Serbian kings. The Russian people's cult of some of their medieval rulers derived much of its force from the fact that they all belonged to the same family – both in the Kievan and the early Muscovite periods the princes were all descended from a common ancestor. Neither the multiplication of the princely branches nor the political fragmentation of the realm ever destroyed that bond between the ruler and his subjects which caused the dynasty to be regarded as a personification of the state and as a symbol of its continuity. The two outstanding examples of this genre in the thirteenth century are the biographies of Daniel of Galicia and of Alexander Nevsky.

The biography of Prince Daniel of Galicia (d. 1264) formed part of the Galician and Volhynian Chronicle and has survived in the Hypatian text of the Kievan Chronicle. Mainly concerned with the military and political history of Western Russia, it describes Daniel's struggle for the throne of the Galician principality and his relations with the Tatars and his neighbours in East-Central Europe. Its author was clearly a learned man who affected an ornate and bookish style, derived in part from translated Byzantine literature and from the Primary Chronicle. Some of his imagery is strongly reminiscent of the *Slovo o polku Igoreve*.

The Life of St Alexander Nevsky (d. 1263) is, by contrast, a less sophisticated and more religiously oriented work. It was probably written in the early 1280s. Whether the more overtly religious elements formed part of the original biography or were inserted by a later writer remains uncertain. Its extant forms suggest that, despite the author's half-hearted attempt to cast it into a hagiographical mould, it is in effect a tale of military valour. It describes the main episodes in the life of Alexander, prince of Novgorod and later grand prince of Vladimir, who defeated the Swedes and the Teutonic Knights and humbled himself before the Tatars to save his subjects from their depredations. In some of the manuscripts Alexander's *Vita* is preceded by a brief text entitled *The Tale of the Ruin of the Russian Land* (*Slovo o pogibeli ruskyya zemli*). It dwells on the natural and man-made beauties of Russia, evokes its past glories (which the author associates mainly with Vladimir Monomakh) and ends with a cryptic reference to grievous events of more recent times. Whether *The Tale of the Ruin* was intended as an introduction to the *Life of Alexander Nevsky*, or – more plausibly – is a salvaged fragment of a separate writing, is still a matter of controversy. But, whatever its origin, this work, in its unaffected lyricism and strong patriotic overtones, epitomizes that nostalgia for the political and cultural achievements of the past which must have been widespread in Russia in the decades following the Mongol invasion. It has been fittingly described as the swansong of Kievan culture.

GUIDE TO FURTHER READING

ANTHOLOGIES AND COLLECTIONS OF TEXTS
The fullest and most representative recent collections are those of N. K. Gudzy, *Khrestomatiya po drevney russkoy literature*, 7th edn (Moscow, 1962), and of A. Stender-Petersen, *Anthology of Old Russian Literature* (New York, 1954). The former offers a wide choice of texts, and is readily accessible. The latter has a wider selection of religious writings, but lacks any specimen of translated literature and is marred by somewhat idiosyncratic editing. Several literary texts of the Kievan period are reproduced from facsimiles of manuscripts in *Khrestomatiya po istorii russkogo yazyka*, ed. S. P. Obnorsky and S. G. Barkhudarov, I, 2nd edn (Moscow, 1952). Several of the more important works are printed with explanatory notes in *A Historical Russian Reader*, ed. J. Fennell and D. Obolensky (Oxford, 1969).

HISTORIES OF EARLY RUSSIAN LITERATURE
The survey of Kievan literature by V. M. Istrin, *Ocherk istorii drevnerusskoy literatury domoskovskogo perioda* (Petrograd, 1922), can be recommended for its incisive and stimulating analysis. A fuller treatment, with a valuable discussion of social and political issues, is provided by M. N. Speransky, *Istoriya drevney russkoy literatury*, I, 3rd edn (Moscow, 1921). Two useful and fairly comprehensive surveys are those of A. S. Orlov, *Kurs lektsiy po drevney russkoy literature* (Moscow–Leningrad, 1939) and N. K. Gudzy, *Istoriya drevney russkoy literatury*, 7th edn (Moscow, 1966). The latter has been translated into English by S. W. Jones, *History of Early Russian Literature* (New York, 1949) and German by F. von Lilienfeld, *Geschichte der russischen Literatur, 11–17 Jahrhundert* (Halle, 1959). Gudzy, however, unduly plays down the religious themes in early Russian literature as well as the extent of foreign influences. The outstanding work in a non-Russian language is by D. Tschiżewskij (Chizhevsky), *Geschichte der altrussischen Literatur im 11., 12. und 13. Jahrhundert* (Frankfurt am Main, 1948). Chizhevsky's book in English, *History of Russian Literature from the Eleventh Century to the End of the Baroque* (The Hague, 1960) is interesting for its concern with literary genres and problems of style, but its value is diminished by unconvincing periodization and the absence of bibliographies. There are valuable essays on selected works of this period in John Fennell and Antony Stokes, *Early Russian Literature* (London, 1974). The first two chapters, by J. Fennell, are particularly recommended for their discussion of textological and formal problems.

THE CULTURAL BACKGROUND OF EARLY RUSSIAN LITERATURE
The best treatment of religious themes in the literature of Kievan Russia is by G. P. Fedotov, *The Russian Religious Mind*, I (Cambridge, Mass., 1966). Written with wide knowledge and understanding, this work, however, exaggerates the differences between the Byzantine and the Russian religious traditions and over-estimates the originality of the latter. The learned and thought-provoking works by D. S. Likhachev repay careful study. They include 'The Type and Character of the Byzantine Influence on Old Russian Literature', *Oxford Slavonic Papers*, XIII (1967), 14–32; *Chelovek v literature drevney Rusi*, 2nd edn (Moscow, 1970); *Poetika drevnerusskoy literatury*, 2nd edn (Leningrad, 1971); and *Razvitiye russkoy literatury X–XVII vekov* (Leningrad, 1973). B. A. Romanov's *Lyudi i nravy Drevney*

Rusi (Moscow–Leningrad, 1966) is an original and stimulating attempt to uncover the social motifs of some of the works of Kievan literature. The rise of literacy in Russia is discussed by D. Obolensky, 'The Heritage of Cyril and Methodius in Russia', *Dumbarton Oaks Papers*, XIX (1965), 47–65.

TRANSLATED LITERATURE
The Gospels
O. Grünenthal, 'Die Übersetzungstechnik der altkirchenslavischen Evangelienübersetzung', *Archiv für slavische Philologie*, XXXI (1910), 321–66, XXXII (1911), 1–48. E. Berneker, 'Kyrills Übersetzungskunst', *Indogermanische Forschungen*, XXXI (1912–13), 399–412.

Liturgical texts
R. Jakobson, 'The Slavic Response to Byzantine Poetry', *Actes du XIIᵉ Congrès International d'Études Byzantines*, I (Belgrade, 1963), 249–67. M. Velimirović, 'The Influence of the Byzantine Chant on the Music of the Slavic Countries', *Proceedings of the XIIIth International Congress of Byzantine Studies* (London, 1967), pp. 119–40.

Patristic writings
There is a good edition of the *Izbornik* of 1076 by V. S. Golyshenko and others (*Izbornik 1076 goda*, Moscow, 1965). See also the article by N. Popov, 'L'Izbornik de 1076 dit de Svjatoslav, comme monument littéraire', *Revue des Études Slaves*, XIV (1934), 5–25, and the general survey by I. Dujčev, 'Medieval Slavic Literature and its Byzantine Background', *Actes du XIIᵉ Congrès International d'Études Byzantines*, I (Belgrade, 1963), 411–29. The vexed problem of the relationship of the *Izbornik* of 1076 to possible Greek models is discussed in two perceptive articles: V. F. Dubrovina, 'O grecheskikh parallelyakh k Izborniku 1076 goda', *Izvestiya Akademii Nauk SSSR, Otdeleniye literatury i yazyka*, XXII, 2 (1963), 104–9; I. Ševčenko, 'On Some Sources of Prince Svjatoslav's *Izbornik* of the Year 1076', *Orbis scriptus: Festschrift für Dmitrij Tschižewskij zum 70. Geburtstag* (Munich, 1966), pp. 723–38.

Hagiography
M. Heppell, 'Slavonic Translations of Early Byzantine Ascetical Literature', *The Journal of Ecclesiastical History*, V (1954), 86–100. I. Dujčev, 'Les rapports hagiographiques entre Byzance et les Slaves', *Proceedings of the XIIIth International Congress of Byzantine Studies*, pp. 363–70.

Apocrypha
The standard edition of the texts is still that of N. Tikhonravov, *Pamyatniki otrechonnoy russkoy literatury*, 2 vols. (St Petersburg, Moscow, 1863; reprinted London, 1973). See also the study by N. Tikhonravov, *Otrechonnyye knigi drevney Rossii*, in the same author's *sochineniya*, I (Moscow, 1898), 127–255.

Josephus' History of the Jewish War
N. A. Meshchersky, *Istoriya Iudeyskoy voyny Iosifa Flaviya v drevnerusskom perevode* (Moscow–Leningrad, 1958). This edition has the text, a linguistic commentary on it, and a detailed historical and literary study. See also the earlier edition, with a French translation: *La Prise de Jérusalem de Josèphe le Juif,*

texte vieux-russe publié par V. Istrin, traduit en français par P. Pascal, 2 vols. (Paris, 1934, 1938).

The Romance of Alexander

V. Istrin, *Aleksandriya russkikh khronografov* (Moscow, 1893). Contains the text of the four principal Russian versions, together with a detailed study of the work. *Aleksandriya. Roman ob Aleksandre makedonskom po russkoy rukopisi XV v.*, ed. M. N. Botvinnik *et al.* (Moscow–Leningrad, 1965).

Digenis Akritas

M. N. Speransky, 'Devgeniyevo deyaniye. Issledovaniye i teksty', *Sbornik Otdeleniya russkogo yazka i slovesnosti Rossiskoy Akademii Nauk*, no. 7 (1922), 1–131. Contains the two main Russian texts, a study of their mutual relationship and their relation to the Greek original. H. Grégoire, 'Le Digénis russe', in *Russian Epic Studies*, ed. R. Jakobson and E. J. Simmons (Philadelphia, 1949), 131–69, argues that the two main Russian versions are closer to the original Greek text than any extant Greek manuscript of the work.

A. Dostál, 'Le Digénis slave, et son importance pour la byzantologie', *Akten des XI. Internationalen Byzantinistenkongresses* (Munich, 1960), 125–30, a brief and cautious summary of the results of the recent scholarship. V. D. Kuz'mina, *Devgeniyevo deyaniye* (Moscow, 1962), a valuable survey of the main problems of the *Digenis* scholarship by the discoverer of the third Russian manuscript of the work. Contains the texts and photographic reproductions of the manuscripts.

Byzantine chronicles

V. Istrin, *Khronika Georgiya Amartola v drevnem slavyanorusskom perevode*, 3 vols. (Petrograd, 1920–2; Leningrad, 1930). This monumental work contains the text, an attempt to establish the place and date of its translation, and a dictionary covering the Greek and Slav versions. V. Istrin, *Khronika Ioanna Malaly v slavyanskom perevode*, kn. 1–5 (Odessa, 1902–9), kn. 6–18 (St Petersburg, 1911, 1913; Petrograd, 1914). M. Weingart, *Byzantské kroniky v literatuře církevněslovanské*, 2 vols. (Bratislava, 1922–3), a study of all Byzantine chronicles translated into Church Slavonic; the whole of the second volume is devoted to the Chronicle of George Hamartolos. Z. V. Udal'tsova, 'Khronika Ioanna Malaly v Kievskoy Rusi', *Arkheograficheskiy yezhegodnik za 1965 god* (Moscow, 1966), 47–58. E. M. Shustrovich, 'Khronika Ioanna Malaly i antichaya traditsiya v drevnerusskoy literature', *Trudy Otdela drevnerusskoy literatury*, XXIII (1968), 62–70.

ORIGINAL LITERATURE
Sermons

The Metropolitan Hilarion: L. Müller, *Des Metropoliten Ilarion Lobrede auf Vladimir den Heiligen und Glaubensbekenntnis* (Wiesbaden, 1962), contains the text and an admirable commentary. There is still no critical edition of Hilarion's *Slovo.* One of the manuscripts – the most complete – has recently been published by N. N. Rozov, 'Sinodal'nyy spisok sochineniy Ilariona – russkogo pisatelya XI v.', *Slavia*, XXXII (1963), 141–75; useful observations, and a good bibliography, will be found in L. Müller, 'Die Werke des Metropoliten Ilarion', *Forum Slavicum*, XXXVII (Munich, 1971); for formal aspects of the work, see R. O. Jakobson, 'Gimn v *Slove* Ilariona *o zakone i blagodati*', *The Religious World of Russian Culture. Russia and Orthodoxy, ii: Essays in honor of Georges Florovsky*, ed. A. Blane (The Hague–Paris, 1975), pp. 9–21. *Clement Smolyatich:* N. K. Nikol'sky,

EARLY RUSSIAN LITERATURE

O literaturnykh trudakh mitropolita Klimenta Smolyaticha, pisatelya XII v. (St Petersburg, 1892). *Cyril of Turov*: his sermons and other didactic works are published by I. P. Yeryomin, 'Literaturnoye naslediye Kirilla Turovskogo', *Trudy Otdela drevnerusskoy literatury*, XI (1955), 342–67; XII (1956), 340–61; XIII (1957), 409–26; XV (1958), 331–48; for a literary study of Cyril's sermons, see I. P. Yeryomin, 'Oratorskoye iskusstvo Kirilla Turovskogo', *ibid.*, XVIII (1962), 50–8; for a more general account of his life and work, see A. I. Ponomaryov, 'Sv. Kirill, episkop Turovskiy i yego ucheniya', *Pamyatniki drevnerusskoy tserkovno-uchitel'noy literatury*, I (St Petersburg, 1894), 87–125; A. Vaillant, 'Cyrille de Tourov et Grégoire de Nazianze', *Revue des Études Slaves*, XXVI (1950), 34–50, is an interesting study of a literary adaptation of a Greek model by a Russian author.

The Lives of Saints Boris and Gleb

D. I. Abramovich, *Zhitiya svyatykh muchenikov Borisa i Gleba i sluzhby im* (Petrograd, 1916), reprinted in *Die altrussischen hagiographischen Erzählungen und liturgischen Dichtungen über die Heiligen Boris und Gleb*, ed. L. Müller (Munich, 1967) (*Slavische Propyläen*, 14), contains the text of the three basic hagiographical works concerned with Boris and Gleb.

The relationship between these texts is discussed by F. von Lilienfeld, 'Die ältesteten russischen Heiligenlegenden', in *Aus der byzantinistischen Arbeit der Deutschen Demokratischen Republik*, I (Berlin, 1957), 237–71, and by L. Müller, 'Studien zur altrussischen Legende der Heiligen Boris und Gleb', *Zeitschrift für slavische Philologie*, XXIII (1955), 60–77; XXV (1956), 329–63; XXVII (1959), 274–322; XXX (1962), 14–44; see also, by the same author, 'Neuere Forschungen über das Leben und die kultische Verehrung der Heiligen Boris und Gleb', *Slawistische Studien zum V. Internationalen Slawistenkongress in Sofia* (Göttingen, 1963), pp. 295–317 (with bibliography).

The Paterikon of the Kiev Monastery of the Caves

The text was published by D. I. Abramovich, *Kievo–Pecherskiy Paterik* (Kiev, 1930), reprinted as *Das Paterikon des Kiever Höhlenklosters*, ed. D. Tschiževskij and others (Munich, 1964) (*Slavische Propyläen*, II). The *Life* of St Theodosius, which forms part of the *Paterikon*, is also published in *Sbornik XII veka Moskovskogo Uspenskogo Sobora*, I, ed. A. A. Shakhmatov and P. A. Lavrov (The Hague, 1957), 40–96 (reprint of the Moscow edn of 1899). An abridged English translation of the *Life* will be found in G. P. Fedotov, *A Treasury of Russian Spirituality* (London, 1950), 15–48. The literary qualities of the work are discussed by I. P. Yeryomin, 'K kharakteristike Nestora kak pisatelya', *Trudy Otdela drevnerusskoy literatury*, XVII (1961), 54–64; an interesting attempt to examine some of its formal aspects is made by J. Börtnes, 'Frame Technique in Nestor's Life of St Theodosius', *Scando–Slavica*, XIII (1967), 5–16.

The Primary Chronicle

The basic works are those of A. Shakhmatov, particularly *Razyskaniya o drevneyshikh russkikh letopisnykh svodakh* (St Petersburg, 1908), and 'Povest' vremennykh let i yeyo istochniki', *Trudy Otdela drevnerusskoy literatury*, IV (1940), 9–150. *Povest' vremennykh let*, ed. V. P. Adrianova-Peretts and D. S. Likhachev, 2 vols. (Moscow–Leningrad, 1950), has an excellent edition of the text, a modern Russian translation and a detailed commentary. The English translation of the Primary Chronicle by S. H. Cross and O. P. Sherbowitz-Wetzor (Cambridge, Mass., n.d.)

contains many inaccuracies and stylistic infelicities, and should be used with caution.

The Writings of Vladimir Monomakh

The text of the *Poucheniye* is printed in *Povest' vremennykh let*, s.a. 1096, ed. V. P. Adrianova-Peretts and D. S. Likhachev, I (Moscow–Leningrad, 1950), 153–63. Vladimir's letter to Oleg, *ibid.*, 163–6. The text of the *Poucheniye* can also be found in *A Historical Russian Reader*, 52–62. Useful commentaries can be found in *Povest' vremennykh let*, II, 425–57 and in A. S. Orlov, *Vladimir Monomakh* (Moscow–Leningrad, 1946). The older commentary by I. M. Ivakin, *Knyaz' Vladimir Monomakh i yego poucheniye* (Moscow, 1901), has not lost its value. There is an interesting attempt at a psychological interpretation of the *Poucheniye* by T. N. Kopreyeva, 'K voprosu o zhanrovoy prirode "Poucheniya" Vladimira Monomakha', *Trudy Otdela drevnerusskoy literatury*, XXVII (1972), 94–108. R. Mathiesen, 'A textological note on the works of Vladimir Monomach', *Ricerche Slavistiche*, XVI (1968–9), 112–25, argues that the prayer which follows Vladimir's letter to Oleg is not the work of Monomakh. There have been many attempts, none of them conclusive, to trace and identify the literary borrowings in the didactic section of the *Poucheniye*. See, in particular, M. P. Alekseyev, 'Anglo-saksonskaya parallel' k Poucheniyu Vladimira Monomakha', *Trudy Otdela drevnerusskoy literatury*, II (1935), 39–80; V. V. Danilov, '*Oktaviy* Minutsiya Feliksa i *Poucheniye* Vladimira Monomakha', *ibid.*, V (1938), 97–107; A. Vaillant, 'Une source grecque de Vladimir Monomaque', *Byzantinoslavica*, X (1949), 11–15; L. Müller, 'Die Exzerpte aus einer asketischen Rede Basilius des Grossen im "Poučenie" des Vladimir Monomach', *Russia Mediaevalis*, I (Munich, 1973), 30–48.

The Pilgrimage of the Abbot Daniel

Text in *Zhitiye i khozhdeniye Daniila russkyya zemli igumena, 1106–1108 gody*, ed. M. A. Venevitinov: *Pravoslavnyy Palestinskiy Sbornik*, t. I, vyp. 3 and 9 (1883). French translation in *Itinéraires russes en Orient*, translated by B. de Khitrowo (Geneva, 1889), 1–83. V. V. Danilov, 'K kharakteristike Khozhdeniya igumena Daniila', *Trudy Otdela drevnerusskoy literatury*, X (1954), 92–105.

The Byliny

Good representative selections of texts can be found in *Byliny*, ed. B. N. Putilov, *Biblioteka Poeta* (Leningrad, 1957) and in *Russian Folk Literature*, ed. D. P. Costello and I. P. Foote (Oxford, 1967). M. Speransky, *Russkaya ustnaya slovesnost'* (Moscow, 1917), an important work by a leading exponent of the view that the *byliny* bear some relationship to historical characters and events. H. M. Chadwick and N. K. Chadwick, *The Growth of Literature*, II (Cambridge, 1936). A. M. Astakhova, *Byliny. Itogi i problemy izucheniya* (Moscow–Leningrad, 1966).

Slovo o polku Igoreve

The literature on the subject is immense. The following may be specially recommended: *Slovo o polku Igoreve*, ed. V. P. Adrianova-Peretts and D. S. Likhachev (Moscow–Leningrad, 1950), contains the text, a facsimile reproduction of the first edition, an excellent commentary and various studies of the work. *La Geste du prince Igor'*, ed. H. Grégoire, R. Jakobson and M. Szeftel: *Annuaire de l'Institut de philologie et d'histoire orientales et slaves*, VIII (New York, 1945–7); reprinted in R. Jakobson, *Selected Writings*, IV (The Hague, 1966), 106–300. This work is particularly notable for Jakobson's essay which provides arguments for

EARLY RUSSIAN LITERATURE

the work's authenticity. Some of Jakobson's arguments are developed further
in his article 'The Puzzles of the Igor' Tale on the 150th Anniversary of its First
Edition', *Speculum*, xxvii (1952), 43–66; *Selected Writings*, 380–410. *Slovo o
polku Igoreve i pamyatniki Kulikovskogo tsikla*, ed. D. S. Likhachev and L. A.
Dmitriyev (Moscow–Leningrad, 1966). The principal aim of this collective work
is to support the *Slovo*'s authenticity by demonstrating the textual dependence of
the *Zadonshchina* upon it. The principal arguments of the 'sceptics', who refuse
to regard the *Slovo* as a medieval work, are summarized by J. Fennell in Fennell
and Stokes, *Early Russian Literature*, pp. 191–206.

The 'Supplication of Daniel the Prisoner'
M. O. Skripil', 'Slovo Daniila Zatochnika', *Trudy Otdela drevnerusskoy literatury*,
xi (1955), 72–95.

The Tale of the Battle on the River Kalka
Text in: *Novgorodskaya pervaya letopis'*, ed. A. N. Nasonov (Moscow–Leningrad,
1950), pp. 61–3; also in *A Historical Russian Reader*, ed. J. Fennell and D.
Obolensky, pp. 73–5.

The Tale of the Ruin of Ryazan'
Convenient editions are: *Voinskiye povesti Drevney Rusi*, ed. V. P. Adrianova-
Peretts (Moscow–Leningrad, 1949), pp. 9–19; *A Historical Russian Reader*, pp. 76–
85. There is a critical edition of the different redactions of the text by D. S. Likhachev, 'Povesti o Nikole Zarazskom', *Trudy Otdela drevnerusskoy literatury*, vii
(1949), 282–405. B. N. Putilov, 'Pesnya o Yevpatii Kolovrate', *Trudy Otdela
drevnerusskoy literatury*, xi (1955), 118–39.

The Sermons of Serapion of Vladimir
E. Petukhov, *Serapion Vladimirskiy, russkiy propovednik XIII veka* (St Petersburg,
1888), contains the text and a literary study of his sermons. On the problem of
where Serapion's sermons were written, compare the opposing views of M. Gorlin,
'Sérapion de Vladimir, prédicateur de Kiev', *Revue des Études Slaves*, xxiv (1948),
21–8, and N. K. Gudzy, 'Gde i kogda protekala literaturnaya deyatel'nost'
Serapiona Vladimirskogo?', *Izvestiya Akademii Nauk SSSR, Otdeleniye literatury
i yazyka*, xi (1952), 450–6.

The Life of St Alexander Nevsky
A critical edition of the text is provided by Yu. K. Begunov, *Pamyatnik russkoy
literatury XIII veka: 'Slovo o pogibeli russkoy zemli'* (Moscow–Leningrad, 1965),
pp. 158–80, who also attempts to reconstruct the original text (pp. 185–94) and describes the principal manuscripts (pp. 195–212). For a study of the relationship between the hagiographical and the secular elements in Alexander's biography see N.
Serebryansky, 'Drevne-russkiye knyazheskiye zhitiya', *Chteniye v imperatorskom
obshchestve istorii i drevnostey rossiyskikh pri Moskovskom Universitete*, 1915, 3,
pp. 175–222.

See also D. S. Likhachev, 'Galitskaya literaturnaya traditsiya v zhitii Aleksandra
Nevskogo', *Trudy Otdela drevnerusskoy literatury*, v (1947), 36–56, who discusses
the similarities between the biographies of Alexander Nevsky and Daniel of
Galicia.

The Tale of the Ruin of the Russian Land

An exemplary study of the work, with texts of the various manuscripts, is provided by Yu. K. Begunov, *Pamyatnik russkoy literatury XIII veka: 'Slovo o pogibeli russkoy zemli'* (Moscow–Leningrad, 1965). For differing views on the origin and nature of the *Tale*, see the studies by A. Soloviev: 'Le Dit de la ruine de la terre russe', *Byzantion*, XXII (1952), 104–32, and 'Zametki k Slovu o pogibeli Russkyya zemli', *Trudy Otdela drevnerusskoy literatury*, XV (1958), 78–115, and by M. Gorlin, 'Le Dit de la ruine de la terre russe', *Revue des Études Slaves*, XXIII (1947), 5–33.

4

LITERATURE IN
THE MUSCOVITE PERIOD
(1300–1700)

NIKOLAY ANDREYEV

After the establishment of Mongol rule in Russia, literature shared the fate of cultural life: its themes were the destiny of the country, her fight for the Christian faith and the preservation and fostering of patriotic feelings. The general tone remained serious, often stern, seldom smiling and for a long time foreign to any recreational aims.

Parchment for manuscripts was extremely costly. Paper appeared in Russia in the fourteenth century, but as it had to be imported from abroad it was expensive. It was only with its more general use and with the introduction of printing in the second half of the sixteenth century that the written word became more accessible. The truly popular literature, however, epic poems (*byliny*), or fairy tales, historical songs, riddles, proverbs continued to be mainly oral.

A survey of literary events in the thirteenth and fourteenth centuries must begin with Tver'. By the end of the thirteenth century, as the political importance of Tver' grew, a parallel development in literature began. Tver' maintained ties with Constantinople and Mount Athos, and received books and icons; its history is characterized by literacy, erudition and love for the written word. Unfortunately, owing to historical upheavals, there is not much left of the cultural heritage of this remarkable Russian centre on the Volga, the preservation of the little that has survived being mainly due to the inclusion of literary works in the Russian chronicles. The regional Tver' chronicles were written from 1285 onwards. Not later than 1294 the icon-painter Prokopiy illuminated George Hamartolos's Chronicle, showing on the title-page Prince Mikhail Yaroslavich and his 'very wise mother' Xenia, who had taught her son 'to love letters and learning'. In 1319 a narrative was written on the assassination of this prince the previous year by Tatars of the Golden Horde. It uses an earlier traditional hagiographical idiom and is in effect a political tract directed against Prince Yury of Moscow. The 1327 rising against the Tatars is reflected in the *Tale of Shevkal*.

In Novgorod the literature of the period is firstly represented by the chronicles, usually short, concise, free from rhetoric and strictly factual. In the entry for 1347 we find the extremely interesting 'Epistle of Vasily Bishop of Novgorod to Feodor Bishop of Tver''. Feodor had affirmed that the concept of paradise is purely mental; to refute him, Vasily, combining Biblical quotations with apocryphal motifs and roving legends, endeavours to locate paradise in Mesopotamia, while Hell, he says, 'is in the West', on 'the Breathing Sea' [the Arctic] and the way there lies along 'the River of Lightning'. A detailed description of the sights of Constantinople in 1348–9 is given in the 'Journey to Constantinople of Stefan of Novgorod'. More interesting still is the anonymous 'Story of Constantinople', in which the Novgorodian author writes extensively about works of art and singles out all that had been destroyed by the crusaders.

Pskov produced a businesslike chronicle, factual and mainly local. It includes a historically significant 'Tale of Prince Dovmont', protector of Pskovian lands. This tale was evidently influenced by the form and style of *The Life of St Alexander Nevsky* (see p. 82).

Translated literature during these centuries was enriched by new works. *The Tale of the Indian Kingdom*, of complicated literary genesis and which presumably reached Russia from Dalmatia, pleased Russian readers (forty-five copies are in existence) with its combination of religion and fable, its reassuring refinement, and also because it was believed to give practical knowledge of 'India the Rich'. India is represented as a happy and fabulously rich land, where everyone is virtuous and pious, the sovereign being the ideal of a servant of Christ and a defender of the Holy Sepulchre. Another popular translated work was the *Tale of Shakhansha's Twelve Dreams*, of eastern Buddhist origin, which came to Russia by way of Serbia and contained eschatological prophecies in the form of enigmatic dreams seen by Shakhansha and their explanation by the 'wise slave' Mamer.

The 'Second South Slavonic Influence' on Russian literature in the fourteenth and fifteenth centuries must be stressed. It came mainly from Constantinople and Mount Athos, where there was at that time a colony of Russian scribes copying manuscripts. Bulgarians and Serbs (Kiprian, Metropolitan of All Russia, Grigory Tsamblak, Metropolitan of Lithuania, and the writer and translator Pakhomy Logofet, a Serb) introduced South Slavonic rhetoric. The outstanding Russian master of this new hagiographical style is Epifany Premudry (the Wise), author of remarkable *Lives* of St Stephen of Perm', teacher of the Zyrian tribes, and of St Sergius of Radonezh. Among translated works a great role was played by the Byzantine World Chronicle of John Zonaras and the Chronicle of Constantine Manasses, which taught the Russians the style encrusted with metaphors, symbols, hyperbole, rhetoric, emotive exclamations and the picturesque imagery of fighting men, which was to influence Russian historical writings until the seventeenth century. The *Tales of Troy* and the *Parable of the Kings*, translated in Serbia, retold the Homeric saga in the style of medieval romances, firing the readers' imagination with information on the daily life of the knights and their special moral code. The same elements were introduced into Russia by the Serbian 'Alexander', translated in Dalmatia from Greek into Church Slavonic, which gives a lyrical interpretation of the romance of Alexander and Roxana and traces a lively picture of action. The Serbian 'Alexander' enjoyed such popularity that it supplanted the Greek Alexander romance of Pseudo-Callisthenes. The didactic sixth-century tale, *Stefanit and Ikhnilat*, of oriental origin, several times worked over, and translated from the Greek in Bulgaria, interested the Russians, for it presented the image of an ideal sovereign and discussed in a lively manner the best methods of ruling a kingdom.

Original Muscovite literature of this period started with the chronicles, first regional and later more general. In 1327, the year after the death of Metropolitan Peter, Prokhor, a bishop of Rostov, wrote his *Life*, which can be considered as the first work embodying a specifically Muscovite political and ecclesiastical style. The first Moscow Chronicle was compiled at the beginning of the fifteenth century, following the indications (and probably with the collaboration) of Metropolitan Kiprian (1390–1406). Besides the regional Russian chronicles, it included for the first time information on the history of the Lithuanian Kingdom, to some of whose territories Moscow laid a claim. In this compilation 'the great peace' brought by Ivan Kalita was extolled. In 1418 or 1423 a further compilation was made, the *Vladimir Polychron*, a more objective account which excluded the scornful references to the people of Tver', Novgorod and Suzdal' found in the earlier Moscow Chronicle: the compilers were evidently aware of the necessity of giving a sober account of events on a nation-wide scale. In the middle of the fifteenth century, the Kievan Primary Chronicle was placed at the beginning of the Moscow Chronicle – a fact of great political significance, as it stressed Moscow's position as representative of the whole of the Russian land. Pakhomy the Serb compiled in 1442 the *Russian Chronograph*, whose narrative goes down to 1441, in which he tried to connect the history of Russia with universal history, using both the Manasses Chronicle and the Serbian *Lives* of St Sava, Stefan Lazarević and others. Stylistically it contains rhetorical features which were taken over by writers of Russian historical tales.

The most remarkable of these tales are four works on the Battle of Kulikovo (1380). The first is the *Story of Mamay's Battle*, which strongly emphasizes the moral aspect of the victory, exalting Prince Dimitri

Donskoy and contrasting him with Prince Oleg of Ryazan', 'the devil's counsellor'. Of special interest is the *Zadonshchina*, based in part on orally transmitted tales of the Kulikovo battle. Stylistically it owes much to the *Slovo o polku Igoreve*, but is a kind of antithesis of the latter in its fundamental idea: in the *Slovo* the Russians are defeated because of lack of solidarity among the princes, in the later work victory is due to national unity. The author of the *Zadonshchina*, Sofony of Ryazan', patently echoes the imagery of the *Slovo*, though at times he gives it an exactly opposite meaning.

Those who question the originality and authenticity of the *Slovo* see in it a work of the eighteenth century, imitating the *Zadonshchina*; but when one reads the two works it is impossible not to sense the stylistic disharmony and, at times, awkward wording in Sofony's poem in comparison with the organic unity of the *Slovo*, whose author was aware of the details of the history of the period to an extent that has only recently been fully realized. In the eighteenth century there was neither sufficient knowledge of medieval Russia nor an author with sufficiently outstanding poetical gifts of this type to have written such an imitation.

The third work on the same theme is the *Tale of the Battle of the Grand Prince Dimitri Donskoy*, written in the middle of the fifteenth century and repeatedly revised. It is longer than the others and contains a number of interesting episodes, such as the visit paid to Prince Dimitri on the eve of the battle by St Sergius of Radonezh and the Metropolitan Kiprian (the latter an imagined detail). The political importance of the grand prince is stressed, as well as his deep piety. Stylistically the work is influenced by the *Zadonshchina* and the *Life of Alexander Nevsky*, and contains echoes of Josephus' *Jewish War*, *The Aleksandriya* and Hamartolos's Chronicle. New features are introduced: episodes in epistolary form, speeches, dialogues, and several literary trends are here united. Structurally and stylistically this influenced the later historical tales of the seventeenth century on the subject of the 'Time of Troubles'. The fourth work concerned with the battle of Kulikovo, the *Tale of the Life and Demise of the Grand Prince Dimitri Ivanovich, Tsar of Russia*, written in the first half of the fifteenth century, is a panegyric of Dimitri Donskoy, in the traditional rhetorical, hagiographic manner; it is only in the widowed princess's lament that the poetry of folk lamentations has very aptly been introduced.

A special place is assigned in the *Polychron*, in the entry for 1425, to the tale *Of the Taking of Moscow by Tokhtamysh*. The tone of the narrative (which has no individual hero), epic in the description of the city's destruction, becomes lyrical when relating the people's and the author's grief. No less original is the *Tale of Temir Aksak* (Tamerlane): in the wholly legendary biography the conqueror is represented as a

93

heroic though malevolent figure ('a ferocious bandit'). The second part, which describes the transfer from Vladimir to Moscow of Russia's palladium, the holy icon of Our Lady of Vladimir, and the miracle, due to her intercession, of the sudden departure of Tamerlane from Russia, shows Vasily I as the counterpart of the 'robber Tamerlane'. Here we find an interesting new motif in literature: the authority of the grand prince of Moscow sanctified by God and therefore morally elevated.

A literary revival is noticeable in Tver' at the end of the fourteenth and the beginning of the fifteenth centuries. The First Tver' Chronicle, known only in fragments, was begun in 1409. It advocates the necessity of ending the conflict between the Princes of Tver' and of Kashin. The Chronicle of the Principality of Tver' was compiled in 1455 and is prefaced by an earlier account of events of universal and Russian history up to 1285. This chronicle demonstrates the autocratic power of the Prince of Tver' and includes a new version of the story of Prince Mikhail Aleksandrovich, written in a hagiographic and laudatory tone. Much more interesting in content and style is *The Eulogy of Prince Boris Aleksandrovich* by the monk Foma, written in 1453. This too stresses the autocracy of the prince of Tver', the 'second Constantine'. It contains in places echoes of church litanies, and is in effect a pattern of words assembled according to various stylistic trends. The various parts of this interesting and original monument of fifteenth-century Tver' literature are bound together by the idea of the continuity of political sovereignty, which in the author's opinion has been transmitted from the rulers of antiquity to the princes of Tver'.

Connected with Tver' is the famous *Journey across Three Seas* by Afanasy Nikitin, who travelled to India and described it thirty years before Vasco da Gama. It can by no means be considered a finished literary work. It consists only of fragments, of material collected and notes made by an observant and intelligent merchant from Tver' during his voyage to the East in 1466–72. This daring and hardy traveller took down in a business-like way all that interested him – from religious rites to ways of conducting trade, from legends to everyday life. His conclusions are severe: the moral level of Indian society is low. He remembered Russia as a land that had no parallel in the whole world. He prayed for her, while admitting that 'her lords were not just'. His notes show him as a man deeply attached to his Orthodox Christian faith, yet remarkably tolerant of other creeds: 'Real and true faith is known to God alone', and 'Real and true faith knows only One God'. Common sense, mother-wit and a critical eye are also likeable traits in Nikitin. His notes, free from literary conventions, and couched in a lively Russian language, at once precise and racy, reveal a man of intelligence and throw a favourable light on the culture of Russia during that period.

94

To judge from his use of Persian, Arabic and Turkish words and idioms, he knew or at least understood several oriental languages. Nikitin died (apparently in the spring of 1473) near Smolensk, on his way home, and his notes were brought directly to Moscow by other merchants. At the beginning of the sixteenth century they were included in the Moscow Chronicles.

In the reigns of Ivan III (1462–1505) and Vasily III (1505–33), a number of works were written on the subject of the rise of Moscow and Russia's 'Byzantine heritage' after the fall of Constantinople in 1453. At the same time Western influences became more and more evident in literature, though Western ideas were resisted. Among translated works one can note *The Tale of Troy* by the Italian poet Guido delle Colonne, written in Latin in 1287. This is the history of the Trojan war retold in terms of a tale of chivalry, and it was quite ably translated in the middle of the fifteenth century. It is full of metaphors and allegories – a style which influenced a number of Russian works from the fifteenth to the seventeenth centuries. *The Tale of Dracula* was translated from German, presumably before 1486. Dracula was a powerful tyrant, and the tale was popular because it touched on the question of the limits of the sovereign's power. *The Dispute between Life and Death* appeared at the beginning of the sixteenth century, translated from the German version of Nicholas Mercator published in Lübeck around 1484, and written in the form of a dialogue. In the hands of the Russian translators and scribes the pre-Reformation spirit of the original was weakened and it was transformed into a more popular work, with the introduction of a new character, Anika the Warrior, in an *intermezzo* dealing with him and death, which became part of the folk plays *Tsar Maximilian* and *King Herod*.

Captured by the Turks and pressed into service in their army, Nestor Iskander, a Russian, described the fall of Constantinople. His originally short *Tale of the Taking of Constantinople* was altered and enlarged by the Russian editors who added the apocryphal prophecy of the transfer of power from Byzantium to a 'fair-haired race' (*Rusiy rod*), which of course soon became *Russkiy rod*, This work would thus be taken to foretell that the Russians would liberate Byzantium. The same idea is developed in *The Tale of the Princes of Vladimir*, probably written in the 1520s. It is a new version of the earlier *Epistle of Spiridon-Savva*, formerly metropolitan of Kiev, on the genealogy of the Russian grand princes who spring from Ryurik – a kinsman, it was alleged, through Prus, of Caesar Augustus. In spite of its flagrantly fictional character, the *Tale* was reflected in official documents of the fifteenth century, and Ivan IV obtained some of his ideas from it.

All these works are evidence of the interest shown by Russian writers in the idea of Moscow as the centre of Orthodox ecclesiastical authority.

The appearance of overtly publicist writings on this subject is therefore not surprising. The most important of these are connected with the name of the monk Filofey of Pskov. Historians do not agree on the date of the earliest of his works, the *Epistle to Ivan Vasil'yevich*. Most of them mistakenly believe that it was written in the reign of Ivan IV, but it would appear that it was originally addressed to Ivan III, when the latter seized extensive tracts of ecclesiastical lands in Novgorod. It is an impassioned defence of church property. As an argument Filofey advanced the idea that Moscow is now the centre of Orthodoxy: 'Two Romes perished because of heresies' and now 'the Third Rome shines in the world more brightly than the sun'; it is therefore the duty of the Moscow sovereign to defend and guard the Orthodox Church and her property. In two further epistles, to Vasily III and to one of the latter's trusted agents in Pskov, Misyur' Munekhin, Filofey expounds only certain aspects of his theory of 'Moscow–the Third Rome'. According to him, 'the Third Rome stands, a fourth there will never be'.

A number of works were written in the fifteenth and the beginning of the sixteenth centuries about the Russian Church, her duties and attributes and her relation to secular power, by Nil Sorsky (*c.* 1433–1508) and Iosif Volotsky (1439–1515), the leaders respectively of the 'Non-Possessors' and 'Possessors', the two main currents of Russian monasticism. Iosif also became famous as a persecutor of the followers of the Judaizers' heresy. After their deaths their disciples continued to write along the lines they had laid down. Nil's disciple Vassian (Prince Patrikeyev) left a number of works defending the Non-Possessors' position. He was eventually condemned as a heretic and died in prison. During the sixteenth century, the partisans of Iosif Volotsky very readily accused all such free-thinking writers of heresy. It seems nearer to the truth to see them simply as men of a critical rationalistic mind and, as such, unacceptable to the 'Iosiflyane'. All this topical literature, which also continually referred to general national and social problems, contributed to the formation of a style midway between church eloquence and the matter-of-fact language of business, at times enlivened by colloquialisms.

Towering above these publicists is the gifted and tragic personality of Maxim (Maximus) the Greek (*c.* 1470–1556), who had been invited to Moscow from Mount Athos to undertake the translation and annotation of the Psalter. Maxim was a man of vast knowledge, diligence and fiery temperament, who in his youth had had contacts with the Italian Renaissance and had become an ardent admirer of Savonarola. In Moscow, from 1518 onwards, aided by a staff of assistants, he not only made translation after translation and corrected liturgical and prayer books, but became a kind of spiritual adviser to all those who needed clarification on the many points which were causing anxiety in Russian society. Not the least of these was the question of church lands, the holding of which Maxim absolutely condemned. The Metropolitan Daniil (1522–1539), a fierce supporter of Iosif Volotsky, soon became Maxim's active enemy, and in 1525 Maxim was condemned by a church council, allegedly for heresies contained in his translations, forbidden the sacraments, and exiled to the Volokolamsk monastery. In 1531 Vassian was tried and Maxim re-tried, both this time in part for their 'Non-Possessor' views. Maxim was accused of treasonable relations with the Turkish authorities and of condemning the Russian Church's recently acquired independence of the Patriarchate of Constantinople. He was exiled to a monastery in Tver', where he remained for twenty years. It was only in 1551, during the 'Stoglav' council, that Ivan IV persuaded Metropolitan Makary to set him free. Maxim ended his life in almost complete freedom at the Monastery of the Holy Trinity, but was not allowed to return to Mount Athos, the Muscovites rightly feeling too ashamed of the treatment meted out to him. He was later canonized.

About 1432 the Sophia Chronicle was compiled in Novgorod, mainly on the basis of local records. The Novgorodian chronicles were codified in 1448; they included nearly the whole of the Sophia Chronicle and much information from other chronicles, the general tendency being to give a commentary not only on the history of Russia but also on that of the Republic of Novgorod. *Lives* and legends appeared which described the events leading to the loss of Novgorod's independence. Such are the *Lives* of Mikhail of the Klopsky monastery and Zosima of Solovki, the mystical *Vision* of Tarasy, the *Tale of Shchil*, and others. One remarkable work is the *Life* of Ioann, Bishop of Novgorod, which includes a description of the Bishop's night-ride to Jerusalem on a demon's back; others are the *Tale* of the unsuccessful attempt by Andrey Bogolyubsky in 1169 to take Novgorod; the *Life* of Antony the Roman, who came sailing on a stone from Rome, where 'orthodoxy had weakened', to Novgorod, described as a flourishing centre of world trade. Of special importance is the *Tale of the White Cowl*, whose authorship is ascribed to Dimitri Tolmach (Gerasimov), the white cowl being a holy symbol of the highest ecclesiastical dignity and power which had passed to Novgorod and whose priority over the secular principle is strongly emphasized. For expressing this idea, the book was put on the Index of 'spurious [banned] books' by the Russian Church Council of 1666–7.

In Pskov a similar tendency to regret the freedom of bygone days is reflected in the *Pskovian Chronicles*, and in the *Tale of the Taking of Pskov by the Grand Prince Vasily III*, which is a moving description, of great lyrical power, of the end of Pskov's independence. Analogous features are found in Yaroslavl' in the *Life of Fyodor the Black*, probably of the end of the fourteenth century, and in the fifteenth century in Rostov in the *Lives* of Leonty and Avraamy and of Isidor the 'Fool in Christ' (Yurodivyy).

Murom produced in the fifteenth or sixteenth century the *Tale of Pyotr and Fevroniya*. This is the story of the love of a prince for a peasant girl, a subject found in the literature of many countries and here adapted to conditions of life in Russia and written in a colloquial style. There are many dialogues, wise sayings and features of folklore. The work was popular and some 150 copies have come down to us.

From Smolensk comes the *Tale of Merkury*. It is a sixteenth-century adaptation of older legends concerned with the fight of the Russian people against nomad invaders. There is a fictitious description of Batu's attack on Smolensk and its defence by the warrior Merkury who, after having carried out his task in the world, is beheaded by an angel, a motif which probably came to Russia from the West.

Muscovite literature in the sixteenth century is characterized by works intended to enhance Moscow's political and ecclesiastical policy of centralization and unification. This is primarily evident in the chronicles which were codified under various titles: the Voskresensky (up to 1541), the Patriarchal or Nikonian (to 1558), and the Lvov Chronicles (up to 1560). To the 1560s belongs the Nikonian Illustrated Compilation, containing some 20,000 pages and 16,000 illuminations. Part of it was used in the so-called *Royal Book* (*Tsarstvennaya kniga*). These compilations extol the greatness of the Muscovite state and at the same time give factual descriptions of events. The Muscovite state is shown to be the product of Russian and universal history.

The compilation of the *Great Chet'i Minei* under the direction of Metropolitan Makary (1542–63), of some 27,000 pages, comprises not only lives of saints, but also includes collections such as the 'Bee', and Josephus' *History of the Jewish War*. In 1563, on Makary's initiative, the *Book of Ranks of the Tsars' Genealogy* was written by the Tsar's chaplain, Makary's successor in the metropolitan see. This is a flowery panegyric of Russian rulers who, it was claimed, were 'tsars' even in the Kievan period and who, through the Emperor Augustus, Prus (his fictional brother) and Ryurik, were said to be related to the rulers of ancient time. The unification of the Russian lands was successful, the author explains, because the princes enjoyed the Lord's support, since the Moscow dynasty had been divinely appointed to rule.

In his sixteen sermons and epistles, Metropolitan Daniil had already sternly castigated the vices of Russian society in a lively vernacular language and 'abusive speech'. This didacticism continued and is reflected in a number of works: in the *Domostroy*, or rules of family life, attributed to the priest Sylvester – though the authorship is now disputed; in part in the *Stoglav*, which deals with church life; and also in the *Alphabet* which attempts to convey to its readers a system of knowledge and opinions.

The conquest of Kazan' served as a pretext for a *History of the Kazan' Kingdom*, written in 1564–5. Its author is a Russian who had been for twenty years a prisoner in Kazan' and was freed at the capture of the city. He was an ardent partisan of Ivan IV. His work, glorifying the tsar and justifying his policies, is written in a bookish, flowery style, combining idiomatic speech and orally transmitted poetry. In the same vein – combining praise of the tsar, contempt for the enemies of Russia, and glorification of all Russians 'from the lowest to the highest' – is the rhetorical *Tale of the Attack of Stefan Batory on Pskov*, presumably written by the Pskovian icon-painter Vasily.

The works of Ivan Peresvetov, long and wrongly considered to have come from the pen of Ivan IV, are polemical and advocate the necessity of strong power; in a sense they seem to foreshadow and urge the measures later taken by Ivan. Peresvetov spoke for the middle stratum of the gentry. Yermolay Erazm in his works defended the peasants' interests. Of particular importance were the letters, exchanged between 1564 and 1579, by Ivan IV and Prince Andrey Kurbsky, who had fled to Lithuania from the tsar's anger. Kurbsky's five letters advance the arguments in favour of a joint rule by the sovereign and the aristocracy, while Ivan in his two epistles offers a fierce and impassioned justification of the absolute power of the monarch, who is responsible solely to his own conscience and to God. The *History of the Grand Prince of Moscow* written by Kurbsky, probably in the early 1570s, is a criticism, at times assuming the style of a polemic, of nearly all the tsar's measures taken after his break with his 'good counsellors' and with the 'Chosen Council', and accusing the whole Muscovite dynasty of being a 'blood-thirsty race'.

The economic crisis in the country, the loss of the Livonian war, the end of the dynasty and the beginning of political unrest seem to have caused a lowering of the literary output in the last quarter of the sixteenth century, though the production of historical folk-songs continued unabated. A revival and growth of literary activity begins again in the seventeenth century.

The *Tale of 1606*, written by an unknown monk to justify the accession of Vasily IV (Shuysky), refers contemptuously to Boris Godunov and the pseudo-Dimitri. Under its new title *Another Story* it was amplified by the *Tale of Father Terenty's Vision*, which tells of the holy Virgin's request of forgiveness for the Russian people, which Christ promises to grant if they 'repent of their sins'. Tales, saints' lives, legends, folk-songs, and epic works record the shattering events of the Time of Troubles. Deep changes occurred in the Russian people's consciousness and were reflected in style, language and ideas. Recent catastrophes were generally viewed as a punishment for sins committed – mainly by Godunov and the first pseudo-Dimitri; on the other hand, the *History* (*Vremennik*), written by Ivan Timofeyev (1619), argues that the real reason for the disasters lies in the lack of unity of the Russians and in their 'speechlessness' before those in power. Avraamy Palitsyn in his *History* (*Skazaniye*) calls these manifestations of servility 'insane silence'. *The Book of Chronicles* by Prince I. M. Katyrev-Rostovsky, a kinsman of the Romanovs, is strictly factual and restrained. Stylistically it owes something to Guido delle Colonne's *History of Troy*. The author is interested in his fellow men and has a talent for describing the outward appearance of historical personages; he is sensitive to nature, and his perception of events is free from imposed church tradition. It is believed by some that he was only the editor of this work, which is written in two markedly different styles, characterized respectively by Ukrainian idioms and rhymed lines. There are many new literary features in the writings of Prince Ivan Khvorostinin. In the *New Tale of the Most Glorious Russian Tsardom*, written by an unknown author in the form of an anonymous letter, an anti-boyar theme is voiced: the boyars are not 'landowners' but 'landeaters'. One should therefore not work for them, they are enemies of Christ's cross, and have betrayed their faith and serve the Poles. Two *Tales* were written about the popular young hero Prince Mikhail Skopin-Shuysky, one about his life, the other about his death. A story about Yermak and the conquest of Siberia also appeared at this time; later works are *The Siege of Azov* and *The Tale of Yeruslan Lazarevich*, conceived likewise among the Cossacks, which described the adventures of a valiant warrior who defends the oppressed. Some of the episodes can be traced to *Shah-Name* by the Persian poet Firdousi, in its Turkish version. The Murom tale of Yulianiya Lazarevskaya is essentially a Life of a saint, though it differs from the usual stereotyped hagiographical model and foreshadows the novel of manners of the end of the century.

The Tale of Grief and Ill-Luck tells in rhythmical prose the story of an obscure young man who, scorning old customs, wanted to live as he pleased, 'tasted of the fruits of the vine' and was finally punished by fate, ending his days in a monastery. The *Tale of Savva Grudtsyn*, written in the 1670s, likewise defends family and tradition, and the hero also ends in a monastery. The background is made up of historical events and there is a demonological explanation of evil. This tale is structurally complex and is sometimes considered to be the first Russian novel of manners with social implications. Demonological themes also appear in the *Tale of the Origin of Tobacco* and the *Tale of Solomoniya the Possessed*, which originated in Russian folklore and partly in western legends. The picaresque novel makes its appearance in the *Tale of Frol Skobeyev*. The *Tale of Karp Sutulov and his Very Wise Wife* deals with the defence of

100

virtue and is told in a moralizing tone. Three historical tales on the beginnings of Moscow combine church themes with romance, the hero being Daniil of Moscow.

Remarkable satirical tales about many aspects of Russian life appeared at the same time. The wittiest is the *Tale of Yersh Yershovich*, a denunciation of bureaucracy. *Shemyaka's Trial*, about a corrupt judge, is one of many such. In the second half of the seventeenth century there was a steady flow of translated literature from Polish, Czech, Latin, German and other languages. The subject is often a love-story with many obstacles but a happy ending (*Vasilisa the Fair, Prince Bova, Pyotr of the Golden Keys*). Some of these translations were collections of jokes, fables, anecdotes, stories of doubtful morality (thus Boccaccio's *Decameron* reached Russia from Poland). Moralistic tracts were also translated (*The Great Mirror*, 1677, *Roman Deeds*, based on *Gesta Romanorum*).

One of the chief events in the literary life of the seventeenth century was the introduction into Russia of syllabic verse forms by the Kiev monk, the White Russian Simeon Polotsky (1629–80), who came to Moscow in 1649 and remained there first as a teacher of Latin, then as a writer of pamphlets against the Old Believers, and finally as a tutor to the tsar's children. He was a gifted teacher, theologian and translator, but became chiefly known as a poet, leaving a large quantity of writings, chief of which are *The Many-Flowered Garden* (1678) and the *Rhythmologion* (1679), in which are given samples of every metre of syllabic versification, from the swift and light six-syllable to the heavy and unwieldy thirteen-syllable verse. Polotsky's influence marked the beginning of the baroque style in Russian literature. He was also a playwright, and two of his plays have survived – *The Comedy of Nebuchadnezzar* and *The Comedy of the Parable of the Prodigal Son*, the latter presenting the eternal problem of fathers clinging to the past and sons defending the present. Simeon's principal followers were Sylvester Medvedev (1641–91) and Karion Istomin.

But the chief and by far the most interesting literary event of the century are the writings of the Archpriest Avvakum (1620–82), one of the leaders of the Old Believers. He left over eighty writings: these include letters, sermons and a remarkable autobiography. All his works are permeated by a fanatical fidelity to the past, hatred of the followers of Nikon, and love for the Russian language. His style, lively and pungent, was an excellent weapon for the dissemination of his ideas. In Avvakum's *Autobiography* the unsophisticated speech of the suburbs and of his own village is combined with the old bookish language, and he achieves such vivid expressiveness, rich linguistic texture, originality in description, and pathetic poignancy that he is rightly considered as standing not so much at the conclusion of the Muscovite period of Russian literature as –

paradoxically – on the threshold of the new epoch. Avvakum was a true master of the language who can still teach Russian writers the art of eloquent story-telling and of dynamic force in the rendering of emotions.

GUIDE TO FURTHER READING

DICTIONARIES AND GLOSSARIES

I. I. Sreznevsky, *Materialy dlya slovarya drevnerusskogo yazyka*, 3 vols. (St Petersburg, 1893–1903, reprint Moscow, 1958). Glossary in *Anthology of Old Russian Literature*, ed. A. Stender-Petersen, third printing (New York and London, 1966), pp. 471–504. Glossary in *A Historical Russian Reader*, ed. J. Fennell and D. Obolensky (Oxford, 1969), pp. 211–28. *Dictionary of Russian Historical Terms from the Eleventh Century to 1917*, compiled by S. G. Pushkarev, ed. G. Vernadsky and R. T. Fisher, Jr (New Haven and London, 1970).

BIBLIOGRAPHICAL WORKS

Bibliografiya sovetskikh rabot po drevnerusskoy literature za 1945–1955 gg., ed. D. S. Likhachev, who gives, in the introduction, an important survey of the progress made – up to 1955 – in the study of early Russian literature. *Bibliografiya sovetskikh russkikh rabot po literature XI–XVII vv. za 1917–1957 gg.*, compiled by N. F. Droblenkova, ed. and with an introduction by V. P. Adrianova-Peretts (Moscow–Leningrad, 1961). N. F. Droblenkova, 'Bibliografiya rabot po drevne-russkoy literature, vyshedshikh v SSSR za 1958–1959 gg.', *Trudy Otdela drevne-russkoy literatury*, XVIII (1962), 499–551. *Bibliografiya sovetskikh rabot po literature XVII veka*, compiled by V. A. Libman, P. A. Borodulin and Ye. V. Parfenova, in the collection *XVII vek v mirovom literaturnom razvitii* (Moscow, 1969), pp. 425–39. I. U. Budovnits, *Slovar' russkoy, ukrainskoy, belorusskoy pis'-mennosti i literatury do XVIII veka* (Moscow, 1962), a useful reference book which covers a wide field. *Bibliografiya russkogo letopisaniya*, compiled by R. P. Dmitriyeva (Moscow–Leningrad, 1962). *A bibliography of works in English on Early Russian History to 1800*, compiled by P. A. Crowther (Oxford, 1969). See section on literature of this period, pp. 131–5. There are also useful yearly surveys of new work published in the *Year's Work in Modern Languages Studies*, section 'Russian Studies: Literature. From the Beginning to 1700'. Material of interest to students of this period appears in *Trudy Otdela drevnerusskoy literatury*, published by the Academy of Sciences of the USSR, Pushkin House, Leningrad.

ANTHOLOGIES

Khrestomatiya po drevney russkoy literature XI–XVII vekov, compiled by N. K. Gudzy, 5th edn (Moscow, 1952). There is an extremely useful collection of texts for this period beginning on p. 137. Also useful are *Khrestomatiya po drevney russkoy literature*, selected by A. D. Stokes from the 7th edn of N. K. Gudzy's *Khrestomatiya* (Letchworth, 1963), and *Anthology of Old Russian Literature*, ed. A. Stender-Petersen, third printing (New York and London, 1966), which has an interesting introduction, notes and glossary. *A Historical Russian Reader. A selection of texts from the XIth to the XVIth centuries*, ed. by J. Fennell and D. Obolensky (Oxford, 1969). Useful notes and a glossary.

Russian Folk Literature, ed. D. P. Costello and I. P. Foote (Oxford, 1967). A good collection of texts, notes and glossary. *Russkiye povesti XV–XVI vekov*, ed.

GUIDE TO FURTHER READING

B. A. Larin (Moscow–Leningrad, 1958), texts with a translation into modern Russian, useful notes. *Russkaya povest' XVII veka*, comp. by M. O. Skripil', ed. I. P. Yeryomin (Leningrad, 1959). A most useful compilation of seventeenth-century texts, with a modern Russian translation, important commentaries and notes. A useful collection of texts and commentaries in *Russische Heiligenlegenden*, ed. E. Benz (Zurich, 1953). *Medieval Russia's Epics, Chronicles and Tales*, ed., translated, and with an introduction by S. A. Zenkovsky, 2nd edn, revised (New York, 1964): a very helpful anthology.

GENERAL HISTORIES OF LITERATURE

As an introduction to the history of the literature of the period, the following will be found useful: Ye. V. Petukhov, *Russkaya literatura. Drevniy period*, 3rd edn (Petrograd, 1916); M. N. Speransky, *Istoriya drevney russkoy literatury*, 2nd edn (Moscow, 1914, also 1924 edn). *Istoriya russkoy literatury*, published by the Academy of Sciences of the USSR, II, part 1 (Moscow, 1945), II part 2 (Moscow, 1948), is the work of several scholars and contains a mass of facts. It is written in the light of historical events, and the work of each writer is usually examined from this point of view. N. K. Gudzy, *Istoriya drevney russkoy literatury*, preferably the 7th enlarged and revised edition (Moscow, 1966), a well-balanced survey, very useful for the analysis of various works. There is an English translation: *History of Early Russian Literature* (New York, 1949). *Istoriya russkoy literatury v tryokh tomakh*, ed. D. Blagoy (Moscow–Leningrad, 1958), is the collective work of several experts. It aims at a study of the literary trends of the period: cf. 156–377. D. S. Likhachev, 'Semnadtsatyy vek v russkoy literature', in the collection *XVII vek v mirovom literaturnom razvitii* (Moscow, 1969), pp. 299–328. An important survey which gives a clear picture of the literary trends in the seventeenth century. D. Čiževskij, *History of Russian Literature from the Eleventh Century to the End of the Baroque* (The Hague, 1960). His approach is idiosyncratic but always interesting. *Istoki russkoy belletristiki. Vozniknoveniye zhanrov syuzhetnogo povestvovaniya v drevnerusskoy literature*, ed. Ya. S. Lur'e (Leningrad 1970). A collective work, which examines works of literature in the context of literary genres. D. S. Likhachev, *Chelovek v literature drevney Rusi*, 2nd edn (Moscow, 1970): for this period see VI, pp. 208–561: a thoughtful and in many ways a pioneering study. See also two pioneering works by the same author: *Poetika drevnerusskoy literatury*, 2nd edn (Leningrad, 1971) and *Razvitiye russkoy literatury X–XVII vekov* (Leningrad, 1973).

THE CULTURAL BACKGROUND OF MUSCOVITE LITERATURE

See under Guide to Further Reading, 'Cultural development in Muscovy', *Companion to Russian Studies*, I, 118.

INDIVIDUAL WRITERS AND WORKS

On Tver': A. N. Nasonov, 'Letopisnyye pamyatniki Tverskogo knyazhestva', *Izvestiya Akademii Nauk SSSR. Otdeleniye gumanitarnykh nauk* (Moscow, 1930), 710–72; Ya. S. Lur'ye, 'Rol' Tveri v sozdanii russkogo natsional'nogo gosudarstva', *Uchonyye zapiski Leningradskogo gosudarstvennogo universiteta no. 36. Seriya istoricheskikh nauk*, III (1939), 85–109; Werner Philipp, 'Ein Anonymus der Tverer Publizistik im 15. Jahrhundert', *Festschrift für Dmytro Čyževsky: zum 60 Geburtstag* (Berlin, 1956), 230–57; N. I. Serebryanski, *Drevnerusskiye knyazheskiye zhitiya* (Moscow, 1915).

103

LITERATURE IN THE MUSCOVITE PERIOD

On Novgorod: N. K. Gudzy provides a carefully chosen critical bibliography on Novgorod writings in *Istoriya drevney russkoy literatury*, 7th edn (1966), 292–307. For the text of 'Poslaniye Vasiliya o zemnom raye' see *Polnoye sobraniye russkikh letopisey*, VI, 87–9; and for a commentary see M. N. Speransky, *Iz starinnoy Novgorodskoy literatury XIV v.* (Leningrad, 1934).

On Pskov: N. I. Serebryansky, *Drevnerusskiye knyazheskiye zhitiya* (Moscow, 1915), contains the text and an analysis of the chronicle's *Tale of Prince Dovmont*.

Translated works mentioned in this chapter: V. M. Istrin, 'Skazaniye ob Indiyskom tsarstve', *Izvestiya Otdeleniya russkogo yazyka i slovesnosti Akademii nauk*, III, 2 (1930); A. N. Veselovsky, 'Slovo o 12 snakh Shakhaishi po rukopisi XV v.', *Sbornik Otdeleniya russkogo yazyka i slovesnosti*, XX, 2 (1879). A. V. Rystenko, *Skazaniye o 12 snakh tsarya Mamera v slavyano–russkoy literature* (Odessa, 1904).

On the 'Second South Slavonic Influence' see in particular: D. S. Likhachev, *Kul'tura Rusi vremeni Andreya Rublyova i Epifaniya Premudrogo* (Moscow–Leningrad, 1962). M. N. Tikhomirov, 'Istoricheskiye svyazi russkogo narodo s yuzhnymi slavyanami s drevneyshikh vremyon do poloviny XVII v.', *Slavyanskiy sbornik* (Moscow, 1947), provides – most usefully – the historical background; Ch. VI, 'Yuzhnoslavyanskiye strany i Rus' v XIX–XV vv.', is particularly important. I. Duychev advances some interesting ideas and observations on the nature of Slavonic interrelationships: 'Tsentry vizantiysko-slavyanskogo obshchcheniya i sotrudnichestva', *Trudy Otdela drevnerusskoy literatury*, XIX (1963), 107–29. Particularly important is D. S. Likhachev's 'Nekotoryye zadachi izucheniya vtorogo yuzhnoslavyanskogo vliyaniya v Rossii', *Issledovaniya po slavyanskomu literaturovedeniyu i fol'kloristike: doklady sovetskikh uchonykh no IV Mezhdunarodnom s'yezde slavistov* (Moscow, 1960), 95–191.

On Metropolitan Kiprian: L. A. Dmitriyev, 'Rol'' i znacheniye mitropolita Kipriana v istorii drevnerusskoy literatury (k russko–bolgarskim literaturnym svyazyam XIV–XV vv.)', *Trudy Otdela drevnerusskoy literatury*, XIX (1963), 215–54; an important work. See also N. Glubokovsky, 'Sv. Kiprian, mitropolit vseya Rossii (1374–1406) kak pisatel'', *Chteniya obshchestva lyubiteley drevney pis'mennosti*, kn. I, yanvar' (Moscow, 1892).

On Grigory Tsamblak: Ya. I. Yatsimirsky, *Grigory Tsamblak* (St Petersburg, 1904). Cf. the critical remarks on Yatsimirsky's work by E. Turdeanu, 'Grégoire Camblak; faux arguments d'une biographie', *Revue des Études Slaves*, XXII (1946), 46–81.

On Epifany Premudry: the text of the *Zhitiya* of St Sergius was published by N. S. Tikhonravov, *Drevniye zhitiya prepodobnogo Sergiya Radonezhskogo* (Moscow, 1892, 1916), and reissued, with a good introduction, by L. Müller: *Slavische Propyläen*, XVII (Munich, 1967); the text of the *Life of Stefan of Perm'* was published by V. G. Druzhinin, *Zhitiye sv. Stefana, yepiskopa Permskogo (napis annoye Epifaniyem Premudrym)* (St Petersburg, 1897), and reprinted in the series *Apophoreta Slavica* (The Hague, 1959), with a brief but useful introduction in English by D. Čiževskij. Historical, theological and literary aspects of these *vitae* are discussed by V. O. Klyuchevsky, *Drevnerusskiye zhitiya svyatykh kak istoricheskiy istochnik* (St Petersburg, 1871), reprinted in *Slavistic Printings and Reprintings* (The Hague–Paris, 1968), 115; V. P. Zubov, 'Epifany Premudry i Pakhomy Serb (K voprosu o redaktsiyakh "Zhitiya Sergiya Radonezhskogo")', *Trudy Otdela drevnerusskoy literatury*, IX 1953), 145–58; G. P. Fedotov, *Svyatyye Drevney Rusi X–XVII st.* (Paris, 1931), 126–52, and by the same author, *The Russian Religious Mind*, II (Cambridge, Mass., 1956), 105–245, and in *A Treasury of Russian Spirituality* (London, 1950). L. A. Dmitriyev, 'Nereshonnyye voprosy

GUIDE TO FURTHER READING

proiskhozhdeniya i istorii ekspressivo–emotsional'nogo stilya xv v.', *Trudy Otdela drevnerusskoy literatury*, xx, 72–89.

For the text and a detailed analysis of the *Tale of Troy* see *Troyanskiye skazaniya: srednevekovyye rytsarskiye romany o Troyanskoy voyne po russkim rukopisyam XVI–XVII vekov*, edited, with an introductory article, by O. V. Tvorogov, and with commentaries by M. N. Botvinnik and O. V. Tvorogov (Leningrad, 1972). *Aleksandriya. Roman ob Aleksandre Makedonskom po russkoy rukopisi XV v.* (Moscow–Leningrad, 1965): the text is edited by M. N. Botvinnik, Ya. S. Lur'ye and O. V. Tvorogov, with a detailed analysis.

For the text and an analysis of the *Tale of Stefanit and Ikhnilat: Stefanit i Ikhnilat: Srednevekovaya kniga basen' po russkim rukopisyam XV–XVII vv.*, ed. O. P. Likhacheva and Ya. S. Lur'ye (Leningrad, 1969). Also L. O. Sjöberg, *Stephanites und Ichnelates: Überlieferungsgeschichte und Text* (Uppsala, 1962).

On the Life of Metropolitan Peter: V. O. Klyuchevsky, *Drevnerusskiye zhitiya*, 72–4.

On the Muscovite chronicles: D. S. Likhachev, *Russkiye letopisi i ikh kul'turno-istoricheskoye znacheniye* (Moscow–Leningrad, 1947), 289–354; M. D. Prisyolkov, *Troitskaya letopis'. Rekonstruktsiya teksta* (Moscow–Leningrad, 1960).

Much has been written about the works connected with the Battle of Kulikovo. The texts and their translation into modern Russian, as well as detailed commentaries, are to be found in *Povesti o Kulikovskoy bitve*, ed. M. N. Tikhomirov, V. F. Rzhiga, L. A. Dmitriyev (Moscow, 1959). Fuller bibliographies can be found in: N. K. Gudzy, *Istoriya drevney russkoy literatury*, 7th edn (Moscow, 1966), 231–4, 240, 243, 244; and A. Mazon, 'La Zadonščina: Réhabilitation d'une oeuvre', in his book *Le Slovo d'Igor* (Paris, 1940); Mazon exaggerates the literary value of the Zadonshchina.

For the *Tale of the Life and Demise of the Grand Prince Dimitri Ivanovich* see M. A. Salmina, 'Slovo o zhitii i prestavlenii velikogo knyazya Dmitriya Ivanovicha, tsarya Rus'skago', *Trudy Otdela drevnerusskoy literatury*, xxv (1970), 81–104.

Texts of the *Taking of Moscow by Tokhtamysh* and of the *Tale of Temir Aksak* are to be found in *Polnoye sobraniye russkikh letopisey*, vi, 98–109, 124–128; viii, 42–8, 65–6; see the commentaries in D. S. Likhachev's *Russkiye letopisi i ikh kul'turno-istoricheskoye znacheniye*, 306–8.

The Tver' chronicles: the texts are printed in *Polnoye sobraniye russkikh letopisey*, xv (St Petersburg, 1863, and Moscow, 1905). A. N. Nasonov, 'Letopisnyye pamyatniki Tverskogo knyazhestva', *Izvestiya Akademii Nauk SSSR. Otdeleniye gumanitarnykh nauk* (1930), pp. 710–72.

The text of the *Eulogy of Prince Boris Aleksandrovich by the Monk Foma* is published with an introduction by N. P. Likhachev in *Pamyatniki drevney pis'mennosti*, clxviii (St Petersburg, 1908); but see A. A. Shakhmatov's criticism of this publication in an appendix to *Otchot o zasedaniyakh Obshchestva lyubiteley drevney pis'mennosti v 1907–1910 gg.* (St Petersburg, 1911). Cf. also D. S. Likhachev, *Russkiye letopisi i ikh kul'turno-istoricheskoye znacheniye*, 321–3.

The best edition of the *Journey across Three Seas* is *Khozheniye za tri morya Afanasiya Nikitina, 1466–1472*, ed. V. P. Adrianova-Peretts, 2nd enlarged and revised edn (Moscow–Leningrad, 1958). This contains all the known variants, a translation into modern Russian, commentaries, helpful introductory articles and a full bibliography. There is an English translation of Afanasy Nikitin's work by Count Wielhorsky in *India in the Fifteenth Century, being a collection of Narratives of voyages to India*, ed. R. H. Major, Hakluyt Society (London, 1857).

LITERATURE IN THE MUSCOVITE PERIOD

Useful articles on Nikitin's journey are by W. Kirchner, 'The Voyage of Athana-sius Nikitin to India', *The American Slavic & East European Review*, v, nos. 14–15 (1946) and V. A. Kuchkin, 'Sud'ba khozheniya za tri morya Afanasiya Nikitina v drevnerusskoy pis'mennosti', *Voprosy Istorii*, 5 (1969), 67–77.

For *The Tale of Dracula*: the texts and a most competent analysis of every aspect of the legends and their subsequent fate are to be found in Ya. S. Lur'ye, *Povest' o Drakule* (Moscow–Leningrad, 1964).

On the *Dispute between Life and Death*, see the interesting commentary by N. K. Gudzy, 'Preniye zhivota i smerti i novyy ukrainskiy spisok yego', *Russkiy Filologicheskiy Vestnik* (1910), nos. 3–4, 315–36; the fullest and most systematic account of the work is by R. P. Dmitriyeva, *Povesti o spore zhizni i smerti* (Moscow–Leningrad, 1964).

The *Tale of the Taking of Constantinople by Nestor Iskander* is published in the series *Pamyatniki drevney pis'mennosti i iskusstva*, vol. 62 (St. Petersburg, 1866) by Archimandrite Leonid: 'Povest' o Tsar'grade Nestora Iskandera'. The work is treated in great detail in G. P. Bolchenko, 'K voprosu o sostave istori-cheskoy povesti o vzyatii Tsar'grada', *Sbornik statey k 40–letiyu uchonoy deya-tel'nosti akademika A. S. Orlova* (Leningrad, 1934).

The Tale of the Princes of Vladimir: the texts, a detailed analysis and a biblio-graphy are to be found in R. P. Dmitriyeva, *Skazaniye o knyaz'yakh Vladimirskikh* (Moscow–Leningrad, 1955).

The works of Filofey of Pskov are published as appendices to V. N. Malinin's *Starets Eleazarova monastyrya Filofey i yego poslaniya* (Kiev, 1901). The origin of the idea of the Third Rome, which Filofey expounded, is discussed by D. Stremooukhoff, 'Moscow the Third Rome: Sources of the Doctrine', *Speculum*, XXVIII, I (1953), 84–101. A re-dating of Filofey's *Epistle to Ivan Vasil'yevich* and a modification of the traditional understanding of the theory of Moscow as the Third Rome were undertaken by N. Andreyev: 'Filofey and his Epistle to Ivan Vasil'yevich', *Slavonic & East European Review*, XXXVIII (1959), 1–31, reprinted in his *Studies in Muscovy* (London, 1970). On the theory of 'Moscow the Third Rome' see also H. Schaeder, *Moskau das dritte Rom*, 2nd edn (Darm-stadt, 1957); G. Olšr, 'Gli ultimi Rurikidi e le basi ideologiche della sovranità dello Stato russo'. *Orientalia Christiana Periodica*, XII (1946), 322–73; D. Obolensky, *The Byzantine Commonwealth* (London, 1971), 362–7.

On the Shearers, Judaizers, Possessors and Non-Possessors as well as Maxim the Greek, there are several useful studies: I. U. Budovnits, *Russkaya publitsistika XVI veka* (Moscow–Leningrad, 1947), 43–166. N. A. Kazakova and Ya. S. Lur'ye, *Antifeodal'nyye yereticheskiye dvizheniya na Rusi XIV – nachala XVI veka* (Moscow–Leningrad, 1955). The latter is a methodical and reliable study, with (in the appendices) an excellent collection of source material – some of it pub-lished for the first time. See also A. I. Klibanov, *Reformatsionnyye dvizheniya v Rossii v XIV – pervoy polovine XVI vv.* (Moscow, 1960). Excellent ideological 'portraits' of Nil Sorsky and Iosif Volotsky are drawn by G. P. Fedotov, *Svyatyye Drevney Rusi*, 166–88, and *The Russian Religious Mind*, II, 265–84, 302–15. See also the translations of some of Nil Sorsky's texts in *A Treasury of Russian Spirituality*, 90–133. Joseph of Volotsk's letters (and a detailed historical and critical commentary on them) are published in *Poslaniya Iosifa Volotskogo*, ed. A. A. Zimin and Ya. S. Lur'ye (Moscow–Leningrad, 1959). Mention should also be made of two important studies by N. A. Kazakova: *Vassian Patrikeyev i yego sochineniya* (Moscow–Leningrad, 1960), and *Ocherki po istorii russkoy obshchestvennoy mysli: pervaya tret' XVI veka* (Leningrad, 1970), which contains a general survey of the period, special attention being paid to Vassian Patrikeyev and Maxim the Greek. See also: Ya. S. Lur'ye, *Ideologicheskaya bor'ba v russkoy publitsistike kontsa XV – nachala XVI veka* (Moscow–Leningrad, 1960).

There is no adequate or complete edition of the writings of Maxim the Greek. The only edition is *Sochineniya prepodobnogo Maksima Greka*, ed. I. Ya. Porfir'yev, 3 vols. (Kazan', 1859–62; 2nd edn, Kazan', 1895–7). There is also a modern Russian translation: *Sochineniya prepodobnogo Maksima Greka v russkom perevode*, 3 vols. (Sergiyev Posad, 1910–11). Nearly half the works attributed to Maxim remain unpublished: see the useful guide by A. I. Ivanov, *Literaturnoye naslediye Maksima Greka. Kharakteristika, atributsii, bibliografiya* (Leningrad, 1969). V. S. Ikonnikov, *Maksim Grek i yego vremya*, 2nd edn (Kiev, 1915), is still indispensable. E. Denissoff's important book, *Maxime le Grec et l'Occident* (Paris–Louvain, 1943), first established the identity between Maxim and Michael Trivolis, thus greatly enlarging our knowledge of the pre-Muscovite period of Maxim's life. Two recent studies are particularly recommended: N. A. Kazakova, *Ocherki po istorii russkoy obshchestvennoy mysli. Pervaya tret' XVI veka* (Leningrad, 1970), 155–243; and J. V. Haney, *From Italy to Muscovy: the Life and Works of Maxim the Greek* (Munich, 1973) (with a copious bibliography). The best and most complete manuscript containing the transcript of the interrogations at Maxim's two trials (discovered in Siberia in 1968) and much fresh evidence on his biography is published (with a long introduction) in *Sudnyye spiski Maksima Greka i Isaka Sobaki*, ed. N. N. Pokrovsky and S. O. Shmidt (Moscow, 1971).

For the texts of the Novgorod chronicles (*Novgorodskaya chetvyortaya* and *Sofiyskaya pervaya*) see the *Polnoye sobraniye russkikh letopisey*, IV, pt 1, sect. 1–3 (Petrograd, 1915; Leningrad, 1925, 1929); V, i (Leningrad, 1925). The best analysis is by D. S. Likhachev, *Russkiye letopisi i ikh kul'turno-istoricheskoye znacheniye*, 308–20.

On Novgorodian themes and legends see *Povesti o zhitii Mikhaila Klopskogo*, ed. with an introductory article by L. A. Dmitriyev (Moscow–Leningrad, 1958); F. I. Buslayev, 'Novgorod i Moskva', *Istoricheskiye ocherki russkoy narodnoy slovesnosti i iskusstva*, II (Moscow, 1861); A. S. Orlov, 'Videniye khutynskogo ponomarya Tarasiya Prokhora', *Chteniya v imper. Obshchestve istorii i drevnostey rossiyskikh* (1908), 4. I. P. Yeryomin, 'Iz istorii russkoy povesti: Povest' o posadnike Shchile', *Trudy komissii po drevnerusskoy literature Akademii Nauk SSSR*, I (Leningrad, 1932). For a bibliography on the *Life* of Ioann, Bishop of Novgorod, and the *Life* of Antony the Roman, see N. K. Gudzy, *Istoriya drevney russkoy literatury*, 7th edn (Moscow, 1966), pp. 295, 296, 307; see in particular on p. 304 the footnotes on *The Tale of the White Cowl*.

For the texts of the Pskovian Chronicles see *Pskovskiye letopisi*, ed. A. N. Nasonov, I (Moscow–Leningrad, 1941), and II (Moscow, 1955). On the manner in which the Pskov Chronicles reflected the feelings of the citizens after the loss of their independence see N. Andreyev, 'O kharaktere tret'ey pskovskoy letopisi', *The Religious World of Russian Culture, Russia and Orthodoxy: Essays in Honor of Georges Florovsky*, II (The Hague–Paris, 1975), 117–58.

For the *Tale of Pyotr and Fevroniya* see the texts published by M. O. Skripil' in *Trudy Otdela drevnerusskoy literatury*, VII (1949), 215–56, and his important study 'Povest' o Petre i Fevronii muromskikh v yeyo otnosheniye k russkoy skazke', *ibid.*, VII, 131–67. There is a brief but fascinating study of the heroes of the Tale in D. S. Likhachev's *Chelovek v literature drevney Rusi*, 2nd edn (Moscow, 1970), ch. 5, 'Psikhologicheskaya umirotvoryonnost' XV v.'.

The Tale of Merkury has aroused a good deal of interest: see the bibliography

LITERATURE IN THE MUSCOVITE PERIOD

in N. K. Gudzy, *Istoriya drevney russkoy literatury*, 7th edn, 312–13, and G. P. Fedotov, *Svyatyye Drevney Rusi*, 233–43.

The texts of the Muscovite chronicles are found in *Polnoye sobraniye russkikh letopisey*, VII (1856), VIII (1859) (*Voskresenskaya*); IX–XIII (1862–1904) (*Patriarshaya ili Nikonovskaya*); XX (1910 and 1914) (*L'vovskaya*). The text of the *Tsarstvennaya kniga* is in vol. XIII, 409–532.

On the *Nikonian Illustrated Compilation* see A. E. Presnyakov, 'Moskovskaya istoricheskaya entsiklopediya XVI veka', *Izvestiya Otdeleniya russkogo yazyka i slovesnosti Akademii Nauk* (1900), 3, 824–7. The main works on the chronicles are listed in N. K. Gudzy's *Istoriya*, 336–7. On the literary activities of Metropolitan Makary see I. U. Budovnits, *Russkaya publitsistika XVI veka*, 188–98. On Makary's ideas see A. A. Zimin, *I. S. Peresvetov i yego sovremenniki* (Moscow, 1958), 71–9. On Makary's activities as a statesman see I. I. Smirnov, *Ocherki politicheskoy istorii russkogo gosudarstva 30–50kh godov XVI veka* (Moscow–Leningrad, 1958), 194–202. The text of the *Great Chet'i Minei* was published in part only in 1868–1917: see the bibliographical information given by N. K. Gudzy in *Istoriya*, 338–9. The text of the *Book of Ranks of the Tsars' Genealogy* is published in *Polnoye sobraniye russkikh letopisey*, vol. XXI. An interesting study is by P. G. Vasenko, *Kniga Stepennaya tsarskogo rodosloviya i yeyo znacheniye v drevnerusskoy istoricheskoy pis'mennosti*, I (St Petersburg, 1904), and by the same author: 'Sostavnyye chasti Knigi Stepennoy tsarskogo rodosloviya', *Letopis' zanyatiy Arkheograficheskoy komissii*, XIX (1908), 1–51.

On Metropolitan Daniil's literary activities see V. Zhmakin, *Mitropolit Daniil i yego sochineniya* (Moscow, 1881); the text of some of his work is printed in the appendix.

The text of the *Domostroy* was published by A. S. Orlov, pt I (Moscow, 1908), pt II (Moscow, 1910). Cf. A. I. Sobolevsky, 'Pop Sil'vestr i Domostroy', *Izvestiya po russkomu yazyku i slovesnosti Akademii Nauk SSSR*, II, 1 (1929). The best account of the Domostroy is by A. A. Zimin: *I. S. Peresvetov i yego sovremenniki* (Moscow, 1958), 55–70. Helmi Poukka, 'O vozmozhnom pol'skom istochnike Domostroya', *Scando-Slavica*, 12 (1966), 119–22, advances the hypothesis that the basis for this code of family life was a literary plagiarism from the works of the Polish author M. Rey.

Stoglav texts are available in various editions (1863, 1887, 1890). For an assessment of the Stoglav: I. N. Zhdanov, *Materialy dlya istorii Stoglavogo sobora, Sochineniya*, I (St Petersburg, 1904); D. Stefanovich, *O Stoglave. Yego proiskhozhdeniye, redaktsiya i sostav* (St Petersburg, 1909); A. A. Zimin, *I. S. Peresvetov i yego sovremenniki*, 91–102.

The History of the Kazan' Kingdom: *Kazanskaya istoriya*, text, introduction and notes by G. N. Moiseyeva (Moscow–Leningrad, 1954).

The Tale of the Attack of Stefan Batory on Pskov, published with an introduction – and an excellent bibliography – by V. I. Malyshev, *Povest' o prikhozhenii Stefana Batoriya na grad Pskov* (Moscow–Leningrad, 1952). Besides Zimin's book on Peresvetov (mentioned above), Peresvetov's writings are published, together with studies of his work by various scholars, in *Sochineniya I. Peresvetova*, ed. A. A. Zimin (Moscow–Leningrad, 1956). See also: W. Philipp, 'Ivan Peresvetov und seine Schriften zur Erneuerung des Moskauer Reiches', *Osteuropäische Forschungen*, N. F. Bd. 20 (Königsberg–Berlin, 1935).

Yermolay Erazm: V. F. Rzhiga, 'Literaturnaya deyatel'nost' Yermolaya Erazma', *Letopis' zanyatiy Arkheograficheskoy komissii*, XXXIII (Leningrad, 1926); the appendix contains the works in which he defended the rights of the peasants.

GUIDE TO FURTHER READING

A. A. Zimin, *I. S. Peresvetov i yego sovremenniki*, ch. III, 'Sotsial'no-ekonomi-cheskiye vozzreniya Yermolaya-Erazma', 109–42, discusses his ideas. G. N. Moiseyeva, *Valaamskaya beseda – pamyatnik russkoy publitsistiki serediny XVI veka* (Moscow–Leningrad, 1958), has published the texts and a detailed study of the historical and literary aspects of this work.

Scholarly literature on Ivan IV and Prince A. M. Kurbsky is fairly extensive. The tsar's own writings are available in the following publications: *Poslaniya Ivana Groznogo*, ed. D. S. Likhachev and Ya. S. Lur'ye, with a modern Russian translation and commentary by Ya. S. Lur'ye (Moscow–Leningrad, 1951); *Sochineniya knyazya Kurbskogo*, ed. G. Z. Kuntsevich in *Russkaya Istoricheskaya Biblioteka*, XXXI (St Petersburg, 1914). *The Correspondence between Prince A. M. Kurbsky and Tsar Ivan IV of Russia, 1564–1579*, ed. with a translation and notes by J. L. I. Fennell (Cambridge, 1955); *Prince A. M. Kurbsky's History of Ivan IV*, ed. with a translation and notes by J. L. I. Fennell (Cambridge, 1965). Useful studies are: S. O. Shmidt, 'Zametki o yazyke poslaniy Ivana Groznogo', *Trudy Otdela drevnerusskoy literatury*, XIV (1958), 256–65; I. Duychev, 'Vizantiya i vizantiyskaya literatura v poslaniyakh Ivana Groznogo', *ibid.*, XV (1959), 159–76. For a background to the 'Correspondence' see: N. Andreyev, 'Kurbsky's Letters to Vas'yan Muromtsev', *Slavonic and East European Review*, XXXIII (1955), 414–36. On Kurbsky's ideas see: Inge Auerbach, 'Die politischen Vorstellungen des Fürsten Andrej Kurbskij', *Jahrbücher für Geschichte Osteuropas*, N. F. 17 (1969) 2, 170–86. E. L. Keenan in *The Kurbskii–Groznyi Apocrypha: The Seventeenth-Century Genesis of the 'Correspondence' attributed to Prince A. M. Kurbskii and Tsar Ivan IV* (Cambridge, Mass., 1971), advanced the strange theory that the 'Correspondence' is a seventeenth-century forgery. His 'heresy' (to use Keenan's own word) was challenged by D. S. Likhachev, 'Sushchestvovali li proizvedeniya Kurbskogo i Groznogo?' in his book *Velikoye naslediye* (Moscow, 1975), 333–48 and R. G. Skrynnikov in his book *Perepiska Groznogo i Kurbskogo: Paradoksy Edvarda Kinana* (Leningrad, 1973). For a thorough survey of the problems involved see N. Andreyev's review article, 'The Authenticity of the Correspondence between Ivan IV and Prince Andrey Kurbsky', *Slavonic and East European Review*, LIII (1975), 582–8, in which the author firmly rebuts the 'heresy'. The only use of this somewhat pointless controversy has been to throw more light (as in the past Mazon did for the 'Slovo o polku Igoreve') on this magnificent polemical correspondence.

On folklore: V. F. Miller, *Istoricheskiye pesni russkogo naroda XVI–XVII vv.* (Petrograd, 1915). An excellent selection of 'historical ballads' is found in *Russian Folk Literature*, ed. D. P. Costello and I. P. Foote, with notes and a glossary (Oxford, 1967), 149–64. See also V. I. Malyshev, *Povest' o Sukhane. Iz istorii russkoy povesti XVII veka* (Moscow–Leningrad, 1956).

On the seventeenth-century tales, see the texts and commentaries in *Russkaya povest' XVII veka*, compiled by M. O. Skripil', ed. I. P. Yeryomin (1953) and *Istoki russkoy belletrisiki* (Leningrad, 1970), chs. XI and XII. On the *Tale of 1606*: A. S. Orlov, 'O nekotorykh osobennostyakh stilya v velikorusskoy istoricheskoy belletristike XVI–XVII vv.', *Izvestiya Otdeleniya russkogo yazyka i slovesnosti Akademii Nauk* (1908), 4. On the *Tale of Father Terenty's Vision*, there is an interesting study in A. A. Nazarevsky's *Ocherki iz oblasti russkoy istoricheskoy povesti nachala XVII stoletiya* (Kiev, 1958), 108–16.

The *Vremennik* of Ivan Timofeyev has been edited with a translation and commentary by O. A. Derzhavina, ed. V. P. Adrianova–Peretts (Moscow–Leningrad, 1951). The *Skazaniye* of Avraamy Palitsyn, prepared with a com-

LITERATURE IN THE MUSCOVITE PERIOD

mentary by O. A. Derzhavina and Ye. V. Kolesova, ed. L. V. Cherepnin (Moscow–Leningrad, 1955). Some of the views advanced by Derzhavina are criticized by N. K. Gudzy on p. 377 of his *Istoriya drevney russkoy literatury*, 7th edn.

On I. M. Katyrev-Rostovsky and I. A. Khvorostinin see S. F. Platonov, *Drevnerusskiye skazaniya i povesti o Smutnom vremeni XVII v. kak istoricheskiy istochnik*, 2nd edn (St Petersburg, 1913).

On the *New Tale of the Most Glorious Russian Tsardom*, see the very detailed study by N. F. Droblenkova, *Novaya povest' o preslavnom Rossiyskom tsarstve i sovremennaya yey agitatsionnaya patrioticheskaya pis'mennost'* (Moscow–Leningrad, 1960) (with excellent bibliography).

On translated works: there is a good bibliography in N. K. Gudzy's *Istoriya*, 7th edn, pp. 450–1, 454, 458, 460–3, 465, 467. See also A. Sobolevsky, *Perevodnaya literatura Moskovskoy Rusi XIV–XVII vv.* (St Petersburg, 1903).

For Simeon Polotsky's works see Simeon Polotsky, *Izbrannyye sochineniya*, ed. I. P. Yeryomin (Moscow–Leningrad, 1953), with a commentary and bibliography. On Russian versification see A. M. Panchenko, *Russkaya stikhotvornaya kul'tura XVII veka* (Leningrad, 1973).

On the Old Believers and on Archpriest Avvakum see P. Pascal, *Avvakum et les débuts du Raskol*, 2nd edn (Parish, 1963); S. A. Zen'kovsky, *Russkoye staroobryadchestvo* (Munich, 1970). Avvakum's own text: *Zhitiye protopopa Avvakuma im samim napisannoye i drugiye yego sochineniya*, edited with a commentary by N. K. Gudzy (Moscow, 1934); reprinted with an introduction by V. E. Gusev, with commentaries by several scholars under the editorship of N. K. Gudzy (Moscow, 1960). A. N. Robinson, *Zhizneopisaniya Avvakuma i Epifaniya. Issledovaniye i teksty* (Moscow, 1963); N. S. Demkova, *Zhitiye Protopopa Avvakuma* (Leningrad, 1974).

For a translation of the *Zhitiye* into English: *The Life of the Archpriest Avvakum by Himself*, translated from the seventeenth-century Russian by Jane Harrison and Hope Mirrlees, with a preface by D. S. Mirsky (London, 1963); *The Life of Archpriest Avvakum by Himself* in a *Treasury of Russian Spirituality*, compiled and edited by G. P. Fedotov, translated by E. Izvolskaya (London, 1950). Mention should be made of the excellent French translation of the *Zhitiye* by P. Pascal, *La vie de l'archiprêtre Avvakum écrite par lui-même* (Paris, 1960).

5

THE AGE OF CLASSICISM

(1700–1820)

M. A. S. BURGESS

The beginning of the eighteenth century finds Russia as a newly installed apprentice in the long established workshop of Europe, employing western traditions and craftsmanship. Russia had been excluded from the Renaissance in Europe after the fall of Constantinople in 1453; the scholars of a Hellenic civilization, preserved under the Eastern Empire, had departed to Venice and the West together with their manuscripts and expertise, while Russia had remained sealed off from the new learning. There was to be no rebirth of culture until the enlightened age, heralded by the reforms of Peter the Great. It is true that western influences had begun to reach Russia during the seventeenth century, but these made little impression. The spiritual authorities often regarded modern works from Europe as heretical.

In Russia, however, there were religious seminaries, one of which, the Kievo-Mogilyansky Academy, provided instruction in Latin and Polish (although little in Greek). In these academies new men of learning were trained, and it was natural for the current literary genre prevalent in ecclesiastical circles to be the one accepted by trained scholars, in this case the mannerist or baroque style. Thus in the early part of the eighteenth century a repetition of an older style which had found favour in the West formed the mode amongst educated Russians.

The mood of the baroque, with its emphasis upon dynamism, the transitoriness of the world, sudden misfortune, excitement, disillusionment, delight in exaggeration and the theatrical, was found to be exactly suited to the condition of mind in Peter's Russia, and to the ebullient character of the emperor himself. The first twenty-five years of the century, until Peter's death, may be designated the age of the baroque. It is a period of experiment, and results must be judged on this level; one cannot, therefore, expect masterpieces. The philosophy and inspiration of the baroque was to inaugurate a flourishing tradition of literary productions. In the church the delivery of the sermon was affected, poetry began, belles-lettres and the drama were influenced. Those anxious

111

to pursue the cultivation of Russian letters could only find help in treatises by foreign theoreticians; intending versifiers therefore delved into mannerist theories. Under the impetus of the baroque a secular literature was begun, allied to a similar movement in scenic production, architecture and the applied arts.[1]

> The optimism of the Renaissance [wrote J. M. Cohen] had yielded to a disbelief in the perfectibility of man, and an equal exploitation of his social blindness by a new race of power politicians, many of whom were churchmen. For the Baroque thinker, poet or religious, life was a flux. What could be observed was no more than appearance, and in describing these appearances the poet could at best only hint at a reality that he was unable to grasp. If the world was unreal what lay behind it could be described only in a metaphor or symbol which might not be entirely clear even to the poet himself.[2]

Amongst early and influential scholars from the religious academies, notice should be taken of the Metropolitan Dimitri Tuptalo (1651–1709), later canonized and known as Rostovsky, from the place of his previous exploits. He had produced his main work, *The Reading Menaea* (*Chet'i Minei*), at Kiev in 1684 and it was reprinted more than once. Dimitri might be considered the first Russian literary research worker, as he made an intelligent and scientific study of the original accounts of western, and particularly Polish, legends, and employed Latin and Greek sources. The *Chet'i Minei* continued to be the main book from which Russians up to the twentieth century learned about the lives of the saints. Dimitri was a great preacher, and his sermons were written in an exuberant baroque style embellished with symbolic constructions and abundant stylistic ornament. Later they became more sentimental and theatrical in tone; he had an eye for effect and an ear for sound. He composed poems, one or two religious epigrams and cycles, and even church hymns. He was also a dramatist; some of his plays were produced in Rostov. He wrote a theological treatise against the Old Believers. For his time he was unusually cultured, and possessed a large library containing the current theological and philosophical treatises of all schools of philosophy.

Next in importance was the Metropolitan Stefan Yavorsky (1658–1722). When the patriarchal see fell vacant in 1700, Stefan was appointed by Peter 'Guardian of the Patriarchal throne'. An opponent of excessive

---

[1] Emphasis upon baroque and mannerist influences in Russian letters has been regarded with disfavour by some Soviet scholars who have preferred to impart a more 'rational' or 'realist' approach to the subject of Russian literary consciousness.

[2] J. M. Cohen, *The Baroque Lyric* (London, 1963), p. 16.

secularization, and hostile towards the tsar's sympathies for Protestantism, he was less talented and erudite than Dimitri Rostovsky. He issued a treatise entitled *The Rock of Faith* (*Kamen' very*), influenced by Catholic theology. A poet and preacher, he also organized the Moscow Academy on the lines of the Kiev Academy. The late baroque style of writing appealed to him; he compiled Slavonic and Latin poems, and wrote a poem to his own library. The trappings of the baroque are readily observed, the curious image and stunning symbolism. He experimented with the religious play, making full use of metaphor, hyperbole, euphonic devices, and strange word sounds. Expressive and imaginative, his imagery was new to Russia. He wrote a text-book of rhetoric, *The Rhetorical Hand*, which included instructions on how to learn combinations of figures according to the various joints of the fingers. His baroque artistry influenced the Russian sermon for the next few generations.

By far the most striking scholar of the first years of the eighteenth century is Feofan Prokopovich (1681–1736), a stalwart champion of Peter the Great and propagandist of all his reforms, a gifted and highly cultivated man. Prokopovich had spent three years in Rome at a Jesuit College, after finishing successfully at the Kievo-Mogilyansky Academy, and the Vatican showed special interest in him. But he soon found himself a bitter enemy of the Roman Catholic Church, and displayed a predilection for Protestant theology. He was a connoisseur of rhetoric, philosophy and theology, became professor and rector of the Kiev Academy after 1705 and was later archbishop of Novgorod. He was befriended by the tsar, for whom he wrote many drafts of a Statute of the Synod, and a *Commentary on the Russian Law of Succession*, making use of Locke, Hobbes and Hugo Grotius. He consorted with foreigners, and built up a large library of 15,000 books, including scientific treatises and works of mathematics. As a politician he was a partisan of enlightened despotism. He engaged in much literary activity: works in Slavonic and Latin, and a tragi-comedy, *Vladimir*, which depicts the baptism of Kiev, the droll characters of heathen priests, Vladimir's vacillations, and panegyrics to the Hetman Mazepa, to the metropolitan and to the Academy of Kiev. This play showed an advance in the development of Russian drama, and although it was written according to the old rules of 'Academic Drama', with a prologue, five acts and an epilogue, it departed from tradition in providing a mixture of the tragic and the comical which imparted a satirical feeling through personification and psychological insight. The use of Polonisms, Church Slavonic and a rather turgid syllabic metre was old-fashioned, but in spite of its inherent weaknesses and conventional construction, the play was an early experiment in Russian historical drama.[1]

[1] See also ch. 8, on 'The Early Theatre'.

Prokopovich published three volumes of sermons, two dialogues, several poems and a Latin manual, *Poetics*. He is also important for his translations of syllabic verse: although he did not write much original poetry, he produced a verse adaptation of the Psalms, a *Laudatory Song* (*Epinikion*), praising Peter's victory over the Swedes, and some elegiac couplets including *A Melancholy Sounding Complaint* against the on-coming period of reaction at the end of Peter's reign. His personal touch is most apparent in his satires and elegies, and in some of his epigrams and nonsense verse. He appears to have been strongly influenced by the eccentricities of the baroque style, and has many of the cardinal qualities of the baroque writer, often incorporating the 'coup de théâtre'. His eloquence could move an audience to tears; his bearing was solemn and his voice resonant. He is the last of the prominent religious writers of the seventeenth century – a true disciple of western learning; his text-books, coloured with Protestant leanings, determined the course of theological instruction for many years, and he was a lasting influence on the first secular author of the eighteenth century, Prince Kantemir.

Antiokh Kantemir (1708–44) was the first original Russian poet of his time. His father Dimitrie was hospodar of Moldavia, an ally of Peter the Great at the time of the Russo–Turkish war. The family claimed Tatar descent, hence possibly the name, a christianized form of *Khan Timur*. His mother, Kassandra Cantacuzene, was Greek. Kantemir was born at Constantinople, but brought up in Russia, where he received for the time an excellent education. At the Moscow Slavo–Graeco–Latin Academy he composed a panegyric in Greek on the Martyr St Demetrios which attracted much praise from the teaching staff. By 1725 he was a student at the Academy of Sciences in St Petersburg, translating from Latin and Greek and composing several lyric poems or love songs. In private, however, he spent more time studying the written works of his country under the direction of the academic translator. Ivan Il'insky who was one of the best teachers at the academy and a poet in rhyme, under whose influence Kantemir wrote *Simfoniya na Psaltyr'*. It was at this time that he became interested in social and political life, where he favoured Peter's reforms. In 1728 he entered the regiment of the Preobrazhensky Guard as lieutenant; and in 1731 he was appointed to London as envoy at the Court of St James. Strongly influenced by Prokopovich, Kantemir wrote a poem dedicated to Peter the Great called *Petrida*, which is perhaps the first exercise in Russian literature in com-posing a historical poem in the spirit of classicism. Kantemir believed in a strong monarchical authority and, together with Prokopovich and the historian Tatishchev, stood at the helm of the Muscovite nobility on the accession of the Empress Anne. She appointed him chamberlain, while Anna Leopol'dovna, the regent, made him a privy councillor. The

Empress Elizabeth confirmed him in these dignities and made him minister. However, his candidature for the post of president of the Academy of Sciences was unsuccessful. He died on 1 March 1744 in Paris of dropsy.

Kantemir is celebrated for his nine satires of thirteen stanzas each written in rhyme and in syllabic metre. They did not appear in print until 1762 at St Petersburg under the title *Satires and Other Little Poems of Prince Antiokh Kantemir with Historical Notes and a Short Biographical Notice of the Author*. Also there were *The Epistles of Horace* together with *An Epistle on the Art of Poetry in Russia* which were printed under the assumed name of *Khariton Makentin*, and *Conversations on the Plurality of Worlds, a Treatise by Fontenelle, with Original Notes by the Translator*.

Apart from these he left many translations in manuscript. He was renowned for his translations of Anacreon. Russia had been untouched by the wave of interest which the Greek *Anacreontea* had caused in western Europe, and it was left to Kantemir, with his knowledge of Greek, to begin a translation. His aim was not so much to produce a version with scholarly notes, but more to introduce Anacreon to an unprepared Russian audience in the simplest way. His version is accurate, but this was perhaps not enough; the charm of the Greek is lacking, and his translation maintains a ponderous dignity throughout. On close examination, Kantemir can be seen to suffer from a certain stylistic insensibility, not only in Greek but also in Russian.

By upbringing Kantemir remained always a foreigner. His activity coincided with a literary vacuum which the Petrine revolution had created in Russia. But Russia owes him two debts – his satires and his cultural and pedagogic work; he was the first real savant and the most widely educated writer Russia had known. Interested in the upbringing of the complete man, and particularly in his moral education, he remained a devout Orthodox believer, in spite of his jibes at the church; he was interested not just in the social problem, but in the human problem. He opposed the introduction of French culture, allied himself with Italian literature of the Renaissance in particular, and came under the influence of the baroque. His versification accepts elements from the Ukrainian–Russo–Baroque and from Poland; an analysis of his style confirms his description as a mannerist poet. He interests the reader of today through his depictions of the Russia of the early eighteenth century and of the manners and customs of provincial and aristocrat, and by his display of the contemporary spoken Russian language.

Vasily Trediakovsky (1703–69), for long regarded as a pedant and a literary failure, was, in fact, one of the most original theoreticians of Russian verse. He has been called the father of the Russian hexameter,

He was fortunate in having received his main education abroad, although in extremely impoverished conditions, and on his return to Russia as a humble intellectual in reduced circumstances, he set out to improve Russian verse form. He was the first to introduce tonic scansion into Russian poetry, and it was through his pioneering work on the hexameter in Russian that the necessary foundation was laid for the famous translations from Homer by N. I. Gnedich and V. A. Zhukovsky in the early nineteenth century. His hexameter, according to Burgi, 'is one of the finest in Russian literature for its rhythm'. It was certainly superior in this regard to the hexameters of Gnedich, Del'vig and Pushkin. His grammatical and philosophical investigations were quite remarkable. His conception of Russian versification was broader than that of many who followed him, and he is renowned for his tract *A New and Brief Method of Composing Russian Verse*. He composed a quantity of operas, prologues, intermezzos and odes, but his poetry is interesting to us now merely as an example of his theories. He performed a service to Russian literature by his translations, particularly the *Argenida* (1751, from the Latin of John Barclay's *Argenis*), Horace's *De Arte Poetica*, and the *Tilemakhida*, a translation into verse of Fénelon's *Télémaque*, a political novel in the guise of a Homeric epic. He also produced *Yezda v ostrov lyubvi* (*Voyage to the Island of Love*) from the French seventeenth-century allegorical novel by Paul Tallemant. His partiality for the techniques of French versification turned into a veneration for the classical heritage mixed with national Slavonic elements.

Trediakovsky's activities are of a transitional character. During the period of reaction he was compelled, like Kantemir, to labour under the most awkward conditions; he was abused and mortified by the leading courtiers of the day, and died in penury, almost forgotten by men of learning and the Academy of Sciences. He perhaps lacked the talent to apply the conclusions of his own theories and assertions to his own works, and his prose is often inelegant and dull, while his verse has been criticized for evincing a total deficiency of taste and poetic talent. The Empress Catherine recommended his *Tilemakhida* as a cure for insomnia, and both this work and his play *Deidamia* have for many remained memorials to his vain endeavours to grasp the laurels of poetry, although others have seen him as the first contributor to the science of Russian prosody.

The way was now paved for the most outstanding Russian savant who had yet appeared, Mikhail Lomonosov (1711–65). The son of a state peasant, he showed early on a partiality for learning and books, and managed to acquire a considerable background of reading as a poor scholar of the Slavo–Graeco–Latin Academy at Moscow and Kiev. A remarkable personality, he was able to turn his hand to most branches of the literary and the applied arts, studying natural science, classical literature, contemporary western poetry and versification; he was well acquainted with the works of baroque theoreticians. He managed to ingratiate himself into aristocratic circles in St Petersburg, and was appointed assistant professor at the Academy of Sciences. There he quarrelled with most of his colleagues – he had a sharp tongue and an arrogant manner – reserving particular venom for Trediakovsky, whom he ruined financially. His sharp invective and explosive temperament precipitated many scandals; his zeal for learning, however, led to the creation of Moscow University in 1755. He carried out scientific experiments, and set up a mosaic studio in 1748; several specimens of his glass and mosaic work still survive.

In St Petersburg, court patronage demanded suitable laudatory verses from the poets laureate, who were, in fact, part of the staff of the court, having to take their place with the decorators and engineers. Naturally the development of their art was severely hampered by their dependence on the court. The ups and downs and intrigues of palace patronage could be dangerous for academicians and writers alike. The collapse of his industrial enterprise and the wrangles within the Academy weakened Lomonosov's spirit, and the outstanding chemist, industrialist, mathematician, and poet died in 1765.

It has been said that with Lomonosov Russian literature really began. He pursued with eager interest all developments of knowledge. He is considered the creator and the zealous protector of the Russian language, the first to bring to it soul, life and motion, by the sheer force of his patriotism and enthusiasm. Lomonosov wrote many philological works, and what interests the reader in these treatises is the way he poses and to what extent he solves the problems of vocabulary and style. He laid down rules for a suitable style to adopt when engaged in composition.

In his poetry, Lomonosov made full use of all normal baroque patterns. He believed that reason should be united with passion, and that the task of eloquence was to arouse or pacify such passion. He believed in *velikolepiye* ('splendour'), and *izobiliye* ('fullness'). Three different styles should be employed, the low, middle and high styles, according to the character of the theme. He took great care to diversify and ornament the architecture of his verses, and would deliberately upset classical poetic canons in order to twist the syntax and split the word order. Most of his poetic work is made up of seventeen odes addressed to the five rulers who occupied the throne in Russia between 1739 and 1765. These odes exactly correspond to his poetic theories. He can be repetitive and often seems to be in a state of ecstasy; there is sweeping imagery, noise and fire, and signs of the turbulence and dynamism of the baroque style. Rhetorical questions and mythological emblems abound; exuberance, rich ornamentation vitalize his work. In his *Letter on the Utility of Glass* (1752), addressed to Count I. I. Shuvalov, he describes 'the birth of glass' in a Vulcan's furnace, and then unfolds the history of its discovery. This is one of Lomonosov's most representative compositions. He also, like Kantemir, made a translation of the *Anacreontea*, which shows considerable inspiration, unlike the earlier version.

A follower of Lomonosov and of the baroque school was the poet Vasily Petrov (1736–99). He was a courtier, and became a reader and translator and finally librarian to the Empress Catherine II. He composed festive odes on the victories, treaties and other celebrations of the times of Catherine and Paul. He also translated Virgil's *Aeneid* in verse. Many of his odes are distinguished by powerful thought and brevity of expression. A poet-philosopher, he belongs to the baroque tradition, which was no doubt inculcated at the seminary where he was brought up. His odes are cultivated, and written in a flowing and melodious metre.

With the arrival of Aleksandr Sumarokov (1718–77) signs of great changes in Russian poetry began to appear. Under his aegis Russian poetry at last began to free itself from the mannerist shackles which Lomonosov had forged and approved. Poetry became more personalized, forms became more diverse, eclogues, idylls and elegies borrowed from Greek and Latin poetry at second hand were introduced. Songs from Russian folk poetry, rondeaux from France, and a few anacreontic verses, became popular. Sumarokov's place in the history of Russian culture is assured by his pioneering work for a national Russian theatre. Most of his life was taken up with writing and directing for the Russian stage. Unfortunately he suffered from a neurotic persecution complex and a temperament that was irascible and intolerant. Proud and overbearing at all times, and lacking in tact, he was apt to irritate his superiors. His disagreeable personality eventually led him to dire distress and poverty.

Sumarokov's stage career was launched by an amateur production of his play *Khorev*; the play was a success, the Empress Elizabeth heard about it, and soon came to patronize the amateur actors together with the director, Sumarokov. After *Khorev* (1747) other plays followed – *Hamlet, Sinav and Truvor, Artistona, Semira, Yaropolk and Demiza*. His comedies included *Tresotinius, The Miracles* and *The Vain Squabble*. He had also compiled the librettos for two operas, *Cephalus and Procris* and *Alcestis*. In 1756 the Empress Elizabeth issued an ukaz establishing a Russian theatre with Sumarokov as official director; in 1759 this patent theatre became the Imperial Court Theatre, thus laying the foundation for the distinguished history of the Russian Imperial theatres.

Sumarokov's theatrical compositions enjoyed a considerable success at first, but the public taste was already beginning to change; new trends from abroad were influencing the reading and theatre-going public. From

England, France and Germany ballad opera and sentimental comedy had spread to Russia. Sumarokov began to appear old-fashioned and pedantic. He inveighed caustically against 'this new and filthy kind of sentimental drama'. Permeated by the traditions of the classical school, the Russian dramatist condemned this 'debasement' of the lofty aims of the Grecian Muse, and never hesitated to rant at what he considered the decadent influence now sweeping the theatre. But Sumarokov was fighting a rearguard action – his style of writing was already outmoded. Other Russian writers such as M. M. Kheraskov (1733–1807), V. V. Kapnist (1757–1823), M. N. Murav'yov (1757–1807), and N. A. L'vov (1751–1803) were already adopting the new genre.

Sumarokov also produced much poetry, in many different kinds of verse, but the laurels he so hardly earned fast faded and withered away. The simplicity in his fables and idylls has been judged affected, the wit in his comedies seems forced; above all the charms of imagination and feeling are few and far between, being enveloped in a difficult and thorny style. A. F. Merzlyakov thus compared Sumarokov and his strongwilled rival in the Academy: 'Lomonosov is a slow, uniform and heavy eagle and floats free. Sumarokov is rather like the bird which flutters above the surface of the earth and pursues its job with the most tortuous and rapid gyrations.' But whatever may be thought of the quality of his prodigious literary output, Sumarokov must be remembered for his pioneering work for the Russian stage. (See chapter 8.)

A dramatist of some importance, Yakov Knyazhnin (1742–91), Sumarokov's son-in-law, wrote comedies, comic operas and tragedies. His most famous ballad operas are *The Coach Accident* (in two acts), *The Honey Tea Seller*, *The Miser* (in one act), *The Pretended Madman* (in two acts). Knyazhnin is often cold, high-flown, forced and much inclined to sublimity. He imitated the French tragedians Corneille, Racine and Voltaire and often reproduced whole extracts from their writings. His most famous work is his tragedy *Vadim of Novgorod*, written after the French Revolution. As it idealized the old democratic institutions of Novgorod and rejected tyranny, copies of the play were destroyed by the government, and it was for a long time prohibited on the stage.

A more original dramatist was Denis Fonvizin (1745–92), of German descent, who came from a well-to-do family. He began his literary work with translations of Voltaire's *Alzire*, Ludwig Holberg's *Fables* and other works. After being appointed a sergeant in the Guards in 1762, he entered the College of Foreign Affairs as a translator, being shortly afterwards sent to Germany. He was soon patronized by the minister, Count M. Panin, which gave him financial security. In 1764 he began to write plays, the first of which, *Korion*, was performed at the Imperial Theatre in St Petersburg in the same year. He also composed, in the French manner,

The Loves of Charita and Polydore, a tale from Barthélemy, and *Sydney*, a poem. He also wrote a satirical fable, *Lisitsa-Koznodey* and *An Epistle to my Servants Shumilov, Van'ka and Petrushka*, a burlesque in which he ridicules the ambition and self-seeking of society people; the latter work was highly commended by the Russian critic Belinsky. Changes in Fonvizin's social views at this time are reflected in his journalistic works, including *On the Freedom of the French Aristocracy*, a poem from Bitaubé entitled *Joseph*, another tract entitled *The Nobility of Commerce Opposed to the Nobility of the Army* from the French, and *A Panegyric Upon Marcus Aurelius*. His first original effort for the stage produced in 1766 a comedy of manners, *The Brigadier*, which discredited the gallomania of the educated circles of his time, and which created a sensation when it was read in the presence of Catherine the Great. An attempt at naturalistic dialogue was made in this work, and its characters are drawn from Russian life. The defects of this play, however, are an artificially contrived and awkward love intrigue, profusion of unnecessary dialogue, insufficient action and one-sided drawing of character (except for the Brigadier's wife). Its importance lies in that it is the first Russian comedy of manners, and as a picture of Russian life at the time it is invaluable.

Fonvizin made several journeys abroad, visiting Poland, Germany and France, but he was disappointed in the West, and dismayed at the poverty which he saw in France. He became a *vol'nodumets* or free-thinker, which made Pushkin call him *drug svobody* and consider that the writer must be *strazh obshchego blaga* – guardian of the common weal. He even drew up a plan for a constitutional government for Russia, but this was shelved by the Empress Catherine. His style had matured by 1782, and he produced a new play, *Nedorosl'* (*The Minor*), on the problem of education. The contrast between two systems of education is exemplified in a young, ignorant and boorish country bumpkin, Mitrofan, and a nicely brought-up young man from the capital. The play gives a picture of ignorant and coarse bourgeois life. This didactic comedy of manners is the first genuinely Russian production to deal with a real aspect of Russian life. It was a tremendous success, and the play is really a historical document in which Fonvizin holds up to public ridicule deficiencies in the social institutions of his time. Comedy of manners though it may be, it cannot rank as great theatre art, but it is the beginning of Russian dramatic satire from which Gogol was later to develop his genius.

Fonvizin's later years were spent in trying to publish his liberal journal, *An Honest People's Friend*, but it was banned, and after the death of Count Panin in 1783 Fonvizin gradually slipped into oblivion. As a result of his failure in the political and social arena he underwent a religious change; palsied and morose, he turned to mysticism. Although not a prolific playwright (a third comedy remained unfinished), he must take his place as the first critical playwright of the newly instituted Russian theatre.

Gavriil Derzhavin (1743–1816) shines as the most original poet in eighteenth-century Russia, the last of the baroque school, and the final pattern for the oncoming generation of truly inspired Russian poets. He was educated privately near Kazan'. Widowed early in life, his mother was tormented by financial worries and persecution, which impressed the future poet with the injustice of the world. He was a brilliant student, of strong visual imagination, and could have chosen to be an architect or a draughtsman.

In 1779 he published his first collection of poems, including a number of translations from the poems of Frederick the Great. His *Ode to Felitsa, Tsaritsa of the Kirghiz Cossacks*, in praise of the empress, won him official recognition, imperial rewards and the hostility of the courtiers whom he satirized. Fortune now smiled and he received one important office after another, although on account of his passionate and choleric temperament, which was strangely united with the most methodical pedantry, he was frequently asked to resign. Just when his affairs were at a low ebb, he produced his *Ode on the Occasion of the Taking of Izmail by Storm*. This inspired the empress anew, and in 1791 she selected him to be her secretary of state; but he tired her excessively in this capacity; Catherine had hoped for eulogies, but her secretary refused to oblige. In 1793 he was promoted to privy councillor and senator, and the next year he was chosen president of the College of Commerce. Derzhavin made pronouncements on the important political happenings of the period, and was prepared to construct odes on the statesmen of the time, and not merely to please: he was perfunctory about Prince Potemkin, satirical about Count A. Orlov, sour about Prince Vyazemsky and S. Naryshkin. Generally he was outspoken and honest. In the reign of Paul I he slipped in and out of favour, but by 1800 he was appointed the imperial treasurer with the dignity of acting privy councillor. He lasted a year in this post, and became minister of justice in 1802. In 1803 he was pensioned off on full salary and an allowance for his table besides. He ended his days as a rich landowner, and died on his estate in 1816.

Derzhavin has been underestimated in the West, and misunderstood by Russian critics. It used to be fashionable to censure his poetry, and he made no appeal to the poets and critics of the early nineteenth century. The trouble was that his poetry was alien to the romantic revival of the nineteenth century. Idealistic poets could not appreciate the dynamism, exuberance and ebullience of the older poet's verses. None the less, he heralded a new tradition in Russian poetry, by breaking away from set rules modelled on mannerist and baroque imagery.

Derzhavin set his own rules. His indefatigable nature could not allow him to be a slave to convention; Sumarokov and his neo-classical echoes were to be thrown overboard. He took the key from Trediakovsky and Lomonosov, but he unlocked a fund of original thought which lay in the Russian heart. Derzhavin is the last writer of the baroque in Russia, and its finest exponent. It can be argued, too, that with his new ideas, his new forms, his fresh imagery and his fine sense of harmony, he represents the first wave of the coming pre-romantic poets. He humanized the literary tradition of his time. He was the first to introduce nature in her personal aspect; whether he was singing of a waterfall, a storm or a forest, he described it in glowing colours far removed from the style of his predecessors. He wrote about individuals; he could be sensual, yet was always appropriate. He employed all the tricks of the baroque, the twisting of the syntax, archaisms, Church Slavonic roots, mythological allusions, a classical erudition, the use of colour, and a fully orchestrated musical verse. Derzhavin remains the greatest and most original poet of eighteenth-century Russia.

Vasily Kapnist (1757–1823), a friend and relation of Derzhavin, wrote lofty odes in the Horatian manner. His poems do not possess the fascination and boldness of Derzhavin's but are not unattractive owing to a certain emotional enthusiasm. His well-known comedy, *The Perverters of Right* (1798), was a savage attack on the dishonesty of judges and court fashions, distinguished by biting satire. Mention should also be made of Vasily Maykov (1728–78) who imported a mock epic genre into his ironic poem *Yelisey, or Bacchus Infuriated* (1771). The style is perhaps a little rough, although there are some realistic descriptions. He also composed a number of odes.

In the last half of the eighteenth century the publishing of satirical journals had become a popular venture. A notable contributor of such journalism was Nikolay Novikov (1744–1818). He had suffered from a defective education, without the aid of the usual foreign tutors, though a local priest taught him the rudiments of grammar, and in 1755 he was sent to the High School attached to Moscow University where he did not complete his course of study. His work in the state service provided Novikov with a wide picture of the social scene throughout the country, which gave him experience which he was able to use in his capacity as a publicist. His first journal was *The Drone* (*Truten'*), followed by *The Painter* (*Zhivopisets*) and a number of other journals. *The Painter* was well regarded, but his *Historical Dictionary*, which has preserved the names of many Russian authors which might otherwise have been lost to posterity, brought him the enmity of many who resented remarks on several of his contemporaries.

Novikov's first labours had attracted the notice of the empress. From

1773 onwards he edited *The Ancient Russian Library* (*Drevnyaya Rossiyskaya vivliofika*), a collection of rare and important documents relating to all periods of Russian history. He founded the first circulating library in Moscow. He also acquired the rights of the newspaper *Moscow Gazette* (*Moskovskiye Vedomosti*) and increased the number of subscribers from six hundred to four thousand. He managed to obtain the lease of the University Press, increased the mechanical facilities of printing, procured the translation of books, established book shops in other towns and tried by every means to infuse into the public the love of reading.

At this time he became a powerful influence in the Masonic movement, which had first appeared in Russia during the reigns of Anne and Elizabeth; a lodge had been set up in 1731. Some people saw in the Masonic movement a solution to the distress caused by the vacuum which followed the break with the tradition of the Church. To others Freemasonry pointed a path to an intense spiritual life, a religious life outside the Church. To others still it was a turning away from the monolithic image of Mother Russia and a looking to the West for revelations and precepts. Mystical and metaphysical ideas were particularly attractive because of their very independence from the teaching of the Church and their superiority over the current philosophies of science. For many people it became a kind of Eleusinian mystery which was to be divulged to no outsider. The Freemasons defended the ideas of the enlightenment, feeling that an individual must be truly enlightened to achieve moral maturity. From the time of its first appearance in Russia Freemasonry progressed rapidly until it was checked in the 1890s by government interference. Its philosophy was generally moral and stressed individual self-perfection. For this reason it drew mystics, pietists, philanthropists, extreme reactionaries, as well as liberals into its net. Novikov found the movement attractive; he first entered a lodge in 1775 in St Petersburg, and henceforth all his publications took on a mystical character. A journal *Morning Light* (*Utrenniy Svet*) was issued in this vein of pietism. He also began philanthropic activities, such as founding two schools for children of the poor. A long list of Masonic periodicals existed under his guidance; he created modern arrangements for his printing works. It was Novikov who popularized the English realistic novel of the eighteenth century and introduced his compatriots to Fielding, Smollett, Swift and Sterne. Novikov's presses turned out text-books for the army and the schools, translations, collections of poetry, prose and dramatic work. However, he began to offend by the publication of his satirical magazines and treatises. Catherine II was herself the editor of a journal *Variety Titbits* (*Vsyakaya Vsyachina*), which aimed at pricking the bubble of the idiosyncrasies of social behaviour, but was in effect naturally on the side of the establishment. Other satirical journals sponsored by Novikov were *The Drone, This and That* (*I to i syo*) edited by Chulkov, *Neither This Nor That* (*Ni to ni syo*) edited by Ruban, *The Post of Hell* (*Adskaya Pochta*) edited by Emin, and *The Medley* (*Smes'*). Catherine looked on these journals benevolently, but *The Drone* had offended right from the start by challenging *Variety Titbits*, and the empress had it closed. Other journals by Novikov, *The Windbag* (*Pustomelya*), *The Painter* and *The Purse* (*Koshelyok*), suffered the same fate. The Moscow Metropolitan, Platon, was obliged to examine Novikov and several hundred of his publications with regard to his Orthodoxy, but he exonerated him for his humane and Christian sympathies. Nevertheless his fate was sealed. In 1788 he was forced to give up the University Press, and in 1791 to close the Typographical Society. The following year he was convicted of criminal thinking and sent to the Fortress of Schlüsselburg, where he remained until the accession of Paul I (1796), who released him under an amnesty. For the last twenty-two years of his life Novikov remained on his estate, forbidden to indulge in any political activities. His offence was the printing of Masonic literature, although Freemasonry itself was not forbidden in Russia. But his real crime lay in his energetic philanthropic exertions and his wide moral influence, the first of its kind in Russia; it was this that troubled Catherine. The Russian Masonic movement, together with Novikov, its champion, were the victims of the panic created in Russia by the French Revolution.

The most important liberal thinker in eighteenth-century Russia was Aleksandr Radishchev (1749–1802). Son of a provincial gentleman, he was given a good education at Moscow University. He was appointed a page of honour to Catherine II, and in 1765, when Catherine required educated jurists, six pages, including the young Radishchev, were sent to study at Leipzig. After four years there Radishchev emerged as a cultivated and westernized young man.

He returned home to find that Catherine was showing herself in her true light, supreme autocrat rather than liberal monarch. He was immediately employed as a clerk to the Senate, which opened his eyes to the abuses and corruption of the government. After the Pugachev revolt (1773–4), he was made 'oberauditor', a kind of president of courts martial on the staff of the St Petersburg commander-in-chief. This placed him in the awkward position of defending the imperial government, which he disliked, but he entered the best St Petersburg society and enjoyed a reputation in the social world. He wrote verses, joined the English Club and moved in literary circles. He seemed all set for a brilliant career in the state service; but this was not to be. Radishchev was at heart a welfare worker and was more interested in people and the improvement of conditions of the down-trodden and oppressed. After the

Pugachev revolt was suppressed he decided he could awaken the social consciousness through publication.

In 1789 he wrote his *Diary of One Week* in which the sentimental trend is carried a stage forward in Russian belles-lettres. In the same year, when Falconet's statue of Peter the Great was unveiled, Radishchev wrote *A Letter to a Friend Resident at Tobol'sk*. The author considered Peter I a great ruler because he gave the first impetus to the massive task of building Russia. He hinted that without revolution there was no limit to autocracy. When Catherine later read this letter she remarked: 'He has long had in mind the path he has taken.'

As early as 1781 Radishchev had begun to write an ode, entitled *Liberty*. This impassioned work would appear to be the earliest revolutionary verse in Russia. He glorified Cromwell for having, as a result of the execution of Charles I, 'taught peoples to avenge themselves'. Radishchev had also published an unsigned article in a magazine *The Citizen in Conversation* entitled 'A Conversation on What is a Son of the Fatherland', which was a firm indictment of all that was wrong in Russian society. Meanwhile, as early as 1772, a few years before Radishchev had set to work on his *Journey from St Petersburg to Moscow* (*Puteshestviye iz Peterburga v Moskvu*), which he had planned over a long time, he contributed a small unsigned extract in the journal *The Painter*. The *Journey* took him ten years to complete, and it incorporated his inmost thoughts and dreams. In 1790 it was published anonymously.

The fact was that Radishchev's ideas were very radical for eighteenth-century Russia. He stands as a forerunner of a trend that was to be characteristic of Russian progressive movements in the nineteenth century, and was expressed in the philanthropy that inspired the populists of the 1860s and 1870s. Thus he is the first representative of the conscience-stricken gentry, the first Russian liberal. The technique followed by the author in his *Journey* was one already used by Sterne in his *Sentimental Journey*, but he differs from Sterne in that he shows little humour; the book is written in a spirit of deadly seriousness. Radishchev set out to expose the shortcomings of the Russian social system, which he does with genuine indignation. In content Radishchev's *Journey* is an account of people and things he saw while travelling through Russia from St Petersburg to Moscow, a simple series of sentimental, truthful pictures drawn without exaggeration. It hardly appears alarming today: in fact the book was not intended to be read by the peasants, but to assist the conscience of their masters in the hope that reformation could come from within Russian society. However, the sovereign is attacked on three occasions in a veiled way; so is America, which serves to introduce a parallel between serfdom and American Negro slavery. The clergy and the censorship also come under fire. The insertion into the work of fragments of his *Ode to Liberty* made the point still clearer. Certainly there are faults in *The Journey*; the style is flat, heavy and tedious. Its real importance lies in its sincerity. It has some claims to be considered an encyclopaedia of Russian life in the late eighteenth century. Princess Dashkov, president of the Academy of Sciences, called it 'the alarum bell of revolution', and Pushkin declared it 'a satirical appeal to insurrection'. The landlords were scandalized. In the Leningrad Public Library a manuscript copy of *The Journey* has been preserved with a note inscribed with these words:

> You are not a well-intentioned author, but a mutineer, a noose for the feebleminded. It was not enough that the Great Catherine exiled you – you should have been hanged as the most harmful reptile . . . This new-baked philosopher should have been sent to a madhouse.

Radishchev was subjected to a severe cross-examination, but refused to retract his opinions and he was condemned to death. A month later, however, Catherine commuted the death penalty to exile in Siberia for ten years. The book was proscribed, and only ten copies of the first edition have survived.

In 1797 Paul I ended Radishchev's exile, and after the accession of Alexander I in 1801 he was reinstated in society with all rights restored, and was appointed a member of the commission for drafting new laws. Radishchev still remained the humanist, the ardent liberal. The commission proved ineffectual, and Radishchev became morose and melancholic, and in 1802 committed suicide.

During the eighteenth century stories of romance and adventure became popular, and the first attempt at the writing of novels was made. Fyodor Emin (1735–70), who imitated Rousseau's sentimental novel *La Nouvelle Héloïse*, is known mainly for his *Letters of Ernest and Doravra* (1766). As a writer Emin became very popular among the general reading public, to whom the adventure story and the sentimental tale appealed, though he was condemned by the classicists. He had a fiery imagination and penetrating intelligence, and was a good linguist, but such talents were neither accompanied by prudence nor built upon a foundation of solid learning, as is witnessed by his uncritical and in part fictitious *History of Russia*.

One Russian writer of burlesque narrative poems and two major works of prose fiction who deserves the attention of the modern reader is Mikhail Chulkov (1743–92). He was responsible for *Peresmeshnik, ili slavenskiye skazki* (The Mocker, or Slavonic Tales), and an engaging picaresque novelette, of which only the first part appeared, entitled *Prigozhaya povarikha, ili pokhozhdeniye razvratnoy zhenshchiny* (1769). This piece of fiction, under the alluring heading of 'The Comely Cook, or the Adventures of a Disreputable Woman', is the author's most satisfying work. There is a hint of Daniel Defoe's vivacious Moll Flanders about Chulkov's dissipated heroine, Martona, the fulsome widowed wench who recites her own story in the novel. The tale thus breaks new ground. There is a greater depth of characterization, some psychological finesse, more human motivation against a fairly realistic background. Important, too, is the mise-en-scène which has now been switched to contemporary Russia. Chulkov was thus an innovator. With his prose fiction he opened up fresh possibilities for aspiring Russian writers.

A more prolific writer, who was interested in all the literary genres of the time, was Mikhail Kheraskov (1733–1807), who became chancellor of Moscow University. Two of his epic poems, modelled on Voltaire's *Henriade*, may be noted – the *Rossiada*, describing the taking of Kazan' in 1552, and *Vladimir Reborn*, which deals with the introduction of Christianity into Russia. They are both attempts to create a national epic style. He also wrote a number of plays. Impartial posterity, however, although giving full praise to his industry, his learning and his taste, should hesitate perhaps before it confers upon him unconditionally the name of poet.

A later writer with a flair for the stage was Ippolit Bogdanovich (1743–1803). His romantic poem *Dushen'ka*, which appeared in 1778, is based on La Fontaine's *Les Amours de Psyché et de Cupidon*. He is one of the first Russian writers to have clothed poetic narrative in a light-hearted and witty style. His minor poems are distinguished by their simplicity and elegance.

Ivan Khemnitser (1745–84) became well known for his fables, which are noteworthy for their simplicity and truth. His versification was light and pure in style, and marked by a characteristic *naïveté*. They are more original than Sumarokov's poems, and made use of the colloquial language. Unfortunately his talents were hardly appreciated in his own time. His position in Russian letters was eclipsed by Ivan Dmitriyev (1760–1837) who published his poems in many political journals. A friend and follower of Karamzin, he applied the latter's new sentimental style to poetry. The structure of his verse is light and clear, and he too is mainly famous for his fables, written in a language more refined than that of Sumarokov or Khemnitser.

It was, however, Ivan Krylov (1769–1844) who finally established the art of the fable in Russian literature. After an inadequate education he became librarian of the Imperial Public Library and a counsellor of state. Apart from fables, he was the author of several dramatic works, and also took to journalism. A first edition of his fables, which established his popularity, had appeared in 1809. Indolent and lazy at his post at the Public Library, he produced no more than two or three fables a year, but they became classics of their kind. Most of them are original, although some are translations or adaptations from La Fontaine or Aesop. They have a simplicity of composition and an unconstrained style interwoven with colloquial expressions. Other Russian fable writers were happy in their imitations of foreign models. Krylov became himself a model for foreigners, and many of his fables have been translated. He showed a common-sense philosophy of life – corruption, career-seeking and boorishness were satirized, and there were veiled social or political allusions. Though not exactly elegant, Krylov's fables are nevertheless racy and attractive, and they are notable for the introduction of ordinary Russian speech.

Towards the end of the eighteenth century the fashion for more emotional and sensitive genres took root. The field for sentimentalism had been prepared by Kheraskov and Radishchev among others, but it was Nikolay Karamzin (1766–1826) who was its foremost exponent.

Karamzin was a great traveller. In 1789 he journeyed abroad and on his return wrote his *Letters of a Russian Traveller*, a vivid account of a journey in western Europe and England. He became editor of the *Moscow Journal* for two years, published various works in prose and verse, and from 1802 produced *The European Messenger* (*Vestnik Yevropy*), a political and literary journal in twelve volumes which inaugurated the long series of *tolstyye zhurnaly* ('bulky journals'), so popular during the nineteenth century.

Karamzin's most important work, to which he devoted the whole of his time from the year 1803, is his *History of the Russian State* (in eight volumes). His political views had undergone a change; at first a stalwart champion of Novikov and a moderate liberal, he became gradually more and more conservative. He became convinced that historical development should proceed gradually, and therefore condemned Peter the Great for his hasty reforms, advocating monarchy for Russia. The impact of his *History* upon the Russian reading public was very great.

With Karamzin a new approach to Russian literature and history begins, since he created modern Russian prose, and in his *History* set an example of a style at once light, clear, pure, elevated and agreeable. For the literary historian he is interesting mainly because he promoted in his writings the new sensitivity, *chuvstvitel'nost'*, compounded of dreamy melancholy and humane, touching sympathy. Atmosphere and places are described fully, and there is a wealth of imagination and colourful descriptions of nature, which for him had a religious quality. Unlike Sterne, he provides not merely a 'sentimental journey' but a rather wider canvas on which reality is depicted, although it is perhaps a subjective, one-sided approach. The *Letters* provide valuable information on Russia at the end of the eighteenth century and on the author's outlook. He describes the thoughts and feelings of the ordinary man. In style he was an innovator: he avoids Church Slavonicisms, constructs his sentences so that feeling takes precedence over syntax, and his style is flexible and fluid.

The sentimental genre encouraged a lachrymose, virtuously self-complacent and decorous sensibility. Karamzin wrote some short stories on peasant, historical and romantic themes, such as *Frol Silin, a Virtuous Man* (1791), where life in the country is extolled and everyone seems terribly kind and very industrious. His most popular story was *Poor Liza* (*Bednaya Liza*, 1792), which became one of the most widely read pieces in Russia. It has all the typical features of sentimentalism. The language is eloquent, languorously musical, lyrical and simple. It is a story of the seduction of a peasant lass by a socialite cad. Deserted by her lover, Liza in the end drowns herself, and so realistic seemed the story to the Russian reader that frequent pilgrimages were made to the pond outside Moscow wherein the sad suicide had taken place. The delicate theme, the neat unfolding of the story, the interest of the plot, and finally the fact that virtue is not rewarded and vice remains unpunished, all contributed to the popularity of *Poor Liza*. If the language now seems a little sugary, the lightness of the style must be commended against Lomonosov's chilly bombast, but the conviction, élan, and vitality of real romanticism had yet to assert themselves. *Poor Liza* had the effect of relaxing Russian prose style and consolidating a language which could now compete with any other sophisticated modern European tongue.

Karamzin also wrote some historical tales, *Natal'ya the Boyar's Daughter* and *Marfa Posadnitsa or the Submission of Novgorod*, where the Russian people make an appearance as part of the *dramatis personae*. In these works Karamzin laid the foundation of Russian historical belles-lettres. Some of his tales show signs of an early romanticism – the 'touching' and 'sensitive' pass into the 'awesome' and the 'terrible'. One of the most characteristic of these tales is *The Island of Bornholm*.

By the time of Karamzin, then, Russian literature had developed from the baroque through the neo-classical to the sentimental, and was thus a field fit for the cultivation of the pre-romantic and the romantic movements.

GUIDE TO FURTHER READING

TEXTS AND ANTHOLOGIES

Biblioteka Poeta, founded by M. Gor'ky: *Demokraticheskaya poeziya XVII veka* (Moscow, 1962); *Vol'naya russkaya poeziya vtoroy poloviny XVIII – pervoy poloviny XIX veka* (Moscow, 1960); *Russkaya sillabicheskaya poeziya XVII–XVIII vv.* (Moscow, 1970); *Poety satiriki kontsa XVIII – nachala XIX v.* (Moscow,

1959); *Stikhotvornaya tragediya kontsa XVIII – nachala XIX v.* (Moscow, 1964); *Stikhotvornaya komediya kontsa XVIII – nachala XIX v.* (Moscow, 1964). For the relevant volumes of authors' works in this series, see: *Biblioteka Poeta, annotirovannaya bibliografiya, 1933–1965, obshchiy plan* (Moscow–Leningrad, 1965).

An Eighteenth Century Russian Reader, eds. C. L. Drage and W. N. Vickery (Oxford, 1969), is a fine handbook for students, containing excellent notes and commentaries on the texts. *Russkaya poeziya*, ed. S. A. Vengerov, vol. 1, vypusk 1–6, vypusk 7 (St Petersburg, 1907). A. V. Kokoryov, *Khrestomatiya po russkoy literature XVIII veka* (Moscow, 1961), is a good anthology of eighteenth-century Russian literature with biographical summaries. *Russkaya proza XVIII veka*, vols. I and II, eds. A. V. Zapadov and G. P. Makogonenko (Moscow–Leningrad, 1950), is a worthy anthology of Russian eighteenth-century prose works. I. T. Pososhkov, *Kniga o skudosti i bogatstve*, ed. B. B. Kafengauz (Moscow, 1951), is a serious study of the text with full notes and commentaries. Simeon Polotsky: *Komediya o bludnom syne*, ed. I. P. Yeryomin in *Izbrannyye sochineniya* (Moscow–Leningrad, 1953), an early Russian play; and *Povest' o rossiyskom matrose Vasilii* in *Russkiye povesti pervoy treti XVIII veka* (Moscow–Leningrad, 1965), 191–210, an early Russian 'tale'. Feofan Prokopovich, *Sochineniya*, ed. I. P. Yeryomin: 'Slovo o vlasti i chesti tsarskoy', 76–93, and 'Slovo na pogrebeniye Petra Velikogo', 126–9 (Moscow–Leningrad, 1961), contains texts and notes. A. N. Radishchev, *Puteshestviye iz Peterburga v Moskvu*, ed. L. B. Svetlov with introduction by D. D. Blagoy (Moscow–Leningrad, 1950), is a well-produced book with illustrations and documents concerning Radishchev and his famous *Journey from Petersburg to Moscow*. A. A. Bestuzhev-Marlinsky, *Sochineniya v dvukh tomakh* (Moscow, 1958), is compiled by P. A. Sidorov, with articles and text annotated by N. N. Maslin. A. V. Kol'tsov, *Polnoye sobraniye sochineniy A. V. Kol'tsova*, ed. and notes by A. I. Lyashchenko (St Petersburg, 1909), and *Sochineniya v dvukh tomakh*, edited with articles and notes by V. Tonkov (Moscow, 1961). M. I. Gillel'son, *P. A. Vyazemsky, zhizn' i tvorchestvo* (Leningrad, 1969), an up-to-date monograph on the life and work of Vyazemsky.

HISTORIES AND MONOGRAPHS

Istoriya russkoy literatury XVIII veka, Bibliograficheskiy ukazatel', ed. P. N. Berkov (Leningrad, 1968). *Istoriya russkoy literatury XIX veka, Bibliograficheskiy ukazatel'*, ed. K. D. Muratova (Moscow–Leningrad, 1962). *Russkiye pisateli: bibliograficheskiy slovar'*, eds. D. S. Likhachev, S. I. Makhinsky, S. M. Petrov, A. I. Revyakin (Moscow, 1971), a useful bibliography of Russian writers which provides a biography for each author. *Svodnyy katalog russkoy knigi grazhdanskoy pechati XVIII veka*, 5 vols. (Moscow, 1962–7), provides a list of books printed in Russian during the eighteeenth century.

Istoriya russkoy literatury, eds. A. S. Orlov, V. P. Adrianova-Peretts and N. K. Gudzy, vol. II, pt 2 (Moscow, 1948), a useful volume for preparing the ground immediately prior to 1700. *Istoriya russkoy literatury*, vols. III and IV, eds. G. A. Gukovsky and V. A. Desnitsky (Moscow, 1941, 1947), a useful and comprehensive history of eighteenth-century Russian literature. A. N. Pypin, *Istoriya russkoy literatury*, vols. III and IV (St Petersburg, 1902–3). G. A. Gukovsky, *Russkaya literatura XVIII veka* (Moscow–Leningrad, 1939), is a fair analysis of the subject. D. D. Blagoy, *Istoriya russkoy literatury XVIII veka* (Moscow, 1955): no scholar or student of eighteenth-century Russian literature should be without this book. D. Čiževskij, *History of Russian Literature* (The Hague, 1960), a readable and learned study of Russian literature until the end of the baroque. *Istoriya russkoy literatury XVII–XVIII vekov*, eds. A. C. Yeleonskaya, O. V. Orlov, Yu. N. Sidorova, S. F. Terekhov and V. I. Fyodorov (Moscow, 1969), a short but adequate summary of the subject. V. Desnitsky, *Izbrannyye stat'i po russkoy literature XVII–XVIII vv.* (Moscow–Leningrad, 1958), a collection of interesting articles relating to the seventeenth and eighteenth centuries in Russian literature. *Problemy realizma v russkoy literature XVIII veka. Sbornik statey*, ed. N. K. Gudzy (Moscow–Leningrad, 1940), various articles. P. N. Berkov, *Istoriya russkoy zhurnalistiki XVIII veka* (Moscow–Leningrad, 1952), an important and full account of journalistic activities in eighteenth-century Russia. *Russkiye satiricheskiye zhurnaly XVIII veka*, compiled by L. B. Lekhtblau, ed. N. K. Gudzy (Moscow, 1940), collected articles, notes and extracts. *Materialy i issledovaniya po leksike russkogo yazyka XVIII veka*, ed. Yu. S. Sorokin (Moscow–Leningrad, 1965). *Literaturnoye nasledstvo*, vols. 9–10, 29–30 (Moscow, 1933, 1937), contains invaluable material for the specialist. *Sbornik XVIII veka*, vols. I, II (repr.), III–X, eds. A. S. Orlov, P. N. Berkov and D. S. Likhachev (Moscow, 1935–1969), a necessary adjunct to every scholar's library pertaining to the study of eighteenth-century Russian culture.

Istoriya russkogo romana, vol. I, chs. 1–3, ed. G. M. Friedlender (Moscow 1962), 3–99, is useful for the history of the eighteenth-century novel in Russia. *Istoriya russkoy poezii*, I, ed. B. P. Gorodetsky (Leningrad, 1968), 5–302, covers the poetry of the period. *Ocherki po istorii russkoy zhurnalistiki i kritiki*, ed. A. V. Zapadov (Moscow, 1950), is a history of Russian eighteenth-century journalism, also A. V. Zapadov, *Russkaya zhurnalistika XVIII veka* (Moscow, 1964). *Problemy russkogo prosveshcheniya v literature XVIII veka*, ed. P. N. Berkov (Moscow, 1961), a series of detailed articles on topics of eighteenth-century Russian culture. *Russkaya literaturnaya rech' v XVIII veke*, ed. I. Yu. Shvedova (Moscow, 1968), a study of language and style in eighteenth-century Russia. A. I. Timofeyev, *Ocherki teorii i istorii russkogo stikha*, chs. 3–4 (Moscow, 1958), 237–360, gives a clear account of the problems of verse in Russia. *Russkiye povesti pervoy treti XVIII veka*, ed. G. N. Moiseyeva (Moscow, 1965) (contains texts), a very useful treatise on the Russian 'tale', with commentaries. R. Burgi, *A History of the Russian Hexameter* (Hamden, Conn., 1954), a well-informed and valuable dissertation. Rimvydas Silbajoris, *Russian Versification* (New York, 1968), is a good treatise on the work of Kantemir, Trediakovsky and Lomonsov. S. Petrov, *Russkiy istoricheskiy roman XIX veka*, chs. I and II (Moscow, 1964), 3–109. N. A. Kotlyarevsky, *Literaturnyye napravleniya Aleksandrovskoy epokhi* (St Petersburg, 1907), a volume to be recommended for the history of literary trends during the first quarter of the nineteenth century. A. N. Pypin, *Kharakteristiki literaturnykh mneniy ot dvadtsatykh do pyatidesyatykh godov*, 2nd edn, ch. I (St Petersburg, 1890), 1–37, a dry but reliable treatise on early nineteenth-century literary trends and thought in Russia.

Literaturnoye tvorchestvo M. V. Lomonosova, ed. I. Z. Serman (Moscow–Leningrad, 1962), a straightforward account of Lomonosov's work. *M. V. Lomonosov v portretakh, illyustratsiyakh, dokumentakh* (Moscow–Leningrad, 1965), an excellent illustrated volume, and *Letopis' zhizni i tvorchestva M. V. Lomonosova* (Moscow–Leningrad, 1961), an invaluable chronological account of Lomonosov's life and work, both edited by V. L. Chenakal. I. P. Shchelykin, *Mikhail Lomonosov: Ocherk zhizni i poeticheskogo tvorchestva* (Moscow, 1969). I. Z. Serman, *Poeticheskiy stil' Lomonosova* (Moscow–Leningrad, 1966), is a useful treatise on Lomonosov's poetry. B. G. Kuznetsov, *Tvorcheskiy put' Lomonosova* (Moscow, 1956), a straightforward survey of Lomonosov's creative work. B. N.

Menshutkin, *M. V. Lomonosov* (Moscow–Leningrad, 1947), is a reliable biography. B. N. Makeyeva, *Istoriya sozdaniya 'Rossiyskoy Grammatiki' M. V. Lomonosova* (Moscow–Leningrad, 1961), a detailed investigation of the 'Russian Grammar'. V. P. Vompersky, *Stilisticheskoye ucheniye M. V. Lomonosova i teoriya tryokh stiley* (Moscow, 1970), an up-to-date treatise on Lomonosov's theories.

J. G. Garrard, *Mixail Čulkov: An Introduction to his prose and verse* (The Hague–Paris, 1970), a sound analysis of the structural, thematic and narrative features of Chulkov's works. A. V. Zapadov, *Masterstvo Derzhavina* (Moscow, 1958), an essential monograph on Derzhavin. Claude Backvis, 'Dans quelle mesure Derzhavin est-il un baroque?' in *Studies in Russian and Polish Literature in Honour of Waclaw Lednicki* (The Hague, 1962), 72–104, an important essay on Derzhavin's style. *G. R. Derzhavin: Stikhotvoreniya*, ed. A. Ya. Kucherov (Moscow, 1958), includes a full discussion of Derzhavin's poetry. A. G. Cross, *N. M. Karamzin: A Study of his Literary Career 1783–1803* (Carbondale, Ill., 1971), a detailed chronological account of Karamzin's literary career. Henry M. Nebel Jr, *N. M. Karamzin: A Russian Sentimentalist* (The Hague, 1967), a fair monograph on Karamzin. G. P. Makogonenko, *Denis Fonvizin* (Moscow–Leningrad, 1961), a straightforward monograph on Fonvizin. K. V. Pigaryov, *Tvorchestvo Fonvizina* (Moscow, 1954), a sensible account of Fonvizin's work. A. I. Kulakova, *Denis Ivanovich Fonvizin* (Moscow–Leningrad, 1966). V. V. Kapnist, *Sobraniye sochineniy*, 2 vols., ed. D. S. Babkin (Moscow–Leningrad, 1960), a thorough compendium of Kapnist's poetry. *Ivan Andreyevich Krylov v portretakh, illyustratsiyakh, dokumentakh*, ed. A. M. Gordin (Moscow–Leningrad, 1966), an excellent aid to teachers and students with many illustrations and documents of interest.

THOUGHT

D. M. Lang, *The First Russian Radical: Alexander Radishchev, 1749–1802* (London, 1959), a readable account of the life and work of Radishchev. A. S. Babkin, *A. N. Radishchev* (Moscow–Leningrad, 1966), a sound monograph. *Aleksandr Nikolayevich Radishchev*, with a preface by V. Kuz'mina, eds. A. G. Mironov and Dudar' (Moscow, 1953), a very nicely produced and illustrated volume. B. B. Kafengauz, *I. T. Pososhkov – zhizn' i deyatel'nost'* (Moscow, 1951), an arid but full account of Pososhkov's life and work. I. A. Fedosov, *Iz istorii russkoy obshchestvennoy mysli XVIII stoletiya, M. M. Shcherbatov* (Moscow, 1967). *Shcherbatov: On the Corruption of Morals in Russia*, ed. A. Lentin (Cambridge, 1969), an excellent dissertation and translation of Shcherbatov's work with parallel Russian text. A. N. Pypin, *Russkoye masonstvo, XVIII i I-aya chetvert' XIX v.* (Petrograd, 1916), is a good history of this influential movement. *N. I. Novikov i yego sovremenniki*, ed. I. V. Malyshev (Moscow, 1961), is important for the literary background to Novikov. G. P. Makogonenko, *Nikolay Novikov i russkoye prosveshcheniye XVIII v.* (Moscow–Leningrad, 1951). A. V. Zapadov, *Novikov* (Moscow, 1968), is a readable biography.

6

FROM THE GOLDEN TO THE
SILVER AGE*
(1820–1917)

V. SETCHKAREV

Karamzin's language reform, which was noted in the previous chapter, did not go unopposed. Admiral Aleksandr Shishkov (1754–1841), a conservative nationalist, saw salvation for the Russian language in its national elements alone, and these elements he found at their purest in Church Slavonic. His occasionally quite witty polemics are written in impeccable Russian and contain much that is valid, but the *Zeitgeist* was against him. The society 'of the Lovers of the Russian Word', which he founded in 1811, became a target of derision for the Karamzinists even though it counted among its members such great names as Derzhavin and Krylov. Important poets of the younger generation such as Griboyedov and Katenin also tended to favour Shishkov's 'archaistic' theory but could not halt the development toward the West. The heart of the major controversy of the nineteenth century – the Slavophiles versus the Westerners – lies in these originally purely linguistic debates.

The most important poet among the young archaists was Aleksandr Griboyedov (1795–1829), whose fame rests on a single work, the comedy *Woe from Wit* (*Gore ot uma*). The content is based on the eternal theme of how a noble idealist comes to grief when confronted with callous philistinism. A love story is very skilfully interwoven into the main plot line. Chatsky, the hero, loses the girl he loves (she finds his ideas suspicious) to a dishonest sycophant who by the end of the action betrays her. Chatsky's brilliant witticisms and tirades against the status quo derive force and life from their connection with his unhappy love affair. Sofia, the heroine, is very realistically portrayed, because Griboyedov eschews all the old literary clichés. Like Molière he succeeds in making his characters convincing both as types and living human beings. His mastery of language is even more amazing; his comedy contains perfectly

* Parts of this chapter are a revised and expanded version of the author's chapter in *Geschichte der russischen Literatur* (Stuttgart, 1962), 77–143, translated by Dr Michael Heim and reprinted by kind permission of Philipp Reclam Verlag.

idiomatic unstrained dialogues in a strictly kept pattern of rhymed iambic lines of varying lengths. It is no wonder that almost every line has become an adage. *Woe from Wit* is still one of the most frequently staged plays in Russia.

Pavel Katenin (1792–1853) sought to reassert the national element in poetry by using rough-hewn realism. His ballads, inspired mainly by the German poet Bürger, influenced Pushkin. He was the last to write a strictly classical tragedy in Russian because here too the trend toward the sentimental took its toll.

A synthesis of classicism and sentimentalism in the drama was attempted by Vladislav Ozerov (1769–1816), who sought to imbue the tired forms of classicism with the new life of the sentimental spirit. His *Fingal*, drawn from Ossian, and *Dmitry Donskoy*, based on Russian history, were great successes, although his final work *Poliksena*, which was coolly received, is much more satisfying aesthetically.

As soon as Shishkov established his society to combat the influence of Karamzin, the poets of the younger generation joined forces to defend the latter's reforms. The most talented among them – Zhukovsky, Batyushkov and Prince Vyazemsky – were in language and theory Pushkin's direct predecessors. The new society called itself 'Arzamas' (after a small provincial city, so as to stress its opposition to the official metropolis) and overwhelmed the representatives of the old school with witty epigrams, satires and parodies. Arzamas was not merely a negative force, however; it accomplished much in the way of drawing up new standards for literature, because some of its members were true poets.

Using Karamzin's reform as a point of departure, Vasily Zhukovsky (1783–1852) furnished the nineteenth century with everything it needed for a definitive poetic language. With him, for the first time in Russian literature, poetry became a direct expression of emotion. The emotion may be monotonous – resignation smiling through tears and hoping for a better fate in the next world – but its formulation is genuine and moving with a mood all its own. These lyrics draped in hushed mourning (the idea of death as a friend is a dominating motif) include many masterpieces of style. Zhukovsky's work is pervaded with the idea that, although God gave us life so that we might be happy, grief is inseparable from life and therefore man must accept the bad with the good in a spirit of thanksgiving. Memories of past happiness can comfort us in our deepest sorrow; sorrow over past happiness binds us to it. And so Zhukovsky comes to regret the short duration of deep sorrow, his only living link with the object he is mourning. Poetry is the reflection of heaven on earth – a very novel idea in Russia. Its duty is to give us a foretaste of the other, better world.

Zhukovsky's original work is not extensive, but he did produce a large number of translations, and to call him the one translator in all world literature who by his translations did most for his own literature is hardly an exaggeration. His translations of Byron, Schiller, Homer (*The Odyssey*) and Goethe come as near as possible to equalling their originals; his translations of Southey, Moore, Walter Scott, Halm, Uhland, Hebel and many other writers leave their originals far behind. His importance for the development of the Russian language (many literary historians date the beginning of the Russian literary language from the appearance in 1802 of his first great translation, Gray's 'Elegy Written in a Country Churchyard') and for the formation of taste cannot be overstated. He made European and some Oriental literature accessible to Russia, providing each of the works he translated with a form which suited it superbly. Alongside Pushkin he remained the leading poet in Russia until well into the 1830s.

Purity of language and clarity of poetic form were the goals which Konstantin Batyushkov (1787–1855) set himself. Light poetry, short pieces, anacreontic, epigrammatic, antique verse require the most precise formal embossment because of the narrow range of subject matter permitted them (jovial company, wine, women and a *joie de vivre* enhanced by rationality). In his love epigrams Batyushkov achieves a high degree of perfection of rhythm and diction. He attempts to blend the precision and brevity of expression of his Latin models with the mellifluence of Italian ('A Friend's Shadow', 'Tasso Dying'). Pushkin very pertinently remarked that Batyushkov did for Russian what Petrarch did for Italian. Of all poets he loved Tasso most and felt that certain of his traits, both personal and poetic, paralleled his own. His poetry might be characterized by the paradox of an elegiac Epicureanism, with the elegiac element gaining in prominence year by year until finally, just before he went mad, his poetry expresses moods of decadence, once again in classical form. In the history of Russian literature Batyushkov is deservedly remembered as a prime moulder of the literary language and poetic form.

The hussar poet Denis Davydov (1784–1839) sings the praises of valour in the face of foe or battle with great inventiveness, passion, wit and dash, but can also find a genuine and unconventional tonality for his love poems. Pushkin wrote that it was Davydov who taught him to write with originality.

THE AGE OF PUSHKIN

In the first two decades of the nineteenth century Russian literature consisted of a chaotic conglomeration of the most varied trends, some of which already showed great promise. The linguistic battle between classical Church Slavonic and sentimental Francophile tendencies was still raging, and neither side had as yet succeeded in elaborating a genuinely Russian literary language.

The archaists accepted the poetic canon of French classicism, while firmly rejecting the French language as a basis for remodelling Russian. The innovators favoured the use of French forms and words, but categorically refused to accept the poetic doctrine of French classicism. The situation was complicated by the fact that both schools had various side currents and lacked theoreticians and poets capable of formulating clear justifications for their theoretical positions and of gaining recognition for these positions with works of high artistic quality.

Russia finally found a brilliant poet and theoretician with the proper requisites in the person of Aleksandr Pushkin (1799–1837), whose first important work, *Ruslan and Lyudmila,* appeared in 1820. It was Pushkin who first synthesized all the prevailing trends and produced great Russian literature by applying this synthesis to his work. Even after one gives his predecessors their due, the fact remains that he was forced to clear new paths at every turn. His concept of poetry went so far beyond anything which had preceded him that before he could even think of putting it into practice he was forced to design the proper tools himself.

To this end he created a new idiom, the Russian literary language, which became the basis for the language that to this day is considered standard. He made decisive reforms in metre. He created the Russian verse narrative and a lyric poetry which encompasses the entire range of emotions. Looking to Shakespeare, he remoulded Russian drama from its very foundations. He developed a prose style which lent itself to both literary and scholarly expression. He was the first to write a Russian novella using modern techniques. He was also a brilliant critic, a highly accomplished literary scholar, a stimulating critical historian, a spirited journalist and a witty virtuoso letter writer.

To give these disparate areas cohesion, Pushkin had first to face the problem of absorbing all the elements affecting Russian literature of his time – influences from East and West, from antiquity, the middle ages and modern times. As far as this titanic task could be accomplished by a single writer, Pushkin succeeded in accomplishing it.

World literature exhibits a great variety of trends, creative methods and technical devices. That Pushkin studied the literature of many nations untiringly is evident from both his works and his notes; a fairly detailed history of literature could be compiled from the critical remarks scattered throughout his poems, notes and letters. The accuracy of his literary judgement and the degree to which his conception of the world was ahead of its time are truly amazing. For example, he predicted the direction Gogol's development would take after reading his first work. In his views on Shakespeare, Goethe and Byron he is every bit as independent and profound as he is in his views on Russian literature. He clearly gave them careful thought and with the sure hand of a great master integrated them fully into the tradition of Russian literature. Whenever he came across a piece of literature, he always seems to have asked himself whether it could be effective in Russian. This attitude doubtless provided the impetus for many of his works. With him everything was creation. Others read, ponder and digest: Pushkin re-created as he read. He went through the creative process a second time. This was his way of coming to grips with a work of art. Very few poets in world literature combine a personal style of such great inner unity with such a wealth of widely differing, sometimes even contradictory, styles.

Pushkin is the classical poet par excellence. If classic literature be defined as the utmost in clarity of thought and perfection of form organically bound to a profound concern with the ultimate questions, then Pushkin's works must be regarded as a supreme example of truly classical poetry.

Lyric poetry is Pushkin's proper domain. He began with light anacreontic verse in the French rococo style – with Parny as his principal model – combining a buoyant *joie de vivre* with melancholy elegiac moods. Witty epistles with distinct Voltairian overtones alternate with passionate, though still largely conventional love poems. Even his earliest verse, despite the occasional shortcomings of the themes, is formally perfect. But behind the formal perfection one is always conscious of the poet's beating heart, his taut nerves and urgent vitality. Pushkin was not long in finding his own style. It is marked by a classically restrained passion, combined with a perfect choice of vocabulary. His words alliterate, assonate and join to form a harmonic organism. As with Mozart's music, no tone may be altered or removed without impairing the whole. Most of his early poems are occasional in subject matter, raising vivid experience to an ideal universal plane. In Pushkin's verse all components of every emotion are turned into pure poetry. Harmony of rhythm and intonation approaches the bounds of possibility.

The later poems tend more and more to discard poetic ornamentation. They become distillations of art at its purest and have been equalled in none but the greatest works of literature. Pushkin raised Russian lyric poetry to heights it has never again recaptured. He mastered the subtleties of all the short poetic genres – from the concise formulation of personal emotion to the ballad. The programmatic poems in which he sets forth his aesthetic ideas deserve special mention. Above all he stresses the poet's right to absolute freedom and independence. Poetry, and art in general, are their own justification; any ulterior motive detracts from their worth. They stand higher than morality or ethics, and the poet must be absolutely free to choose his own thematic material; no one may prescribe to him the object of his inspiration. Pushkin was the first Russian poet to place such strong emphasis on the principle of art for art's sake, the conviction that artistic talent has its origins in the supernatural. He illustrated his aesthetic philosophy with powerful images (e.g. 'The Prophet').

The narrative poem, *Ruslan and Lyudmila*, was the first extensive work in verse of great poetic significance to appear since Karamzin's reform. Even at this early stage in his career Pushkin's language was quite faultless; it combined Church Slavonic and French elements with colloquial Russian in an organic synthesis. The melodic, subtle, supple and expressive Russian literary language had finally come of age. On the level of content *Ruslan and Lyudmila* serves Pushkin as a vehicle for superimposing the fantastic arsenal of Ariosto's magic world onto a precise historical background (the action is set in Kievan Russia) in an elegantly ironic tone and with a number of lyrical digressions. The result is a work of the highest order which rightfully created a sensation when it first appeared.

Pushkin's next two narratives in verse, *The Prisoner of the Caucasus* and *The Fountain of Bakhchisaray*, treated Byronic themes. The hero of the former is a disenchanted young man whose past (although veiled in deep secrecy) overflows with turbulent passions and who loses the ability to return the love of a child of nature. The hero of the latter poem, an oriental despot, is destroyed by unrequited passion. In both, the oriental mood of the Caucasus and the Crimea comes to life in colourful descriptions. The language is a highly successful combination of soft melodious rhythm and extreme lexical precision.

A tribute to Voltaire and to Parny follows in the *Gavriliyada*, a poetic spoof on biblical tradition which disarms all moralistic criticism with the magic of its brilliant linguistic virtuosity. But Pushkin reaches a new high point in his verse narrative *The Gypsies*, which deals with a young man entangled in guilt (because he cannot help but follow his own destiny) which is purged by a higher form of justice. The graphic power and beauty of its doomed characters are reminiscent of Greek tragedy. The inserted Ovid saga is a beautiful elegy on a historical theme, and from a formal point of view the harmony between narrative passages and dramatic dialogue is worthy of special note.

Count Nulin, a kind of delightful intermezzo, parodies fateful and serious historical tradition (the rape of Lucretia) with a sharp punch line at the end. *Poltava* deals with a romantic case of a young girl's violent love for an old man – on an historical background full of dramatic pathos. Romanticism prevails in episodes characterized by only half-told action, resplendent baroque in the broadly drawn historical characters and battle scenes.

The Little House in Kolomna is a unique work of art: a swift-moving anecdote told in perfectly wrought, ironic *ottava rima* with an admixture of comments on versification problems, open scorn for readers who are always after morals, and glimpses into the very depths of the subconscious. In no other work except *Eugene Onegin* is the essence of Pushkin the poet reflected so clearly.

The verse narrative *Angelo* is an attempt at ridding Shakespeare's *Measure for Measure* of all its baroque accessories. It stands as a milestone in Pushkin's development toward the ultimate in poetic expression.

His last work in this genre, *The Bronze Horseman*, is remarkable in all respects. With forceful images it tackles the problem of whether the common weal justifies the destruction of the happiness of the individual The great Petersburg flood of 1824 provides the backdrop. The problem remains unsolved.

The novel in verse, *Eugene (Yevgeny) Onegin*, is a perfect combination of the objective force of the realistic novel with the subjectivity of lyrical poetry and worldly wise irony. The subsequent Russian novel owes much to this one work. After Pushkin perhaps only Tolstoy in *War and Peace* succeeded in depicting the development of his heroes throughout the course of the novel with comparable objective artistry. The atmosphere of Russian high society, bent on external appearance and detached from all higher values, from God and its own people, finds moving expression in one of its most typical representatives. Without faith or ideals, without any vital bond with his people or country, without any inner resources, completely wrapped up in himself, and bored by everything, Onegin ends in despair. By overestimating the power of human reason and repressing his emotions and feelings, he has scorned the love of the heroine Tat'yana and destroyed her entire life. All he has left after a senseless flare up of passion is a feeling of his own emptiness. The whole of the work is penetrated by a flowing lyricism which runs especially rich in the surprising, spirited digressions. The verses flow together into Pushkin's original fourteen-line 'Onegin stanzas', but each verse is an impeccable, rhythmically perfect unit of its own.

Pushkin wrote the tragedy *Boris Godunov* to give Shakespearean-type theatre a foothold in Russia, but the censors would not allow it to be staged. Several weak points in the dramatic structure notwithstanding, it has great poetic beauty. Meanwhile, in his *Little Tragedies* (*Mozart and Salieri, The Stone Guest, The Covetous Knight, A Feast During the Plague*), Pushkin turned to an unusual poetic genre. Each of these vignettes is a concentrated portrayal of a human passion raised to its highest power. His fairy tales in verse are perfect gems. Taken from literary patterns (e.g. Grimm, Washington Irving), they are masterworks of language which young and old can enjoy with equal relish.

In his prose writings Pushkin sought precision in brevity without functionless words, but infused with concentrated thought. The *Tales of Belkin*, a cycle united by the person of the ostensible narrator, are all based on anecdotes which, when intensified by Pushkin's inventive twists, turn into absorbing novellas with a spirited and convincing cast of characters. Scholars have only begun tapping the depths of the metaphysical atmosphere behind the glistening classical surface clarity. *The Queen of Spades* is generally accepted as a classic example of the novella: in content, composition and language it is unquestionably Pushkin's prose masterpiece. *The Captain's Daughter* – the first important Russian novel – is distinguished by its exciting, swiftly developing plot and interesting, skilfully developed characters. The large number of fragments of novels which Pushkin left behind give some idea of how much Russia lost when he died. *A History of the Village of Goryukhino*, an unfinished satire describing village conditions in the official, solemn style of historiography, shows him to be a master in this field as well.

Pushkin's significance for the development of Russian literature can scarcely be overrated. He succeeded in bringing about the decisive linguistic synthesis as well as the definitive union of classicism and romanticism which allowed Russian literature to enter the literature of Europe on an equal footing. His position in Russia can only be compared with that of Goethe in Germany. Many poets and writers looked to him for inspiration; a few names among many must suffice here.

The importance of Prince Pyotr Vyazemsky (1792–1878) lies in his enthusiastic propagation of the romantic movement. Although he does not seem to have grasped its essence too well (romanticism's speculative aspects rarely received more than casual attention in Russia), he championed its forms in splendidly written articles. He was one of Pushkin's best friends. Their correspondence glistens with wit and perceptive literary criticism. Vyazemsky's early poems are quite insignificant and entirely unromantic. It was not until he grew older that they began to take on an original note.

Though Baron Anton Del'vig (1798–1831) is also chiefly known for his close friendship with Pushkin, his talent as a poet is considerable. His idylls in classical metres and his songs in the folk vein show him at his best, although his poetry gives the impression of excessive polishing.

The poetry of Nikolay Yazykov (1803–46) radiates a cold splendour. His skill in transforming visual impressions into harmonious word cascades is astonishing. But neither his inebriate student songs nor the largely Slavophile-oriented lyric poetry of his later period amount to much more than fine rhetoric.

Philosophical poetry was introduced into modern Russian literature by Dmitry Venevitinov (1805–27), the leader of a group of young men who in the twenties were enthusiastic followers of Schelling's philosophy. He succeeded in blending genuine lyric poetry with acute philosophical and aesthetic reflections. His main themes are the mystery of art and the high calling of the poet, but he could also write excellent poems in a cutting, highly naturalistic style (*Rodina*, *Domovoy*) that points to an entire gamut of untapped poetic possibilities and makes his early death that much more unfortunate.

Another philosophical poet, Yevgeny Boratynsky (or Baratynsky) (1800–44) is metaphysical in a different sense, his philosophy harking back to the French enlightenment. His poems combine the logical construction of a syllogism with the vibrant ardour of a deeply sensitive poet. Pessimism pervades his entire work. Characteristically, his love lyrics contain many renunciations of his loved one, but there is more passion in these renunciations than in many more conventional love songs. He strove to form a style of his own and succeeded completely. His finely honed, deeply pondered stanzas are the ultimate in precision: each word corresponds to a clear thought. He did not shun syntactical archaisms, which give his poetry an unmistakably characteristic diction. A similar precision in expressing emotions runs through his narrative poems. Critics are only now beginning to give Boratynsky his due.

Russia's most important nineteenth-century poetess, Karolina Pavlova (1807–93), also belongs to the group of Pushkin's successors who combined internal dynamism with skilfully polished form. She differs from the rest, however, in that she often uses psychological motifs.

Metaphysics and love are joined in the lyric poetry of Fyodor Tyutchev (1803–73), a very important figure in Russian literature despite his small output. Although some of his poems appeared in Pushkin's journal *The Contemporary* (1836–8), they went unnoticed, and it was not until his first volume of poetry was published in 1854 that he became known in wider circles. In subject matter, vocabulary and style he is diametrically opposed to Pushkin – a direct descendant of the Lomonosov and Derzhavin tradition. His rhetorical, elevated, and yet passionate metaphysical and love lyrics express a sharply dualistic *Weltanschauung* in words which have seldom – before or since – conveyed such force. His main philosophical theme (inspired by Schelling) is the battle between cosmos and chaos in both the universe and the human soul. His poems, aphoristic and precise, display a highly developed feeling for form, and with the exception of his patriotic pieces they rank with the best in Russian poetry.

It is difficult to characterize the unripe genius of Mikhail Lermontov (1814–41), who was killed in a duel at the age of twenty-seven. His lyric poetry is extremely uneven, but some poems are flawless in every respect. Lermontov writes about deep sorrow stemming from the conviction that the world and all its values are imperfect and senseless. For the sensitive soul the result is an insatiable, all-consuming desire for the other world. Why is man made as he is? Why does he act against his better judgement and emotions? Such are the problems which excited the poet. He posed them in starkly subjective, emotionally coloured verses, but did not attempt a solution. Controlled by an acute feeling for form, his dynamism and fervour led him to great rhetorical achievements (the poem on Pushkin's death, for example), and his increasing concern for turning realistic detail into poetry resulted in some excellent works in the ballad style (like 'Tamara' or 'The Bequest'). His emphasis on emotion, even to the point of consciously allowing it to cloud the clarity of diction, links him to Zhukovsky. His narratives in verse are modelled on Byron and are on the whole rather weak. He was much more successful with his 'Tsar Ivan and the Merchant Kalashnikov', an epic poem in the old Russian narrative style in which the people and customs of Muscovite Russia come alive.

Lermontov's greatest achievement, however, is his prose novel *A Hero of Our Time* (*Geroy nashego vremeni*), which carries the problems raised by Pushkin in *Eugene Onegin* a stage further. An exceptional man who cannot fit into the world around him, disaffected, bored and contemptuous, turns in toward himself. And when love for his fellow men fails to save him, he becomes lost to both the world and himself. His heart becomes a wasteland, exposed to all the highest existential forces – life, guilt, love, death. He finds they elicit no response – he feels himself a 'superfluous man'. In the character of Pechorin, the hero, Lermontov anticipated the trend toward a new type of personality, a type which had lost all vital belief in power from above and could do no more than replace it with his own self, which in turn founders in the void of egoism. In *A Hero of Our Time* Lermontov created Russia's first psychological novel, which Turgenev, Tolstoy and Dostoyevsky studied closely.

The composition of the novel deserves special notice. It consists of five time segments, each of which has its own title. In chronological order they are 'Taman'', 'Princess Mary', 'The Fatalist', 'Bela', 'Maksim Maksimovich', but Lermontov chose a different order, the better to unveil Pechorin's character bit by bit. So first Maksim Maksimovich, the man with 'the heart that knows', tells us about him. Then Pechorin himself comes on the scene. Finally we read his intimate diary. His views on friendship, love and death become gradually clear, as do the hopelessness and indifference in his nature – it is the unveiling of this nature and not the development of a character that determines the succession of the segments. Lermontov's language fulfils Pushkin's demand for tightness and precision, but a certain lyricism belonging to Lermontov alone pervades his prose, and one can well understand why Chekhov claimed he knew no more beautiful language than Lermontov's.

Folksong imitations, a genre very popular in the eighteenth century, reach a certain degree of excellence during this period. Sumarokov had achieved some pretty effects, and Del'vig continued the tradition successfully. But not until Aleksey Kol'tsov (1809–42) did this genre find a poet capable of securing for it a niche of its own. Most of his songs are placed in the mouths of peasant girls or women: their plaints, touching in their naïveté and dramatic quality, make up the bulk of the songs. There are also effective descriptions of nature and of the harshness of peasant life, written chiefly in rhymeless stanzas. Kol'tsov has one disturbing characteristic, however: he tends to idealize peasant existence, a trait never found in genuine folk songs.

The age of Pushkin also saw an upsurge in the quality of journalism, which was then beginning to play a decisive role in literature, a role very different from its cultural and moral mission in the eighteenth century. Besides several almanacs – the Schelling-oriented *Mnemosyne* (1824–5) published by Wilhelm Kyukhel'beker and Vladimir Odoyevsky is the most significant – journals like Del'vig's *Literary Gazette* (1830–1), Nikolay Polevoy's *Moscow Telegraph* (1825–34), Mikhail Pogodin's *Moscow Messenger* (starting 1827) and Pushkin's *Contemporary* (starting 1836), did much to propagate foreign literature in Russia and provide the reader with salutary criticism. Journalism in Petersburg was less satisfying because it was inspired by an insignificant writer named Faddey Bulgarin and struck a servile pro-government note.

THE AGE OF GREAT PROSE

The fact that Tyutchev's poetry evoked so little response is symptomatic. The thirties saw a decisive shift toward prose. Almost two decades earlier Vasily Narezhny began to popularize the picaresque and adventure novel, and by the late twenties and early thirties Mikhail Zagoskin and Ivan Lazhechnikov were writing novels from Russian history in the style of Sir Walter Scott. Aleksandr Bestuzhev-Marlinsky tried to convey the pose of the Byronic hero in prose and often set his novels and short stories in a romanticized version of the Caucasus. Aleksandr Vel'tman wrote novels which exhibit romantic irony and bear the imprint of the styles of Laurence Sterne and Jean Paul. Their importance for the development of the Russian novel is becoming increasingly clear. In the work of Vladimir Odoyevsky (1803–69) ideas from Schelling's philosophical system are elaborated in the style of E. T. A. Hoffmann. Odoyevsky seems to have exerted some influence on Dostoyevsky's early works. His peculiar *Russian Nights*, composed in dialogue form, introduced the philosophical novella cycle into Russia. His principal theme is the philosophy of the arts and especially the decisive role of music.

For the magnificent synthesis of all these trends Russian literature is indebted to Nikolay Gogol (Gogol') (1809–52). Almost all the great writers of the nineteenth and twentieth centuries reveal the influence of his materials and technique, much of which he found in E. T. A. Hoffmann. Unlike Pushkin's classical prose, Gogol's language exhibits a deliberate mixing of the most varied levels. By confronting 'high' with 'low' words, he creates effects which in 'classical' prose were achieved by the common devices of rhetoric.

It is impossible to appreciate Gogol's work without understanding his deep attachment to religion and his struggle to contend with problems of theology and – in his later period – mysticism. The world as seen by Gogol is a tool of the devil. Satan is ever striving to turn man away from all he really needs – i.e. from God – with the utmost cunning. Only through his relationship to God can man stake a sure claim for his due place in the cosmos. If his thoughts cling to the things of this earth, he falls prey to the power of evil, which entangles him more and more deeply in the snares of the devil. The devil's most powerful tool is earthly beauty, and beauty finds its most powerful incarnation in the body of a beautiful woman (cf. *Viy*, *Nevsky Prospekt*). By the same token earthly oriented art is nothing less than evil's larva. Artistic perfection borders on the demonic, and beyond its borders lurks a dreadful new reality beset by an 'impure force' (cf. *The Portrait*).

The devil, who might be called the main figure in all of Gogol's work, knows only too well which snares to apply to each individual in order to bring about his fall most effectively. Gogol is not interested in great men or the celebrated snares of burning passion and lust for power or fame; his concern is with the little man and his little idols. Men are so stupid and shallow, so completely uninformed as to the true value of existence, so insensible to the divine sparks they all possess, that the devil needs no more than everyday home-grown expedients to sink them deep into the mire of petty earthly cares. Sometimes an ordinary everyday necessity – an overcoat, for example – is enough to satisfy the aspirations of a human soul and destroy it by leading it from the path of salvation. *The Overcoat* has no philanthropic intent whatsoever: its aim is to demonstrate how the devil can turn the most paltry object to his own advantage in his efforts to bring about his victim's ruin. Men cling to the surface of things and thereby forfeit the divine element. Once the usual surface equilibrium is upset, the man with nothing inside loses his stability and very soon his mind as well (e.g. *The Nose*). Gogol portrays mankind's complacent inferiority with what may seem at first glance to be approval, but is actually devastating irony (one of his surest devices). The way he goes about it is unique. His work is a model of irreconciled oppositions. The basic conflict of Gogol the realist versus Gogol the romantic remains unresolved. He turns apparently impossible combinations into most persuasive reality: lyricism and naturalism join forces in his early stories from the Ukraine; heroic pathos and coarse humour in *Taras Bul'ba*; horror and good-natured tomfoolery in *Viy*; burlesque comedy and hopeless pessimism in *The Tale of how Ivan Ivanovich quarrelled with Ivan Nikiforovich*. Gogol does not try to describe real life. Instead of depicting it as such, he depicts his own reality, that of an imagination with a weird phantom-like relationship to concrete reality because it reproduces the most insignificant details of its phantoms with extreme realism. The concrete phantoms of his works become increasingly terrifying as he expands the catalogue of comic devices he wields with such unerring virtuosity: juxtaposition of the significant and insignificant, conjunctions which set up climaxes that never come, intentional disruptions of logical connections, obvious absurdities treated with the utmost solemnity or even in the style of a scholarly treatise – these are only a handful from his bag of tricks. Gogol's masterful comic effects lie like a shimmering transparent net over the sombre subsoil of his works.

An abundance of characters illustrating the most diverse aspects of the sorrow of human existence have sprung from Gogol's inexhaustible imagination. *Dead Souls* (*Myortvyye dushi*) is his masterpiece, and the title refers to more than the activities of his swindler hero, who uses the names of dead serfs for purposes of shady but lucrative business transactions. It is also meant to characterize the average man as Gogol saw him. There is no life except in God, but all the characters in *Dead Souls* have fallen prey to the devil's petty enticements. Both Gogol's masterly comedies, *The Government Inspector* (*Revizor*) and *The Marriage* (*Zhenit'ba*), have the same basic theme. From the point of view of both stage and literary technique they may be compared only with the greatest of plays in the repertory.

Worn out by his spiritual struggles, Gogol came more and more to believe he had been chosen as a teacher to warn mankind of its errors and free it from the power of the devil. His didactic *Selected Passages from Correspondence with Friends* cannot be considered a work of art. He burned the second part of *Dead Souls*: the fragments which have survived are sketches which the author discarded.

The tendency to regard literature as a mouthpiece for social and political theories gained an increasing number of adherents during the thirties and forties, and the damage Russian literature suffered from it – even among its greatest representatives – is enormous. Very soon two opposing interpretations of history and of Russia's destiny began to crystallize: those of the Slavophiles and the Westerners. The Slavophiles maintained that old Europe, decaying as she was from within, would be cured by the Russian Orthodox spirit, and that it was time to return to the old Russian, pre-Petrine tradition. In this tradition alone was to be found the true Orthodox regenerative faith in Christ, a faith which would overcome the destructive chaos-oriented atheism of the West and lead mankind on to new salvation. The Westerners felt that progress in Russia would be possible only if certain western ideals and ideas, just then in first bloom, were assimilated. In one way or another every writer of the nineteenth century owes allegiance to one or another of these factions.

Slavophilism's exponents in literature were Ivan Kireyevsky (1806–56), an essayist, Aleksey Khomyakov (1804–60), noteworthy – as a writer – chiefly for the clear, pure Russian of his articles (his poetry does not exceed the level of harmonious eloquence), and Sergey Aksakov.

Aksakov (1791–1859) proved himself an artist of considerable stature in his *Family Chronicle*, *Memoirs* and *The Childhood Years of Grandson Bagrov*. With objectivity and epic breadth he tells of the patriarchal, tradition-laden life of a Russian landowner. Though scarcely any events of significance break up the routine of everyday existence, his works hold one's attention from the first page to the last with their character portrayals, nature descriptions and the palpable forcefulness of their 'genre' pictures. The figures in these chronicles are living men and women with all their good and bad qualities. The grandfather, both lovable and terrifying, and the young boy, who observes the world around him from the vantage point of the child he is, are especially impressive portraits. Aksakov's representation of a child's internal development holds its own even against Tolstoy's trilogy (*Childhood, Boyhood, Youth*). His language is pure, supple and artless.

Important exponents of Westernism in literature include the cultural philosopher Pytor Chaadayev (1794–1856), the critic Visarion Belinsky (1811–48) and Aleksandr Herzen (1812–70). Chaadayev stressed the superiority of Roman Catholicism over Russian Orthodoxy, explaining by this fact the backwardness of Russian culture in comparison with the excellencies of the West. Belinsky has the reputation of being Russia's greatest literary critic, and it is true that his influence on the development of literature was extremely important. At the same time it cannot be denied that he directed Russian literature into channels which proved harmful to it. It is his fault that the sixties were nearly devoid of poetry. It is he who established the norm requiring poetry to be judged according to extra-aesthetic social criteria, and he is to blame for the increasing neglect of form in favour of tendentious content. While certain elements of Belinsky's aesthetic judgements are sometimes very much to the point, the whole of his work is vulnerable and often displays surprising short-sightedness. Constantly switching his philosophical allegiances, he underwent a bizarre development from half-understood Schelling *via* not understood Fichte to misunderstood Hegel – all to arrive finally at Feuerbach. To be sure, Belinsky was never dishonest. Whatever ideal he happened to be defending *was* his ideal. The spirit with which he serves his ideas is always sincere, but his criticism does not proceed from aesthetic criteria. Belinsky did perform a great service, however, by contributing to the creation of a Russian philosophical vocabulary.

Aleksandr Herzen engaged in fiction, journalism, philosophy, science, criticism and sociology, and displayed great mastery of style in them all. His political revolutionary ideas, expounded in his usual clear and lively manner (chiefly in *From the Other Shore*), do not concern us here. His novel *Who is to Blame?* and the satire *The Notes of Doctor Krupov* are somewhat too socially oriented (the latter is an attempt at winning over the romantic idealists with sceptical rationalism), but even here the command of characterization which distinguishes his memoirs comes through. In his memoirs, *My Past and Thoughts* (*Byloye i dumy*), Herzen tells the story of his life with an elegant Voltaire-like irony. He paints psychologically perfect portraits of his contemporaries and condemns the Tsarist regime with real passion. His language is straightforward; it gives the impression of the speech of a brilliant conversationalist, and is never insipid.

The poet Apollon Grigor'yev (1822–64), who is particularly known for his gypsy songs, also originated a new trend in criticism. Defending his own concept of literature against that of his time, he refused to seek aesthetic criteria in ideas outside the domain of art. It was his contention that no work of art might be considered for criticism as long as it remained isolated. Much of his poetry is remarkable, though little known. Aleksandr Blok, leader of the symbolists, was much influenced by it.

Two of the four great novelists of the nineteenth century, Turgenev and Goncharov, made their débuts in the forties. Ivan Turgenev (1818–83) began his literary career with lyric and narrative verse and was for a time considered a ray of hope for the revival of poetry. From 1843 to 1852 he wrote (besides short stories) comedies and dramas which compensate for their lack of external action by complex psychic tensions, thereby anticipating Chekhov's technique by almost half a century. He did not find his true niche in literature, however, until he turned to narrative prose. His works may be divided into novels with a social background and stories dealing with purely human relationships. The latter are unquestionably more important.

147

Turgenev's first great prose work, *A Sportsman's Sketches* (*Zapiski okhotnika*), occupies a special place among his works. Each sketch is a beautiful miniature put together from the author's impressions as he wanders throughout the countryside, but the whole is a biting pamphlet against serfdom. Turgenev manages to take a definite stand on a political issue without in the least sacrificing the aesthetic side of his work. His most successful novels are *Rudin* and *A Nest of Gentlefolk* (*Dvoryanskoye gnezdo*). In *Rudin* he portrays a typically Russian idealist who, though noble and selfless, an excellent theorist and fascinating speaker, has very little practical knowledge and falls to pieces when it is time to act. *Rudin* established the 'superfluous man' type which – in numerous variations – dominated Russian literature well into the twentieth century. The heroine of *A Nest of Gentlefolk*, Liza, is often extolled as the incarnation of Russian womanhood because she is always ready to place what she considers her duty before what is patently her happiness. It takes a good deal of empathy, however, to accept her character as valid.

The figure of Bazarov, the hero of the novel *Fathers and Sons* (*Ottsy i deti*), is important in terms of cultural history; this portrait of a noble positivist and utilitarian nihilist served as a model for many similar characters in 'liberal' and Soviet literature. Unlike Dostoyevsky and Tolstoy, Turgenev does not penetrate into the souls of his characters. Instead, he characterizes them by catching the atmosphere peculiar to each of them (and surrounding every individual), their effect on their environment and those tiny, imponderable gestures which do so much to reveal the true man. He is much more concerned with individual character portrayals than with an absorbing plot, yet his stories are captivating from the first word to the last. He has the gift of raising very human situations to a poetic, artistic plane without idealizing them or departing from reality. In this respect he is once again a forerunner of Chekhov.

Turgenev's social novels, *On the Eve* (*Nakanune*), *Fathers and Sons*, *Smoke* (*Dym*), *Virgin Soil* (*Nov'*), are on the whole disappointing, despite many well-described details, impressive portraits and absorbing episodes. The structure of his novels is rather uniform, their plots somewhat too transparent. All possible objections notwithstanding, however, the atmosphere which only Turgenev can create (e.g. the human relationships in *Smoke* – so passionate and yet so delicate) makes these shortcomings seem less important. He is at his unrivalled best, however, when leaving ideas behind and concentrating on people in the throes of the deepest and most unsettling of emotions – people in love. He is most successful in his portrayal of women, whose charm he conveyed so well. *First Love* (*Pervaya lyubov'*), *Asya* and above all *The Torrents of Spring* (*Veshniye vody*), which combine irony with delicate tenderness, are among the most beautiful love stories in Russian literature. Turgenev also wrote a great number of stories and novellas, distinguished by absorbing plot lines, lucid characterizations, sensitive, finely-shaded nature descriptions and an acute sense of style.

As Turgenev grew older, he turned to a new province – the fantastic, supernatural and mysterious. The suggestive force of his characters is transferred to the unknown – the enigmatic power behind events – and lays open human existence to uneasy queries. His masterpieces in this type of story are *The Song of Love Triumphant*, *The Dream* and *Klara Milich*.

In beauty and purity Turgenev's Russian is second only to Tolstoy's. For his technique of handling plot development he is much indebted to his friend Flaubert. His personal philosophy is very close to that of Schopenhauer, whom he greatly esteemed, and his pessimism comes through very clearly in his last work, *Poems in Prose*, which draws on Leopardi and Baudelaire. Yet, though almost all his works end sadly and in spite of all his pessimism, Turgenev still believes that salvation is somehow possible.

Ivan Goncharov (1812–91) wrote only three novels, increasing his depth with each one. In *A Common Story* he chronicles the familiar process by which a young romantic idealist is transformed into a matter-of-fact pragmatist. But, as the practical uncle who works the boy's transformation looks back over his own life, he is forced to concede that his own utilitarian principles are untenable and have actually ruined his life. By the end of the novel the heroes, whose spirited conversation makes up a great portion of the work, have nearly changed places.

The title character of Goncharov's second novel, *Oblomov*, is usually considered the incarnation of Russian inertia, the inability to act which leads to senseless vegetation. His significance, however, goes much deeper. He may be regarded as a continuation of the Onegin and Pechorin type: his is the tragedy of an individual stripped of all beliefs and ideals, isolated from human society and lacking even the strength to feel contempt for his environment. In other words, the ultimate in apathetic egoism results in hopeless boredom. But here too Goncharov is rather ambiguous. No matter how much Oblomov vegetates, he remains quite happy, and despite his inactivity he never loses the reader's sympathy. Moreover, there is no evidence in the text to prove that Goncharov meant his death to be anything but a perfectly acceptable end for a perfectly acceptable path to self-fulfilment. When seen from this angle, the practical world of bustle and success as represented by his hero's opposite, Stolz, no longer looks so rosy, and following his general policy, Goncharov refrains from giving any hint of a happy ending. The first three parts of the novel, which contain a certain amount of plot movement, are not as artistically successful as the last part, in which almost nothing happens. Goncharov's fastidious attention to detail and his sure sense of style generate tension, dynamism, even eroticism with what would seem to be the most paltry resources. For a striking example one has only to recall the role played by the elbows of Oblomov's would-be mistress.

The idea of boredom as the necessary consequence of the disintegration of all values, itself a result of the reign of reason, completely dominates Goncharov's outstanding novel, *The Precipice (Obryv)*. Here the hopelessly grey undercoat of existence without spiritual values, the senselessness of life for people with neither the strength nor the will to forge and follow their own ideals, becomes almost tangibly clear. The nihilists, who rejected all values, were a phenomenon very much to be reckoned with in Goncharov's day, and he felt their movement could only end in nothingness. Even the hero Raysky, who is not a nihilist, can be saved from demoralizing boredom only by believing in an ideal. In its ideology the novel displays a striking parallel to the writings of Pascal, who sees the only redemption from the pit of boredom in faith. But whereas Pascal preaches faith in God and Christ, Goncharov seeks salvation in faith in art. Exact and slightly ironical characterizations, a masterful treatment of plot development, but above all the description of passionate love superimposed on infinite boredom make *The Precipice* a powerful, artistic triumph whose significance has not yet been fully appreciated.

Besides several excellent critical essays Goncharov wrote an exquisitely witty and ironic description of a trip to Japan on a sailing vessel, *The Frigate Pallada*, in the years 1852–3. This original, spirited and exciting 'log' is almost unknown outside Russia.

Although the literary stature of Aleksey Pisemsky (1821–81) is much more modest, his novels (of which *A Thousand Souls* is the most important) are noteworthy for their rich plots and the uncompromisingly naturalistic means he uses to advance them. His fundamental premise is that men are base, and he illustrates it with alarming clarity. His writings are the clearest reflection in Russia of the French naturalist school. His comedies and tragedies sometimes carry this naturalistic tendency too far, but they succeed very well on the stage and display a compelling and logical development of action. The most successful of his plays is *A Hard Lot*, a tragedy dealing with love and serfdom.

Quite devoid of merit from an artistic point of view, the novels of Pavel Mel'nikov (1818–83), whose pseudonym was Andrey Pechersky, are nonetheless interesting for their descriptions of the life and customs of the Old Believers along the Volga. *In the Woods* and *On the Mountains* provide the folklorist with an imposing collection of highly instructive material. The life of the peasant was also central to the extensive work of

Dmitry Grigorovich (1822–99), who left behind several stories of village life.

The fifties and sixties witnessed a steady decline in the quality of literary criticism. Belinsky's seed was beginning to bear fruit, and Chernyshevsky, Dobrolyubov and Pisarev, and their followers, almost succeeded in stamping out what was left of a once flourishing poetry. Crass utilitarianism, 'social interests', 'demands of real life' and coarse materialism were declared the only acceptable criteria of literary values. This so-called 'enlightenment' suffered from an almost unbelievable dearth of ideas. The level of its ideological outlook is well illustrated by the notion that 'a real apple is better than a painted apple because it can be eaten'. This 'ideology' generated a psychosis which affected an extraordinary number of writers. Because aesthetic criteria were made to appear ridiculous and all attempts at evaluating a work's artistic merit were turned topsy-turvy, genuine talents were throttled and hopeless mediocrities praised to the skies. When Nikolay Chernyshevsky (1828–89) set about formulating his social and utopian theories in the novel *What is to be Done?* (*Chto delat'?*), the result was a lifeless abstraction devoid of the most basic artistic qualities. Yet it was read like the Bible.

It is only natural for lyric poetry to founder in such an atmosphere. Only one real poet was able to cope with the critics' insistence that poetry should be 'social'. Nikolay Nekrasov (1821–77) had no trouble in complying with their demands because they so deeply mirrored his own convictions. His main theme was the Russian people, for whose hard lot he felt genuine and profound compassion. His greatest work is the satiric social epic *Who Lives Well in Russia?* Although his verse is inspired by social problems, this compassion imbues it with a subjective, lyrical quality, a poetic impetus, a sort of kinetic energy which results in unmistakable originality. Nekrasov was unfortunately endowed with a prodigious facility for writing verse, and although most of his work is nothing more than rhymed journalism, his best poems are extremely effective. His language is very colourful, and he was not averse to dropping a coarse prosaism into the middle of a tender lyric passage. In this respect he greatly influenced the style of poetry which succeeded him.

Despite the intolerant condemnation of pure lyric poetry, several poets did make names for themselves. In fact, a new school was even established in the 1850s and 1860s and underwent a development parallel to that of the French Parnassians. Its members called for 'thinking in images' and worked in classical and nature themes which they found particularly suited to their ideas. In practice, however, their attempts rarely amounted to more than eclectic imitations, chiefly of Pushkin. The most important among them were Apollon Maykov, Nikolay Shcherbina and Lev Mey. Lermontov's subjective, highly emotional style found a

151

follower in Yakov Polonsky (1819–98), who was expert at turning everyday trifles into genuine lyric poetry. His now forgotten novels have the merit of combining psychological insight with captivating plots.

Two poets stand far above all the rest in the second half of the century: A. K. Tolstoy and Fet. Count Aleksey Tolstoy (1817–75) advocated art for art's sake with the greatest conviction. In form much of his verse may be classed among the most successful in the Russian language. His narrative poems such as *The Dragon* (in perfect and resounding *terza rima*) and *Ioann Damaskin* (which extols the divine calling of the true poet in rapturous verses) have genuine grandeur. As a writer of ballads – most of his themes come from early Russian history – he has no rival in Russia. Moreover, his lyrics are excellent (e.g. 'Amid the Noise of the Ball'), and his comic verse is unmatched in wit, irony, imagination and purity of form. His narrative poem *The Portrait* combines romanticism with irony, and the flawless stanzas of *Popov's Dream* deliver satirically pointed, yet humorous jabs at the political foibles of his time.

Aleksey Tolstoy and the brothers Aleksey and Vladimir Zhemchuzhnikov parodied the intellectual poverty of the period by composing devastating imitations of its literary banalities and publishing them under the name of a fictitious civil servant, Koz'ma Prutkov. The self-righteous insipidity of 'Prutkov's' poetry and prose – which for all their absurdities were most skilfully contrived – provides an excellent picture of literary conditions during a period quite hostile to poetry.

The established critics in this period could only scoff at a poet of the calibre of Afanasy Fet (1820–92), whose lyrics are distinguished by their mellifluous language. Purity of pitch and subtlety of instrumentation place them among the most musical poems in Russian literature; they are essentially delicate variations on three major themes: nature, love and death. Like Turgenev, Fet was much influenced by Schopenhauer, whose magnum opus, *Die Welt als Wille und Vorstellung*, he translated into Russian.

After the great comedies of Griboyedov and Gogol the Russian theatre produced few really good plays. Pisemsky has already been mentioned, as have Turgenev's attempts at psychological drama. The hopelessly pessimistic Aleksandr Sukhovo-Kobylin (1817–1903) wrote three biting satirical comedies in which clever scoundrels triumph over dull virtue. All three have won a permanent place in standard classical repertory. Aleksey Tolstoy's famous historical trilogy contains brilliant character studies (e.g. *Tsar' Fyodor*) and is written in faultless verse.

The theatre of the second half of the nineteenth century was dominated by Aleksandr Ostrovsky (1823–86). To this day he is the most often produced playwright in Russia. His plays, approximately forty in all, peculiar blendings of tragedy and comedy, are so intimately bound up with Russian social conditions that for all their excellent qualities it is unlikely they will ever attract much of an audience outside Russia. Ostrovsky usually focuses on the milieu and customs of Moscow merchants and petty officials, though he sometimes switches to their counterparts in the provinces. Without an understanding of the patriarchal tyranny, the incredibly limited intellectual horizon and the superstitious attachment to tradition which formed the outlook of this class, it is impossible to make much sense of the characters' behaviour. They parade before the spectator in all their petty narrow-mindedness and malice because Ostrovsky knows no compromises. Evil nearly always prevails. The fact that he can make his moral victory clear in the face of the grievous losses suffered by the good is proof of his poetic gift (cf. *The Forest*). His restriction of the action to a single milieu necessarily leads to a certain degree of monotony of plot, and it is hence not surprising to find in his plays quite a lot of uninteresting material, alongside such effective works as *The Thunderstorm* (*Groza*). All the plays, however, capture with complete accuracy the speech patterns of the social strata they treat.

While in the second half of the nineteenth century lyric poetry underwent a considerable decline, and dramatic writing did not develop as it might have, Russian prose could vaunt not only Turgenev and Goncharov, but also the powerful figures of L. Tolstoy and Dostoyevsky.

Lev Tolstoy (1828–1910) is Russia's greatest writer after Pushkin. His ability to turn fact into art and to raise reality to a permanently valid aesthetic order puts him on a par with the greatest authors. By intuitively selecting certain material and psychological details, he imparts his own brand of poetry to reality. He can also dredge up long-obscured memories, psychic associations and fleeting emotions to the surface of the consciousness – feelings which everyone recognizes as his own but which, seemingly unimportant, have hitherto lain dormant in the unconscious – and show how they belong to the most important components of the human personality. Tolstoy noticed what would otherwise have gone unobserved. He did not lay bare the world of the unconscious in the form of spontaneous revelations; rather, he conquered it gradually with the sharply analytic light of his intellect. A dyed-in-the-wool rationalist, he rejected all the accepted definitions of objects, events and emotions. By describing them as if they were occurring for the first time, he 'estranged' them from their usual contexts, thereby putting them in a new light. Because we see them much more sharply and distinctly than we normally see things, they take on an entirely new meaning.

Unlike most of his contemporaries, Tolstoy was more concerned with moral and psychological problems than with social issues. Society is a burden on the man seeking something higher; it hinders him from following the only true way – the way of the Good. Tolstoy describes the psyche of an individual in the process of breaking away from society. His characters usually belong to the aristocracy, the educated class, and his aim in subjecting them to such a minute dissection is to lay bare their vices. Tolstoy actively opposes civilization and culture; they falsify, debase, mechanize and complicate all direct communion. He opposes even art: no good can come of beauty which serves exclusively to veil the essence of life, i.e. the value of morality. It is not within the scope of this survey to analyse his philosophy. His entire literary output reveals an artist whose great objectivity overshadows all the philosopher's theories.

Tolstoy's earliest stories, *Childhood*, *Boyhood*, and *Youth*, bring together the main attributes characteristic of his technique: the transformation of the raw materials of everyday experience into an artistically viable form and the pinpointing and generalization of the most intimate feelings and perceptions. But while a poetic atmosphere of subtle hints predominates in the first story, the other two exhibit an increasing admixture of cold analysis. The Caucasian sketches and reports from the siege of Sevastopol' 'estrange' romantic war clichés. By replacing the officially accepted labels and catchwords for battle descriptions with his own style, rich in straightforward, unheroic detail, Tolstoy proved that only in retrospect does an agglomeration of repulsive particulars take on a romantically magnanimous aura. The same type of deromanticization of themes is evident in sketches such as *The Wood Felling*, which deals astringently with the supposed romanticism of life in the Caucasus. But false artificial romanticism is a product of 'civilized' man. In all Tolstoy's stories the uneducated man of the people stands high above the representatives of culture because his natural, unconscious humanity highlights the only worthwhile quality in man – the feeling of a deep bond with the whole of life. Impulses which he genuinely experiences, like courage in battle, represent for civilized man a complex pattern of the most diverse motives which have nothing in common with the names usually attached to them. All of his short novels and stories which appeared between 1856 and 1861 comment on this thesis in one way or another. The most important among them are *Three Deaths*, a novella which contrasts the natural, 'beautiful' death of a tree with the ugly, 'affected' death of a woman 'of culture' (the death of a peasant serving as an intermediate stage); the novel *Family Happiness*, which parodies the usual literary treatment of the love story, while analyzing various aspects of love (falling in love, flirting, love between man and wife, love between mother and child, etc.) in its own way; and *The Cossacks*, a story which examines the nature–culture opposition in all its trenchancy: there is no return to nature for the corrupt representative of culture, no matter how much he may desire it.

It was not until the novel *War and Peace* (*Voyna i mir*), however, that Tolstoy reached the peak of his faculties. All the achievements of his own special narrative technique, all the best qualities of his style are here raised to the highest power. The characters live uncannily genuine lives. The transformation of reality into high art is complete, without residue. *War and Peace* preaches a belief in natural, primordial life forces; there is no reason for man to hesitate or brood when all he has to do is trust that the Good resides in things themselves. The contrast between faith in life, triumph and eminence on the one hand and brooding capitulation and inconsequence on the other holds every bit for the private life of the individuals as for the events of world history.

War and Peace has been rightly described as a 'heroic idyll'; it is a basically optimistic epic of Russia's educated class. The action takes place during and shortly after the Napoleonic wars, between 1805 and 1820. Each of the novel's heroes, Pierre Bezukhov and Prince Andrey Bolkonsky, is seeking the meaning of life in his own way; each of them discovers it in the devotion of the self to the service of others. Long digressions treating topics in the philosophy of history underline the epic character and form which Tolstoy intentionally gave the novel. Although the ideological content of these passages may well be contested, it does counterbalance the ebullience of the plot development and is therefore justified as far as form is concerned. Among the many characters whose destinies meet and who influence one another throughout the novel, the figure of the heroine Natasha stands out clearly. Her unexpected development from the enchanting, ethereal creature she was as a girl to a rather narrow-minded, dutiful materfamilias is a model of character portrayal which has few equals in literature. The novel is full of episodes and scenes which are unforgettable in their subtle finish and yet never obstruct the main line of action. In *War and Peace* Tolstoy created one of the most impeccable works in the whole of world literature.

For his second great novel, *Anna Karenina*, Tolstoy reassembles his vast repertory of technical devices, but the mood they combine to produce is – in contrast to that of *War and Peace* – profoundly pessimistic. The tragic atmosphere of this incisive analysis of passion is clearly marked by Tolstoy's imminent internal transformation. While *War and Peace* with its faith-backed exuberance could still find a perpetual continuity in life, *Anna Karenina* ends with a desperate cry of anguish. It is a novel of manners set during the 1870s in the upper circles of Petersburg aristocracy. Tolstoy provides a picture of the time in all its diversity – statesmen, career officers, officials, lawyers, scholars and artists, all take an active part – but finds their aspirations and very existence basically senseless and doomed to failure. Both couples – Anna and Vronsky, Kitty and Levin (each couple serves to 'estrange' the other) – end in grief, the former cut off by the suicide of the brilliantly characterized Anna, the latter threatened by the disappointing tedium of day-to-day existence. Levin's 'resurrection' does not ring true.

Tolstoy meanwhile had begun to find life itself problematic, and in his search for its rational meaning he turned to a dogmatic, rationally constructed religion for a system corresponding to his inner experiences. He now denounced all art which does not serve moral ends and does not contribute toward the propagation and recognition of the ethical principles which he had come to accept as valid. Despite its clear design, however, the 'morally good' literature which marks his last period (1880–1910) is far from inferior to the literature of his great period and stands on the same high artistic level. Even the *Confession*, which he wrote to provide a theoretical foundation for his new theses, is an admirable work of art, and in his last great novel, *Resurrection*, characterization approaches the limits of precision. The novel's structure shows Tolstoy as a superb master: it parallels the crime and atonement of the hero Nekhlyudov with a many-faceted spiritual portrait of Russia and, figuratively, of life in general.

The same may be said of his short stories and novellas, of which *The Death of Ivan Il'ich* is probably the most powerful. Using a well-educated but by no means extraordinary man as his model, he demonstrates that of all the phenomena accompanying human existence only death has not succumbed to conventionalization: every man must face death on death's own terms. Because the egocentric 'civilized man' leads a life of conventions and has neither the inner harmony nor the faith to come to grips with death, he sees it as a mysterious concretization of horror. Not until the last moment when, despite all his suffering, the hero manages to forget about himself for an instant does he suddenly realize that death is deliverance from life. Tolstoy generates the same urgency when handling the problems of conventional marriage (in *The Kreutzer Sonata*) and conventional lovers (in *The Devil*). The long story *Khadzhi Murat* opposes natural freedom to the convention of the modern state. In *The Divine and the Human* he reduces the very idea of a state system to absurdity. What men hold sacred and inviolable is a system of fulsome self-imposed inanities, such as fatherland, church, or any of the conventions or institutions they imply. In simpler, more transparent form, Tolstoy's folk tales once again confirm his enormous creative genius.

Tolstoy was forever polishing his rich and clear style. For beauty and precision it is matched only by that of Pushkin and Turgenev. His language is the language of logic and thought, prose in contrast to poetry, composed in the pure Russian of the educated class, which lets no nuance pass unnoticed and unexploited. Tolstoy's naturalist tragedies and comedies, although not as powerful as the novels in all respects, derive their effect from the artless diction which captures speech styles of several levels of society with amazing accuracy.

Fyodor Dostoyevsky (1821–81) has been studied almost exclusively as a philosopher and religious thinker – even by literary historians. In fact his works do constitute a philosophical drama; his novels are philosophy in action, an exhibition of active evolving ideas. Although the ideological foundation for this monumental tragedy of ideas is the doctrine of the Orthodox Church, Dostoyevsky far oversteps its boundaries. His philosophy of compassion and humility, his doctrine of the responsibility of each for all, his attitude toward the beautiful as a great and perilous force, his solution to the problem of social conflict – all these make him a powerful and original thinker who does not hesitate to tackle an issue at its sorest point and refuses to gloss over the least detail in his search for absolute truths. His faith proceeds from moral necessities (although he prefers to classify his characters as humble or proud instead of the usual good–bad distinction) and has its roots in an ailing conscience grieved by the existence of evil in the world. He draws almost every realm of philosophy into his struggles, and the stimulus he has given philosophy is still growing and constantly developing new aspects (most recently in existentialism).

It is therefore all too easy to overlook Dostoyevsky's literary importance. And yet he introduced a new technique of novel-writing which made a clean break with the classical tradition of the novel. Instead of constructing a uniform, symmetrically balanced plot which seems to be carved from a single block, he consciously mixes the most incongruous, sometimes diametrically opposed elements, the better to subordinate them in the end to the unity of his philosophical system and to the stormy stream of the novel's action. Within the confines of one work he combines philosophical confessions and the adventures of a detective story, injects a religious drama into a melodrama and turns the narrative technique of the penny dreadful into a vehicle for the manifesto of a new mysticism. He intentionally rejects the canon of traditional aesthetics which calls for homogeneity at any price, and assembles a new art from dissimilar components. When Dostoyevsky joins apocalypse and journalism, there is no reason to invoke the 'Russian soul'; he is simply feeling his way toward new aesthetic laws. A comparison of novel-technique in world literature before and after Dostoyevsky will reveal a deep and wide schism which can only be attributed to his influence.

Dostoyevsky confronts the characters of his novels – absolute, 'prefabricated', almost blatant representatives of a well-defined and uncompromisingly complete *Weltanschauung* – with the turmoil of life and gives us a breathtaking account of how and why they falter or triumph. They are by no means specifically Russian; they are exaggerations of universal, human personalities, although of course in Russian dress. All excesses are meant to clarify philosophical and religious theories. Despite his keen, intuitive psychological insight Dostoyevsky attaches little importance to psychology – Tolstoy is the undisputed master of psychological analysis. Instead, he concentrated on man's ultimate concerns. History sees him as a great innovator in the technical fields, but his philosophical acumen takes him far beyond the boundaries of literary criticism.

Many of the motifs of his great novels are apparent in Dostoyevsky's earliest works. His first story, *Poor Folk*, is full of compassion for poor, downtrodden people who bear the noble seed of their divine origins deep within their being. In *The Double* he explores the psychological and metaphysical ramifications of one personality usurping the cosmic ground allotted to another in the social order of modern times, and traces the gradual development of insanity in his hero with life-like accuracy and tortuous penetration. In man mere intellect does not suffice; personality takes precedence. The exclusively 'intellectual' man or the member of an intellectually-oriented, ant-hill type political system becomes replaceable and loses his ground, his spiritual footing. At this early stage the 'cruel' Dostoyevsky has already reached one of his high points. Next, in *Mr Prokharchin* he portrays the death of a miser who suddenly becomes aware of his responsibility for his fellow men after losing contact with them early in life. In the 'sentimental novel' *White Nights*, on the other hand, he paints a sympathetic picture of an idealist who dreams his life away. In the novella *The Landlady* he raises the question of whether science, creative and intuitive forces, philosophy and poetry may be advantageously combined in one work. The demonic force of beauty unnerves the intellect and drives it towards crime with elemental power. Delirium's ominous twilight, psychotic murder with no basis in reality, the fateful stream of events, the ebb and flow of impulses in a sick brain, the breakdown and intimated regeneration of the hero – all these are seeds from which the rich visions of his later work were to spring.

Ten years of silence followed (1849–59) during which Dostoyevsky descended into the depths of human suffering. The most extreme sensations man can be subjected to were piled in heavy layers onto his already pathologically sensitive disposition. *Notes from the House of the Dead*, a reworking of impressions from his life in prison, gives at least some idea of the horrors he experienced. Yet the more hopeless and repulsive the human condition appeared to him, the more clearly did he feel that love of Christ as preached in the Gospel left the way to salvation wide open – even for the last among men. *Notes from the Underground* polemicizes with the socialist theories of his youth. In place of the proposition that happiness can be organized, Dostoyevsky proclaims absolute, anarchistic freedom of the human will – a transitional phase in his development, which soon becomes inseparably bound with the love of Christ, and in this new form serves as the cornerstone of his views of life.

Crime and Punishment (*Prestupleniye i nakazaniye*), the first of Dostoyevsky's great novels, illustrates what happens when the forces of self-will and love clash within an individual. Raskol'nikov, his hero, founders because, even while believing himself a superman and testing his ability for titanic deeds by committing murder, he cannot prevent himself from having compassion for the insulted and the injured or suffering along with the underprivileged and enslaved. Similarly, *The Idiot* is an attempt to transplant the ideally good man, as Dostoyevsky saw him, into contemporary society. He founders because the absolute good is an inhuman property which can only lead to one-sidedness, to a break with the inherently human qualities Dostoyevsky fought for.

Dostoyevsky's last three novels – *The Possessed* (*Besy*), *A Raw Youth* and *The Brothers Karamazov* – are actually fragmentary studies for a broadly conceived but never completed work dealing with atheism. The fact that they are nonetheless self-contained organic works of art is yet another proof of the prodigious artistic vigour of their creator. These novels raised the issues with which Dostoyevsky was ultimately concerned: man's proper relationship to God and to his fellow men, and the individual's proper relationship to society. He reaches the peak of his descriptive faculties in 'The Grand Inquisitor', a chapter from *The Brothers Karamazov*, which may well be the most valid representation of the figure of Christ in the whole of world art. Dostoyevsky's ultimate goal is the unification of all humanity in Christ's love. To attain it, he takes his readers through all the agonies of the human condition.

Only time will tell whether the formal side of his novels will prove durable. In comparison with the other great novelists of his time, Dostoyevsky's language is choppy and unkempt, but since its very awkwardness helps to emphasize the powerfully primordial, incomplete quality of his concepts, it is probably the only language suitable to him. His breathless, yet involved and extraordinarily nuanced jargon falls together with the dynamic, driving action to form an organic whole. The novels are full of dialogues which sometimes reduce the role of the narrator to little more than setting the scene with the economy typical of stage directions. The speeches of his protagonists bring to life the ideas which obsess them. Cut off from the agitated human voice delivering them, they would lose much of their thrust.

Nikolay Leskov (1831–95), a peerless *raconteur*, had a never-ending supply of subject matter and a vast collection of technical resources at his command. His novella *The Enchanted Wanderer* is so rich in anecdotes worthy of further development that it could easily be broken up into twenty short stories. Leskov is particularly skilful in his use of the *skaz* technique: he sets up a fictional narrator whose particular way of speaking (*skaz*) makes his presence distinctly felt throughout the work. This narrator addresses an imaginary group of listeners as well as the reader and therefore enjoys 'twice the audience' of a normal storyteller. Because most of Leskov's narrators are illiterate or at best semi-educated, the *skaz* includes many dialect forms and folk etymologies. Translations are all but impossible. Leskov's images and characters are penetrating. He wrote both tragic and humorous stories which often display more than a touch of satire and always capture the Russian way of life (and its most disreputable representatives) with loving accuracy. Of his novels only *Cathedral Folk* deserves mention; the rest are tendentious and quite uninspired. Leskov was especially interested in the life of the clergy. He frequently uses ecclesiastical themes in his novellas (e.g. the masterly *Sealed Angel*) and among his late stories there are impressive and absorbing paraphrases of saints' lives. The first request he makes of his narrators is that they should hold the reader's attention. To achieve this end he sometimes overloads them with entertaining material and is prone to accumulate details for their own sake. Very few of his novellas are entirely free from stylistic mannerisms. He tends to squeeze too many anecdotes into the framework of a single story and succumbs too easily to prolixity; nor is his feeling for form very highly developed. These qualifications hold only for a part of his work, however, and several of his stories (e.g. *A Lady Macbeth of Misensk*, *The Toupee Artist*) are masterpieces in every respect.

The satirist Mikhail Saltykov-Shchedrin (1826–89), one of Russia's most remarkable prose writers, was very popular in the seventies. Much of his audience misunderstood (and still misunderstands) the ideological basis of his works, which is incontestably Christian rather than socialist or communist. From the standpoint of the true Christian he lashes out at social conditions in the Russia of his time. His satires are exceptionally biting. No matter what fantastic or absurd heights his exaggerations reach, they never lose touch with reality. It is this close contact with the ordinary world that makes them so ominously effective. They are so dependent on the trends of the day, however, that they can scarcely be read at present without the aid of a running commentary, and many of his writings border on journalism. His best known work is *The Story of a City*, a satire *à clef* in which he rewrites the history of Russia and her rulers on a 'municipal' scale with pitiless scorn and an admirable talent for hitting the nail on the head. Saltykov's sole novel, *The Golovlyov Family*, is a work of great literary distinction. In macabre tones it depicts the fall and degeneration of a family of landowners. It is probably the most morose work in all Russian literature. Saltykov describes men who have lost all human values: the main character (whose nickname, Iudushka, means 'little Judas') can compete with the darkest incarnations of depravity in world literature. Saltykov brings his social message across by demonstrating the bestiality and spiritual poverty of 'civilized' serf owners. The novel's unity of composition and its characters who always ring true have ensured for it a notable place in Russian literature.

The sketches of Gleb Uspensky (1843–1902), even more closely linked to day-to-day events, have suffered from age more obviously than Saltykov's satires. Uspensky is still remembered, however, for the humour and understanding he brings to his descriptions of life among the provincial proletariat and the peasants. By refraining from idealizing them, he avoids a common failing of the time.

In contrast to the voluminous prose epics of Tolstoy and Dostoyevsky, whose followers produced long-winded, minutely detailed imitations in the naturalist vein, a number of writers who saw much greater possibilities in the concentrated form of the short story began publishing during the seventies and eighties. Vsevolod Garshin (1855–88) depicts man's inner world and then confronts him with crass reality. His first novella, *Four Days*, is the inner monologue of a soldier who has just lain four days beside the rotting corpse of an enemy he has killed. All Garshin's stories deal with mental and physical suffering and with its impact on characters of an almost morbidly receptive nature. Insanity, murder, suicide and disease are his subject matter, and he portrays them all masterfully with stark naturalism. And yet one feels his deep compassion, the torment which plagued him in the face of the incurable ills of the world. His symbolic stories such as *Attalea Princeps* and *What Never Was* are pervaded with an enchanting lyrical irony. An early death put an end to the growth promised by his last stories (e.g. *Nadezhda Nikolayevna*) and war memoirs.

In form and content he is the forerunner of Anton Chekhov (1860–1904), one of the greatest names in Russian literature. Chekhov's medical practice laid bare life's terror, nature's horrors and man's defencelessness in all their intensity. He sees man as nothing more than a sick animal. Life's nobility, man's dignity are illusions. Life is senseless, colourless, man is malicious and moronic. People basically do not understand each other. Nor do they see that their endeavours bear none of the fruits they had anticipated. One ray of hope does break through his gloomy picture: somewhere deep within every man the need for actively loving his neighbour lies concealed. Man naturally strives for perfection. He knows about the Good and instinctively feels that this Good lies in renouncing the self. He is constantly working towards a better future, even though he often admits that it will not be for him. For all life's cruelty man has demonstrated such humility and magnanimity that his inborn predatory nature is vindicated in advance by his capacity for heroic renunciation. Chekhov the atheist thus turns out to be one of the most Christian of writers. His greatness lies in his love for man, which overcomes loathing.

From his earliest humorous sketches, the first pieces he ever wrote, it is clear that precision and succinctness of expression are essential qualities of his art. He compresses a cleverly conceived anecdote into as few words as possible and clinches it with an effective and often unexpected punch line. But behind each joke stands a shadow of awareness that someone has been hurt by it, that one or another of the participants is suffering – even if needlessly or in jest. One wonders about the ways of a world which allows such situations to come about. In these early sketches Chekhov is more sharply critical and much less forgiving than he is in his later, more serious works. Although he had an unerring sense of the comical side of life, humour implies a realization of the senselessness of existence which can all too easily turn laughter into tears. And so we have the paradox that Chekhov, perhaps the most humorous of all Russian writers, also wrote the most tragic stories that Russian literature has known. His novellas record life's endless stream of woe and the hope for a better future in great resonant words whose beauty offers consolation. The literary historian Leonid Grossman wrote that Chekhov's language seems like a flood of tears during the first wave of grief: although painful, it somehow unburdens the soul, numbs the sorrow and seeks reconciliation with the depths of misery.

It is difficult to choose the best from among the wealth of Chekhov's stories. Each one is a miniature masterpiece in its own way. The longer works, such as *The Steppe*, *My Life*, or *The Duel*, keep their hold on the reader from the first word to the last. They envelop him in a mood of sweet depression and enchant him with their wistfulness. Yet in their own curious way they deal with all life's sharpest conflicts. Chekhov's main characteristic is a special brand of melancholia with a slight admixture of irony. It is a gentle, delicate melancholy, but it is never monotonous. The basic tone of his moods is grey, but a grey with an amazingly wide range of shades which shows off other colours to great advantage. His stories are usually put together with small, precise strokes, from details drawn from the everyday life or the psyche of his characters. At first they may seem insignificant as individual strokes, but in their ensemble they create a meticulously premeditated atmosphere which is much more effective and instructive in the ethical sense that any openly tendentious style could possibly be. His narrative technique and his general style might be compared to impressionism in painting. His choice of strokes is carefully thought out and corresponds exactly to the content of the stories. For example, to illustrate his premise that hopes are never fulfilled, that things we gear our whole lives to are no longer what they seemed to be when we started out to work for them (even if they eventually become reality), Chekhov colours his stories with the frequent use of passive constructions and impersonal expressions such as 'it seemed', 'it was as if', etc.

Following very much the tenor of the stories, Chekhov's plays are largely undramatic and almost without action. All they seem to offer is mood and superficial details. Yet it is impossible to remain unmoved in the presence of the magic which emanates from them. Grief, depression and despair are transmuted by the author's artistic energy into a sweet melancholy to which it is only too pleasant to yield. Chekhov raises this melancholy to a kind of Platonic idea which his characters then contemplate, whether they wish to or not. The recurring summons to work (the only way out of their hopeless melancholy) is insufficient to tear either the characters or the audience away from the fascinating spell of Chekhov's atmosphere. Every role in these plays has great possibilities because every character is alive, even if his existence is limited to several lines. The best known are *The Seagull (Chayka)*, *Uncle Vanya (Dyadya Vanya)*, *The Three Sisters (Tri sestry)* and *The Cherry Orchard (Vishnyovyy sad)*. The world-famous Moscow Art Theatre acquired its reputation from Stanislavsky's interpretations of these plays.

Vladimir Korolenko (1853–1921) expressed a personal ideology opposed to Chekhov's. His works are optimistic, infused with a belief in the good in man. For Korolenko evil is a result of social inequality. His novellas and sketches are characterized by vivid nature descriptions and an ability to capture moods in nature which is reminiscent of Turgenev. A profound sense of poetry and a delicate lyricism produce a euphonious rhythm in his prose; it consciously avoids sharp accents. He also has a fine sense of humour, free of any intention to satirize or offend. The effectiveness of his character portrayals depends on psychological depth, persuasive power and a curiously muted technique which tends to imply rather than state outright. Novellas like *Makar's Dream*, *In Bad Company* and *The Forest Rustles* are clear examples of how he blends these qualities. His memoirs, *The Story of My Contemporary*, are witty and in some ways recall Herzen's great achievement in this genre.

THE AGE OF SYMBOLISM

Towards the end of the century there was an upsurge of the long-neglected lyric, and with the poets of the symbolist movement Russian poetry reached new heights.

An early attempt to break with the still binding romantic conventions was made by Konstantin Sluchevsky (1837–1904), who tried to open poetry to new subjects. His images are sometimes highly original and effective (e.g. 'After an Execution in Geneva'), but his skill as a technician is not always on the level of his gifted and poetic imagination.

Sergey Andreyevsky (1847–1919), an excellent literary critic who also wrote well-formed, melancholic poems, and whose prose masterpiece *The Book on Death* has remained almost unknown despite its artistic and philosophical import, called 'beauty and melancholy' the main themes of Russian pre-symbolist poetry. The pre-symbolists were second-rate poets, but their popularity was enormous. The best known are Semyon Nadson, Aleksey Apukhtin, Arseny Golenishchev-Kutuzov (who was strongly influenced by Buddhist philosophy), Konstantin Fofanov and Mirra Lokhvitskaya.

The most influential forerunner of symbolism was the religious philosopher and poet Vladimir Solov'yov (1853–1900). His love lyrics, infused with mystic motifs, combine warm feeling with striking poetic images and a beautifully rhythmic, flowing line. For Solov'yov, Sophia – God's wisdom personified as the feminine element of the Trinity – was an object of erotic worship. Philosophy and love merge into a single emotion, and it is often difficult to tell when his poems lean towards the mystical and when they express a more terrestrial yearning. His mysticism was combined with a fine sense of humour. His sparkling nonsense verses, parodies and comic poems are in no way inferior to the works of Koz'ma Prutkov. Sometimes Solov'yov even mixes the two genres. The mystical poem *Three Encounters* and the comic piece *The White Lily* illustrate the success of this unusual technique. Solov'yov was also a distinguished writer of prose. His *Three Conversations* on the theme of evil in the world are of lasting literary worth, remarkable for their power of language and subtlety of characterization, their wit and intellectual penetration.

Russian symbolism arose as a reaction to the hostility which poetry encountered throughout the second half of the century when 'reality' was considered the be-all and end-all of literature. Symbolism saw reality merely as a symbol of something else, something more real which lay behind it. For Russians symbolism was not only an aesthetic theory as it had been in France, but a personal ideology. For inspiration and technique it depended partly on Russian poets such as Boratynsky and Tyutchev and partly on the French symbolist movement. Baudelaire's poem 'Correspondances' became the watchword of the Russian movement's early stages. The older school, headed by Valery Bryusov, was strongly influenced by the French and adhered strictly to their aesthetic criteria. The younger school – Vyacheslav Ivanov and Blok in particular – developed its own philosophy with a decidedly mystical character. But for all symbolists art was divine and self-sufficient, and poets were the priests of its mysteries. The very sound of words, the mood created by their form began to take on as much importance as their meaning. Occasionally they became even more important. The resulting logical obscurity was mitigated by the poetic fluidity of the whole and by the music of the line, which communicated to the sensitive reader more than simple reason. To abandon control by the intellect was a dangerous step, and only the greatest of the symbolists succeeded in creating artistically perfect poetry. But even they went for long periods without true inspiration, and many poets never passed the 'harmonious but empty' stage. Almost all the Russian symbolists were also distinguished masters of prose and literary criticism.

Valery Bryusov (1873–1924) was the theoretician of the older school of symbolists. He preferred classical motifs to themes from the Russia of his time and elaborated them in chiselled phrases and impeccable form. His sonnets are formally close to perfection. He turned to more contemporary subjects for his lyric poetry, and certain of his limitations became more apparent here. A notable experimentalist and a skilled craftsman in the workings of language, he explored a good many poetic possibilities without claiming for them the distinction of great poetry. The journal he edited, *The Scales* (*Vesy*), was an effective organ for the promotion of symbolism. His brilliantly conceived first novel, *The Fiery Angel*, is set in sixteenth-century Germany and deals with demonology. It achieves its effectiveness by the combination of a calm chronicle report and scenes of fiery passions and thrilling action. His second novel, *The Altar of Victory*, is set during Rome's decline and is far superior to the better-known historical novels of Dmitry Merezhkovsky (1865–1941), whose *Leonardo da Vinci* was once quite popular in Europe and America. Merezhkovsky was on close terms with the symbolists; it was he who first proposed that French symbolist poetry serve as a model for the revival of the Russian lyric. He evolved a curious mystical philosophy which equated the Greek and Roman world with the body and Christianity with the spirit, and saw in this antithesis the main source of strife in the world. All his writings – novels, plays and criticism (the study of Tolstoy and Dostoyevsky is his most important critical work) – are meant to illustrate this philosophy.

Most of the poetry of Konstantin Bal'mont (1867–1943) offers little besides beautiful sounds and a pompous pretence at profundity. Some of his poems, however, especially those written towards the beginning of his career, are of real value, and the progress he made towards a more supple poetic language, along with his talent for composing melodious verse, should not be overlooked.

Fyodor Sologub (1863–1927), on the other hand, is an outstanding poet and novelist. His lyric poetry is the expression of a self-contained dualistic

view of the world which posits two realities: that of the good and beautiful and that of evil. The former is the realm of death, the latter the realm
of life in all its forms. Sologub expresses this idea and its many ramifications in a flowing classical line of the utmost harmony and purity. The
careful finish of his philosophical system calls for great precision in
choosing words; words have a meaning beyond their usual one, a special
meaning which follows from the poet's philosophy. In this respect Sologub
is a pure symbolist. He was also influenced by Schopenhauer and found
sensual love the most important as well as the vilest source of evil in the
world. In describing it, he is always on the verge of slipping into overdone
eroticism, and this tendency is probably the only blemish on his otherwise
delicately balanced poetry.

Sologub was also a master of prose, and wrote one of the outstanding
modern Russian novels, *The Petty Devil*. Life in a Russian provincial
town here becomes a symbol of life as such. For all its repulsiveness it is
nonetheless a convincing work of art; all the characters have an inner
veracity, and the portrayal of the main character's fast-progressing
paranoia is extraordinary. Sologub's complex trilogy *A Legend in the
Making* is surely one of the most curious works in Russian literature.
With astonishing fantasy and its own brand of stylistic magic this novel
sets out to create a modern mythology.

A distinguished Russian poetess, Zinaida Gippius (1869–1945),
expressed her ideas in almost tangible form. Her intellectual poetry is
passionate; her abstractions live. Her longing for faith is subject to tormented scepticism, and she gives penetrating accounts of their battle with
one another. Her later political poems are also significant. Her poetry is
distinguished by its highly original approach to composition and verse
technique. She also wrote novels, plays and witty literary essays.

The most outstanding poet of the older school of symbolism is
Innokenty Annensky (1856–1909). His poetry is closely related to that of
the French *décadence*, and comparable to that of Verlaine and Mallarmé,
its greatest representatives. He combines a mastery of all the devices of
the French 'decadents' with an intimate familiarity with the typical
themes of Russian literature. Most of his poems are concise statements of
an overpowering fear of life and death and of the redemptive qualities of
beauty (which cannot, however, redeem this world). Their unusual
symbolism is inexhaustible, unpredictable and compelling. Although
deceptively simple, each poem is structured into a carefully conceived
organism capable of conveying messages of great suggestive force.
Annensky's lyrics have greatly influenced a number of post-symbolist
poets, and his influence today surpasses that of Blok.

In addition to lyric poetry Annensky wrote four tragedies which handle
classical themes with the most refined resources of modern psychology

and a rich, nuanced use of language. Although they are practically unknown, they belong to the outstanding achievements of Russian drama.
He also wrote two volumes of essays in which various phenomena of
European and Russian literature are viewed through the prism of his
rather wilful personality.

The poets of the older school of Russian symbolism saw in art the
highest degree of accomplishment man may attain. The younger school,
while never contesting art's significance, felt it more as a first step to
higher regions whose secrets would be revealed through religion,
mysticism, ethics or even rationalism, depending on the intentions of the
poet. The reaction against symbolism, which became evident in 1909,
focused mainly on this philosophical and religious subspecies of the
movement.

The mystical tendency in symbolism found its greatest representative in
Vyacheslav Ivanov (1866–1949). For him writing poetry is creating
myths patterned after models from times long past which the poet carries
in his soul. Reality fuses with the beyond in mystical ethos, and their
complex correspondences may be unravelled only by artistic inspiration.
Ivanov's teaching, which in essence claims that true religion will unite all
religions, had considerable influence on his symbolist contemporaries.

Aleksandr Blok (1880–1921) is considered the most distinguished poet
of Russian symbolism; however, he himself stated repeatedly that his
poetry could be truly understood only by those able to enter into his
mystical experiences. Whoever does not partake of this congruity of
sensation and mood will respond to little more than their word music.
Blok's mystical experiences have their origin in Solov'yov, but develop
into a curious kind of mystical realism which, like realistic irony in
general, became – together with a soft romantic lyricism – the most
characteristic feature of his poetry. Like Solov'yov, he parodies, especially
in his plays, his own mystical experience. His ideal, 'the Beautiful Lady',
gradually became a symbol of Russia, which his passionate love lyrics
describe in all its ugliness. Blok's role in the development of the formal
aspects of Russian poetry is important. He makes extensive use of in-
exact rhyme, thereby opening new possibilities of expression. He often
counts stressed syllables only, thereby disrupting the 'syllabic-accentual'
metre. The smooth flow of his vowel harmony is quite intoxicating. He is
also a master of poetic rhythm. His celebrated poem *The Twelve*,
although in content and intent an ambiguous and rather forbidding work,
derives a good deal of poetic thrust from his skilful rhythmic alternations.
Blok is a typical representative of his time, a period of surfeited
pessimism and vague hopes for the future which sought for an outlet in
hazy mysticism or political manifestos.

The poetry of Andrey Bely (1880–1934) lacks the intense passion of

167

Blok's finest work. He too combines a mystical quest – which led him to Rudolf Steiner's anthroposophy – with deep pessimism, which often ends in vicious cynicism. Too many of his poems are experiments in verse technique, and his prose is far more important. Bely's 'ornamental style' is not without its influence even today. Instead of merely imitating the way Gogol or Leskov use the *skaz* technique, he expanded it to suit his own purpose. He also developed the complex theory of text instrumentation, which plays on the emotional reactions evoked by consonantal sounds. In his novel *Petersburg* the real and the unreal, the logical and the metaphorical, the comic and the tragic levels constantly glide in and out of one another. To recreate the atmosphere during the hours preceding the explosion of a time bomb, Bely invents a technique which occasionally anticipates Joyce's *Ulysses*. The similarities between them become even clearer in *Kotik Letayev*, in which Bely records the stream of consciousness of a child from the time its faculties of perception begin to grow. His memoirs make interesting reading, despite their mannered style, for their glittering, if not always reliable, portraits of well-known contemporaries.

During the same period there were a number of writers who had nothing in common with the symbolists and who concentrated entirely on prose. Their short stories and plays enjoyed great popularity (seldom justified in terms of their artistry), which was largely due to their exploitation of racy or other 'interesting' themes (executions and floggings, burials, etc.) and facile liberalism. Sensuality is their dominant motif; writers of this period either preached unbounded amorality and refused to curb their obsessions on principle, or interpreted the sex drive (following Schopenhauer's example) as the root of all evil, going to great lengths to describe its ill effects in lurid detail, ostensibly to discourage their readers from indulging in these excesses.

The most important member of this group was Maksim Gor'ky (1868–1936). He began his literary career with novellas which combined coarse naturalism with sensitive romanticism and contained scenes of strong, fresh vitality and genuine originality (*Makar Chudra, Mal'va, Chelkash*). He then began to involve his characters in arguments over the 'meaning of life', and since he was unable to reconcile his own quite chaotic, pessimistic views with the optimism required of him as an exponent of the rising communist movement – even though he tried very hard to accept that optimism – his 'philosophy' lacks the power of his convictions and therefore falls flat. His novels can hardly be regarded as successful despite many positive qualities (which are usually concentrated in the first few pages). They are especially weak in structure and reach their lowest ebb when political considerations dominate artistic formulation (as is the case in the tiresome, tasteless novel *The Mother*). Gor'ky's plays are weak imitations of Chekhov which lack even a trace of the latter's inner dynamism. However, the first two volumes of his fictionalized autobiography, *Childhood* and *In the World*, with their unforgettable portraits, are excellent. His diary and his reminiscences of Tolstoy and Leonid Andreyev are extremely interesting and on a very high artistic level.

Leonid Andreyev (1871–1919), an author very well known in his time, provides an illuminating example of what happens to art when great talent and a striking lack of taste come together in one person. All values are relative. The only reality is death. In a stale, overtly rhetorical style Andreyev accumulates example after repulsive example to drive home his point. The subject-matter and the angle from which he examines it demonstrate great powers of creative imagination, but the results defy description. While several of the novellas may be read without too much distaste, the plays – the philosophical *The Life of Man*, for example, was an enormous success – are deadly dull.

Mikhail Artsybashev (1878–1927), another member of the school of bad taste, was much less gifted than Andreyev. His novel *Sanin*, which preached that love is a fiction and that everyone should abandon himself unrestrainedly to his sexual impulses, enjoyed a success which is hardly comprehensible from today's standpoint. The novels and novellas of Aleksandr Kuprin (1870–1938) were also very successful. His descriptions of barracks existence are lifelike, but his later works sometimes depend on rather cheap effects.

Amidst these escapades in the name of originality Ivan Bunin (1870–1953) maintained the tradition of Turgenev, Goncharov, Tolstoy and Chekhov. His superb poems, and especially the highly wrought prose of his novels and novellas, proved that it was not impossible to treat social, metaphysical and sexual problems in all candour without plunging into bathos as long as artistic ends remained paramount. Bunin concentrates on Russia's village and provincial life, but despite his naturalist descriptions he maintains a classically compelling form. The masterly novella *The Gentleman from San Francisco* has the texture of heavy, rich brocade. It relates how civilization's most exquisite refinements crumble to dust before the hegemony of death. Bunin's work – the best of it was written in emigration – brings a great tradition to a noble end. He is the last champion of a style which retained its coherence from the time of Pushkin and, even with the stylistic elements introduced by Gogol, preserved its classical form.

Aleksey Remizov (1877–1957) developed the *skaz* technique of individualized speech to the utmost. Very early in his career he became addicted to pose and to virtuoso craftsmanship which (when combined with his unclear mysticism) produce a disagreeable impression. Of his

169

voluminous writings the most successful are the legends, which re-create the old Russian style in colloquial everyday language. His *Dreams*, of greater poetic value, are nothing more than re-tellings of real dreams which have some kind of symbolic meaning – even if it is not the kind which can be put into words.

Although Vasily Rozanov (1856–1919) is more of a thinker and journalist than a literary figure, he had a considerable influence on the writers of his generation. His aphorisms were sometimes brilliant, sometimes catchpenny, but always stylistically original. Most of them deal with the relationship between sexuality and religion or try to reconcile Nietzsche's ideas with Russian orthodoxy. The effectiveness of his intimate style is due to his startling formulations, unusual nature descriptions and striking character portraits.

Mikhail Kuzmin (1875–1936) occupies a special position very close to the symbolists on account of his exquisitely stylized prose. Prose never entered into the elaborate theories which the symbolists constructed, and it soon became normal for prose writers to imitate styles from the past so as to transmit to their medium the distinctive tone of the lyric with a wide range of artistic devices. Bryusov's novels are successful attempts at prose of this kind. Kuzmin carried this technique still further. He imitates the styles of the Greek Alexandrian school and of the eighteenth century, imbuing them with religious and ritual-bound sympathies. Frivolous sensuality and religious devotion lend to his prose and artistic verse a certain piquant flavour. His novels of contemporary life – *The Quiet Guard* is probably the most important – are marked by a subtle feeling for characterization, a somewhat 'perverse' choice of theme (consistently handled with finesse) and cleverly stylized diction. His novellas are gems of delicately chased structure.

In his poetry too Kuzmin soon made a conscious break with symbolism to lay the foundations of a new school of poetry which has come to be known as 'acmeism'. Its votaries emphasized above all the tangible nature of the world. Acmeism differs from symbolism in that it believes in the autonomy and the value of this world and of its forms; things are beautiful for their own sake, not because they symbolize abstract, mystical ideas. Kuzmin consciously directs his poetry towards the beautiful minutiae of this richly variegated life. His poetic diction retained its precise elegance even after he turned to mystical gnosticism in his later volumes.

No matter how vehemently the acmeists insisted on the validity of the 'here and now', it is clear that they learned much from the symbolist experience. One might almost say that by ruling out the beyond, they perceived correspondences in this world all the more sharply – between reality and the psyche, for example. One of the most enthusiastic acmeist poets was Nikolay Gumilyov (1886–1921), who traced his affinities back to the Parnassians, the forerunners of French symbolism. He shares their predilection for the exotic, for precise images of the distant past, but adds to it an admiration for the superman type (surely under Nietzsche's influence). His finely nuanced verse displays amazing technical skill and still holds a fascination for younger poets. Gumilyov also wrote brilliant theoretical expositions of the acmeist position.

But the greatest of the acmeist poets is undoubtedly Osip Mandel'shtam (1891–1938). In Mandel'shtam's verse lofty diction acts as a catalyst for the poeticization of colloquial diction. Striking juxtapositions of staid archaism and irreverent vulgarism, elevated rhetoric and down-to-earth vernacular give it a well-burnished formal lacquer. For thematic material Mandel'shtam looks mainly to European literature, and to Mediterranean and western culture (Greece, Rome, Byzantium, the middle ages). His second volume, *Tristia*, introduced impressionistic, expressionistic and even surrealistic elements into the laconic clarity of his first, *Stone*. Like Gumilyov, Mandel'shtam was an outstanding theoretician. They both published in the acmeists' journal *Apollon* (1909–17).

Anna Akhmatova (1889–1966) is chiefly known for her short poems which capture a world of intimate feelings and thoughts with the utmost terseness. Although she almost never provides more than hints or outward signs of her inner life, they clearly reflect a background of tumult and passion. In the ballad *The Grey-eyed King*, for example, a complex love drama is revealed in half-statements. At first Akhmatova wrote almost exclusively about woman's love. She later widened her scope to include poetry of a religious and prophetic nature which also bears on political events. Maksimilian Voloshin was a less important representative of the same school.

Alongside the west-European-oriented acmeists there was another less consequential movement contending for the honour of replacing symbolism. Its members wrote poetry based on Russian folk themes in folk song and epic rhythms. After Sergey Gorodetsky (1844–1967), who founded the movement, its most important adherents were Nikolay Klyuyev (1887–1937) – whose florid 'peasant poetry', heavily influenced by symbolism, preached a Russian heathen folk mysticism – and Sergey Yesenin (1895–1925). Yesenin was a talented poet who sang the praises of the Russian soil and the Russian village in fresh verses redolent of true folk songs. Outrageous verve alternates with deep melancholy in his city poems, which despite their coarseness reveal a forceful authenticity of feeling. Yesenin's poetry is a vital, convincing reflection of the spirit of the Russian people vacillating from one extreme to the other under the pressures of the time.

Acmeism was soon superseded by futurism, a movement which set out

171

to effect a complete break with all poetic conventions of the past. It aimed more particularly at revising the vocabulary of poetry. In futurism the poet discards the priesthood of the symbolists to become an artisan whose task it is to lift his craft out of the complex of ideas which used to be accepted as poetry and to free it from all the emotional associations of the then prevalent poetic diction. Although this sort of revolutionary action usually infuses poetry with new stimuli, it must be followed by the appearance of a great poet able to bring about a fruitful synthesis.

Futurism was sponsored by Viktor Khlebnikov (1885–1922), who felt that each word had its own life and evolved according to its own set of laws. He endeavoured to create a world of new words. In his view, words beginning with the same consonant are united by a common basic concept; they tend towards a common point in the consciousness. By accepting these or similar premises, a poet limits himself to wordplay, which Khlebnikov called 'metalogical' (*zaumnyy*) poetry; Khlebnikov's work must be valued chiefly for its virtuosity and for the role it played in creating a new poetic language for future poets. His non-experimental verse shows evidence of great poetic talent.

Futurism's most famous representative is Vladimir Mayakovsky (1893–1930). He too was an ingenious experimentalist, but whereas Khlebnikov worked with vocabulary, Mayakovsky experimented primarily with rhythm and rhyme. The majority of his poems consist of political propaganda and satire. He is particularly skilful at updating poetic figures, e.g. the highly original 'realization of metaphor and hyperbole', which clothes baroque images like the flaming heart in modern dress by describing in minute detail a modern fire engine hard at work extinguishing a flaming heart. Mayakovsky's poetry is shrill, oratorical, sensational and often vindictive. He went further than Blok in his technical innovations and had a decisive influence on all the important poets who followed him. To record in print the way he wanted his poems declaimed, he broke up his verses into echelonned lines – with the result that many of his poems resemble staircases, an affectation which many Soviet poets were quick to adopt. In his intimate love lyrics Mayakovsky proved himself a great poet. The frantic shrieks of his public poetry may well be a reaction to inner resistance.

Boris Pasternak (1890–1960) was also for a time a futurist, although his poems were never patterned after any ready-made prototype. His poetry has an inner mellifluence which everyday expressions only serve to heighten. His metres are exact, and the structure of his poems is transparently clear. Because the acuteness and originality of his vision tend to make his images seem odd at first, his poetry is not easily comprehensible. But once the reader has penetrated his world, he will be amply rewarded. Profundity of thought and freshness of expression are the hallmark of his lyric poetry. Condemned to a long silence by conditions in Russia, he turned to translating and reaffirmed his great mastery of language in versions of many Shakespeare tragedies and of Goethe's *Faust*, to mention only his most striking achievements.

Futurism spawned a minor movement called egofuturism, which was led by Igor' Severyanin (1887–1941). The 'ego' in egofuturism is meant to indicate the absolute originality of the poetry of the future. Severyanin deals in the rather cheap daydreams of the man in the street – from ice-cream to private aeroplanes. Yet he has his own type of charm; even though he is mostly after effects, the effects he devises are quite successful. Their lack of variation and breadth, however, exclude many from the realm of serious poetry.

GUIDE TO FURTHER READING

GENERAL WORKS

D. S. Mirsky, *A History of Russian Literature* and *Contemporary Russian Literature* (London, 1926–7). One may disagree with some of the author's evaluations, but this history is still the best survey in English of the period discussed above. Marc Slonim, *The Epic of Russian Literature from its Origins through Tolstoy* (New York, 1950), less original and less reliable than Mirsky, but still very readable. *Istoriya russkoy literatury*, Akademiya Nauk SSSR, vols. V–IX (Moscow–Leningrad, 1941–56). Very detailed, but at the same time extremely tendentious; to be used with great caution, because many facts are distorted. A. Stender-Petersen, *Geschichte der russischen Literatur*, 2 vols. (Munich, 1957), the fullest discussion of the period in an overall history of Russian literature in German. A. Bagry, *Russkaya literatura XIX – pervoy chetverti XX vv.* (Baku, 1926; reprint, Düsseldorf, 1970), a reliable, if slightly tendentious, presentation leaning towards a formalistic approach. D. Tschižewskij, *Russische Literaturgeschichte des 19. Jahrhunderts*, vol. I: *Die Romantik*; vol. II: *Der Realismus* (Munich, 1964, 1967), a very stimulating presentation of the period by a distinguished scholar.

MAIN EDITIONS AND WORKS ABOUT SINGLE AUTHORS AND SHORTER PERIODS

N. M. Karamzin, *Sochineniya*, vols. I–IX (St Petersburg, 1834–5). V. V. Sipovsky, *N. M. Karamzin, avtor 'Pisem russkogo puteshestvennika'* (St Petersburg, 1899). A. G. Cross, *N. M. Karamzin: a study of his literary career, 1783–1803* (Carbondale, Ill., 1971).

K. Skipina, 'O chuvstvitel'noy povesti', *Russkaya proza, Sbornik statey*, eds. B. Eykhenbaum and Yu. Tynyanov (Leningrad, 1926).

P. Brang, *Studien zur Theorie und Praxis der russischen Erzählung 1770–1811* (Wiesbaden, 1960).

V. A. Zhukovsky, *Polnoye sobraniye sochineniy* (St Petersburg, 1902). Aleksandr Veselovsky, *Zhukovsky. Poeziya chuvstva i serdechnogo voobrazheniya* (St Petersburg, 1904; 2nd edn, Petrograd, 1918). Marcelle Ehrhardt, *V. A. Joukovski et le préromantisme russe* (Paris, 1938). Boris Zaytsev, *Zhukovsky* (Paris, 1951), a beautifully written and reliable introduction to Zhukovsky's personality and art.

I. A. Krylov, *Polnoye sobraniye sochineniy*, vols. I–III (Moscow, 1944–6). V. Kenevich, *Bibliograficheskiye i istoricheskiye primechaniya k basnyam Krylova* (St Petersburg, 1878). N. Stepanov, *I. A. Krylov: zhizn' i tvorchestvo* (Moscow, 1958).

A. S. Griboyedov, *Polnoye sobraniye sochineniy*, vols. I–III (St Petersburg, 1911–17). N. Piksanov, *Griboyedov. Issledovaniya i kharakteristiki* (Leningrad, 1934). I. Goncharov, *Mil'yon terzaniy*, any edition, still the best interpretation of Griboyedov's famous comedy. J. Bonamour, *A. S. Griboiédov et la vie littéraire de son temps* (Paris, 1965).

B. Tomashevsky, 'K. N. Batyushkov' in *Biblioteka poeta, Malaya seriya* (Moscow, 1948), pp. v–lx.

I. Zamotin, *Romantizm 20-kh godov 19-ogo stoletiya v russkoy literature*, 2 vols. (St Petersburg–Moscow, 1911–13). Valuable as a compilation of material; its conclusions are of dubious validity. P. Sakulin, *Iz istorii russkogo idealizma. Knyaz' V. F. Odoyevsky*, vol. I, pts. 1 and 2 (Moscow, 1913), contains much material on the history of Russian romanticism.

A. S. Pushkin, *Polnoye sobraniye sochineniy*, vols. I–XVII (Moscow, 1937–59). D. S. Mirsky, *Pushkin* (London, New York, 1926, 1963), a much too brief critical biography, but containing some interesting psychological insights and original aesthetic evaluations of single works. *Eugene Onegin, A Novel in Verse by Aleksandr Pushkin*, translated from the Russian, with a commentary, by Vladimir Nabokov, 4 vols. (London, 1964). A brilliant commentary going far beyond the limits of one work. If carefully read, one of the very best introductions to Pushkin. J. Bayley, *Pushkin* (Cambridge, 1971), is a good recent study. G. Chulkov, *Zhizn' Pushkina* (Moscow, 1938), the most reliable and least tendentious of Soviet biographies of Pushkin. L. Grossman, *Etyudy o Pushkine* (Moscow, 1923), a brilliant and erudite study by a distinguished Pushkin scholar. B. Tomashevsky, *Pushkin*, 2 vols. (Moscow–Leningrad, 1956, 1961). The first volume contains an excellent discussion of Pushkin's early works; the second, *Materials for the Monograph*, consists of disjointed, though useful, fragments put together after the author's death. V. Vinogradov, *Yazyk Pushkina. Pushkin i istoriya russkogo literaturnogo yazyka* (Moscow–Leningrad, 1935). V. Shklovsky, *Zametki o proze Pushkina* (Moscow, 1937). *Pushkin. Vremennik Pushkinskoy Komissii*, 6 vols. (Moscow–Leningrad, 1936–41). This collection contains many excellent studies dealing with all aspects of his work. V. Bryusov, *Moy Pushkin* (Moscow–Leningrad, 1929), stimulating and perspicacious studies by the great symbolist poet. M. Gershenzon, *Mudrost' Pushkina* (Moscow, 1919), a somewhat controversial but interesting presentation of Pushkin's outlook, stressing his leanings towards mysticism. V. Veresayev, *Pushkin v zhizni*, 2 vols. (Moscow, 1936), an excellent compilation of comments on Pushkin by contemporaries. V. Setschkareff, *Alexander Puschkin. Sein Leben und sein Werk* (Wiesbaden, 1963).

Ye. A. Boratynsky, *Stikhotvoreniya, poemy, proza, pis'ma* (Moscow, 1951). M. Gofman, *Poeziya Ye. A. Baratynskogo* (Petrograd, 1915).

F. I. Tyutchev, *Polnoye sobraniye stikhotvoreniy*, vols. I–II (Leningrad, 1957). K. Pigaryov, *Zhizn' i tvorchestvo Tyutcheva* (Moscow, 1962), an exemplary monograph by an excellent scholar.

GUIDE TO FURTHER READING

M. Yu. Lermontov, *Polnoye sobraniye sochineniy*, vols. I–II (Moscow–Leningrad, 1947–8). B. Eykhenbaum, *Lermontov. Opyt istoriko-literaturnoy otsenki* (Leningrad, 1924; reprint, Munich, 1967). Undoubtedly the best discussion of Lermontov's works. B. Eykhenbaum, *Stat'i o Lermontove* (Moscow–Leningrad, 1961), contains a brilliant discussion of Lermontov's plays and several highly pertinent articles about his prose and poetry.

N. V. Gogol', *Polnoye sobraniye sochineniy*, vols. I–XIV (Moscow, 1937–52). V. Gippius, *Gogol'* (Leningrad, 1924; reprint, Providence, R.I., 1963), has claims to be the most perceptive study of Gogol's work. V. Setchkarev, *Gogol. His Life and Works* (New York, 1965). Vladimir Nabokov, *Nikolai Gogol* (New York, 1944, 1959, 1961), a somewhat controversial, but brilliantly written and spirited study. V. Erlich, *Gogol* (New Haven and London, 1969), a reliable introduction to problems presented by Gogol's works. Abram Tertz (A. Sinyavsky), *V. teni Gogolya* (London, 1975). B. de Schloezer, *Gogol* (Parish, 1932, 1946, 1952), an unjustly forgotten French biography which stresses the tragic aspects of Gogol's life and art. V. Vinogradov, *Gogol' i natural'naya shkola* (Leningrad, 1925). V. Vinogradov, *Evolyutsiya russkogo naturalizma. Gogol' i Dostoyevsky* (Leningrad, 1929).

S. T. Aksakov, *Sobraniye sochineniy*, vols. I–IV (Moscow, 1955–6). R. E. Matlaw, *Introduction to Sergey Aksakov, 'The Family Chronicle', 'The Genius of Ingenuousness'* (New York, 1961), a short but informative essay.

P. Ya. Chaadayev, *Sochineniya i pis'ma*, vols. I–II (Moscow, 1913–14). C. Quenet, *Tchaadaev et les Lettres philosophiques: contribution a l'étude du mouvement des idées en Russie* (Paris, 1931).

V. G. Belinsky, *Polnoye sobraniye sochineniy*, vols. I–XIII (Moscow, 1953–9). H. E. Bowman, *Vissarion Belinsky. A Study in the Origins of Social Criticism in Russia* (Cambridge, Mass., 1954).

A. J. Gertsen [Herzen], *Sochineniya*, vols. I–IX (Moscow, 1955–8). A. Veselovsky, *Gertsen-pisatel'* (Moscow, 1909).

I. S. Turgenev, *Polnoye sobraniye sochineniy i pisem*, vols. I–XXVIII (Moscow, 1960–1968). A. Yarmolinsky, *Turgenev, The Man, His Art and His Age* (New York, 1959, 1961), a simple, well-written introduction. R. Freeborn, *Turgenev: The Novelist's Novelist. A Study* (Oxford, 1960), a useful book, containing an analysis of Turgenev's art. M. Gershenzon, *Mechta i mysl' I. S. Turgeneva* (Moscow, 1919; reprint, Providence, R.I., 1970), a persuasive presentation of Turgenev's philosophy of life. *Venok Turgenevu 1818–1918. Sbornik statey* (Odessa, 1919), a collection of essays by different authors covering very competently several aspects of Turgenev's art. Marina Ledkovsky, *The Other Turgenev: From Romanticism to Symbolism* (Würzburg, 1973), stimulating discussion of Turgenev's usually neglected leanings towards mysticism.

I. A. Goncharov, *Sobraniye sochineniy*, vols. I–VIII (Moscow, 1952–5). L. S. Utevsky, *Zhizn' Goncharova* (Moscow, 1931), an intelligently compiled collection of documents illustrating Goncharov's life. N. I. Prutskov, *Masterstvo Goncharova romanista* (Moscow–Leningrad, 1962), a competent, though ideologically somewhat slanted, discussion of Goncharov's novels. V. Setchkarev, *Ivan Goncharov: His Life and His Works* (Würzburg, 1974).

A. F. Pisemsky, *Sobraniye sochineniy*, vols. I–IX (Moscow, 1953). C. A. Moser, *Pisemskiy. A Provincial Realist* (Cambridge, Mass., 1969).

175

N. A. Nekrasov, *Polnoye sobraniye sochineniy i pisem*, vols. I–XII (Moscow, 1948–52). K. Chukovsky, *Nekrasov, kak khudozhnik* (Petrograd, 1922), a short but excellent discussion of Nekrasov's art. Sigmund S. Birkenmayer, *Nikolay Nekrasov: His Life and Poetic Art* (The Hague, 1968).

B. Bukhshtab, *A. A. Fet. Vstupitel'naya stat'ya. Polnoye sobraniye stikhotvoreniy* (Leningrad, 1959).

A. N. Ostrovsky, *Sobraniye sochineniy*, vols. I–X (Moscow, 1959–62). N. Dolgov, *A. N. Ostrovsky. Zhizn' i tvorchestvo* (Petrograd, 1923). Lidiya Lotman, *A. N. Ostrovsky i russkaya dramaturgiya yego vremeni* (Moscow, 1961).

L. N. Tolstoy, *Polnoye sobraniye sochineniy*, vols. I–XC (Moscow–Leningrad, 1928–59). Aylmer Maude, *The Life of Tolstoy*, 2 vols. (London, 1929–30). B. Eykhenbaum, *Molodoy Tolstoy* (Petrograd–Berlin, 1922; reprint, Munich, 1968); translation: *The Young Tolstoy* (Ann Arbor, Mich., 1972). B. Eykhenbaum, *Lev Tolstoy* (Leningrad, 1928–31; reprint, Munich, 1968). B. Eykhenbaum, *Lev Tolstoy. Semidesyatyye gody* (Leningrad, 1960). Eykhenbaum's works on Tolstoy are outstanding models of literary interpretation. V. Shklovsky, *Lev Tolstoy* (Moscow, 1967), without doubt the best Russian biography of Tolstoy. M. Aldanov, *Zagadka Tolstogo* (Berlin, 1923; reprint, Providence, R.I., 1969), a stimulating, brilliantly written and highly informative discussion of Tolstoy's thinking, personality and art. K. Leont'yev, *Analiz, stil' i veyaniye. O romanakh gr. L. N. Tolstogo* (Moscow, 1912; reprint, Providence, R.I., 1965), a classic essay dealing mainly with *War and Peace* and *Anna Karenina*. R. F. Christian, *Tolstoy's War and Peace. A Study* (Oxford, 1962). John Bayley, *Tolstoy and the Novel* (London, 1966). *Tolstoy. A Collection of Critical Essays*, ed. R. E. Matlaw (Englewood Cliffs, N.J., 1967), an excellent selection of articles on Tolstoy's art and thought. V. Veresayev, *Zhivaya zhizn'* (Moscow, 1928), one of the most interesting comparisons of Tolstoy and Dostoyevsky.

F. M. Dostoyevsky, *Sobraniye sochineniy*, vols. I–XIII (Leningrad, 1926–30). K. Mochulsky, *Dostoevsky: His Life and Work* (Princeton, 1967); translation of the same author's *Dostoyevsky. Zhizn' i tvorchestvo* (Paris, 1947), a classic biography and an excellent introduction to Dostoyevsky's work. Jessie Coulson, *Dostoevsky. A Self-Portrait* (London, 1962), chronologically arranged excerpts from Dostoyevsky's letters with competent connecting text. L. Grossman, *Dostoyevsky* (Moscow, 1965), a slightly tendentious but very erudite biography by one of the most brilliant Dostoyevsky scholars, written in a readable style; contains a good short bibliography. E. Wasiolek, *Dostoevsky. The Major Fiction* (Cambridge, Mass., 1964), a sound, competent and well-written analysis of Dostoyevsky's novels. *Dostoevsky. A Collection of Critical Essays*, ed. R. Wellek (Englewood Cliffs, N.J., 1962), an excellent selection of short essays dealing with different aspects of Dostoyevsky's work. *O Dostoyevskom. Stat'i*, ed. D. Fanger (Providence, R.I., 1966), valuable discussions of Dostoyevsky's work by V. Komarovich, P. Bitsilli and others. M. Bakhtin, *Problemy poetiki Dostoyevskogo* (Moscow, 1963), perhaps the most stimulating study of the form of Dostoyevsky's novels, stressing their 'polyphonic' quality. The second expanded edition of Bakhtin's *Problemy tvorchestva Dostoyevskogo* of 1929; translation: *Problems of Dostoyevsky's Poetics* (Ann Arbor, Mich., 1973). Ya. O. Zundelovich, *Romany Dostoyevskogo* (Tashkent, 1963), a highly original book filled with stimulating observations on Dostoyevsky's technique.

N. S. Leskov, *Sobraniye sochineniy*, vols. I–XI (Moscow, 1956–8). Andrey Leskov,

GUIDE TO FURTHER READING

Zhizn' Nikolaya Leskova, po yego lichnym, semeynym i nesemeynym zapisyam i pamyati (Moscow, 1954), though slightly biased, contains the fullest biographical material on Leskov. L. Grossman, *N. S. Leskov. Zhizn', tvorchestvo, poetika* (Moscow, 1945), a model of what an introduction to a writer should be. V. Setschkareff, *N. S. Leskov. Sein Leben und sein Werk* (Wiesbaden, 1959).

M. Ye. Saltykov-Shchedrin, *Sobraniye sochineniy*, vols. I–VI (Moscow–Leningrad, 1926–8). N. Strelsky, *Saltykov and the Russian Squire* (New York, 1940). Ya. El'sberg, *Stil' Shchedrina* (Moscow, 1940).

A. P. Chekhov, *Polnoye sobraniye sochineniy i pisem*, vols. I–XX (Moscow, 1944–1951). P. M. Bitsilli, *Anton P. Čechov. Das Werk und sein Stil. Aus dem Russischen übersetzt und mit Ergänzungen aus anderen Arbeiten des Autors herausgegeben von Vincent Sieveking* (Munich, 1966), a translation of Bitsilli's brilliant work *Tvorchestvo Chekhova: Opyt stilisticheskogo analiza*, published in *Godishnik na Universitet Sv. Kliment Okhridski-Sofia*, istoriko-filologicheski fakultet, vol. XXXVIII, 6 (1942), contains also two other special studies by Bitsilli (as difficult of access in the original language as his main work) and an excellent bibliography. R. Hingley, *Chekhov. A Biographical and Critical Study* (London, 1950). *Idem, A New Life of Anton Chekhov* (London, 1976). *Letters of Anton Chekhov*, translated from the Russian by Michael Henry Heim in collaboration with Simon Karlinsky. Selection, Commentary and Introduction by Simon Karlinsky (New York, 1973), the best introduction to Chekhov's life and work. Ivan Bunin, *O Chekhove* (New York, 1955), an original and rewarding book by the great writer. *Chekhov. A Collection of Critical Essays*, ed. R. L. Jackson (Englewood Cliffs, N.J., 1967).

I. A. Bunin, *Sobraniye sochineniy*, vols. I–IX (Moscow, 1965–6).

B. Mikhaylovsky, *Russkaya literatura XX veka. S devyanostykh godov XIX veka do 1917 g.* (Moscow, 1917), a good, but onesidedly critical introduction to the main features of Russian symbolism and acmeism. Biased and unreliable on all other topics. Innokenty Annensky, *O sovremennom lirizme*, in the journal *Apollon*, vols. 1–3 (1909), an exquisite and spirited study by the great symbolist poet. S. Makovsky, *Na Parnase 'Serebryanogo veka'* (Munich, 1962), personal reminiscences and criticism by an important figure of the period. Georgy Ivanov, *Peterburgskiye zimy* (New York, 1962), a factually unreliable, but well-written book by a distinguished poet, conveying the atmosphere of the early decades of this century. I. F. Annensky, *Stikhotvoreniya i tragedii* (Leningrad, 1959). V. Setchkarev, *Studies in the Life and Works of Innokentiy Annenskiy* (The Hague, 1963). A. A. Blok, *Sobraniye sochineniy*, vols. I–XII (Moscow–Leningrad, 1932–6). K. Mochul'sky, *Aleksandr Blok* (Paris, 1948). A. N. Bely, *Stikhotvoreniya i poemy* (Moscow–Leningrad, 1966). K. Mochul'sky, *Andrey Bely* (Paris, 1955), an excellent monograph. V. Markov, *Russian Futurism: A History* (Berkeley and Los Angeles, 1968), an exhaustive, highly reliable and erudite study.

INDIVIDUAL AUTHORS (see also pp. 214–30)
Akhmatova (pseudonym of Gorenko), Anna Andreyevna (1889–1966): *Evening (Vecher)*, 1912; *Rosary (Chotki)*, 1914; *The White Flock (Belaya staya)*, 1917; *Anno Domini MCMXXI*, 1922; *The Willow (Iva)*, 1940.

Aksakov, Sergey Timofeyevich (1791–1859): *Family Chronicle, Memoirs (Semeynaya khronika, Vospominaniya)*, 1856; *The Childhood Years of Grandson Bagrov (Detskiye gody Bagrova vnuka)*, 1858; *Literary and Theatrical Reminis-*

177

cences 1812–1830 (Literaturnyye i teatral'nyye vospominaniya 1812–1830 gg.), 1858; *History of my Acquaintance with Gogol (Istoriya moyego znakomstva s Gogolem)*, 1890.

Andreyev, Leonid Nikolayevich (1871–1919): short stories since 1898; plays: *The Life of Man (Zhizn' cheloveka)*, 1907; *Black Masques (Chornyye maski)*, 1909; *Anathema*, 1910.

Andreyevsky, Sergey Arkadiyevich (1847–1919): lyrical poetry; critical essays; *The Book on Death (Kniga o smerti)*, 1922.

Annensky, Innokenty Fyodorovich (1856–1909): *Quiet Songs (Tikhiye pesni)*, 1904; *The Cypress Chest (Kiparisovyy larets)*, 1910; *Posthumous Verses (Posmertnyye stikhi)*, 1923; plays: *Melanippe, the Philosopher (Melanippa-filosof)*, 1901; *Tsar Ixion (Tsar' Iksion)*, 1902; *Laodamia*, 1906; *Thamyras, the Cythara Player (Famira Kifared)*, 1913; critical essays: *Book of Reflections (Kniga otrazheniy)*, 1906; *The Second Book of Reflections (Vtoraya kniga otrazheniy)*, 1909.

Apukhtin, Aleksey Nikolayevich (1840–93): *Poems (Stikhotvoreniya)*, 1886.

Artsybashev, Mikhail Petrovich (1878–1927): short stories from 1901; novels: *Sanin*, 1907; *Millions (Milliony)*, 1910.

Bal'mont, Konstantin Dmitriyevich (1867–1943): *A Collection of Poems (Sbornik stikhov)*, 1890; *Under a Northern Sky (Pod severnym nebom)*, 1894; *Let Us Be Like the Sun (Budem kak solntse)*, 1903; *Nothing but Love (Tol'ko lyubov')*, 1903; *The Liturgy of Beauty (Liturgiya krasoty)*, 1905.

Baratynsky: *see* Boratynsky.

Batyushkov, Konstantin Nikolayevich (1787–1855): *Experiments in Verses and Prose (Opyty v stikhakh i proze)*, 1817.

Belinsky, Visarion Grigor'yevich (1811–48): literary criticism: e.g. *Literary Dreams (Literaturnyye mechtaniya)*, 1834.

Bely, Andrey (pseudonym of Bugayev, Boris Nikolayevich) (1880–1934): *Gold in Azure (Zoloto v lazuri)*, 1904; *Ashes (Pepel)*, 1909; *The Urn (Urna)*, 1909; narrative in verse: *First Meeting (Pervoye svidaniye)*, 1921; novels: *The Silver Dove (Serebryannyy golub')*, 1910; *Petersburg*, 1912; *Kotik Letayev*, 1922; *Moscow (Moskva)*, 1926; Memoirs, 3 vols., 1929–33.

Bestuzhev-Marlinsky, Aleksandr Aleksandrovich (1797–1837): *Ammalat-Bek*, 1832.

Blok, Aleksandr Aleksandrovich (1880–1921): *Poems on the Beautiful Lady (Stikhi o prekrasnoy dame)*, 1905; *The Unexpected Joy (Nechayannaya radost')*, 1907; *The Snow Mask (Snezhnaya maska)*, 1907; *Earth in Snow (Zemlya v snegu)*, 1907; *The Scythians (Skify)*, *The Twelve (Dvenadtsat')*, 1918; plays: *The Puppet Show (Balaganchik)*, *The Unknown Lady (Neznakomka)*, 1906; *The Rose and the Cross (Roza i krest)*, 1912; critical essays.

Boratynsky, Yevgeny Abramovich (1800–44): lyrical poetry; narratives in verse: *Eda*, 1824; *The Ball (Bal)*, 1828; *The Gipsy Woman (Tsyganka)*, 1831.

Bryusov, Valery Yakovlevich (1873–1924): *Chefs d'oeuvre*, 1895; *Tertia Vigilia*, 1901; *Urbi et Orbi*, 1903; *Stephanos*, 1905; novels: *The Fiery Angel (Ognennyy angel)*, 1908; *The Altar of Victory (Altar' pobedy)*, 1911; critical essays.

Bunin, Ivan Alekseyevich (1870–1953): lyrical poetry; novels and narratives: *The

GUIDE TO FURTHER READING

Village (Derevnya), 1910; *Dry Valley (Sukhodol)*, 1912; *The Chalice of Life (Chasha zhizni)*, 1914; *The Gentleman from San Francisco (Gospodin iz San Frantsisko)*, 1916; *Mitya's Love (Mitina lyubov')*, 1925; *Arsenyev's Life (Zhizn' Arsen'yeva)*, 1952.

Chaadayev, Pyotr Yakovlevich (1794–1856): *Philosophical Letters (Filosoficheskiye pis'ma)*, 1836 et seq.

Chekhov, Anton Pavlovich (1860–1904): short stories from 1880: *Ward No. 6 (Palata No. 6)*, 1892; *Kashtanka*, 1892; *My Life (Moya zhizn')*, 1896; *In the Ravine (V ovrage)*, 1900; *The Bishop (Arkhierey)*, 1902; *The Bride (Nevesta)*, 1904; plays: *Ivanov*, 1889; *The Seagull (Chayka)*, 1896; *Uncle Vanya (Dyadya Vanya)*, 1897; *The Three Sisters (Tri sestry)*, 1901; *The Cherry Orchard (Vishnyovyy sad)*, 1904.

Chernyshevsky, Nikolay Gavrilovich (1828–89): *The Aesthetic Relations of Art to Reality (Esteticheskiye otnosheniya iskusstva k deystvitel'nosti)*, 1855; *Sketches from the Gogol Period of Russian Literature (Ocherki Gogolevskogo perioda russkoy literatury)*, 1856; novel: *What is to be Done? (Chto delat'?)*, 1863.

Davydov, Denis Vasil'yevich (1784–1839): lyrical poetry.

Del'vig, Anton Antonovich (1798–1831): idylls; poetry in antique metres; epigrams; songs.

Dmitriyev, Ivan Ivanovich (1760–1837): lyrical, religious and patriotic poetry; fables, songs; satire in verse: *Gossip (Chuzhoy tolk)*, 1794; 'contes': e.g. *A Modern Wife (Modnaya zhena)*.

Dobrolyubov, Nikolay Aleksandrovich (1836–61): *What Is Oblomovism? (Chto takoye oblomovshchina?)*, 1859; *The Dark Realm (Tyomnoye tsarstvo)*, 1859.

Dostoyevsky, Fydor Mikhaylovich (1821–81): *Poor Folk (Bednyye lyudi)*, 1846; *The Double (Dvoynik)*, 1846; *Mr Prokharchin (Gospodin Prokharchin)*, 1846; *The Landlady (Khozyayka)*, 1847; *A Weak Heart (Slaboye serdtse)*, 1848; *White Nights (Belyye nochi)*, 1848; *Netochka Nezvanova*, 1849; *The Village of Stepanchikovo and its Inhabitants (Selo Stepanchikovo i yego obitateli)*, 1859; *The Humiliated and the Insulted (Unizhennyye i oskorblyonnyye)*, 1861; *Memoirs from the House of the Dead (Zapiski iz myortvogo doma)*, 1861–3; *Notes from the Underground (Zapiski iz podpol'ya)*, 1864; *Crime and Punishment (Prestupleniye i nakazaniye)*, 1866; *The Gambler (Igrok)*, 1868; *The Idiot (Idiot)*, 1868; *The Eternal Husband (Vechnyy muzh)*, 1870; *The Possessed (or The Devils) (Besy)*, 1871; *A Raw Youth (Podrostok)*, 1875; *The Gentle Creature (Krotkaya)*, 1876; *The Brothers Karamazov (Brat'ya Karamazovy)*, 1879–80.

Fet, Afanasy (pseudonym of Shenshin, Afanasy Afanas'yevich) (1820–92): lyrical poetry 1840; late collections of verse: *Evening Lights (Vecherniye ogni)*, since 1883.

Garshin, Vsevolod Mikhaylovich (1855–88): short stories: *Four Days (Chetyre dnya)*, 1877; *The Coward (Trus)*, 1879; *A Meeting (Vstrecha)*, 1879; *Artists (Khudozhniki)*, 1879; *Attalea princeps*, 1880; *The Red Flower (Krasnyy tsvetok)*, 1883; *Nadezhda Nikolayevna*, 1885.

Gippius, Zinaida Nikolayevna (1869–1945): poems, 1904, 1910; literary essays.

Gogol', Nikolay Vasil'yevich (1809–52): idyll: *Hans Küchelgarten*, 1829; tales: *Evenings on a Farm near Dikanka (Vechera na khutore bliz Dikan'ki)*, 1831–2;

179

Arabesques (*Arabeski*), *Mirgorod*, 1835; *The Nose* (*Nos*), 1836; *Dead Souls* (*Myortvyye dushi*), 1842; *The Overcoat* (*Shinel'*), 1842; plays: *The Government Inspector* (*Revizor*), 1836; *The Marriage* (*Zhenit'ba*), 1842; *Selected Passages from Correspondence with Friends* (*Vybrannyye mesta iz perepiski s druz'yami*), 1847.

Golenishchev-Kutuzov, Arseny Arkad'yevich (1848–1913): lyrical poetry.

Goncharov, Ivan Aleksandrovich (1812–91): *The Same Old Story* (*Obyknovennaya istoriya*), 1847; *The Frigate 'Pallada'* (*Fregat Pallada*), 1858; *Oblomov*, 1859; *The Precipice* (*Obryv*), 1869.

Gor'ky, Maksim (pseudonym of Peshkov, Aleksey Maksimovich) (1868–1936): tales and novels: *Makar Chudra*, 1892; *Mal'va*, 1897; *Foma Gordeyev*, 1899; *The Mother* (*Mat'*), 1907; *Childhood* (*Detstvo*), 1913; *In the World* (*V lyudakh*), 1915; *The Artamonov Business* (*Delo Artamonovykh*), 1925; *The Life of Klim Samgin* (*Zhizn' Klima Samgina*), 1936; plays: *The Lower Depths* (*Na dne*), 1902; *Vassa Zheleznova*, 1910.

Gorodetsky, Sergey Mitrofanovich (1884–1967): lyrical poetry.

Griboyedov, Aleksandr Sergeyevich (1795–1829): *Woe from Wit* (*Gore ot uma*), completed 1823, first published 1833.

Grigorovich, Dmitry Vasil'yevich (1822–99): *The Village* (*Derevnya*), 1846; *Anton-Goremyka*, 1847; *Migrators* (*Pereselentsy*), 1855; *The Gutta-percha Boy* (*Gutta-perchevyy mal'chik*), 1883.

Grigor'yev, Apollon Aleksandrovich (1822–64): poetry from 1846; critical essays; *My Literary and Moral Wanderings* (*Moi literaturnyye i nravstvennyye skital'chestva*), 1864.

Gumilyov, Nikolay Stepanovich (1886–1921): *The Way of the Conquistadors* (*Put' konkvistadorov*), 1905; *Romantic Flowers* (*Romanticheskiye tsvety*), 1908; *Pearls* (*Zhemchuga*), 1910; *Foreign Sky* (*Chuzhoye nebo*), 1912; *The Quiver* (*Kolchan*), 1916; *The Tent* (*Shatyor*), 1921; literary criticism.

Herzen (Gersten), Aleksandr Ivanovich (1812–70): *Who is to Blame?* (*Kto vinovat?*), 1847; *The Notes of Dr Krupov*, 1847; *My Past and Thoughts* (*Byloye i dumy*), 1851–67.

Ivanov, Vyacheslav Ivanovich (1866–1949): *Pilot Stars* (*Kormchiye zvyozdy*), 1903; *Translucency* (*Prozrachnost'*), 1904; *Eros*, 1907; *Cor ardens*, 1911; critical essays: *Furrows and Boundaries* (*Borozdy i mezhi*), 1916; *The Evening Light* (*Svet vecherniy*), 1962.

Izmaylov, Aleksandr Yefimovich (1779–1831): fables, 'contes'.

Karamzin, Nikolay Mikhaylovich (1766–1826): *Poor Liza* (*Bednaya Liza*), 1792; *The Island of Bornholm* (*Ostrov Borngol'm*), 1793; *The History of the Russian State* (*Istoriya Gosudarstva Rossiyskogo*), 1816–26.

Katenin, Pavel Aleksandrovich (1792–1853): ballads; tragedy: *Andromache*, 1827; critical essays.

Khemnitser, Ivan Ivanovich (1745–84): fables.

Khlebnikov, Viktor Vladimirovich (1885–1922) – called himself Velimir Khlebnikov: lyrical poetry and verse narratives.

Khomyakov, Aleksey Stepanovich (1804–60): lyrical, mainly religious, poetry; theological works.

Kireyevsky, Ivan Vasil'yevich (1806–56): literary essays; philosophical treatises.

Klyuyev, Nikolay Alekseyevich (1887–1937): Lyrical poetry.

Kol'tsov, Aleksey Vasil'yevich (1809–42): lyrical poetry (from 1835).

Korolenko, Vladimir Galaktionovich (1853–1921): *Makar's Dream (Son Makara),* 1885; *In Bad Company (V durnom obshchestve); The Forest Rustles (Les shumit),* 1886; *The Story of My Contemporary (Istoriya moyego sovremennika),* 1906–8.

Krylov, Ivan Andreyevich (1769–1844): 205 fables.

Küchelbecker (Kyukhel'beker), Wilhelm (Vil'gel'm Karlovich) (1797–1846): lyrical poetry; critical essays.

Kuprin, Aleksandr Ivanovich (1870–1938): *The Duel (Poyedinok),* 1905; *The Pit (Yama),* 1912; *Jeanette,* 1933.

Kushchevsky, Ivan Afanas'yevich (1847–76): *Nikolay Negorev or the Happy Russian (Nikolay Negorev ili blagopoluchnyy Rossiyanin),* 1871.

Kuzmin, Mikhail Alekseyevich (1875–1936): *Alexandrian Songs (Aleksandriyskiye pesni),* 1906; *The Carillon of Love (Kuranty lyubvi),* 1906; *Nets (Seti),* 1908; *Clay Doves (Glinyanyye golubki),* 1914; *Unearthly Evenings (Nezdeshniye vechera),* 1921; novels: *Wings (Kryl'ya),* 1906; *The Deeds of Alexander the Great (Podvigi Velikogo Aleksandra),* 1910; *The Adventures of Aimé Lebœuf (Pokhozhdeniya Eme Lebefa),* 1907; *The Quiet Guard (Tikhiy strazh),* 1916; critical essays: *Conventions (Uslovnosti),* 1923.

Lazhechnikov, Ivan Ivanovich (1792–1869): *The Ice House (Ledyanoy dom),* 1835.

Lermontov, Mikhail Yur'yevich (1814–41): lyrical poetry; narratives in verse: *The Novice (Mtsyri),* 1840; *The Demon (Demon),* 1841; *The Song about the Tsar Ivan Vasil'yevich, the Young Oprichnik and the Brave Merchant Kalashnikov (Pesn' pro tsarya Ivana Vasil'yevicha, molodogo oprichnika i udalogo kuptsa Kalashnikova),* 1837; novel: *A Hero of Our Time (Geroy nashego vremeni),* 1840; play: *Masquerade (Maskarad),* 1835–6.

Leskov, Nikolay Semyonovich (1831–95): novels: *No Way Out (Nekuda),* 1864; *Cathedral Folk (Soboryane),* 1872; short stories (among many others): *A Lady Macbeth of the Mtsensk District (Ledi Makbet mtsenskogo uyezda),* 1866; *The Enchanted Wanderer (Ocharovannyy strannik),* 1874; *The Mountebank Pamphalon (Skomorokh Pamfalon),* 1887.

Lokhvitskaya, Mirra (Mariya Aleksandrovna) (1869–1905): lyrical poetry from 1888.

Mandel'shtam, Osip Emil'yevich (1891–1938): *Stone (Kamen'),* 1913; *Tristia,* 1922; prose: *The Egyptian Stamp (Yegipetskaya marka),* 1928; critical essays.

Mayakovsky, Vladimir Vladimirovich (1893–1930): lyrical poetry: long poems: *Cloud in Trousers (Oblako v shtanakh),* 1915; *War and the World (Voyna i mir),* 1916; *150,000,000,* 1920; *About This (Pro eto),* 1923; play: *The Bedbug (Klop),* 1928.

Maykov, Apollon Nikolayevich (1821–97)): lyrical poetry; tragedy: *Two worlds (Dva mira),* 1873.

Mel'nikov-Pechersky, Pavel Ivanovich (1818–83): *In the Woods (V lesakh),* 1872; *On the Mountains (Na gorakh),* 1881.

Merezhkovsky, Dmitry Sergeyevich (1866–1941): lyrical poetry; novels: *Trilogy: Julian the Apostate, Leonardo da Vinci, Peter and Alexis*, 1896, 1901, 1905; literary criticism: *Tolstoy and Dostoyevsky*, 1901–2.

Mey, Lev Aleksandrovich (1822–62): ballads; lyrical poetry; *The Tsar's Bride* (*Tsarskaya nevesta*), 1849; *The Girl from Pskov* (*Pskovityanka*), 1860.

Nadson, Semyon Yakovlevich (1862–87): lyrical poetry.

Narezhny, Vasily Trofimovich (1780–1825): *The Russian Gil Blas* (*Rossiyskiy Zhilblaz*), 1814; *The Seminarist* (*Bursak*), 1824; *The Two Ivans or the Passion for Lawsuits* (*Dva Ivana ili strast' k tyazhbam*), 1825.

Nekrasov, Nikolay Alekseyevich (1821–77): lyrical poetry; long poems: *The Pedlars* (*Korobeyniki*), 1861; *Who Lives Well in Russia?* (*Komu na Rusi zhit' khorosho?*), an unfinished epic, 1863–77.

Nikitin, Ivan Savvich (1824–61): *Poems* (*Stikhotvoreniya*), 1856; *The Kulak*, 1858.

Odoyevsky, Vladimir Fyodorovich (1803–69): *Russian Nights* (*Russkiye nochi*), 1844; short stories.

Ostrovsky, Aleksandr Nikolayevich (1823–86): *The Bankruptcy* (*Bankrot*), 1849; *It's a Family Affair* (*Svoi lyudi — sochtyomsya*), 1850; *The Poor Bride* (*Bednaya nevesta*), 1853; *Poverty is no Crime* (*Bednost' ne porok*), 1854; *The Thunderstorm* (*Groza*), 1860; *The Wood* (*Les*), 1871; *Wolves and Sheep* (*Volki i ovtsy*), 1877; *Talents and their Admirers* (*Talanty i poklonniki*), 1882.

Ozerov, Vladislav Aleksandrovich (1769–1816); *Oedipus in Athens* (*Edip v Afinakh*), 1804; *Fingal*, 1807; *Dmitry Donskoy*, 1807; *Poliksena*, 1816.

Pasternak, Boris Leonidovich (1890–1960): poetry: *My Sister, Life* (*Sestra moya zhizn'*), 1922; *Themes and Variations* (*Temy i variatsii*), 1923; *Second Birth* (*Vtoroye rozhdeniye*), 1932; novel: *Dr Zhivago*, 1958.

Pavlova, Karolina Karlovna (1807–93): lyrical poetry.

Pisarev, Dmitry Ivanovich (1840–68): critical essays.

Pisemsky, Aleksey Feofilaktovich (1821–81): *Boyarshchina*, 1847; *A Thousand Souls* (*Tysyacha dush*), 1858; *Troubled Sea* (*Vzbalamuchennoye more*), 1863; *Men of the Forties* (*Lyudi sorokovykh godov*), 1869; play: *A Hard Lot* (*Gor'kaya sud'bina*), 1859.

Pleshcheyev, Aleksey Nikolayevich (1825–93): lyrical poetry.

Polonsky, Yakov Petrovich (1819–98): lyrical poetry; novel: *The Confessions of Sergey Chalygin* (*Priznaniya Sergeya Chalygina*), 1871.

Pushkin, Aleksandr Sergeyevich (1799–1837): lyrical poetry; narratives in verse: *Ruslan and Lyudmila*, 1820; *The Prisoner of the Caucasus* (*Kavkazskiy plennik*), 1821; *Gavriliyada*, 1821; *The Fountain of Bakhchisaray* (*Bakhchisarayskiy fontan*), 1823; *The Gypsies* (*Tsygany*), 1824; *Count Nulin* (*Graf Nulin*), 1825; *Poltava*, 1829; *The Little House in Kolomna* (*Domik v Kolomne*), 1830; *Angelo*, 1833; *The Bronze Horseman* (*Mednyy vsadnik*), 1833; novel in verse: *Eugene Onegin* (*Yevgeny Onegin*), 1823–31; plays: *Boris Godunov*, 1825; *The Covetous Knight* (*Skupoy rytsar'*), *Mozart and Salieri, The Stone Guest* (*Kamennyy gost'*), *The Feast during the Plague* (*Pir vo vremya chumy*), all 1830; fairy tales in verse, 1831–3; prose: *Tales of Belkin* (*Povesti Belkina*), 1830; *Dubrovsky*, fragment, 1832; *The*

GUIDE TO FURTHER READING

Queen of Spades (Pikovaya dama), 1833; *The Captain's Daughter (Kapitanskaya dochka)*, 1836; *Egyptian Nights (Yegipetskiye nochi)*, fragment, 1835; *The Journey to Arzrum (Puteshestviye v Arzrum)*, 1829; critical essays.

Remizov, Aleksey Mikhaylovich (1877–1957): *The Devil's Ravine and the Midnight Sun (Chortov log i polunoshchnoye solntse)*, 1908.

Rozanov, Vasily Vasil'yevich (1856–1919): *The Legend of the Grand Inquisitor (Legenda o Velikom Inkvizitore)*, 1890; *The Dark Visage (Tyomnyy lik)*, 1911; *Solitaria (Uyedinyonnoye)*, 1912; *Fallen Leaves (Opavshiye list'ya)*, 1913–15.

Saltykov-Shchedrin, Mikhail Yevgrafovich (1826–89): *The Story of a City (Istoriya odnogo goroda)*, 1869–70; *The Golovlyov Family (Gospoda Golovlyovy)*, 1880.

Severyanin, Igor' (pseudonym of Lotarev, Igor' Vasil'yevich) (1887–1941): *The Thunder-Seething Cup (Gromokipyashchiy kubok)*, 1913; *Pineapples in Champagne (Ananasy v shampanskom)*, 1915; *Classic Roses (Klassicheskiye rozy)*, 1931.

Shcherbina, Nikolay Fyodorovich (1821–69): lyrical poetry.

Shishkov, Aleksandr Semyonovich (1754–1841): *Treatise on the Old and New Style of the Russian Language (Rassuzhdeniye o starom i novom sloge rossiyskogo yazyka)*, 1803.

Sluchevsky, Konstantin Konstantinovich (1837–1904): lyrical poetry.

Sologub, Fyodor (pseudonym of Teternikov, Fyodor Kuz'mich) (1863–1927): lyrical poetry from 1896; novels: *Bad Dreams (Tyazholyye sny)*, 1896; *The Petty Devil (Melkiy bes)*, 1905; *A Legend in the Making (Tvorinmaya legenda)*, 1908–12; plays: *The Gift of the Wise Bees (Dar mudrykh pchol)*, 1907; *The Victory of Death (Pobeda smerti)*, 1908; *Van'ka the Housekeeper and the Page Jean (Van'ka klyuchnik i pazh Zhan)*, 1909.

Solov'yov, Vladimir Sergeyevich (1853–1900): lyrical poetry; critical essays; *Three Conversations (Tri razgovora)*, 1900.

Sukhovo-Kobylin, Aleksandr Vasil'yevich (1817–1903): *Krechinsky's Wedding (Svad'ba Krechinskogo)*, 1855; *A Case (Delo)*, *The Death of Tarelkin (Smert' Tarelkina)*, 1869.

Tolstoy, Aleksey Konstantinovich (1817–75): lyrical poetry; ballads; narratives in verse: *John of Damascus (Ioann Damaskin)*, 1859; *The Portrait (Portret)*, 1874; *The Dragon (Drakon)*, 1875; *The Dream of Popov (Son Popova)*, 1874; plays: *Don Juan*, 1862; trilogy: *The Death of Ivan the Terrible (Smert' Ioanna Groznogo)*, 1865, *Tsar Fyodor (Tsar' Fyodor)*, 1868, *Tsar Boris (Tsar' Boris)*, 1870; novel: *Prince Serebryany (Knyaz' Serebryanyy)*, 1863.

Tolstoy, Lev Nikolayevich (1828–1910): *Childhood (Detstvo)*, 1852; *Boyhood (Otrochestvo)*, 1854; *Youth (Yunost')*, 1854; *The Raid (Nabeg)*, 1853; *Sebastopol in December (1854)*, *Sebastopol in May (1855)*, *Sebastopol in August (1855)*, 1856; *Two Hussars (Dva gusara)*, 1856; *Three Deaths (Tri smerti)*, 1859; *Family Happiness (Semeynoye schast'ye)*, 1859; *The Strider (Kholstomer)*, 1861; *Polikushka*, 1866; *War and Peace (Voyna i mir)*, 1864–9; *Anna Karenina*, 1873–6; *The Death of Ivan Il'ich (Smert' Ivana Il'cha)*, 1885; *The Kreutzer Sonata (Kreytserova sonata)*, 1890; *Master and Servant (Khozyain i rabotnik)*, 1895; *Resurrection (Voskresen'ye)*, 1899; *Khadzhi Murat*, 1904; *The Divine and the Human (Bozhestvennoye i chelovecheskoye)*, 1905; *What for? (Za chto?)*, 1906; *There are no Guilty People (Net v mire vinovatykh)*, 1910; *The Devil (D'yavol)*, 1911; *My Confession (Moya*

183

ispoved'), 1881; *What Is Art? (Chto takoye iskusstvo?*), 1898; plays: *The Power of Darkness (Vlast' t'my)*, 1886; *The Fruits of Enlightenment (Plody prosveshcheniya)*, 1893; *The Living Corpse (Zhivoy trup)*, 1911.

Turgenev, Ivan Sergeyevich (1818–83): lyrical poetry from 1838; novels: *Rudin*, 1855; *A Nest of Gentlefolk (Dvoryanskoye gnezdo)*, 1859; *On the Eve (Nakanune)*, 1860; *Fathers and Sons (Ottsy i deti)*, 1862; *Smoke (Dym)*, 1867; *Virgin Soil (Nov')*, 1876; short stories from 1844: *The Diary of a Superfluous Man (Dnevnik lishnego cheloveka)*, 1850; *A Sportsman's Sketches (Zapiski okhotnika)*, 1852; *Asya*, 1857; *First Love (Pervaya lyubov')*, 1861; *Torrents of Spring (Veshniye vody)*, 1871; *The Dream (Son)*, 1877; *The Song of Love Triumphant (Pesn' torzhestvuyushchey lyubvi)*, 1882; *Klara Milich*, 1883; plays: *A Month in the Country (Mesyats v derevne)*, 1855; *A Dependant (Nakhlebnik)*, 1857.

Tyutchev, Fyodor Ivanovich (1803–73): lyrical poetry from 1836.

Uspensky, Gleb Ivanovich (1843–1902): *Morals and Manners of the Rasteryayeva Street (Nravy Rasteryayevoy ulitsy)*, 1866; *The Power of the Soil (Vlast' zemli)*, 1882.

Vel'tman, Aleksandr Fomich (1800–70): *The Wanderer (Strannik)*, 1831; *Adventures Drawn from the Sea of Everyday Life (Priklyucheniya, pocherpnutyye iz morya zhiteyskogo)*, 1846–8.

Venevitinov, Dmitry Vladimirovich (1805–27): lyrical poetry; philosophical and critical essays.

Voloshin, Maksimilian Aleksandrovich (1877–1932): lyrical poetry.

Vyazemsky, Pyotr Andreyevich (1792–1878): lyrical poetry; critical essays.

Yazykof, Nikolay Mikhaylovich (1803–43): lyrical poetry from 1822.

Yesenin, Sergey Aleksandrovich (1895–1925): lyrical poetry.

Zagoskin, Mikhail Nikolayevich (1789–1852): *Yury Miloslavsky, or the Russians in 1612 (Yury Miloslavsky, ili russkiye v 1612 godu)*, 1829; *Roslavlev, or the Russians in 1812 (Roslavlev, ili russkiye v 1812 godu)*, 1831; *Askold's Grave (Askol'dova mogila)*, 1833.

Zhemchuzhnikov, Aleksey Mikhaylovich (1821–1908): lyrical poetry.

Zhukovsky, Vasily Andreyevich (1783–1852): lyrical poetry and translations, e.g. Gray's 'Elegy Written in a Country Churchyard', 1802; August Bürger's *Lenore*, 1808; Schiller's *Jungfrau von Orleans*, 1824, and ballads; Homer's *Odyssey*, 1849.

7

LITERATURE IN THE SOVIET PERIOD

(1917–1975)

MAX HAYWARD

Soviet literature is essentially an extension into the post-revolutionary period of the Russian tradition, and one should more properly speak of Soviet *Russian* literature. The term 'multi-national Soviet literature', in so far as it might imply that various strands from the non-Russian cultures of the Caucasus, Central Asia and other areas have been brought together in some process of mutual enrichment, is only of rhetorical significance. The fact is that, so far, Russian culture has remained predominant throughout the Soviet period, and Stalin's famous slogan 'national in form and socialist in content' was in practice an assimilationist one. Campaigns against 'bourgeois nationalism' in the 1930s destroyed whatever promise of free development might have been held out to non-Russian cultures in the 1920s.

In formal, aesthetic terms Soviet Russian literature of the 1920s largely grew out of trends – at first allowed to compete more or less freely with each other – which had arisen before the revolution. No new style developed that was not rooted in symbolism, futurism, or in run-of-the-mill realism in the nineteenth-century manner. Most of the leading Soviet poets of the early 1920s were living representatives of these pre-revolutionary trends. Thus, for example, Aleksandr Blok, Andrey Bely, and Valery Bryusov were associated with symbolism, Vladimir Mayakovsky and Boris Pasternak with futurism. In prose, Gor'ky, Serafimovich and Veresayev carried on the 'realist' tradition. This is not to say that some post-revolutionary movements could not claim originality by virtue of setting themselves up in opposition to trends that were dominant in the old era. There were attempted new beginnings which have left their mark on the modern history of Russian literature. Noteworthy in this respect was the group founded in Petrograd in 1921 and called the 'Serapion Brothers' (from the Hermit Serapion in a tale by E. T. A. Hoffmann). Its avowed aim was to free Russian prose from ideological trammels and to break away from traditional psychological realism by putting more emphasis on structure and plot. Their manifesto was written by a literary scholar and playwright, Lev Lunts, who died prematurely in 1924. Some major Soviet prose writers, such as Mikhail Zoshchenko, Konstantin Fedin, Yevgeny Zamyatin and Veniamin Kaverin, were closely connected with this movement (which had ceased to exist as such by the mid-1920s), but in later years the original programme of the 'Serapion Brothers' was fiercely denounced by party critics because of its 'apolitical' premises, and its members went very different ways in the second decade after the revolution.

Another significant movement in the 1920s which is sometimes thought of as special to the Soviet period (though it started in 1916 as the Society for the Study of Poetic Language [OPOYAZ]) was the school of literary criticism usually referred to by its enemies as 'formalist'. Its exponents, who included some leading literary scholars and writers such as Viktor Shklovsky and Yury Tynyanov, preferred to speak of the 'formal method'. By the end of the 1920s it had proved to be ideologically unacceptable, and in later decades the word 'formalist' came to be applied indiscriminately as a term of abuse to any kind of stylistic experiment or supposed originality of form. Shklovsky was a founding member of the 'Serapion Brothers' and gave them theoretical support by emphasizing that literary criticism should concern itself first of all with formal or artistic quality, treating content or the message of a work of art as secondary or incidental. Such a challenge to the Russian tradition was bound to provoke a fierce reaction – particularly as the message was so important to the new rulers. But until it began to disintegrate in 1927, the formalist movement was a fertile source of new critical ideas, and a stimulus to many writers (whatever group they may have been associated with) whose main allegiance was to literature as such, rather than to any particular set of social and political values.

For the most part, however, the various groupings and 'isms' which arose in the 1920s were shortlived or unproductive, failing to attract major talents or provide a new point of departure for them. Some were little more than echoes of foreign trends, while others were attempts to revive or refurbish pre-revolutionary ones. Such endeavours were less an indication of new creative vigour than of a frenetic desire to exploit (or adapt to) a post-revolutionary situation which, as time was soon to show, became increasingly uncongenial to any form of intellectual or artistic avant-garde – such things can flourish only under the patronage of an affluent, ideologically tolerant bourgeoisie. All the early Soviet movements with pretensions to aesthetic innovation thus died of inanition or were suppressed, but since they contributed to the comparatively heterogeneous flavour and vocabulary of the 1920s, the main ones must be briefly described. *Imaginism*, which borrowed its name from the English 'imagists', was launched in 1919 and petered out in 1927. Its adherents believed in the primacy of images in poetry, and their major theme – an obvious one at a time of rapid urbanization – was the doom of the lonely individual in the modern city. Sergey Yesenin, the only major poet to be associated with them, no doubt joined the imaginists largely because their manifesto stressed important elements that already existed in his own poetry; in the hands of lesser poets (A. Mariengof, V. Shershenevich), imaginism degenerated into the piling on of images, often outrageous or vulgar, for their own sake. The result was like a cheapened version of Mayakovsky. An extreme, even more sterile form of imaginism was the group calling themselves *Nichevoki*, who proclaimed their affinity with the western dadaists and rejected any kind of social purpose or content: art was to be in the name of 'nothing'. *Constructivism*, a popular catchword throughout Europe in the 1920s, was applied to a wide range of modernist tendencies in all the arts (notably, the Russian followers of Le Corbusier in architecture, and Naum Gabo – who emigrated from the Soviet Union in 1922 – in painting and sculpture). In literature it appears as a further development of some trends in part of the futurist movement: worship of modern technology, and the belief that a poem is a 'construction', to be designed and put together like a product of the engineer's drawing-board. As an organized movement (the so-called 'Literary Centre of the Constructivists', founded in 1924), it attracted several poets such as E. Bagritsky and I. Sel'vinsky. The constructivists were unable to compete seriously as a left-wing avant-garde with the heirs of futurism grouped round the journal *LEF* ('Left Front of the Arts', 1923–5, later renamed *Novyy LEF*, 1927–8). Under the editorship of Mayakovsky, *LEF* inevitably became the main focus for those who combined the avant-garde temperament with militant commitment to the cause of the revolution and the new regime, and it could boast more talented young recruits (Aseyev and Kirsanov, among others) than any other left-wing movement in literature. Apart from the dominating presence of Mayakovsky, *LEF*'s great asset was the support of the formalists (which perpetuated an old alliance with the futurists). Being in some ways politically more royalist than the king, the *LEF* group was bound to run into trouble at the end of the decade and to come under attack as an assembly of 'petty-bourgeois' intellectuals from even more militant claimants to be the true representatives of the proletariat in literature (see RAPP below).

In retrospect one can see that the 1920s were distinguished from the pre-revolutionary period less by the emergence of any new concepts than by certain overriding factors extraneous to literature and the arts, which were now on the way to losing whatever autonomy they had once possessed. What decisively marks off Soviet literature from Russian literature is a radically altered relationship between writers, society and the state, and the fact that the choice of *subject matter* was inevitably dictated by the great historical and social changes wrought by the October Revolution. In this sense, there was not much essential difference between those who passionately believed in 'commitment' (such as the members of *LEF*) and those who balked at it (such as the Serapions): the overwhelming preoccupation of Russian writers after 1917, whatever literary grouping they might previously have belonged to or now joined, was with the sense of the historical cataclysm through which they had lived, with their attitude to the new society, and with its attitude to them. The stuff of literature was hence furnished by the revolutionary events themselves, by their aftermath in the civil war, and then by the gradual emergence of a new society with a vastly changed fabric and texture.

From 1918 to 1929 the literary life of the country was not yet subject to the harsh and direct political interventions of later years. Censorship was formally re-established by a decree of the Council of People's Commissars in 1922, under the name *Glavlit* ('Chief Directorate for Literary Affairs'), but like its tsarist predecessor it was preventative in character and for most of the 1920s nobody was *required* to give public assent to beliefs not sincerely held. In July 1925 the party central committee issued a judicious-sounding resolution in which it declared its intention not to arbitrate – at least for the time being – between the various warring literary groups. With the tolerant and sophisticated Anatoly Lunacharsky in charge of cultural affairs, and with a high proportion of the Bolshevik leaders (Lenin, Trotsky, Bukharin, etc.) being intellectuals – even though expressing contempt for their own kind – it was taken for granted that the creative process was not amenable to crude administrative control. It was also understood that in the arts, as well as in science and technology, the new society would have to lean on pre-revolutionary tradition and achievement. Workers from the factory bench and peasants from the plough could not be magically converted into engineers, writers and painters. An attempt to create a specifically proletarian culture by the so-called 'Proletkul't', through which workers and peasants were to be rapidly trained as poets and novelists, was discountenanced by the party and abandoned as early as 1923; the whole idea was politically obnoxious to Lenin since it presupposed that there could be autonomous or spontaneous 'proletarian' activity not subject to party control. In literary terms, as is evident from the products of *Kuznitsa* ('The Smithy', founded as a splinter group of *Proletkul't* in 1920), the proletarian poets were derivative in their techniques, freely borrowing from the idiom of the futurists and the symbolists in their hymns of praise to the revolution and the machine; their calls for the depersonalization of man in the collective and for a radical break with the old culture seemed like a parody of Mayakovsky, and were probably not very appealing to the flesh-and-blood proletariat. (Some members of the group, such as Mikhail Gerasimov, Vladimir Kirillov and Vasily Kazin, could claim to be genuine proletarians, or peasants by birth, but their most militant theoretician, Aleksey Gastev, was the son of a school-teacher.)

Just as in science, technology and industrial management the party had to rely in the early years of the revolution on 'bourgeois specialists', so in the field of literature and the arts it invited the collaboration of 'uncommitted' writers, some of them inherited from the old regime, and known as 'fellow travellers' (*poputchiki*), putting up for the time being with their vacillating unreliability in ideological matters and their tendency to put artistic integrity above mere political considerations. The party's basic policy in the first decade after the revolution, until the last years of the 1920s when Stalin triumphed completely over his rivals, was to work for the adherence of writers to the revolutionary cause, to lead them to a social and political commitment which, it was hoped, would make them real allies (and not just ineffectual, false conformists) in the attainment of the party's distant goals, as well as in its day-to-day struggle to achieve moral authority over the population. In these conditions of relative latitude, Soviet literature of the 1920s seems rich and varied by comparison with what it was to become. Some of it even helped to create an atmosphere, conveyed in artistically effective terms, of genuine revolutionary fervour, which, however, faded as the years went by. The October Revolution itself was greeted at the time in ecstatic, even religious terms by several poets who already before the revolution had tended to view the universe and human history as mere reflections of the transcendental. The symbolists Blok and Bely, for instance, interpreted the revolution as a millennial event, equalled only by the coming of Christ. Sergey Yesenin mistook the grand designs of the Bolsheviks for a plan to build a rural Utopia in which there would be universal reconciliation and brotherly love. Only Mayakovsky was able to combine a beatific vision of the future promised by October with a political understanding of the revolution's true nature. Already in April 1917 he had written: 'Today, the great heresy of the socialists is coming true as an unheard-of reality.' He was contemptuous of the mysticism which saw the hand of God in the great historical events, and he accepted with enthusiasm the crucial idea of class warfare *à outrance*. It is interesting to contrast Blok's 'Twelve', with its glimpse of Christ invisibly leading the revolutionaries, with the cheerful blasphemy of Mayakovsky's 'Mystery-Bouffe', staged by Meyerhold in 1918 in honour of the first anniversary of the revolution. In this boisterous mock mystery play, entry into the proletarian kingdom on earth is forbidden 'to the poor in spirit' and granted only to him 'who has calmly planted a knife in the enemy's body and walked away with a song'. During its whole existence, the Soviet regime has never found a better literary ally than Mayakovsky – though his flamboyant self-identification with it was a mask for personal unhappiness. As Andrey Sinyavsky has pointed out in his essay 'On Socialist Realism', Mayakovsky was the only Soviet poet to create a style fully in tune with, and expressive of, the new epoch. Stalin had good reason to proclaim him the greatest poet of the Soviet era.

In many ways, this earliest period in Soviet literature was its finest. Certainly there were never again to be such poetic tributes to the revolution as then rang out in unmistakably genuine accents. It was, however, only a small minority of Russian writers who wholeheartedly accepted October. The Bolshevik seizure of power was seen by many Russian intellectuals as a usurpation. When Lunacharsky, shortly after his appointment as People's Commissar of Enlightenment, invited more than 120 writers and artists to a conference in December 1917, only five appeared (they included Blok, Mayakovsky and Meyerhold). Some of Russia's greatest writers were cool or hostile. Even Maksim Gor'ky, one of the future sponsors of 'socialist realism', denounced Lenin in his newspaper *Novaya Zhizn'* during 1917–18. Nikolay Gumilyov, the leader of the 'acmeists' (who favoured clarity of diction and concreteness of image as opposed to the diffuseness of the symbolists), was shot as a counter-revolutionary, and his wife, Anna Akhmatova, saw the revolution as the beginning of a time of troubles in which poetry would be 'like a hungry beggar, knocking at the door of strangers who will not open up'. Osip Mandel'shtam (who had been associated with Gumilyov and Akhmatova in the acmeist Poets' Guild formed in 1912) also soon found himself hopelessly at odds with the new regime. Boris Pasternak already in 1917 had the reservations about man's ability to transform his own nature, or to direct the course of history, which he was to articulate in *Dr Zhivago* four decades later. A number of Russian writers (Ivan Bunin, Aleksey Remizov, Dmitry Merezhkovsky) emigrated for good; others (Aleksandr Kuprin, Marina Tsvetayeva) emigrated only to return much later in the 1930s. Yet others (Aleksey Tolstoy, Il'ya Ehrenburg) emigrated briefly and returned in the early 1920s, when it seemed that Russia was safe for the progressive literary intelligentsia and indeed more congenial in some ways than before. In his satirical novel *Julio Jurenito* (1922) Ehrenburg had remarked sardonically that Bolshevik prisons would not differ greatly from bourgeois ones. It was perhaps in this spirit that the majority of the fellow travellers settled down in the years of NEP to a relatively detached consideration of recent history and of the new social realities. The apocalyptic days had gone by. Blok died in 1921, already deaf to the 'music of the Revolution'; Yesenin committed suicide in 1925; and only Mayakovsky seemed able to sustain the epic charge which the revolution had given his poetry (*Vladimir Il'ich Lenin*, 1924, and *All Right*, 1927).

The prose of the 1920s is for the most part lacking in clear-cut commitment to the revolutionary cause. The outstanding early prose work on the theme of revolution and civil war, Isaak Babel''s *Red Cavalry*, was even at the time of publication (1926) attacked for the author's apparent detachment from the grandiose events he had witnessed. But Babel''s purposes were literary, not political or didactic. He wanted to lift Russian prose out of the rut of psychological realism, and to introduce 'southern' colour and flamboyance into the traditional Russian 'greyness'. He believed that his native Odessa might become a new literary capital which would be in conscious opposition to the coldness and drabness of the north. As he said in his programmatic literary essay 'Odessa' (1917): 'Doesn't it seem that in Russian literature there has so far been no real ... description of the sun?' Although Babel' himself soon fell silent and was arrested in the late 1930s, his idea did bear some fruit in the Soviet period. If there is any Soviet prose with a specific flavour not entirely derivative of the pre-revolutionary styles, it is to be found in this southern Russian 'school of Odessa' with its colourful, romantic flavour. Valentin Katayev and Konstantin Paustovsky, for example, managed to carry some of its quality even into the 1930s and 1940s (e.g. Katayev's *Lone White Sail*, 1936). Another writer associated with this group – although he was not born in Odessa and stood somewhat apart from the others – was Aleksandr Grin, who in his rejection of Russian realism went so far as to invent his own romantic country of 'Grinland'.

Apart from this exotic element, soon to wither in the cold climate of Stalinism, the most memorable prose of the 1920s is perhaps that which exploited the rich social incongruities of post-revolutionary society. The satire of Il'f and Petrov (also 'Odessans'), Bulgakov and Zoshchenko triumphantly revived the spirit of Gogol – to whom some of them were explicitly indebted for their literary manner and devices. The Russia of Lenin could vie with that of Nicholas I in its comic potentialities.

At a more solemn level, the prose literature of the 1920s was preoccupied with recent history and the changed status of the individual (particularly the intellectual) in society. In the novels of Boris Pil'nyak, Leonid Leonov, Aleksandr Fadeyev, Mikhail Sholokhov, Vsevolod Ivanov and Yury Olesha, to mention the best of the chroniclers of the civil war and post-revolutionary life, there is a search for self-definition which provides a certain thematic continuity with the pre-revolutionary Russian prose tradition, where the problem of national and individual identity was always a paramount concern. There are often also conspicuous formal influences of the past (Dostoyevsky in the case of Leonov, Tolstoy in that of Sholokhov and Fadeyev). Pil'nyak, Ivanov and some others strove to elaborate an original style, but their so-called 'ornamental' manner, with its elaborate ringing of the changes on verbal

191

motifs, also had antecedents in pre-revolutionary writing (notably that of Bely and Remizov).

Common to most of this fellow-traveller prose of the 1920s was the implication that the revolution, however disagreeable or even squalid it may have been, was nevertheless something that flowed naturally from Russian history. Pil'nyak, in what was chronologically the first Soviet novel, *The Naked Year* (1922), established the cliché of the revolution as an unleashing of elemental cleansing forces which were sweeping away the past like a raging blizzard. He also coined the phrase 'men in leather jackets' to denote the Bolsheviks – who were at first depicted by him and other fellow travellers as an emanation of revolutionary anarchy. Soon, however, as in Pil'nyak's later novel, *Machines and Wolves* (1923–4), the commissars are shown more realistically as representatives of a powerful organizing will essentially in conflict with revolutionary turmoil. By the mid-1920s the clash between old and new, town and country, man and machine, anarchy and discipline, is the predominant theme of Soviet prose. The attitude of the individual writer to the new regime, which began to look less ruthless as the unheroic years of NEP went by, could be benevolently neutral (Leonov), fervently pro-Bolshevik (Fadeyev), or sceptical to the point of hostility (Pil'nyak). But almost all the leading novelists of the time shared a feeling that they were witnesses of a process beyond good and evil – a contest between implacable historical forces which individual human beings could scarcely influence. Society was seen as an arena for the interplay of impersonal forces against whose background individual self-assertion was a futile gesture. The fellow travellers thus helped to create a public mood in which dissent, even the clinging to one's personal idiosyncrasies, was at the best quixotic and comic, and at the worst the reprehensible posturing of doomed solipsists. The puny eccentrics who resisted were bound, in the current phrase of the time, to be thrown on to 'the rubbish-dump of history'. Even where the author sympathizes with such characters, as Olesha does in his *Envy* (1927), the lone, romantic rebel is made to wallow hopelessly in his own debasement. Olesha's anti-hero says: 'We envy the coming epoch. It is the envy of old age.' Such last-ditch individualism was frequently identified with *meshchanstvo* – a petty concern with one's own private life and feelings, a longing to hide in what Mayakovsky called the 'musty mattresses of time'. As opposed to this we soon see the 'positive hero', the brash 'new man', portrayed sympathetically, if rarely convincingly. He may be an iron-willed civil war leader, as in Fadeyev's *Rout* (1927), or an industrial manager, as in Olesha's *Envy*. The inevitable doom of those individuals or social groups who fail to march 'in step with history' is a major theme of Sholokhov's *Quiet Flows the Don* (vols. 1–3, 1928–33; vol. 4 only 1940), though there is an underlying assumption running through the novel that ultimately the doings of men are subordinated to the higher judgements of nature.

Yet with all this there was generally a strong element of doubt and ambiguity in the literature of the NEP period. Throughout the 1920s there was no certainty that the 'new' would really triumph. The Bolsheviks may have held the commanding political heights, but in social terms the daunting question of 'who – whom?' – as Lenin had put it – was still conspicuously unresolved. In Leonov's *Badgers* (1924), for instance, the victory of the leather-jacketed Bolsheviks from the town looked by no means assured, and there semed to be much foolhardiness about their challenge to peasant Russia. Leonov was typical in his ambivalence, and the reader is never sure whether he was more impressed by the super-human doggedness of the commissars or by the seemingly invincible inertia of the masses.

The 1920s – particularly the second half – were an unhappy and, at least in terms of publication, a rather barren time for poetry. The centre of the stage was held by Mayakovsky and some of his admirers and imitators (notably Semyon Kirsanov and Nikolay Aseyev), but their bravura was in sharp contrast to the mutedness or silence of most of Russia's lyric voices. It is now known that, despite the relative mildness of censorship during the 1920s, some poets, in particular Mandel'shtam, were virtually banned from publishing in the Moscow literary periodicals, though they were sometimes able to appear in print in the less 'vigilant' provinces. Such proscription could sometimes be overcome by appeals to powerful patrons (Mandel'shtam was able to publish a volume of verse in 1928, thanks to the help of Bukharin), or concessions of an ideological nature, but an even graver problem was that the general atmosphere caused a kind of 'dumbness' which affected Akhmatova, Pasternak and Mandel'shtam in varying degrees. Mandel'shtam was able to write no new verse, only some prose, between 1924 and 1930. Akhmatova published nothing between 1924 and 1940. Pasternak deliberately turned from lyrical poetry to an epic style which he felt was more in keeping with the era. His two long poems *1905* (1925–6) and *Lieutenant Schmidt* (1926–7) were attempts to come to grips with the theme of revolution and were, as such, a concession to the spirit of the times. It is perhaps significant that the most affecting lyrical poetry was Yesenin's – his agonized but submissive disillusionment was powerfully conveyed in such poems as 'Return to my Native Place' and 'Soviet Russia', written a year before his suicide in 1925. The romantic prose of such writers as Babel' and Ivanov was paralleled in the poetry of Eduard Bagritsky and Nikolay Tikhonov, both of whom wrote epics on heroic themes in exotic settings which showed some influence of the 'counter-revolutionary' Gumilyov. A highly original poet of the 1920s was Nikolay Zabolotsky whose work is, on the surface, a kind of bizarre verbal genre painting, but embodies a pessimistic philosophy that brought him into official disfavour in the later years.

At the turn of the decade, Stalin's 'revolution from above', the first Five-Year Plan and the beginning of collectivization temporarily resolved the doubts of several of the leading fellow travellers. There was even a resurgence of the millennial fervour which had been felt by some at the time of the October Revolution. Maksim Gor'ky's decision around this time (1929) to return to Russia and lend his authority to the Soviet regime was combined with evident approval of Stalin's measures to push Russia towards a future which, it was confidently expected, would see real social justice and an end to the cultural schism between people and intelligentsia. The more sceptical some writers had been, the more enthusiastic they now appeared to be. Leonov in his *Sot'* (1929), Katayev in *Time Forward!* (1932) and Pil'nyak in *The Volga Flows to the Caspian Sea* (1930) seemed to proclaim the imminence of victory over the physical environment and human nature itself. One of the most remarkable novels of this period was Ehrenburg's *Second Day* (1932) in which the author argued that the intellectual who still gave priority to the claims of conscience and independent moral judgement was, in effect, betraying the higher cause of socialism. In a debased and vulgarized form, the theme of this novel by Ehrenburg was typical of much 'socialist realist' literature in the 1930s. Those who would not submit or see the light – so the message ran – would be unmasked and destroyed.

The actual doctrine of 'socialist realism' was launched only in 1932. The idea, and the term itself, were introduced to the literary community, without any previous public debate, in a leading article in *Literary Gazette* in May that year. In the previous month the party had suddenly announced the liquidation of all the existing literary organizations and groups. By this time, because of the worsening political atmosphere, the existence of some of them was already largely nominal, but they had all once reflected important and genuine differences. Mention has been made of movements which in one way or another claimed to be innovatory. But there were also voices, representing perhaps the majority of the leading Soviet writers, which spoke out strongly in favour of a more conventional view of the nature and function of literature. Chief amongst these was the Marxist literary critic and editor, Aleksandr Voronsky, the guiding spirit of a group calling itself *Pereval* ('The Pass'), which arose at the end of 1923 and was associated with the literary journal *Krasnaya Nov'* ('Red Virgin Soil'). A declaration published there in 1927 spoke of the need to preserve continuity with Russian and world classical literature. In his theoretical writings, Voronsky developed the view that art could not be seen as a mere social instrument, or reduced to the sum of the techniques employed in its production (as both the constructivists and *LEF* – with support from the formalists – maintained), but sprang from intuitive or subconscious impulses beyond rational control or explanation. This implied that art was above the class struggle, and Voronsky was accused by the militant left of deviating from Marxism in favour of Bergson's intuitivism. (More seriously, he was later denounced – perhaps for reasons unconnected with his literary views – as a Trotskyist, and he disappeared during the purges.) Although Voronsky came to grief because of his theoretical arguments, his spirit of compromise as editor of *Krasnaya Nov'* (from 1921 until his dismissal in 1927) accorded well with the actual party line almost to the end of the 1920s. Apart from the neutrality implied in the party's resolution of 1925, the 'conservative' literary tastes of Lenin and other Soviet leaders tended to favour middle-of-the-road resistance to both 'bourgeois-intellectual' and 'proletarian' intransigence of the left. After the collapse of *Proletkul't*, the cause of proletarian militancy in literature had been taken up by the 'Russian Association of Proletarian Writers' (RAPP), formed at a conference of proletarian writers in January 1925. Bowing to the party's resolution of July that year, RAPP modified its aggressive attitude to the fellow travellers, but it never lost sight of its aim of 'proletarianizing' Soviet literature. (Few of its members were actual proletarians by origin, least of all Leopol'd Averbakh, its general secretary from 1926 till its dissolution, or Fadeyev, the most notable writer connected with it.) RAPP prepared the way for socialist realism by insisting that Soviet writers must abandon the 'wait-and-see' attitude of the fellow travellers, and make a positive commitment to communist ideology. They also elaborated what was to be the main aesthetic requirement of socialist realism, namely that writers must 'learn from the classics', putting the literary techniques of nineteenth-century Russian realism at the service of the proletariat and the party.

Although, typically, he was to liquidate its authors, Stalin found this formula well-suited both to his political aims and his personal tastes. In 1929, after the final breaking of his opponents in the party, Stalin allowed RAPP to start a campaign of intimidation against uncommitted writers. Two leading fellow travellers, Boris Pil'nyak and Yevgeny Zamyatin, both of them officials of the largest literary organization, the Union of Writers, little more than an ordinary professional association (not to be confused with the later Union of Soviet Writers after 1934), were hounded on account of work which had been published abroad. Zamyatin's anti-utopian novel *We* had been written in 1920 and was published abroad in 1924. Pil'nyak's *Mahogany* appeared in Berlin in 1929. There was no law against Soviet writers publishing abroad, but these two particular cases were used as a pretext for impugning the political reliability of the two authors in question and of the fellow travellers in general. This was the first such concerted campaign against intellectuals designed to cow them and force their allegiance. Pil'nyak recanted, in a manner that was to become familiar, but Zamyatin refused to yield and was allowed to emigrate (in 1931).

Although it took some time for the lesson to sink in, this was the point of no return for Soviet intellectuals. Paradoxically, however, the party resolution of 1932, which condemned the 'excesses' of RAPP and ordered its liquidation, looked at first like a gesture of reconciliation. It was announced that writers were now to belong to a 'unified' organization which would be open to all, irrespective of their class antecedents (i.e. whether they had been proletarians or fellow travellers), as long as they were prepared to give their general assent to party policy and to the literary doctrine of socialist realism. At first it looked as though the party was simply providing a relatively loose organizational and doctrinal framework which, almost in the spirit of *Pereval*, would give scope to a wide range of individual talent – from, say, Fadeyev to Pasternak. The first Writers' Congress in 1934, which was held to inaugurate the new Union of Soviet Writers, seemed to confirm this impression. Furthermore, the rise of Hitler and the beginnings of the 'popular front' policy appeared to dictate ideological tolerance in an anti-fascist camp which had to embrace liberal opinion on an international scale. But things soon took a very different turn. The progressive deterioration of the political situation in Russia after the murder of Kirov (1934) destroyed the conditions for independent creative activity of any kind, and by 1939 the best that any Soviet writer who wished to keep his integrity could hope for was to be allowed to fall silent. Babel', Pil'nyak and many other Soviet writers were arrested and died in camps. Akhmatova chose silence, Pasternak took refuge in translation, and Mandel'shtam, who in 1934 had written and read to some friends a poem condemning Stalin, spent three years in exile before being finally sent to his death in a concentration camp at the end of 1938. After Stalin walked out of the first performance of Shostakovich's opera *A Lady Macbeth of Mtsensk* in 1936, it was made plain that socialist realism had to be interpreted as a crass and eclectic style which reminded some Russians of the folksy vulgarity associated with the reign of Alexander III. 'Formalism' (widened to mean any kind of stylistic originality) was now treated as a political crime, and when Meyerhold, in a final gesture of despair, publicly refused to accept socialist realism in a speech in 1939, he was arrested and disappeared. When it was first launched, socialist realism was supposedly meant to denote a literary manner which had arisen spontaneously, as a natural development of nineteenth-century 'critical' realism, differing from it only in the vital respect that it was optimistic or affirmative in its view of the progress of

196

mankind towards socialism. It was held to have been exemplified in Gor'ky's *Mother* (1906) and later in some of the fellow-traveller writing of the 1920s – Fedin, Leonov, Sholokhov and others were regarded as having written socialist realist novels well before the term had become a standard one. In fact the doctrine has always been definable less in literary terms than in terms of the political demands made of writers and artists at various periods. Anybody who in the 1920s had supported the Soviet regime or given an optimistic appraisal of its prospects was later described as a socialist realist (unless he was swept away in one of the recurrent purges). In the 1930s, to qualify as a good socialist realist it was safest to write historical chronicles, such as those of Aleksey Tolstoy on Ivan the Terrible and Peter the Great, which contained thinly disguised flattery of Stalin. The most widely acclaimed product of socialist realism on a contemporary theme was the pedestrian but uplifting novel by Nikolay Ostrovsky, *How the Steel was Tempered* (1935).

As has often been pointed out, the war brought relief to writers in the sense that nothing more was required of them than to play a minor part in a clear-cut struggle for national survival which overrode or made irrelevant the question of artistic integrity. Some of the semi-documentary fiction of the wartime period had at least a certain graphic immediacy which ensures its survival: Konstantin Simonov's *Days and Nights* (1944), Vasily Grossman's *The People is Immortal* (1942) and particularly Pyotr Vershigora's *People with a Clear Conscience* (1946), an uncompleted novel about the partisans, are refreshingly superior to some of the blatantly falsified accounts of the war which appeared later. Although, by the nature of things, only rhetorical or epic poetry was called for (Aleksandr Tvardovsky's long ballad about the ordinary Soviet soldier Vasily Tyorkin was immensely popular), there was also a revival of true lyric poetry; this was the heyday of the middle generation of poets, such as Aleksey Surkov, Margarita Aliger and Konstantin Simonov, who wrote poems with a personal ring, less encumbered by the obligatory official stereotyped sentiment which disfigured most of the poetry published after the war until Stalin's death. In these conditions of comparative relaxation, Akhmatova and Pasternak (his collection *On Early Trains* (1943) contains poems on topical wartime themes) were able to publish again after years of silence; this gave rise to a widespread feeling among the intelligensia that peace might bring with it a change for the better.

But all hopes were dashed by the Central Committee decrees (1946–8) on art and literature associated with the name of Zhdanov, the member of the Politburo who dealt with cultural matters. Akhmatova was denounced by Zhdanov as 'half-nun, half-whore' and the journal that had published her verse was liquidated. For the remaining years of

Stalin's life the Soviet creative intelligentsia lived in a constant state of fear, and the political demands made on writers were so excessive as to destroy even the propaganda value of literature. Socialist realists were now required to ignore the grim realities of Soviet post-war life and present instead fanciful pictures of material abundance and social harmony.

In the years since Stalin's death in 1953, Soviet literature has benefited from a gradual abatement of the paralysing terror which had been the chief instrument of rule since the early 1930s. In theory the party has continued to maintain that literature must be regulated by ideological and administrative controls, but in the absence of total terror these controls became progressively less effective, particularly after Khrushchev's selective denunciation of Stalin's 'mistakes' at the Twentieth Party Congress in 1956 – this was a fatal blow to the myth of the party's infallibility. There have been three major attempts to set the clock back: in 1954 as a reaction to the first cautious challenges after Stalin's death to official doctrine (Vladimir Pomerantsev's essay 'On Sincerity in Literature' in *Novy Mir*, December 1953, and Ehrenburg's novel *The Thaw* in *Znamya*, May 1954); then, in 1957, in panic at the Hungarian revolution and the literary response to the Twentieth Congress (e.g. Vladimir Dudintsev's *Not by Bread Alone* and Aleksandr Yashin's short story 'The Levers'); and finally, in 1962–3, when Khrushchev, provoked by an exhibition of what he took to be modern painting, for a brief while set about checking the 'liberal' trend set in motion by his own impetuous initiatives.

The capacity of the Soviet leadership to exploit literature for its own ends continued to decline after Khrushchev's fall in 1964, despite clumsy efforts by his successors to restore a measure of ideological discipline. The party still disposes of a formidable apparatus of cultural control and repression, but its will to use it has weakened in the face of a greater independence of spirit at home and the need to achieve at least an appearance of respectability abroad. In the mid-1970s, the conflict with China and the concurrent policy of détente with the United States clearly imposed certain restraints in the handling of the consequences of 'destalinization' and of some of Khrushchev's specific interventions in literary matters, particularly his speech to the Third Writers' Congress in 1959. On this occasion he said that the writers should not come running 'to the government' for the settlement of all their disputes, thus implicitly (and perhaps unwittingly) suggesting that literature and the arts were an area of Soviet life which could not, or should not, be an object of absolute party control. Whatever his reasons for this concession, the immediate result was a certain tolerance – apart from the interlude of a few months in 1962–3 – for the public airing in circumspect language of differences of opinion in literary matters. An open fissure was thus allowed to develop in the 'monolith' of ideological unity which Stalin had maintained by repeated waves of terror. In this unprecedented situation, the party began to pursue a policy of holding a balance between the so-called 'conservatives' (or 'dogmatists' as they are often styled by their opponents in the Soviet Union) and the 'liberals' who sometimes refer to themselves as 'progressives'. The former are joined together by a vested interest in maintaining the rule of mediocrity and are clearly nostalgic for the straightforward situation of Stalin's time; they militantly uphold the doctrine of socialist realism, put loyalty to party discipline above artistic independence and are identified with a scarcely-veiled nationalist, even chauvinist (and anti-semitic), mood. There were signs in the second half of the 1960s that some of the 'dogmatists' were as disenchanted with the post-Stalin leadership as the 'liberals', and that the Politburo of Brezhnev and Kosygin, trying to steer a 'centrist' course, was at times as disturbed by opposition from the right as by opposition from the left. Some novels by right-wingers, such as Vsevolod Kochetov (*What do you want?*, 1969) and Ivan Shevtsov (*Love and Hatred*, 1970), called unambiguously for the restoration of strong rule and ideological order. Both novels provoked controversy in the Soviet press, some critics attacking and others defending them. This in itself was a good example of how radical divisions in literary (and by implication political) opinion could now be revealed in public.

Apart from Mikhail Sholokhov, there are few writers of genuine literary achievement among the 'conservatives'. Not surprisingly their ranks contain a high proportion of provincials who tend to be resentful of the more sophisticated metropolitan writers. Office-holders in the various writers' organizations are also, needless to say, predominantly conservative. They are especially strong and militant in the Writers' Union of the RSFSR, which was set up in 1958 as a counterweight to the Writers' Union of the USSR where the liberals (particularly in its Moscow branch) were occasionally able to exert influence, and even get themselves elected to the board. But by and large the liberals have been excluded from positions of authority in the cultural establishment and, like their counterparts in the last century, they have made their voices heard mainly through certain literary periodicals, especially *Novy Mir*.

During the editorship of the poet Aleksandr Tvardovsky (who resigned under pressure in 1970) the monthly *Novy Mir* became a latter-day equivalent of *Fatherland Notes* (*Otechestvennyye Zapiski*) in the period (1868–77) when it was edited by N. A. Nekrasov. By its choice of authors (Solzhenitsyn among others) and the skilful use in articles on current affairs of the kind of veiled language which in Russia is traditionally called 'Aesopian', *Novy Mir* gave expression to the liberal position during the 1960s. Its principal demand, sometimes defined editorially in so many words by Tvardovsky himself, was quite simply for truth and sincerity. In the liberal view a writer's loyalty can only be to his own conscience. Believing that there is nothing incompatible between patriotism and an openness to outside influences, the liberals have also been in favour of breaking down cultural barriers between Russia and the West. Unlike the 'westernizers' of the last century, probably few of them are naïve enough to think that the West can offer some ready-made solution to Russia's political and social problems. They appear to believe, however, that literature and the arts, by gradually changing the general climate of opinion, can contribute to a slow process of reform.

The moral commitment of the post-Stalin liberal writers and the consequent need to relate their work to the general political background make it difficult to assess their achievement in purely literary terms. There has been little writing in prose to compare with the best work of the 1920s. Novels and stories that created a stir in the immediate post-Stalin years represent at best a kind of inverted socialist realism. Ehrenburg's *Thaw* (1954), which gave its name to this period, can be interpreted as a polemic with his own earlier *Second Day*: its implicit conclusion is that in times of conformism imposed by terror the only honourable course for the individual is to try to maintain, at least privately, some kind of personal integrity of intellectual and moral judgement. The next important work of the 'thaw' period, Dudintsev's *Not By Bread Alone*, appeared in the auspicious climate created by Khrushchev's revelations about Stalin at the Twentieth Party Congress in 1956. Flat and ill-constructed, with a schematic conflict between 'good' and 'bad', it is distinguished from a standard socialist realist novel only by its reversal of the values that had hitherto been obligatory. Instead of being vested abstractly in the party, 'good' now resides, according to Dudintsev's reappraisal, in the conscience of individuals who are prepared to fight for the truth as they see it. The characters in Ehrenburg's *Thaw* had been passive in their resistance to 'collective' pressures, but Dudintsev's hero fights actively and heroically for what he believes to be right. The highlight of the first phase of post-Stalin 'liberalization' – and a contributing factor in its abrupt suspension – was the publication in the second half of 1956 of two volumes of a literary almanac entitled *Literary Moscow*. Edited by Veniamin Kaverin, Konstantin Paustovsky and others, it was something in the nature of a collective gesture on the part of a whole group of Soviet writers. A novel by Emmanuil Kazakevich in the first volume, 'The House on the Square', gave a revealing description of the atmosphere in the Soviet army of occupation in Germany. The second volume contained what was perhaps the most explosive work to appear by the end of 1956: Aleksandr

Yashin's short story 'The Levers', a study in the falsity of public attitudes engendered by Stalinism.

In the following years the 'new wave' Soviet prose gradually shifted the focus of its interest from public values (roughly speaking, the question of how individuals should behave as members of society or of the party) to the exploration of more private aspects of life. The typical genre was now the long short story or short novel (*povest'*). This was partly a reaction against the long-windedness of Stalinist literature, but it also reflected a lessening concern with the broad social background against which small private dramas may be acted out. At first this low-key fiction, of which some of the most successful practitioners are Vladimir Tendryakov, Yury Kazakov, Vasily Aksyonov, I. Grekova (Yelena Ventuel'), Vitaly Syomin, Yury Nagibin, Yury Trifonov, Andrey Bitov, Nikolay Dubov, Georgy Vladimov, Anatoly Gladilin, Viktor Nekrasov and Vladimir Voynovich, was met with great hostility, and it is still frowned on by the conservative critics, who complain about its 'abstract humanism' and concern with the trivia of human existence, rather than with the grand perspectives of the 'building of communism'. What is most offensive to its enemies about this new prose is the absence of 'positive heroes' who, in classical socialist realism, were supposed to serve as inspirational models to Soviet readers. This is not to say that the new fiction does not raise, if only by implication, some of the broader issues of Soviet society. There are of course specific problems which arise from the havoc caused by the years of Stalinism. The extent, for example, to which the Russian countryside was pillaged in order to pay for industrialization has been demonstrated in an impressive body of writing, mainly in the form of sketches (*ocherki*) and short stories. Reminiscent of the populist prose of the last century in their frank documentation of the country's major social problem, the writings of Valentin Ovechkin, Yefim Dorosh, S. Zalygin, Fyodor Abramov, B. Mozhayev and others came close to saying outright that the party's agricultural policy has been a disastrous failure from beginning to end.

Some of the writers in this group (often referred to collectively as the *derevenshchiki*, 'village writers') have tended to emphasize a more positive aspect of the countryside as a repository of traditional values which are disappearing in the towns. This is a remarkable feature of some of Tendryakov's stories. Sometimes there are distinctly religious or Slavophile undertones, as in the sketches and stories of Vladimir Soloukhin. Other interesting 'village' prose has been written by Vasily Belov, Valentin Rasputin and Vasily Shukshin.

Little of literary worth has been published by way of humorous or satirical prose-writing on contemporary themes – in this, as in other respects, the post-Stalin years have not been able to match the 1920s. All that springs to mind are some of the stories by Fazil' Iskander (who in less constraining circumstances might have blossomed into a writer of major satirical talent), and one story by Vasily Aksyonov. A humorous prose epic by Vladimir Voynovich remains unpublished in the Soviet Union.

An important branch of prose in the last decade or so have been retrospective and relatively unvarnished accounts, in the form of semi-memoirs or fiction, of the wartime experience. Some of the assiduously fostered myths of the Stalin period have been disposed of by Konstantin Simonov and – most effectively of all from a literary standpoint – by Vasil' Bykov.

Some of the older fellow-traveller writers have also made noteworthy contributions to post-Stalin prose. Like Ehrenburg, both Leonov and Katayev have published novels in which they seem to take issue with their earlier attitudes and rationalizations. From the literary point of view the most rewarding of these works is Katayev's *Holy Well* (1966), a dream-journey into the author's own past with a curious (and avowed) indebtedness to Fellini's film technique. There is a devastating portrait of a literary time-server who may well embody some of the features of his own past that Katayev now most regrets. The story also contains a gruesome image for the Soviet writer obedient to Stalin's whims: a cat which had been trained to speak by its Georgian owner and dies while trying to mouth the latest polysyllabic catchword. Leonov's *Evgenia Ivanovna* (1963) is a similar study in fellow-traveller 'revisionism', though the implications are deeply buried beneath layers of characteristic ambivalence. The heroine is a Russian woman taken into emigration at the end of the civil war by her husband and then abandoned by him. After marrying a distinguished English archaeologist (she presumes her Russian husband is dead), Evgenia Ivanovna goes with him to Soviet Georgia where she meets her ex-husband, who has now become an exponent of the crass 'national Bolshevism' which was the author's own credo in the late 1920s and 1930s. Not all surviving novelists of the older generation have gone so far in rebutting their own earlier beliefs; some who no doubt had fewer illusions, such as Kaverin and Paustovsky, have made telling contributions to the liberal re-appraisal of the Stalinist past. Sholokhov, on the other hand, in speeches at Writers' and Party Congresses had adopted an outspokenly right-wing line (in 1966, for instance, at the Twenty-Third Party Congress, he called for stern measures against dissident intellectuals).

The greatest and most original achievement of post-Stalin prose to be published in the Soviet Union is undeniably Solzhenitsyn's short novel on Stalin's concentration camps, *One Day in the Life of Ivan Denisovich* (November 1962). It is ironical that this work, which must be judged primarily for its lasting worth as a work of literature in the grand Russian tradition, should have appeared as the result of a squalid political intrigue. There seems no doubt that Khrushchev personally sanctioned its publication by *Novy Mir* because he thought that a frank account of Stalin's concentration camps would help mobilize public opinion behind him at a moment when his position was threatened by his rivals in the praesidium. Once again, in order to gain a tactical advantage – as in his revelations about Stalin in 1956 – Khrushchev failed to take into account the long-term effect of his actions. By exploding the limits of what, thematically speaking, had hitherto been possible for Soviet writers, and by giving the stamp of quasi-official approval to a work which implicitly questioned the legitimacy of all the Soviet regime's basic claims, Khrushchev prepared the ground for the opposition to the party's control of literature which spread among the Soviet literary intelligentsia during the following years. Solzhenitsyn himself, in an open letter to delegates at the Writers' Congress in May 1967 and in a subsequent letter to the Board of the Writers' Union in December 1967, denounced the censorship of Soviet literature and the failure of the Union of Writers to protect the interests of its members.

But the literary significance of *One Day in the Life of Ivan Denisovich* is far greater than its political impact. As in any true work of art, the aesthetic quality transcends the content, i.e. the documentary, ideological or political aspects of the raw material. Even the best of other post-Stalin prose writing tends to rely in considerable degree for its literary effect on the reader's awareness of the peculiar social and political context in which it is written. If such awareness of the context were to be taken away, much of this writing would seem far less significant. Without the knowledge that it is written in defiance of certain previously imposed standards, and that a challenge to them still involves difficulties or hazards for the author, one would lose the odd sense of tension which Soviet literature derives from its non-literary context: it is the difference between watching a man walking on a tightrope and watching a man walking on the ground. The remarkable feature of this first published work of Solzhenitsyn is that, though his subject matter is peculiarly Soviet, it is at the same time independent of the geographical and historical context. In other words the political implications of his novel, as well as the time and place in which the action is set, are incidental to the author's achievement of having fashioned a statement of universal application out of the squalid material of life in a concentration camp. One day in the life of Ivan Denisovich seems uncannily symbolic of one day in *anybody's* life. Like Kafka's *Trial*, Solzhenitsyn's novel shows the human condition as a captive state from which there is no escape and for which there is no rational explanation. The feeling of being trapped and doomed is considerably heightened by making the reader see the concentration camp through the eyes of an illiterate peasant who is unable to rationalize his predicament as an intellectual would. To achieve this effect, Solzhenitsyn resorted to the device known as *skaz*, in which the language of the narrative is the same – in a slightly stylized form – as that of the main characters and of the particular milieu in which they live (in this case the speech of a peasant from Central Russia intermixed with concentration-camp slang). This in itself raises the novel to a higher literary level than any other prose published in the post-Stalin period. It was the first challenge in many years to the drab, emasculated idiom of socialist realism from which few of the younger prose writers referred to above have succeeded completely in emancipating themselves.

After 1966, when his short story, 'Zakhar-kalita', appeared in *Novy Mir*, Solzhenitsyn was unable to have any further work published in the Soviet Union. His two long novels *Cancer Ward* and *The First Circle* circulated in manuscript, as a result of which copies found their way abroad where they were published in Russian and other languages (1968 and 1969). Both these novels are more directly autobiographical than *One Day in the Life of Ivan Denisovich*. Nerzhin, the main character in *The First Circle* (which was written over a period of ten years, 1955–66), clearly to some extent represents the author himself, as does Kostoglotov in *Cancer Ward*. After his arrest at the front in 1945 Solzhenitsyn was sentenced to eight years' imprisonment, the first four of which he spent mainly in the peculiar institution described in *The First Circle* – a prison on the outskirts of Moscow in which scientists and technologists were confined in comparatively mild conditions, as long as they agreed to work on special projects – such as new spying gadgets – commissioned by Stalin and Abakumov, the head of the secret police. Solzhenitsyn was sent there on the strength of his knowledge of physics and mathematics. Disobedience meant being consigned to a forced labour camp of the type described in *One Day*, and this is what happened to Solzhenitsyn at the end of 1949. On his release in 1953 he was required to live in exile in Kazakhstan. After falling ill with some form of cancer he was allowed to go to a hospital in Tashkent, the scene of *Cancer Ward* (written in 1963–6), which thus forms the third part of a trilogy. *The First Circle* and *Cancer Ward* are much longer, more ambitious and consequently less sharply focused than *One Day*, but they give a revealing panorama of Soviet life during the late Stalin years and the first two or three years after his death. They lack the peculiar effect of distance achieved in *One Day* by the interposing of a semi-literate narrator between the author and his experiences. Owing a good deal in language and technique to the influence of Tolstoy, they belong to a more conventional tradition of Russian prose. In the summer of 1971, Solzhenitsyn authorized the publication in Paris of a new novel, *August 1914*, the first part of a series of volumes whose purpose is to explore the roots of the Russian revolution, and to call in question the official version of Soviet history. At the end of 1973, Solzhenitsyn further released for publication in Paris the first part of *The Gulag Archipelago*, a vast study of the Soviet prison and penal system from the revolution to the present day, written between 1958 and 1967. The publication of this impassioned work, which contains passages of remarkable descriptive power, was the last straw for the Soviet government. Evidently not daring to apply harsher measures for fear of the effect on world opinion, the authorities stripped him of Soviet citizenship and forcibly exiled him to Western Germany in February 1974. (For works published in exile, see the Guide to Further Reading.)

It is to the poets rather than to the prose writers (with the exception of Solzhenitsyn) that one must look for new departures in language and style in the post-Stalin era. The revival of Russian poetry in the last fifteen years or so can perhaps be explained in part as a spontaneous revolt against the stultification and debasement of the Russian language under Stalin. It was the poets who had been most sensitive to the destruction or mutilation of the sort of private values which are the natural realm of poetry. Poetic language had become hopelessly bombastic and public. From the prosodic point of view it was required to be so conventional that even imitation of Mayakovsky was viewed as dangerous 'formalism'. Most authentic poetic voices – those of Pasternak and Akhmatova, for instance – had again been silenced after the brief interlude of wartime, and such poets as continued to publish were virtually indistinguishable from each other. It was not until after 1956 that this torpor gradually came to an end and new voices were heard. At first, as in prose, the new wave of post-Stalin poetry was remarkable more for *what* it said than for its style – which remained, on the whole, unadventurous. Yevgeny Yevtushenko made his début as a 'civic' poet concerned above all to expose the evils of Stalinism, voicing the moral revulsion of his generation in a somewhat eclectic manner but with skill and courage. He was one of the first to speak frankly of many important issues, such as anti-semitism ('Babiy Yar', 1961) and the danger of a reversion to Stalinism ('Stalin's Heirs', 1962). Yevtushenko's early achievements may now seem less remarkable with the passage of time, and he has been criticized for his supposed triteness and failure to find a distinctive accent of his own. But he is a genuine lyric poet, sometimes resembling Yesenin in his candour about himself, who has felt forced to speak out urgently in a manner that did not always do justice to his best qualities. These have found expression in his more intimate, lyrical poems which attracted less attention than the 'civic' ones. In his mature work of later years he shows himself to be master of a firm and fluent poetic manner unmistakably his own.

Andrey Voznesensky, who burst on the scene a little later than

Yevtushenko, immediately created an impression of considerable originality. If Yevtushenko had been concerned with the moral enlightenment of his audience, Voznesensky aimed rather at re-invigorating the idiom and accents of poetry. In his early verse he caught the attention by his virtuosity in handling the Russian language, his ability to exploit the connotative associations of words in such a way as to achieve unusual effects of irony and ambiguity.

It is impossible to give here any idea of the range and quality of Russian poetry at the present day. Yevtushenko and Voznesensky created an atmosphere in which poets sometimes achieved the status of popular idols. In the early 1960s public hunger for verse was such that the sports stadium of Luzhniki in Moscow could be packed by almost 15,000 people for a poetry recital (although in the post-Khrushchev era the authorities have discouraged appearances by 'controversial' poets at large public gatherings and on television).

Among the younger poets who have made a name for themselves in recent years one may mention Bella Akhmadulina, Viktor Sosnora, Yunna Morits, Yevgeny Vinokurov, Aleksandr Kushner, Vladimir Kornilov, David Samoylov and Naum Korzhavin (who emigrated to the West in 1974). Iosif Brodsky, perhaps the most accomplished and original of the post-Stalin generation, has never been published in the Soviet Union, apart from several short items which appeared in anthologies in 1966 and 1967. In 1964 he was tried as a 'parasite' and banished to the Archangel region where he worked on a collective farm before being released the following year in the wake of a world-wide outcry. From the two collections of his work that have appeared in the West it is evident that his talent is in a different mould from that of Voznesensky, Yevtushenko and his other contemporaries. This may in part be due to its having been nurtured not in Moscow but in Leningrad, where the finer reverberations of Russia's 'Silver Age' of poetry never entirely died away through decades of terror, war and famine. Mandel'shtam once defined acmeism as 'nostalgia for world culture', and although Brodsky cannot be described as an acmeist in any meaningful sense, he does appear consciously to have adopted the acmeist concern for Russia's links with Europe and with 'Judeo–Christian culture' (Mandel'shtam's phrase). The futurists and some of the symbolists (including Blok) were more inclined to stress Russia's cultural separateness. Like Mandel'shtam and Akhmatova (to whom he was very close in the last years of her life) Brodsky is a true European, as can be clearly sensed in the very texture of his poetry. It has a 'classical' intonation, as opposed to the frenetic 'romantic' quality of Voznesensky, Akhmadulina and others. In 1972 Brodsky emigrated from the Soviet Union and went to live in the United States.

206

Although they are not perhaps poets in the strict sense of the word, there are several writers and performers of songs who in recent years have achieved great popularity – for the most part unofficially – with the Soviet public. Resembling French *chansonniers*, they comment on many aspects of Soviet life in sharply satirical fashion. The most lyrical of them is Bulat Okudzhava. Aleksandr Galich is noteworthy for his effective use of a racy Moscow vernacular.

Several poets of the 'middle generation' who survived the Stalin era deserve mention together with the younger poets whom they sometimes encouraged and defended. Such are Boris Slutsky, Ol'ga Berggol'ts, Leonid Martynov, Arseny Tarkovsky and Aleksandr Tvardovsky. The latter is best known for his editorship of *Novy Mir*, but his two epic poems *Into the Far Distance* (*Za dal'yu dal'*) and the satirical *Vasily Tyorkin in the Other World* are major landmarks of post-Stalin literature. Tvardovsky was not an innovator, but his handling of conventional verse forms, in such a way as to achieve an easy colloquial effect, is masterly.

No survey of the Soviet period of Russian literature would be complete without a consideration of two features which are perhaps the most striking result of the relaxation of Stalinist controls. The first is the 'discovery' of works which were written many years ago, by authors long since dead, and which have been published in the Soviet Union after their 'rehabilitation'; the second is the process already alluded to by which works circulate in manuscript, later finding their way abroad to be published there.

In prose the most significant of the belatedly published works is Mikhail Bulgakov's *The Master and Margarita* (1966–7). It was finished not long before the author's death in 1940 and is a comic masterpiece unsurpassed in Soviet literature. Outwardly it is a picaresque novel about the adventures of the Devil and his companions in Moscow at some indeterminate time in the late 1920s or early 1930s. As the title implies, it is also a retelling of the Faust legend in a Soviet setting, but the most extraordinary feature, interwoven as a sub-plot, is a brilliantly imaginative version of the condemnation and execution of Christ. If Bulgakov had been known only by his earlier works he would rate as no more than a gifted satirist, a Soviet imitator of Gogol, but the publication of *The Master and Margarita* revealed him as a great Russian writer who at first sight seems out of place in the shallows of Soviet prose. No Soviet writer has ever dared approach the problem of evil – a central preoccupation of nineteenth-century Russian literature – in such a direct and challenging fashion. A lesser, unfinished novel by Bulgakov, *Black Snow* (*Teatral'nyy roman*), was published in 1965, a quarter of a century after it was written. Apart from being very funny, it is interesting for its satirical portraits of Stanislavsky and Nemirovich-Danchenko. It is only in recent years that any word of criticism has been voiced about the stultifying effect their apotheosis under Stalin had on the Soviet theatre, and the belated appearance of Bulgakov's novel has contributed to the slow emancipation of the Soviet stage from 'the Method'.

Another prose writer who has to some extent been 'revealed' by posthumous (but still very selective) editions of his work is Andrey Platonov. He published a certain amount in the 1920s and early 1930s, but later found it more and more difficult to get into print. Platonov has the rare distinction for a Soviet writer of having been a true proletarian. His father was a mechanic in a railway workshop, and he himself went to work at the age of fifteen. The heroes of his stories and novels are also often skilled workers and mechanics, and it is immediately apparent that he writes from a sense of personal identification with them. Like many real workers he was dismayed by the bureaucratization of the 'workers' and peasants'' state and gave vent to his feelings in a mordant satire *The City of Gradov* (1926) which is modelled, as one sees from the title, on Saltykov-Shchedrin's famous mock chronicle of Russian despotism, *The Story of a City* (1869–70). Like the poet Nikolay Zabolotsky, Platonov has a philosophical concern with the interplay of *homo faber* and nature: the mechanic, or any creative person, is seen as an organizing, harmonizing element in the apparent chaos of the world. The eerie quality of the situations and environments he describes, matched by a deliberate quaintness of language reminiscent of some *skaz* writers (such as Leskov in the nineteenth century and Zoshchenko in the Soviet period), create an effect of conspicuous originality against the general background of socialist realist prose. Although never imprisoned, he was publicly denounced several times for 'slander', and in the post-war years his name, like that of Babel', Zamyatin, Pil'nyak, Bulgakov and others, was expunged from the record. The re-publication of his earlier writings and posthumous publication of some later work have made him into an exciting 'discovery' for a younger generation of readers in the Soviet Union. But at least two important long works have still to appear there: *Chevengur*, a novel about the early years of the revolution, and *The Building Site* (*Kotlovan*).

Several other outstanding works of Russian literature have so far been published only in the West – though in a few cases western publication has been followed by full or partial publication in the Soviet Union. The most famous example is Pasternak's *Dr Zhivago*. Having failed to get it published in the Soviet Union shortly after Stalin's death, Pasternak deliberately arranged for its appearance abroad. It was the first time in many years that anyone had dared to do this: ever since the persecution of Zamyatin and Pil'nyak in the late 1920s there had been no greater mortal sin for a Soviet writer than to send a work out of the country. It required uncommon courage on Pasternak's part to come forth as a witness – thereby easing the way for others – after all the silent years of terror. His anguished decision to 'break the spell of the dead letter' is described in 'Hamlet', the first of the cycle of Zhivago's poems at the end of the novel. Some of these poems have been published over the years in the Soviet Union. 'Hamlet' was even quoted in full in an article by Voznesensky on Pasternak as a translator – in this context the censor evidently thought it was a translation from Shakespeare! But the novel itself remains under a ban, though it is probably no more anti-Soviet than *The Master and Margarita* or *One Day in the Life of Ivan Denisovich*, the only two novels published in the Soviet Union which stand comparison with it. Like all great works, it has several levels of meaning, some of them too deep, perhaps, to be appreciated by the present generation of readers. At the first and most superficial level, it is a *roman à thèse*. This aspect need not be thought unworthy of discussion, since it was Pasternak's conscious intention to condemn not only Marxism (dismissed by Zhivago in a few contemptuous phrases), but also what might be called the *Russian* ideology which in the nineteenth century made possible the uncritical adoption of ready-made doctrines in general. The unspeakable tragedies of the Soviet period were seen by Pasternak as to some extent a consequence of the maximalist temperament of the Russian intelligentsia, of its belief in the possibility of all-embracing solutions. He makes it quite clear that in his view there has been only one revolution in human history, namely the coming of Christ with the simple assertion of the freedom of the individual personality. From this larger view the seizure of power by the Bolsheviks in 1917 was, he implies, an attempt at *counter*-revolution, throwing us back to Roman times when there were leaders ('pock-marked Caligulas' – Pasternak's only reference to Stalin) and herd-like peoples. At deeper levels, Pasternak tries to reach beyond the perspective of mere history, in which the Soviet episode appears only as a single day, to the even broader context of eternity and nature – this is the real background against which Zhivago's temporal ordeal is to be seen. *Dr Zhivago* must be considered a *Soviet* novel because its starting point is the author's own experience of the Soviet era, but by making his readers view it in the light of poetic infinity, he achieves a singular effect of transcendence.

For a similar reason two long poems by Akhmatova, also published in full only abroad, are essentially 'Soviet'. *Requiem* (written between 1935 and 1940) is a lament for her second husband, her son, and all her compatriots who disappeared into concentration camps in the 1930s (her son survived a second imprisonment after the war). It is a work of simple dignity which, as befits a memorial, needs no comment or explanation. The same cannot be said of *Poem without a Hero*, written between 1940 and 1942, but published for the first time in New York in 1961 (the first part, under the title *A Petersburg Tale*, was published in the Soviet Union in 1965). This is a cryptic work which is not easy to understand without some knowledge of the St Petersburg social scene in 1913. As has been pointed out by Korney Chukovsky and others, Akhmatova, even in her intimate lyric poetry, has a keen sense of history and likes to record events and exact dates in the manner of a chronicler. The events may seem personal or trivial, but she has a way of making them significant in relation to the wider context of the era. In *Poem without a Hero*, a series of narrative episodes interspersed with lyrical digressions, she allows herself the scope of an epic poet in order to try to make sense of the era; the result is a remarkable work in which personal and national destiny are intertwined. In the tradition of Pushkin's *Bronze Horseman* and Blok's *Retribution*, she sets out to illuminate the present and future in the light of the past. The poem was written at a particularly terrible time for Akhmatova personally and for her country. At a precise moment in 1940 – it happened, as she tells us, while she was looking through some old papers – she thought back beyond the years of revolution, famine and mass arrests to 1913, the last peace-time year after which 'the real, not the calendar, twentieth century' was to begin. She remembered, in particular, the suicide of a young poet which shocked the glittering, morally corroded intellectual world to which she belonged. She appears to suggest that everybody was guilty, that the young poet was sacrificed on the altar of his contemporaries' vanity and wickedness. The idea that the catastrophes to come were a collective punishment on a society that scarcely deserved to survive gains from being conveyed with Akhmatova's usual restraint and matter-of-factness. Though her view is less Olympian than Pasternak's in *Dr Zhivago* (perhaps because her personal ordeal was greater) she too transcends the Soviet experience, making it bearable to herself in religious terms as one link in a chain of sin, retribution and possible redemption.

The widespread circulation in typescript of many other works not published in the Soviet Union has resulted in the appearance of an extensive literature parallel to the officially sanctioned one, and sometimes misleadingly referred to abroad as 'underground'. In Russia it is known jokingly as *samizdat* ('self-publishing' by analogy with *gosizdat* – 'state publishing'). Many of these works are not, in any real sense, politically subversive and have in some cases been submitted for publication to literary journals or state publishing houses; but having been rejected by censorship, they circulate, with or without the knowledge of their authors, in the manner of chain letters – that is, they are typed out in several copies, passed on to others and then typed out again. Though there are penalties for the circulation and harbouring of material judged to be 'anti-Soviet', there is nothing in Soviet law that forbids the copying out and passing on of manuscripts as such. Inevitably, however, the growth of *samizdat* has led in recent years to several trials of writers accused of 'slander' against the Soviet system. The first was that of Andrey Sinyavsky and Yuly Daniel' in February 1966. Then, at the beginning of 1968, several young writers were tried and sentenced because they had edited a *samizdat* literary journal and organized protests against the harsh sentences passed on Sinyavsky and Daniel'.

It is impossible to give here a comprehensive account of *samizdat*, but some of the more important examples are quoted in the Guide below. Perhaps its most successful literary products, apart from those already mentioned, have been the stories of Sinyavsky and Daniel', first published abroad under their pseudonyms, Abram Tertz and Nikolay Arzhak. Stylistically Daniel''s stories have much in common with the 'new wave' prose of his contemporaries, such as Tendryakov, Nagibin and others. In *This is Moscow Speaking* (1962) and *Atonement* (1964), he deals in a vivid manner with the moral damage inflicted by Stalinism. Sinyavsky, as he emphasized at his trial, writes in a consciously experimental fashion, seeking to revive an element of fantasy which had been largely lost in the later Soviet period. In his essay 'On Socialist Realism' (1960), he wrote that he put his hope in 'a phantasmagoric art . . . in which the grotesque will replace realistic descriptions of ordinary life'. Most of Sinyavsky's work (*Fantastic Tales, Lyubimov, Pkhents*) illustrates this proposition and reveals him as a writer of unusual imaginative gifts and deep literary culture. The articles published under his own name before his arrest, and his book on *The Poetry of the First Years of the Revolution* (written with A. Menshutin, 1964), show him also to be a critic and scholar of rare quality. In 1972 he was released from imprisonment after serving six years in a concentration camp, and in the following year he was allowed to leave the Soviet Union for France.

The exile of Solzhenitsyn and the emigration of other Soviet writers – indeed, the whole chain of events begun by the imprisonment of Sinyavsky and Daniel' in 1966 – are symptomatic of total estrangement between an important section of the Soviet literary community and the authorities. On the surface order has been restored: *Novy Mir* has ceased to play the role it played under Tvardovsky as the focus of 'liberal' opinion; editorial and censorship controls have been progressively tightened up; and a number of active dissidents have been expelled from the Union of Soviet Writers (e.g. Lidiya Chukovskaya and Vladimir Maksimov) or forced into emigration. By the standards of Stalin's times, these are mild sanctions, but they have had their effect: the threat to deprive a writer of his status and livelihood can sometimes be used to extract statements condemning colleagues or renouncing work published abroad. But this has become much harder; few writers of consequence (with the exception of Katayev) joined in the campaign mounted against Solzhenitsyn before

211

his exile, and some – including Yevtushenko – spoke up in his support. There is now a wholly new and unprecedented situation in which the party can impose its will on writers only in a quite negative and self-defeating way. By rigorously controlling publication through its mono-poly of the press, it stimulates the further growth of *samizdat* – a process it seems powerless to stop without the reintroduction of full-scale police terror. By victimizing writers who have become too openly defiant, it provokes further discontent and resistance. Though it is unlikely that there can be any resumption of the 'liberal' trend in literature without a general political change, there seems to be even less chance that the party can reassert its authority over the writers or force them to give up all the considerable gains of the last twenty years: they are still very much better off than they were in 1953. The present party leadership is no doubt mainly concerned to limit the political consequences of literary dissent, and it must be sadly aware of the futility of trying to do more.

GUIDE TO FURTHER READING*

GENERAL WORKS, REFERENCE BOOKS

The best and most comprehensive account of Soviet Russian literature in English is Gleb Struve, *Russian Literature under Lenin and Stalin 1917–1953* (London, 1972). An excellent brief survey is Edward J. Brown, *Russian Literature since the Revolution*, 2nd edn (London, 1969). Other general outlines which may be con-sulted are: Marc Slonim, *Soviet Russian Literature* (Oxford, 1964), a discussion of particular problems or movements, and of individual authors; *Literature and Revolution in Soviet Russia, 1917–1962*, eds. Max Hayward and Leopold Labedz (Oxford, 1963), a collection of essays by various authors on the different periods into which Soviet literature may be divided; William E. Harkins, *Dictionary of Russian Literature* (London, 1957), has useful entries relating to the Soviet period. From the early 1930s till Stalin's death, surveys of the Soviet period by Soviet critics and scholars had to take account of the frequent shifts, often conveyed in secret party instructions, in the official attitude. As time went on, particularly after the terror of 1937–8, more and more leading writers, such as Isaak Babel', Boris Pil'nyak, Pasternak and Akhmatova, were either passed over in silence or dismissed in scurrilous terms. Hopelessly unreliable and inadequate as they are, however, Soviet sources for that period may be consulted for the light they throw on the official attitude of the moment. There are reference works of the late 1920s which are still quite objective. Very useful, for instance, as a biblio-graphical guide to the movements and writers of the first decade after the revolution is I. N. Rozanov's *Putevoditel' po sovremennoy russkoy literature* (Moscow, 1929). In recent years there has again been a return to relative objectivity in the treatment of Soviet literature. Despite continuing ideological pressures, there are now reliable works of reference which can be consulted with profit. Foremost among these is the eight-volume *Kratkaya literaturnaya entsiklopediya*

* I wish to thank Mrs Valerie Jensen for her invaluable assistance in the prepara-tion of this Guide.

(Moscow, 1962–75). Some of the volumes have been severely attacked in the Soviet press for their impartial treatment of writers such as Mandel'shtam, Babel', Pasternak and Zamyatin. The pre-war *Literaturnaya entsiklopediya*, vols. 1–9 and 11 (Moscow, 1929–39), planned in twelve volumes, was never completed. The earlier volumes, fervently Marxist in tone, often have informative and stimulating entries on writers of the 1920s.

The most ambitious survey of Soviet literature to appear since Stalin's death is the *Istoriya russkoy sovetskoy literatury*, vols. 1–4, second revised and enlarged edition (Moscow, 1967–71), which covers the whole period up to 1965. There are useful chronologies and an index. Another useful work published by the Academy of Sciences is the two-volume *Istoriya russkogo sovetskogo romana* (Moscow, 1965). As can be seen from the index, it is fairly comprehensive, and even 'negative' works and authors are treated with some approach to objectivity. *Istoriya sovetskoy mnogonatsional'noy literatury*, vols. 1–6 (Moscow, 1970–4), written by various hands, deals with all the numerous non-Russian Soviet literatures, parallel with, and in addition to, Russian. Most of the contributions seem to present a fairly 'orthodox' point of view. A helpful descriptive bibliography of articles and monographs in English is: George Gibian, *Soviet Russian Literature in English. A Checklist Bibliography* (Ithaca, N.Y., 1967).

MONOGRAPHS ON PARTICULAR PERIODS, MOVEMENTS OR EPISODES

The best Soviet work on the early poetry of the Soviet period (1917–20) is A. Menshutin and A. Sinyavsky, *Poeziya pervykh let revolyutsii* (Moscow, 1964). Robert A. Maguire, *Red Virgin Soil – Soviet Literature in the Twenties* (Princeton, 1968), is a helpful study of the prose, criticism and literary controversies of the period. Sheila Fitzpatrick's *The Commissariat of Enlightenment* (Cambridge, 1970) is a pioneering account of cultural policy under Lunacharsky. There is very little on the 1930s and second world war period that may be recommended, except the contribution by E. J. Simmons to *Literature and Revolution in Soviet Russia*. A brilliant study and critique of the underlying philosophy and spirit of the Stalinist years is Andrey Sinyavsky's essay 'On Socialist Realism', originally published abroad in French and English in 1956 and 1960 under the pseudonym 'Abram Tertz' and available in Russian in *Fantasticheskiy mir Abrama Tertsa* (New York, 1967). There are a number of good studies of the post-war period until Stalin's death and beyond to the 'thaw' of 1956, though the emphasis is inevitably on questions of political and ideological control. The most thorough of these works is Harold Swayze, *The Political Control of Soviet Literature, 1946–1959* (Cambridge, Mass., 1962). Covering a slightly shorter period, but devoting more attention to literature as such, is Walter N. Vickery, *The Cult of Optimism* (Bloomington, 1963). The literature of the 'thaw' is amply covered in George Gibian's *Interval of Freedom: Soviet Literature during the 'Thaw', 1954–57* (Minneapolis, 1960). A well-documented study of Khrushchev's erratic handling of literature and the arts is Priscilla Johnson's *Khrushchev and the Arts – The Politics of Soviet Culture, 1962–64* (Cambridge, Mass., 1965). An excellent study of the transition from the 1920s to the 1930s and the short-lived dictatorship of RAPP is E. J. Brown's *The Proletarian Episode in Russian Literature, 1928–1932* (New York, 1953). Avrahm Yarmolinsky, *Literature under Communism* (New York, 1957), is a handy short survey of the period from the end of the war to Stalin's death. An illuminating study of post-war Stalinist fiction is Vera Dunham, *In Stalin's Time: Middle Class Values in Soviet Fiction* (Cambridge, 1976). A comprehensive work on the various literary doctrines of the 1920s and early 1930s is

LITERATURE IN THE SOVIET PERIOD

Herman Ermolayev, *Soviet Literary Theories, 1917—1934: The Genesis of Socialist Realism* (Berkeley, 1963). The Formalists are authoritatively treated in Victor Erlich's *Russian Formalism: History, Doctrine*, 2nd revised edn (The Hague, 1965); Vladimir Markov, *Russian Futurism: a History* (Berkeley, 1968), is a masterly study of the most dynamic pre-revolutionary movement, whose momentum carried over into the first years of the Soviet regime. The 'Serapion Brothers' are dealt with in H. Oulanoff, *The Serapion Brothers: Theory and Practice* (The Hague, 1966).

Other useful studies are: Helen Muchnic's *From Gorky to Pasternak – Six Writers in Soviet Russia* (New York, 1961; London, 1963), essays on Gor'ky, Blok, Mayakovsky, Leonov, Sholokhov and Pasternak, with an emphasis on critical evaluation; Ernest J. Simmons, *Russian Fiction and Soviet Ideology* (Columbia, 1958), is a detailed study of Leonov, Fedin and Sholokhov; Rufus W. Mathewson Jr, *The Positive Hero in Russian Literature* (New York, 1958), is a valuable attempt to trace the genesis in older Russian literature of the central aesthetic values of the Stalinist period. Boris Thomson, *The Premature Revolution, Russian Literature and Society 1917-1946* (London, 1972), contains studies of various aspects of Soviet literary life. *The Soviet Censorship*, eds. Martin Dewhirst and Robert Farrell (Metuchen, N.J., 1973), is an up-to-date guide on the subject.

INDIVIDUAL AUTHORS (see also pp. 177–84)

Most authors referred to earlier are here listed in alphabetical order, with dates and other pertinent details, and in some cases further brief descriptions. As a general rule only the latest collected (or selected) editions in Russian, where they exist, are given; attention is drawn to the main works recommended for further reading, and to important English-language studies in book form. (References to English-language articles published up to 1967 may be found in George Gibian's *Soviet Russian Literature in English*, in the alphabetical list of Soviet authors.) There are considerable textological problems with the works of some Soviet authors: later editions may be different from first editions because of changes insisted on by the censorship, or because the author has himself rewritten the book, usually under pressure, to make it conform to changed political or literary doctrine. It is advisable to read the first edition, particularly of novels originally published in the 1920s and early 1930s.

Abramov, Fyodor Aleksandrovich (1920–): writer on kolkhoz themes whose documentary story 'Vokrug da okolo' in the literary monthly *Neva* (1963) is remarkable for its stark portrayal of village problems. Also the author of novels: *Dve zimy i tri leta* (1968), and *Puti-pereput'ya* (1973), both published in *Novy Mir* and included in the trilogy *Pryasliny* (Moscow, 1974).

Akhmadulina, Bella Akhatovna (1937–): one of the most popular of the younger women poets, noted particularly for her longer poems such as *Skazka o dozhde* (1964), *Oznob* (1963) and *Moya rodoslovnaya* (1963). These are included in the Soviet collection of her poetry *Uroki muzyki* (1969), but a more complete edition of her work (including some not published in the Soviet Union) is *Oznob, Izybrannyye proizvedeniya* (Frankfurt/Main, 1968). *Stikhi* (Moscow, 1975) has a few new poems.

Akhmatova, Anna Andreyevna (1889–1966): leading acmeist poet whose major post-revolutionary volumes are *Podorozhnik* (1921), *Anno Domini MCMXXI* (1922), *Iz shesti knig* (1940). The latter is a selection of work written between

1924 and 1940, and shows that she never ceased writing, even though it became more and more difficult for her to publish. After a brief wartime interlude, when a number of poems were printed in literary magazines, she was again silenced by Zhdanov's attack on her in 1946. Several collections of her poems appeared after Stalin's death. The best is *Beg vremeni* (1965), which includes all the above-mentioned volumes. However, two of her major works of the Soviet period, *Rekviyem* (1935–40) and *Poema bez geroya* (1940–2), have not been published in full in the Soviet Union. The latter is a cryptic work and commentaries are helpful, such as those in the French bilingual edition by Jeanne Rude: *Anna Akhmatova, Poème sans Héros* (Paris, 1970). There are also useful notes and commentaries in the most complete edition of Akhmatova's work so far to be published: *Sochineniya*, eds. G. Struve and B. Filippov, vol. 1, 2nd edn (1967), vol. 2 (1968). An important publication containing hitherto unpublished poems by Akhmatova and the first completed version of *Poema bez geroya* together with an informative introduction and notes is: *Tale Without a Hero and Twenty-two Poems by Akhmatova*, eds. Jeanne van der Eng-Liedmeier and Kees Verheul (The Hague, 1973). Further new poems, with a memoir by Lidiya Chukovskaya, are in *Pamyati Anny Akhmatovoy* (Parish, 1975). See also A. Haight, *Anna Akhmatova. A Poetic Pilgrimage* (New York and London, 1976).

Aksyonov, Vasily Pavlovich (1932–): novelist and short-story writer, *Zvezdnyy bilet* (1961) dealt with the problem of the gap between the generations and stirred much controversy, not least because of the use of modern slang. Collection of later stories: *Na polputi k lune – Kniga rasskazov* (Moscow, 1966); his satirical tale 'Zatovarennaya bochkotara' appeared in *Yunost'* in 1968.

Aliger, Margarita Iosifovna (1915–): poetess famous for her wartime epic *Zoya* (1942). Her wartime lyric poems were gathered together in *Leningradskaya tetrad'* (1942). Collections of verse are *Siniy chas* (1960) and *Stikhotvoreniya i poemy*, vols 1–2 (Moscow, 1970).

Antokol'sky, Pavel Grigor'yevich (1896–): poet noted for ballads of somewhat dramatic quality (he was originally an actor and producer of the Vakhtangov theatre), e.g. his famous *Syn. Izbrannoye*, vols. 1–2 (Moscow, 1966); *Sobraniye sochineniy*, vols. 1–4 (Moscow, 1971–3).

Aseyev, Nikolay Nikolayevich (1889–1963): poet, associate of Mayakovsky to whom his best-known work is dedicated: *Mayakovsky nachinayetsya* (1940). *Sobraniye sochineniy*, vols. 1–5 (Moscow, 1963–4).

Babel', Isaak Emmanuilovich (1894–1941): Russian–Jewish short-story writer famous for *Konarmiya* (1926) and *Odesskiye rasskazy* (1927). Since his rehabilitation after Stalin's death, two editions have appeared of his selected works in Moscow: *Izbrannoye*, with a preface by Il'ya Ehrenburg (Moscow, 1957), and *Izbrannoye*, with an introduction by L. Polyak (Moscow, 1966). The second collection is somewhat fuller, but both should be supplemented by the English-language volumes edited by his daughter: *Isaac Babel: the Lonely Years, 1925–29 – Unpublished Stories and Correspondence*, edited and with an introduction by Nathalie Babel (New York, 1964), and *You Must Know Everything* (London, 1969). The latter contains important material of various periods not easily available elsewhere, and includes invaluable notes and commentaries. A comprehensive study of his life and work is: James E. Falen, *Isaac Babel, Russian Master of the Short Story* (Knoxville, 1974). See also Patricia Carden, *The Art of Isaac Babel* (London, 1972).

LITERATURE IN THE SOVIET PERIOD

Bagritsky, Eduard Georgiyevich (1895–1934): an important poet of the 'Southern' school, whose influence can be seen in the work of some younger poets today. Like other writers associated with Odessa he represents a romantic strain with a liking for colourful narrative and exotic themes, particularly in his earlier work (*Ptitselov, Til' Ulenshpigel', Traktir, Arbuz*), all included in his first collected volume *Yugo-zapad* (1928). His best-known epic poem is *Duma pro Opanasa* (1926). In his later work he comes to terms with sobering post-revolutionary reality and after a period of disillusionment, expressed in such poems as *Noch'*, *Stikhi o solov'ye i poete*, becomes a whole-hearted partisan of the 'new' (cf. his 2nd and 3rd collections: *Pobediteli* (1932) and *Poslednyaya noch'* (1932)). Collected verse: *Stikhotvoreniya i poemy* (Moscow, 1964).

Bedny, Dem'yan (pseudonym of Pridvorov, Yefim Alekseyevich) (1883–1945): a vigorous and prolific versifier. *Sobraniye sochineniy*, vols. 1–8 (Moscow, 1963–1965).

Belov, Vasily Ivanovich (1932–): author of stories about the northern Russian countryside, noted for their lyrical emphasis on the preservation of simple human values in a rural setting, e.g. 'Privychnoye delo' (1966), 'Plotnitskiye rasskazy' (1968), and 'Bukhtiny vologodskiye' (1969): the latter two were published in *Novy Mir*. Collection: *Sel'skiye povesti* (Moscow, 1971).

Bely, Andrey (pseudonym of Bugayev, Boris Nikolayevich) (1880–1934): symbolist poet whose work in the Soviet period consisted mainly of prose. He responded to the October Revolution with a poem entitled *Khristos voskres* (1918). Most of his post-revolutionary prose was autobiographical, *Kotik Letayev* (1922) and *Kreshchonyy kitayets* (1927), or historical, *Moskva* (1926) and *Maski* (1932). He also wrote important memoirs: *Na rubezhe dvukh stoletiy* (1930), *Nachalo veka* (1933) and *Mezhdu dvukh revolyutsiy* (1934). Collected verse: *Stikhotvoreniya i poemy* (Moscow, 1966). See J. D. Elsworth, *Andrey Bely* (Letchworth, 1972).

Bitov, Andrey Georgiyevich (1937–): talented representative of 'new wave' prose, such as the short stories in *Bol'shoy shar* (Moscow, 1963); his latest collection is *Obraz zhizni: povesti* (Moscow, 1972).

Blok, Aleksandr Aleksandrovich (1880–1921): outstanding symbolist poet. Apart from the two famous poems *Dvenadtsat'* and *Skify* (both 1918), he wrote very little after the revolution except an important essay 'Intelligentsiya i revolyutsiya' (1918), and parts of the long poem *Vozmezdiye*, begun in 1910, but finished only in 1921. See Sergei Hackel, *The Poet and the Revolution: Aleksandr Blok's 'The Twelve'* (Oxford, 1975).

Bondarev, Yury Vasil'yevich (1924–): novelist whose *Tishina* (*Novy Mir*, 1962) is an interesting study of the 'cult of personality'. Other novels, such as *Goryachiy sneg* (1969), deal with wartime themes.

Brodsky, Iosif Aleksandrovich (1940–): outstanding poet of the younger generation whose work has scarcely been published at all in the Soviet Union, but only abroad, e.g. in *Ostanovka v pustyne: Stikhotvoreniya i poemy* (New York, 1970). He now lives in the United States.

Bryusov, Valery Yakovlevich (1873–1924): leading symbolist poet who joined the Communist Party after the revolution and made a sustained effort, through his choice of themes and his treatment of them, to be accepted as a Soviet poet, e.g. *K russkoy revolyutsii* (1920); *U Kremlya* (1923); *Lenin* (1924). His work of

216

the Soviet period is fully represented in *Izbrannyye sochineniya*, vols. 1–2 (Moscow, 1955). A seven-volume edition of his works is now in progress.

Bulgakov, Mikhail Afanas'yevich (1891–1940): leading novelist and playwright. His brilliant satires in the 1920s often had strong political undertones: *Diavoliada* (1925); *Rokovyye yaytsa* (1925). His major early novel *Belaya gvardiya* (1925) is an impressive study of the impact of the revolution and civil war on the intelligentsia – it formed the basis of his most famous play: *Dni Turbinykh* (1926). Shortly before his death he completed *Master i Margarita*, undoubtedly his greatest work which, despite its fantastically ingenious picaresque plot, is a serious philosophical novel unique in Soviet literature. It was published a quarter of a century after his death, in 1966–7, in two instalments, with cuts, in the journal *Moskva*. His unfinished *Teatral'nyy roman* was published in *Novy Mir* (1965). Most of his early fiction is now easily available only in *Izbrannoye* (New York, 1950). *Sobach'ye serdtse*, an early satirical story, written but never published in the Soviet Union, has also appeared in the West (Paris, 1969). A one-volume Soviet edition of three novels appeared in Moscow in 1973; it contains *Belaya gvardiya*, *Teatral'nyy roman* and *Master i Margarita* – the latter in a full, uncut version for the first time.

Bykov, Vasil' (Vasily) Vladimirovich (1924–): though strictly speaking a Belorussian writer, Bykov has entered into Russian literature through the outstanding stories about the last war which have appeared in Russian translation in *Novy Mir*: *Myortvym ne bol'no* (1966) and *Sotnikov* (1970). The latter was apparently written in Russian, not Belorussian.

Chukovskaya, Lidiya Korneyevna (1907–): author of two *samizdat* autobiographical stories which have been published abroad: 'Opustelyy dom' (Paris, 1965), also published under the correct title 'Sofiya Petrovna' in *Novyy Zhurnal* (New York, 1966), and 'Spusk pod vodu' (New York, 1972). The first gives a vivid picture of the purge in Leningrad in 1937, and the second describes the atmosphere among Soviet writers and intellectuals at the end of the 1940s.

Daniel', Yuly Markovich (1925–): prose writer; under the pseudonym 'Nikolay Arzhak' he wrote several stories whose publication abroad led to his imprisonment in 1966 together with Andrey Sinyavsky (q.v.), on charges of 'defaming' the Soviet social and political system. He was released in 1970. All four stories have been published in book form in the United States: *Govorit Moskva* (Washington, 1962); *Ruki* and *Chelovek iz Minapa* (Washington, 1963); *Iskupleniye* (New York, 1964). His verse, written in the camp, has been published in Amsterdam (1971): *Stikhi iz nevoli*.

Dombrovsky, Yury Osipovich (1910–): author of a novel *Khranitel' drevnostey* (*Novy Mir*, 1964) which successfully re-creates the atmosphere of the pre-war terror in 1937.

Dudintsev, Vladimir Dmitriyevich (1918–): though undistinguished in style, his novel *Ne khlebom yedinym* (*Novy Mir*, 1956; in book form, 1957 and 1968), was an important milestone in the post-Stalin 'thaw'. It was the first exposure of some of the social consequences of Stalin's rule, and the name of the bureaucrat Drozdov became for a time a standard way of referring to the type. In 1960 he published a curious allegorical tale, *Novogodnyaya skazka*, which seems to hint obscurely that Khrushchev's exposure of Stalin in 1956 was due to a crisis of conscience. Collected stories are available in *Rasskazy* (1963).

Ehrenburg, Il'ya Grigor'yevich (1891–1967): novelist, journalist and poet. His long residence abroad (1909–17, and then 1921–41 as European correspondent of *Izvestiya*) accounts for the marked cosmopolitan flavour of his writing. He also vividly exemplifies the dilemma of the fellow traveller with a foot in both camps. Notable among his vast output of novels, stories, essays, etc. are: *Neobychaynyye pokhozhdeniya Julio Jurenito* (1922), *Den' vtoroy* (1934), *Padeniye Parizha* (1942), *Ottepel'* (in the journal *Znamya*, 1954). His memoirs, published in *Novy Mir* (1960–5) under the title *Lyudi, gody, zhizn'*, despite the inevitable reticences, give a fascinating picture of the fate of the Russian intelligentsia in Soviet times. Together with some of his essays (on Chekhov, Stendhal), they did much to demolish large areas of Stalinist mythology. It is advisable to read his main novels in the original editions, rather than in his *Sobraniye sochineniy*, vols. 1–9 (1962–7). A selection of verse, *Stikhotvoreniya*, was published in Moscow in 1972.

Fadeyev, Aleksandr Aleksandrovich (1901–56): one of the more successful 'socialist realist' novelists. His *Razgrom* (1927), a novel about the Civil War, did much to establish a literary model for the Communist 'positive hero'. His most famous work, *Molodaya gvardiya* (1945), is about the heroism of young resistance fighters under German occupation in the second world war. Stalin made him rewrite it because it allegedly failed to bring out the 'leading role' of the party, and a second edition appeared in 1951. Fadeyev was secretary of the Union of Soviet Writers, 1946–53, and as such bore a share of the responsibility for the purges of fellow writers in the last years of Stalin's life. In 1956, after the Twentieth Party Congress, he shot himself. *Sobraniye sochineniy*, vols. 1–7 (Moscow, 1969–71).

Fedin, Konstantin Aleksandrovich (1892–): leading fellow traveller and member of the 'Serapion Brothers'. In 1959 he was appointed secretary and then chairman of the board of the Union of Writers. His best-known novel is *Goroda i gody* (1924), a study of intellectuals caught up in revolution. *Brat'ya* (1928) is also concerned with the problem of intellectual adjustment to the new regime. His post-war novels *Pervyye radosti* (1945), *Neobyknovennoye leto* (1948) and *Kostyor* (1961–5) constitute a historical trilogy about Russian life between 1910 and 1941. *Sobraniye sochineniy*, vols. 1–10 (Moscow, 1969–73).

Furmanov, Dmitry Andreyevich (1891–1926): author of documentary novels about the Civil War, *Chapayev* (1923) and *Myatezh* (1925).

Galich (Ginzburg), Aleksandr Arkad'yevich (1918–): poet, playwright and *chansonnier*. Collections of his songs have been published only in the West: see especially *Pokoleniye obrechonnykh* (Frankfurt/Main, 1972). In 1974, after being expelled from the Union of Soviet Writers, he emigrated to Norway.

Gerasimov, Mikhail Prokof'yevich (1889–1939): son of a railway worker and proletarian poet; one of the founders of the *Kuznitsa* group. Disillusioned by NEP, he left the party in 1921. He was arrested in 1937 and died in a camp. *Stikhotvoreniya* (Moscow, 1959).

Gladilin, Anatoly Tikhonovich (1935–): talented younger prose writer. His *Khronika vremyon Viktora Podgurskogo* (*Yunost'*, 1956; and as a book, Moscow, 1958) is one of the first noteworthy contributions to the 'new wave' fiction. Like Aksyonov, he is much concerned with the problems of post-Stalin youth, and his *Istoriya odnoy kompanii* (*Yunost'*, 1966) gives a valuable picture of its development. His *Vechnaya komandirovka* (Moscow, 1963) portrays in rather unusual fashion an official of the secret police.

GUIDE TO FURTHER READING

Gladkov, Fyodor Vasil'yevich (1883–1958): one of the few older Soviet writers of any importance who could claim to have a genuine proletarian background (though he was a peasant's son). His novel *Tsement* (1925), about the reconstruction of a factory after the civil war, is a Soviet classic. The first edition was mildly criticized by Gor'ky for its naturalistic language, and subsequent editions were revised by the author. *Sobraniye sochineniy*, vols. 1–8 (Moscow, 1958–9).

Gor'ky, Maksim (pseudonym of Peshkov, Aleksey Maksimovich) (1868–1936): the main link between the pre-revolutionary 'realist' tradition and 'socialist realism' of which his novel *Mat'* (1906), with its portrayal of the proletariat as an ultimately victorious social force, is still held up as a model. After an initial period of doubt and hostility, Gor'ky put the weight of his immense prestige behind the Soviet leaders – first Lenin, and then Stalin – and became the presiding spirit of orthodox Soviet literature. His own work in the Soviet period is for the most part retrospective – chronicles of pre-revolutionary life in the form of novels and plays which try to show how the social trends of the time had inevitably culminated in the October Revolution. The most ambitious of these works is *Zhizn' Klima Samgina*, which he began in 1925 and did not quite finish before his death in 1936. *Delo Artamonovykh* (1925) is an effective account of the life of a merchant family from 1861 to the revolution. Some of his most important autobiographical writing, *Moi universitety* (1922), and literary reminiscences, e.g. *Lev Tolstoy* (1919), also fall in the Soviet period. *Polnoye sobraniye sochineniy*, vols. 1–25 (Moscow, 1968–74), contains fiction, poetry, etc.; two further series, covering journalistic writings and letters, are promised.

Granin (German), Daniil Aleksandrovich (1919–): novelist and short-story writer who specializes in the moral problems of scientists: *Iskateli* (1954) and *Idu na grozu* (1962). He made an important contribution to the literature of the 'thaw' period with his short story 'Sobstvennoye mneniye' (*Novy Mir*, 1956). *Izbrannyye proizvedeniya* (Moscow, 1969). *Kto-to dolzhen: Povesti i rasskazy* (Leningrad, 1970).

Grin, Aleksandr (pseudonym of Grinevsky, Aleksandr Stepanovich) (1880–1932): a 'romantic' *par excellence*, many of whose works are set in the country of his imagination, 'Grinland'. Behind the exotic trappings and intricate plots there is, however, a serious moral purpose and devotion to a system of values which runs counter to orthodox Communist ones. His consequent popularity with the intelligentsia and his 'cosmopolitan' flavour meant that his work was virtually banned in the later Stalinist years. A very prolific writer; his best-known works in the Soviet period were the short novels *Alyye parusa* (1923) and *Begushchaya po volnam* (1928). The best selection is *Izbrannoye*, vols. 1–2, with an introduction by K. Paustovsky (Moscow, 1956). *Sobraniye sochineniy*, vols. 1–6 (Moscow, 1965). An excellent brief study is N. J. L. Luker, *Alexander Grin* (Letchworth, 1973).

Grossman, Vasily Semyonovich (1905–64): novelist best known for his war novel *Narod bessmerten* (1942). In *Za pravoye delo* (1952) he attempted to give a broader picture of events, but publication was interrupted by a violent attack in *Pravda* which accused the author of 'Manichaeism' (presenting the war as one more episode in the struggle between eternal forces of good and evil). It appeared in book form after Stalin's death (Moscow, 1954). Sections originally forbidden and confiscated in Moscow have been published in the émigré journal *Kontinent* (1975). He is also the author of a short unfinished novel, *Vsyo techot* (Frankfurt/Main, 1970), which has circulated in *samizdat* since his death; it contains severe criticism of Lenin.

219

Gumilyov, Nikolay Stepanovich (1886–1921): leading acmeist poet and co-founder with Anna Akhmatova of the Poets' Guild. He was shot for 'counter-revolutionary' activity before he had time to contribute significantly to early Soviet literature, but he was a powerful influence on others (particularly Bagritsky). *Sobraniye sochineniy*, vols. 1–4, ed. Struve and Filippov (Washington, 1962–8).

Il'f, Il'ya (pseudonym of Fainzil'berg, Il'ya Arnol'dovich) (1897–1937) and Petrov, Yevgeny (pseudonym of Katayev, Yevgeny Petrovich) (1903–42): the most success-ful and popular of Soviet satirists who (until the premature death of Il'f) always wrote together. Their best-known works are: *Dvenadtsat' stul'yev* (1928) and *Zolotoy telyonok* (1931), about the adventures of the master rogue Ostap Bender, a kind of Soviet Chichikov. *Sobraniye sochineniy*, vols. 1–5 (Moscow, 1961).

Iskander, Fazil' Abdulovich (1929–): a native of Abkhazia, Iskander brings a Caucasian colour and vividness to his writing. His *Sozvezdiye kozlotura* (*Novy Mir*, 1966), which pokes fun at Khrushchev's agricultural policies and scientific charlatanism of the Lysenko type, is a rare example of a political satire to be published in the Soviet Union. Selected works: *Derevo detstva. Rasskazy i povesti* (Moscow, 1970). Also very readable, despite heavy censorship, is the picaresque tale *Sandro iz Chegema* (*Novy Mir*, 1973). Poetry collection: *Letniy les. Stikho-tvoreniya* (Moscow, 1969).

Ivanov, Vsevolod Vyacheslavovich (1895–1963): the most colourful of the civil war novelists, not least because of the Asiatic setting of his stories and novels: *Partizany* (1921), *Bronepoyezd 14–69* (1922), *Tsvetnyye vetra* (1923). The expres-siveness of his style was toned down in later editions, and in the 1930s he moved from 'ornamentalism' to 'socialist realism' (in *Parkhomenko*, 1939). *Sobraniye sochineniy*, vols. 1–8 (Moscow, 1958–60).

Kamensky, Vasily Vasil'yevich (1884–1961): futurist poet (and also one of the first Russian aviators) who went from extreme linguistic experimentation to a straightforward ballad style. *Stikhotvoreniya i poemy* (Moscow, 1966).

Katayev, Valentin Petrovich (1897–): veteran fellow-traveller novelist and play-wright. His early work is coloured by the 'romanticism' and vividness of the 'Southern' school (like Babel', Bagritsky, and his brother Petrov, Il'f's collaborator, he came from Odessa) which he never completely lost. His satirical gifts and love of the picaresque are demonstrated in *Rastratchiki* (1927), one of the best novels about the NEP period. His *Vremya vperyod* (1932) is perhaps the most genuinely lyrical contribution to the literature of the first Five-Year Plan. In the 1930s, as a typical response to the increasing pressure of 'socialist realism', he turned to historical themes and wrote an engaging novel, *Beleyet parus odinokiy* (1936), about two boys who became involved in the 1905 Revolution. This eventually proved to be the first part of a tetralogy under the general title *Volny chornogo morya* which deals with events up to the Second World War; pt 2: *Khutorok v stepi* (1956); pt 3: *Zimniy vecher* (1960–1); pt 4: originally published under the title *Za vlast' sovetov* (1949), but after party criticism – like Fadeyev he had allegedly underplayed the role of the party in wartime resistance – he brought out a 'revised' version in 1951, which appeared under the title *Katakomby* as pt 4 of the tetralogy. Two other works published after Stalin's death are note-worthy: *Svyatoy kolodets* (*Novy Mir*, 1966), a dream journey into his own past, and *Travy zabveniya* (*Novy Mir*, 1967), reminiscences which include portraits of Bunin and Mayakovsky. His *Sobraniye sochineniy* in 10 vols. was begun in 1962.

Kaverin, Veniamin Aleksandrovich (1902–): leading member of the 'Serapion Brothers', whose early novels obey the Serapions' injunction to learn from the Western adventure story or thriller: *Konets Khazy* (1926); *Bol'shaya igra* (1926); *Skandalist* (1929). In a rather different vein, his *Khudozhnik neizvesten* (1931) is an important discussion of the artist's moral dilemma at a time when it was becoming acute. In the 1930s and 1940s he continued to write novels of adventure intended for younger people. The most popular was *Dva kapitana*, books 1–2 (1938–44). In the years since Stalin's death he has written a number of interesting stories such as *Dvoynoy portret* and *Sem' par nechistykh* (1962) which are vivid and outspoken comments on Soviet life. Most of these stories came out in the collection *Kosoy dozhd'* (Moscow, 1963). His latest novel is *Pered zerkalom* (1971). *Sobraniye sochineniy*, vols. 1–6 (Moscow, 1963–6). Kaverin's early work is the subject of D. G. B. Piper, *V. A. Kaverin. A Soviet Writer's Response to the Problem of Commitment* (Pittsburgh, n.d.).

Kazakevich, Emmanuil Genrikhovich (1913–62): originally a Yiddish writer who switched to Russian only after the war. Author of a series of novels based on his experiences in the Soviet army, notably *Dom na ploshchadi*, the main contribution to *Literaturnaya Moskva*, vol. 1 (1956), of which he was one of the editors. *Sochineniya*, vols. 1–2 (Moscow, 1963).

Kazakov, Yury Pavlovich (1927–): one of the most accomplished short-story writers of the younger generation who have made their mark since Stalin's death. His characters are often people who are at odds with society, or have fallen out of it: *V gorod* (1961), *Otshchepenets* (1959), also under the title *Trali-vali* (1961), *Adam i Yeva* (1962). Collection: *Severnyy dnevnik* (Moscow, 1973).

Kazin, Vasily Vasil'yevich (1898–): proletarian poet and member of *Kuznitsa*. *Stikhotvoreniya i poemy* (Moscow, 1964); *Stikhi* (Moscow, 1966).

Kharms, Daniil Ivanovich (1905–42?): a writer of 'absurd' stories and nursery rhymes for children. He was one of a small group of Leningrad writers who founded a modernist movement with the name OBERIU (standing for 'The Association for Real Art'; its members were known as '*Oberiuty*'). The group did not long survive its manifesto of 1928, and most of its members took refuge in writing for children. It was a last quixotic attempt to assert the independence of literature. Kharms was arrested shortly after the outbreak of the war and apparently perished in 1942. He has been 'rediscovered' in the Soviet Union in recent years and a few of his stories have been published. See George Gibian, *Russia's Lost Literature of the Absurd* (Ithaca, 1971).

Khlebnikov, Viktor Vladimirovich (Velimir) (1885–1922): one of the leading figures of the futurist movement whose influence, particularly in linguistic innovation, was great. His *Nochnoy obysk* (1918) is a curious pendant to Blok's *Dvenadtsat'*; in *Noch' pered sovetami* (1921) he expressed his enthusiasm for the October Revolution. *Sobraniye sochineniy*, vols. 1–5 (Leningrad, 1928–33). An important monograph on him in English is: Vladimir Markov, *The Longer Poems of Velimir Khlebnikov* (Los Angeles, 1962).

Kirillov, Vladimir Timofeyevich (1890–1943): proletarian poet and member of *Kuznitsa. Stikhotvoreniya i poemy* (Moscow, 1970).

Kirsanov, Semyon Isaakovich (1906–72): an associate of Mayakovsky and very much influenced by him. After Stalin's death he published a long poem, *Sem' dney nedeli* (1956), which caused a stir because of its satirical treatment of

LITERATURE IN THE SOVIET PERIOD

Stalinist bureaucracy (it appeared not long after Dudintsev's *Ne khlebom yedinym,* also in *Novy Mir*). *Stikhotvoreniya i poemy, 1923–1965* (Moscow, 1967).

Klychkov (pseudonym of Leshenkov, Sergey Antonovich) (1889–1940): poet and novelist, associated with Yesenin and Klyuyev. In the post-revolutionary period he wrote mainly prose in a Gogolian spirit of grotesque fantasy: *Sakharnyy nemets* (1925); *Chertukhinskiy balakir'* (1926). He died in a concentration camp.

Klyuyev, Nikolay Alekseyevich (1887–1937): 'peasant' poet associated for a time with Yesenin, whose visionary-Utopian attitude to the October Revolution he at first shared. In the early 1930s he was exiled and died in a concentration camp. The only collection of his work is: *Sochineniya,* ed. Struve and Filippov, vols. 1–2 (Munich, 1969).

Kochetov, Vsevolod Anisimovich (1912–73): novelist who was a leading spokesman of the anti-liberal wing in post-Stalin Soviet literature. Two of his novels, *Brat'ya Yershovy* (1958) and *Chego zhe ty khochesh'?* (1969), are pamphlets against the 'liberal' intelligentsia, the latter work being an interesting example of the influence of the cheap Western thriller on some neo-Stalinist writers (see also Ivan Shevtsov's *Lyubov' i nenavist'*, Moscow, 1970).

Kornilov, Vladimir Nikolayevich (1928–): poet. His *Shofyor* appeared in *Tarusskiye stranitsy* (1961; see Paustovsky); selected verse, 1948–64, in *Pristan'* (Moscow, 1964). He has published a *samizdat* novel *Bez ruk, bez nog* in the émigré literary journal *Kontinent* (1974), edited by Vladimir Maksimov (q.v.).

Korzhavin, (Mandel') Naum Moiseyevich (1925–): lyric poet who wrote anti-Stalinist verse while Stalin was still alive, and was banished for doing so. Collection of verse, *Gody* (1963). In 1974 he emigrated to the West, where he has published a new volume, *Vremena* (Frankfurt/Main, 1976).

Kushner, Aleksandr Semyonovich (1936–): Leningrad poet. Collection of verse: *Primety* (1969). For a description of his work see Suzanne Massie, *The Living Mirror* (London, 1972).

Kuznetsov, Anatoly Vasil'yevich (1929–): novelist, author of a documentary novel *Babiy Yar,* first published in censored form in *Yunost'* (1966); after the author's defection while on a visit to England in 1969 the full text was published in the West (Frankfurt/Main, 1970). A comparison between the complete and the censored text gives a good idea of the workings of literary censorship in the Soviet Union. An interesting short story 'Artist mimansa' has also been published in censored form in the Soviet Union in *Novy Mir* (1968) and in the full version abroad (*Novyy Zhurnal*, New York, 1970).

Leonov, Leonid Maksimovich (1899–): fellow-traveller novelist and playwright whose work reflects the successive stages of the development of Soviet literature. *Barsuki* (1924), *Vor* (1927; and in a considerably modified version, 1959) and *Sot'* (1929) are major studies of the Civil War period, NEP and the beginning of the First Five Year Plan. Later novels, such as *Skutarevsky* (1932), *Doroga na okean* (1936) and *Russkiy les* (1953), though written under the increasing constraints of the Stalinist period, are nevertheless still of interest. After Stalin's death Leonov has published no major novel, but the long story *Evgenia Ivanovna* (*Znamya*, 1963) is a revised version of a work begun in 1935. *Sobraniye sochineniy,* vols. 1–9 (Moscow, 1960–2).

Maksimov, Vladimir Yemel'yanovich (1932–): after an adventurous early life as an itinerant labourer, started to write in the early 1950s and made his name with a number of plays and novels (particularly *Zhiv chelovek*, 1965), most of them published in the conservative journal *Oktyabr'*. His major novel *Sem' dney tvoreniya*, a sombre chronicle of Soviet life, could not be published in the Soviet Union and came out in Germany in 1971, to be followed by *Karantin* and *Proshchaniye s niotkuda*, both of which give revealing pictures of Soviet life. In 1973 he was expelled from the Union of Writers and in 1974 allowed to leave for France. In the same year he became editor of a new journal, *Kontinent*, which publishes work by emigrants as well as *samizdat* manuscripts by authors still living in the Soviet Union (e.g. Kornilov and Voynovich).

Mandel'shtam, Osip Emil'yevich (1891–1938): leading acmeist poet. His post-revolutionary verse, collected in *Stikhotvoreniya* (1928), shows him hopelessly at odds with the new era. In 1934 he wrote a poem denouncing Stalin and was arrested and exiled. While in exile in Voronezh he wrote a brilliant cycle of poems (1935–7), but on his return to Moscow in 1937 he was arrested once more and sentenced for 'counter-revolutionary activity'. He died in a transit camp near Vladivostok at the end of 1938. After Stalin's death a little of his work was published in the Soviet Union. A long-promised volume of his verse in the series *Biblioteka Poeta* finally appeared in 1973, with a highly misleading introduction by A. Dymshits. His widow was able to preserve most of his work after his death – see her memoirs, *Vospominaniya* (New York, 1970), and *Vtoraya kniga* (Paris, 1972), translated as *Hope against Hope* (London, 1971) and *Hope Abandoned* (London, 1974) – and it has been published in *Sobraniye sochineniy*, vols. 1–3: 2nd enlarged editions of vol. 1 (1967); vol. 2, containing his prose, (1971); vol. 3, articles and letters, etc. (1969), eds. G. P. Struve and B. A. Filippov (New York). See Clarence Brown, *The Prose of Osip Mandelstam* (Princeton, 1967), and *Mandelstam* (Cambridge, 1973).

Mariengof, Anatoly Borisovich (1897–1962): imaginist poet, heavily influenced by both Mayakovsky and Yesenin. His first book of poems, *Vitrina serdtsa*, was published in Penza in 1918. *Stikhi i poemy* (Moscow, 1926).

Martynov, Leonid Nikolayevich (1905–): poet. His verse is noted for its fantasy, e.g. in *Lukomor'ye* (1945). *Stikhotvoreniya i poemy*, vols. 1–2 (Moscow, 1965); *Giperboly* (Moscow, 1972).

Mayakovsky, Vladimir Vladimirovich (1893–1930): associated with the futurists before the revolution, achieved fame with *Oblako v shtanakh* (1915), a messianic denunciation of the old regime. After the revolution he wrote epic poems as well as many *agitprop* jingles in support of it: *Misteriya-buff* (1918), *150,000,000* (1921), *Lyublyu* (1922), *Pro eto* (1923), *Vladimir Il'ich Lenin* (1924), *Khorosho* (1927). The agonized lyrical vein of his pre-revolutionary verse reappeared towards the end of his life in *Pis'mo tovarishchu Kostrovu iz Parizha o lyubvi* and *Pis'mo Tat'yane Yakovlevne* (1928). Two satirical plays, *Klop* (1928) and *Banya* (1929), showed his disillusionment at the revival of the petty-bourgeois mentality during NEP. *Polnoye sobraniye sochineniy*, vols. 1–13 (Moscow, 1955–1961). See Edward J. Brown, *Mayakovsky. A Poet in the Revolution* (Princeton, 1973).

Morits, Yunna Petrovna (1937–): lyric poet. Collections: *Mys zhelaniya* (1961); *Loza. Kniga stikhov, 1962–1967* (Moscow, 1970).

Mozhayev, Boris Andreyevich (1923–); author of an important kolkhoz novel, *Iz zhizni Fyodora Kuz'kina* (*Novy Mir*, 1966).

LITERATURE IN THE SOVIET PERIOD

Nagibin, Yury Markovich (1920–): writer of short novels and stories; leading representative of 'new wave' post-Stalin prose, who contributed a notable story, 'Khazarsky ornament', to *Literaturnaya Moskva*, vol. 2 (1956). *Izbrannyye proizvedeniya*, vols. 1–2 (Moscow, 1973).

Nekrasov, Viktor Platonovich (1911–): author of several war novels, *V okopakh Stalingrada* (1946), and *V rodnom gorode* (1954), who has given support to the 'liberal' cause in the post-Stalin years. His novel *Kira Georgiyevna* (1961) is an interesting study of the moral and psychological damage caused by Stalinism. In 1974 he emigrated to the West, where he has published some of a series of sketches, *Zapiski zevaki*, in *Kontinent* (1975).

Okudzhava, Bulat Shalvovich (1924–): poet, prose-writer, and *chansonnier*. His 'Bud' zdorov, shkolyar' in *Tarusskiye stranitsy* (1961), was one of the first frank accounts of the wartime experience. The only complete collection of his work has been published abroad: *Proza i poeziya*, 3rd edn (Frankfurt/Main, 1968), and *Dva romana* (Frankfurt/Main, 1970).

Olesha, Yury Karlovich (1899–1960): novelist and playwright, best known for his novel *Zavist'* (1927) and its stage version *Zagovor chuvstv* (1929). *Izbrannyye sochineniya* (Moscow, 1956). See Elizabeth K. Beaujour, *The Invisible Land, a study of the artistic imagination of Iurii Olesha* (New York, 1970).

Ostrovsky, Nikolay Alekseyevich (1904–36): novelist whose *Kak zakalyalas' stal'* (1935) is still held up as a model of socialist realism.

Ovechkin, Valentin Vladimirovich (1904–68): writer on kolkhoz themes. His *Rayonnyye budni* (1952–6), begun before the death of Stalin, was the first attempt at an honest treatment of life in the countryside. *Izbrannyye proizvedeniya*, vols. 1–2 (Moscow, 1963). *Zametki na polyakh* (Moscow, 1973).

Panfyorov, Fyodor Ivanovich (1896–1960): socialist realist novelist, best known for his epic work on collectivization: *Bruski*, books 1–4 (1928–37). Some of his late works, e.g. *Volga matushka reka* (1953–60), are of sociological interest.

Panova, Vera Fyodorovna (1905–72): novelist and playwright, notable for her relatively subtle approach to human problems, even in the Stalin years: *Sputniki* (1946); *Vremena goda* (1953); *Seryozha* (1955). Later works are on historical themes, e.g. *Kto umirayet?* (1965).

Pasternak, Boris Leonidovich (1890–1960): poet and novelist. In the immediate post-revolutionary years Pasternak wrote several epic poems on historical themes: *Devyat'sot pyatyy god* (1925–6); *Leytenant Shmidt* (1926–7). These define his early attitude to the revolution and were followed by a 'novel in verse', *Spektorsky* (1931), which shows his reservations about the use of violence, and his belief in the primacy of art over history. Major lyrical cycles published after the revolution were *Sestra moya zhizn'* (1922) and *Vtoroye rozhdeniye* (1932). In the 1930s he turned increasingly to translation (Shakespeare, Goethe, Shelley, Verlaine and Georgian poets) which he regarded as integral to his own work. Two wartime collections of verse, *Na rannikh poyezdakh* (1943) and *Zemnoy prostor* (1945), were the last original work he was to publish until after Stalin's death. *Doktor Zhivago*, on which he had worked intermittently since before the war, was announced for publication in the Moscow monthly magazine *Znamya* in 1954, but in the upshot the novel was rejected for publication in the Soviet Union (except for a small selection of the Zhivago cycle of verse, printed in the same issue of *Znamya* which announced forthcoming publication of the novel).

It appeared abroad, first in Italian translation in November 1957. Various editions of the Russian text appeared shortly afterwards (Feltrinelli, Milan, 1957; University of Michigan Press, 1958). Since there was then no copyright protection for books originating in the Soviet Union, the text has appeared in several pirated editions. The only edition authorized by Pasternak himself is the one by Feltrinelli. The most complete edition of Pasternak's work is the three-volume edition by G. Struve and B. Filippov (Ann Arbor, 1961). An important, but by no means complete, collection of Pasternak's verse appeared in the Soviet Union in 1965: *Boris Pasternak – Stikhotvoreniya i poemy.* The introductory article by A. D. Sinyavsky is the best critical interpretation of Pasternak's work. An uncompleted play, *Slepaya krasavitsa,* was published posthumously in 1969 (Collins and Harvill Press, London) and a few months later in the Soviet Union in the magazine *Prostor* (October 1969). An autobiographical sketch was published with some slight cuts posthumously in *Novy Mir* under the title *Lyudi i polozheniya* (January 1967); full text in English: *An Essay in Autobiography* (London, 1959). Olga R. Hughes, *The Poetic World of Boris Pasternak* (Princeton, 1974).

Paustovsky, Konstantin Georgiyevich (1892–1968): prose-writer. Though a native of Moscow, associated with the 'romantic' school of Odessa. Played an important part in the post-Stalin 'liberal' movement, as an editor of *Literaturnaya Moskva,* vols. 1–2 (1956), and of *Tarusskiye stranitsy,* a collection of prose and poetry which appears to have been published with remarkably little interference from the censorship (Kaluga, 1961). His most successful work in the postwar years has been his autobiography, *Povest' o zhizni,* published in six books (1945–63). See also *Izbrannaya proza* (Moscow, 1965) for earlier work.

Petrov, *see* Il'f.

Pil'nyak, Boris Andreyevich (1894–1937): novelist. His *Golyy god* (1922) was the first Soviet novel and a good example of the so-called 'ornamental' style with its elaborate contrapuntal shifts and repeated motifs. *Mashiny i volki* (1923–4) gives a more sober account of post-revolutionary life. His *Povest' nepogashonnoy luny* (*Novy Mir*, 1926) caused a political scandal by hinting that a Soviet army commander (evidently Frunze) had been assassinated by being made to undergo an unnecessary operation. In 1929 the publication in Berlin of his story *Krasnoye derevo* was used as an excuse for a purge of fellow-traveller writers. The text of the story is now most easily available in *Opal'nyye povesti* (New York, 1955). In a reworked form it was incorporated in the long novel *Volga vpadayet v Kaspiyskoye more* (1930). Pil'nyak's submission to Party criticism did not save him, and he was apparently executed in 1937. Although he has been formally 'rehabilitated' since Stalin's death, scarcely any of his work has been republished. *Sobraniye sochineniy,* vols. 1–8 (Moscow, 1929–30).

Platonov, Andrey Platonovich (1899–1951): outstanding prose-writer. Neglected and virtually suppressed in Stalin times, he has been reprinted in recent years and now enjoys great popularity among Soviet readers. However, his best novel, *Kotlovan,* an eerie, almost surrealistic view of 'socialist construction', as seen through the eyes of building workers, has not been published in the Soviet Union – it is available in the émigré journal, *Grani,* no. 70 (Frankfurt/Main, 1969). Part of another important novel, *Chevengur,* has been published only abroad (Paris, 1972). The most recent Soviet edition of his work is: *Smerti net – Rasskazy* (Moscow, 1970). A good introduction to his work is an essay by Yevtushenko in the English-language volume *This Fierce and Beautiful World* (London, 1970).

Polevoy, Boris Nikolayevich (1908–): socialist realist novelist, known mainly for his *Povest' o nastoyashchem cheloveke* (1946).

Prishvin, Mikhail Mikhaylovich (1873–1954): a writer of nature stories, author of a long novel *Kashcheyeva tsep'* (1923–8). Like Aleksandr Grin he was popular with Soviet readers because he offered escape into a non-Soviet world and sketched out in symbolic language an alternative system of non-Marxist values.

Samoylov (Kaufman), David Samuilovich (1920–): a lyric poet who has written particularly on wartime themes. Collections: *Blizhniye strany* (1958), *Vtoroy pereval* (1963), *Dni* (1970).

Sel'vinsky, Il'ya L'vovich (1899–1968): one of the founders of the constructivist movement in the 1920s. Best known for his two epic poems *Ulyalyayevshchina* (1927) and *Pushtorg* (1928). *Izbrannyye proizvedeniya* (Leningrad, 1972).

Serafimovich, Aleksandr Serafimovich (1863–1949): a protégé of Gor'ky, author of a famous civil war novel *Zheleznyy potok* (1924).

Shaginyan, Marietta Sergeyevna (1888–): novelist known chiefly for her contribution to the literature of the first Five-Year Plan: *Gidrotsentral'* (1930). In the 1920s she was associated with an unsuccessful attempt to launch detective fiction (known as *krasnaya pinkertonovshchina!*) in the Soviet Union: *Miss Mend ili Yanki v Petrograde*, published in 1926 under the pseudonym 'Jim Dollar'. *Sobraniye sochineniy*, vols. 1–9 (Moscow, 1971–).

Shershenevich, Vadim Gabriyelevich (1893–1942): originally an 'ego-futurist', became a leader of the imaginist school after 1919. *Kooperativy vesel'ya* and *Korobeyniki schast'ya* (Moscow, 1921) contain his imaginist verse.

Sholokhov, Mikhail Aleksandrovich (1905–): author of the Soviet classic *Tikhiy Don*, the first three volumes of which appeared between 1928 and 1933, the last in 1940. In 1954 a new edition, politically and stylistically reworked by the author himself, was published. Later editions are closer to the original version, but it is advisable to read prewar editions for the unadulterated text. Sholokhov's novel about collectivization, *Podnyataya tselina* (1931), also appeared in a bowdlerized form in the late Stalin years. *Sobraniye sochineniy*, vols. 1–9 (Moscow, 1965–). See D. H. Stewart, *Mikhail Sholokhov, a Critical Introduction* (Ann Arbor, 1967). Allegations first made in the 1930s that Sholokhov appropriated someone else's manuscript of *Tikhiy Don*, or that he had an unacknowledged co-author, have been revived in recent years. The somewhat inconclusive evidence is reviewed in Roy Medvedev, *Problems of the Literary Biography of Mikhail Sholokhov* (Cambridge, 1977).

Shukshin, Vasily Makarovich (1929–74): before his premature death one of the most promising of the 'village' writers. Several of his stories appeared in *Novy Mir* between 1963 and 1967; after 1971 he published further stories in *Nash Sovremennik*. His *Kalina krasnava* was made into an outstandingly successful film.

Simonov, Konstantin Mikhaylovich (1915–): novelist, poet and playwright. His *Dni i nochi* (1944) was one of the best wartime novels. His retrospective studies of the war are: *Zhivyye i myortvyye* (1959), *Soldatami ne rozhdayutsya* (1963–4) and *Posledneye leto* (1970–1). *Sobraniye sochineniy*, vols. 1–6 (Moscow, 1966–70).

Sinyavsky, Andrey Donatovich (1925–): scholar and literary critic who, under the pseudonym Abram Tertz, published several short stories and short novels in the

West. All these, as well as his essay 'Chto takoye sotsialisticheskiy realizm?' are available in *Fantasticheskiy mir Abrama Tertsa* (New York, 1967). After his emigration to France in 1973, he published *Golos iz khora* (London, 1973). See also: *On Trial: The Soviet State versus 'Abram Tertz' and 'Nikolay Arzhak'*, eds. Leopold Labedz and Max Hayward (London, 1967), for an account of Sinyavsky's trial in 1966.

Slutsky, Boris Abramovich (1919–): poet noted particularly for his verse about the war. Many of his anti-Stalin poems have still not been published in the Soviet Union. Collection: *Pamyat' – Stikhi. 1944–1968* (Moscow, 1969).

Soloukhin, Vladimir Alekseyevich (1924–): poet and prose-writer. His verse collections, *Kak vypit' solntse* (1961) and *Zhit' na zemle* (1965), and documentary prose such as *Vladimirskiye prosyolki* (*Novy Mir*, 1957) and *Chornyye doski* in the collection of stories *Zimniy den'* (1969), are marked by a liberal Slavophile tendency. A harrowing autobiographical story *Prigovor* in the journal *Moskva* (1975) is of interest.

Solzhenitsyn, Aleksandr Isayevich (1918–): *Odin den' Ivana Denisovicha* first appeared in *Novy Mir* in November 1962, and was followed by a paperback edition, with very slight textual variants, in 1963. The two stories *Matryonin dvor* and *Sluchay na stantsii Krechetovka* were published in *Novy Mir* in January 1963. *Dlya pol'zy dela* appeared in *Novy Mir* in July 1963. The last work by Solzhenitsyn to appear in the Soviet Union was the short story *Zakhar-kalita* (*Novy Mir*, January 1966). Since then all his work has appeared only in foreign editions, some of them corrupt, most of them unauthorized. The best editions of *Rakovyy korpus* and *V kruge pervom* are those of the YMCA press (Paris, 1968 and 1969). The YMCA press also published, with Solzhenitsyn's express authority, the first part of *Avgust chetyrnadtsatogo* (1971). A six-volume collection, *Sobraniye sochineniy*, has been published by *Possev* (Frankfurt/Main, 1969–71). *Arkhipelag Gulag* has appeared in three volumes in Paris (1973–6). Several chapters on Lenin omitted in the original edition of *Avgust 14-ogo* have been published separately, together with other chapters on Lenin from forth-coming volumes in the series, as *Lenin v Tsyurikhe* (Paris, 1975). *Bodalsya telyonok s dubom* (Paris, 1975) is an autobiographical account of the author's later years in the Soviet Union, ending with his forcible exile. See C. Moody, *Solzhenitsyn* (Edinburgh, 1973).

Sosnora, Viktor Aleksandrovich (1936–): Leningrad poet distinguished by his originality of language and preoccupation with pre-Petrine historical themes, particularly in the collection *Vsadniki* (Leningrad, 1969). For some verse unpub-lished in the Soviet Union, see Suzanne Massie, *The Living Mirror* (London, 1972).

Syomin, Vitaly Nikolayevich (1927–): neo-realist prose-writer who made a stir in 1965 with his *Semero v odnom dome* (*Novy Mir*), a description of working-class life.

Tarkovsky, Arseny Aleksandrovich (1907–): accomplished poet and translator of the older generation who began to publish his original verse only in the 1960s. Collection: *Vestnik* (Moscow, 1969).

Tendryakov, Vladimir Fyodorovich (1923–): one of the best 'new wave' prose writers whose stories and short novels show a concern with moral dilemmas: *Ukhaby* (1958), *Troyka, semyorka, tuz* (1960), *Sud* (1961), *Podyonka – vek korotkiy* (1969), *Perevyortyshi. Povesti* (Moscow, 1974).

227

LITERATURE IN THE SOVIET PERIOD

Tertz, *see* Sinyavsky.

Tikhonov, Nikolay Semyonovich (1896–): poet and prose-writer. His early romantic verse on civil war themes (*Orda* and *Braga*, 1922) showed the influence of Gumilyov. He was a leading member of the Serapion Brothers. *Sobraniye sochineniy*, vols. 1–7 (Moscow, 1973–).

Tolstoy, Aleksey Nikolayevich (1882–1945): his main works in the Soviet period were on historical themes: *Pyotr I* (pt 1: 1929–30; pt 2: 1933–4; pt 3: 1944–5) and *Ivan Groznyy* (1943). His epic trilogy *Khozhdeniye po mukam*, written between 1919 and 1941, is a study of Russian society before and after the revolution. *Polnoye sobraniye sochineniy*, vols. 1–15 (Moscow, 1946–53).

Trifonov, Yury Valentinovich (1925–): novelist and story-writer known particularly for his studies of the moral and psychological dilemmas of the intelligentsia: *Utoleniye zhazhdy* (1963); the long stories *Obmen* (1969), *Predvaritel'nyye itogi* (1970), *Dolgoye proshchaniye* (1971), *Drugaya zhizn'* (1975) were published in *Novy Mir.*

Tvardovsky, Aleksandr Trifonovich (1910–71): poet and editor. His epic poem about a Soviet soldier, *Vasily Tyorkin* (1941–5), won him great popularity during the war. *Vasily Tyorkin na tom svete*, a sequel in which Stalinism is brilliantly satirized, circulated for some years in manuscript before being published in *Izvestiya* (18 August 1963), with Khrushchev's permission, and with an introduction by his son-in-law, A. Adzhubey. A slightly different version of the poem had previously appeared in the émigré journal *Mosty* (no. 10, Munich, 1963); the text also appeared in *Novy Mir* (no. 8, 1963). Another long ballad, *Za dal'yu dal'* (1953–60), was an important contribution to the literature of the 'thaw'. His lyrical poetry is less well known than his epic ballads, but it conveys a remarkable impression of simplicity, strength and integrity. See, for example, *Iz liriki etikh let* (Moscow, 1967). As editor of *Novy Mir* (1950–4 and 1958–70) he published many of the most important works of the post-Stalin era (including Solzhenitsyn's). *Sobraniye sochineniy*, vols. 1–5 (Moscow, 1966–71).

Tynyanov, Yury Nikolayevich (1894–1943): leading formalist literary scholar and novelist. His historical novels, in striking contrast to those of Aleksey Tolstoy, stress the liberal aspect of Russian history: *Smert' Vazir-Mukhtara* (1928), about the death of Griboyedov in Persia; *Kyukhlya* (1925), about Pushkin's friend Vil'gel'm Kyukhel'beker. Particularly noteworthy are his two historical fantasies, *Podporuchik Kizhe* (1928) and *Voskovaya persona* (1930), about Paul I and Peter the Great respectively. *Sochineniya*, vols. 1–3 (Moscow, 1959). Tynyanov is the subject of an outstanding critical biography by A. Belinkov, 2nd edn (Moscow, 1965).

Veresayev, pseudonym of Smidovich, Vikenty Vikent'yevich (1867–1945): a realist of the Gor'ky school. After the revolution he wrote two novels about the intelligentsia, *V tupike* (1922) and *Syostry* (1933). *Sobraniye sochineniy*, vols. 1–5 (Moscow, 1961).

Vershigora, Pyotr Petrovich (1905–63): author of an important documentary novel about the war: *Lyudi s chistoy sovest'yu* (1946).

Vinokurov, Yevgeny Mikhaylovich (1925–): poet of philosophical bent. Collection: *Zhest – Novyye stikhi* (Moscow, 1969).

Virta, Nikolay Yevgen'yevich (1906–76): author of a vivid documentary novel about the Tambov uprising, *Odinochestvo* (1935).

228

Voynovich, Vladimir Nikolayevich (1932–): 'new wave' prose writer whose stories have a working-class background: *Khochu byt' chestnym* (*Novy Mir*, 1963); *Dva tovarishcha* (*Novy Mir*, 1967). Collection: *Povesti* (1972). The first two parts of his satirical novel about the life of a soldier, *Zhizn' i neobychaynyye priklyucheniya soldata Ivana Chonkina*, appeared in Paris in 1975.

Voznesensky, Andrey Andreyevich (1933–): his first verse was printed in 1958. Several collections have been published: e.g. *Ten' zvuka* (Moscow, 1970), *Vzglyad: Stikhi i poemy* (Moscow, 1972), *Dubovyy list violonchel'nyy* (Moscow, 1975).

Yashin, Aleksandr Yakovlevich (1913–68): prose writer and poet. His short story 'Rychagi' appeared in *Literaturnaya Moskva*, vol. 2 (1956). He is also the author of 'village' prose: *Vologodskaya svad'ba* (*Novy Mir*, 1962). *Izbrannyye proizvedeniya*, vols. 1–2 (Moscow, 1972–).

Yesenin, Sergey Aleksandrovich (1895–1925): three poems written in 1918 show acceptance of the revolution as a peasant utopia: *Nebesnyy barabanshchik*, *Iordanskaya golubitsa* and *Inoniya*. His disillusionment in subsequent years is reflected in the cycle *Rus' kabatskaya* (1921–4), *Vozvrashcheniye na rodinu* (1924), *Rus' sovetskaya* (1924) and *Rus' ukhodyashchaya* (1924). Collected works: *Sobraniye sochineniy*, vols. 1–5 (Moscow, 1966–8).

Yevtushenko, Yevgeny Aleksandrovich (1933–): apart from his many lyrics, the first of which were published in 1949, he has written several epic poems, such as: *Stantsiya Zima* (1956), *Bratskaya GES* (1964–5), and *Kazanskiy universitet* (*Novy Mir*, April 1970), on the occasion of Lenin's hundredth anniversary. Some of his more controversial poems, *Babiy Yar* (*Literaturnaya Gazeta*, 19 September 1961), and *Nasledniki Stalina* (*Pravda*, 1 October 1962), do not appear in his collections, such as: *Vzmakh ruki* and *Nezhnost'* (both 1962), and *Idut belyye snegi* (1969). His *Precocious Autobiography* was published in Paris in 1963 and has never appeared in the Soviet Union (in Russian, Toronto, 1963). For later verse see *Poyushchaya damba* (1975), *Ottsovskiy slukh* (1975).

Zabolotsky, Nikolay Alekseyevich (1903–58): one of the most original poets of the Soviet era whose bizarre manner and pessimistic view of human affairs, as in his first collection *Stolbtsy* (1929), and *Torzhestvo zemledeliya* (1933), brought him into disfavour during the Stalin era. Banished to Central Asia in 1938, he was allowed to return to Moscow in 1946, after which he published verse written in a more 'optimistic' vein. The most complete collection of his work is: *Stikhotvoreniya*, eds. G. Struve and B. Filippov (Washington–New York, 1965). *Izbrannyye proizvedeniya*, vols. 1–2 (Moscow, 1972).

Zalygin, Sergey Pavlovich (1913–): writer on kolkhoz themes. His short novel *Na Irtyshe* (1964, in *Novy Mir*) is a vivid study of collectivization.

Zamyatin, Yevgeny Ivanovich (1884–1937): novelist and playwright, a member of the 'Serapion Brothers', who went into voluntary exile in 1931. His anti-Utopian novel *My* (*We*) (first full Russian edition, New York, 1952) was never published in the Soviet Union, but the bulk of his work appeared there in a collected edition before he left: *Sobraniye sochineniy*, vols. 1–4 (Moscow, 1929). See also *Litsa* (New York, 1955) for his literary essays, and one or two items unpublished in the Soviet Union.

Zoshchenko, Mikhail Mikhaylovich (1895–1958): before his denunciation by Zhdanov in 1946 for the first part of his autobiographical tale *Pered voskhodom solntsa*, published in the literary monthly *Oktyabr'*, nos. 6–7 and 8–9 (1943), and his short story 'Pokhozhdeniya obez'yany', in the monthly *Zvezda* (nos. 5–6, 1946), Zoshchenko was perhaps the most widely-read Soviet prose-writer in the Soviet Union. He was a founder member of the 'Serapion Brothers'. His comic stories about Soviet daily life, narrated in the semi-literate language of the Leningrad *obyvatel'*, are notable examples of the *skaz* form (e.g. the cycle *Golubaya kniga*, 1934). There is still some reticence about republishing his work in the Soviet Union, but some incomplete collections have appeared in recent years, e.g. *Povesti i rasskazy*, vols. 1–2 (Leningrad, 1968). The second half of *Pered voskhodom solntsa* was finally published in *Zvezda* (Moscow, 1972) under the title *Povest' o razume*, without any indication of its connection with the first half. The two halves have been published together as one book in New York (1973).

8

THE EARLY THEATRE

M. A. S. BURGESS

Before the seventeenth century a *theatre* in Russia can hardly have been said to exist. The retarded development of a Russian stage was caused by certain traits in the national tradition – the bigotry and illiteracy of the population, the hostility of the Orthodox Church and the absolutism of the tsar. Puritanism frowned on dramatics: miming was sinful, players were evil or corrupt.

Nomadic performers, however, surely entertained at feudal households on particular occasions. Diversions evolved at Byzantium influenced such early essays in Russian histrionics. Frescoes in the Cathedral of St Sophia at Kiev depict a representation of a musical or semi-theatrical occasion. Yet wandering *jongleurs* who seem to have been countenanced by the Church in the eleventh century were, from the fourteenth century onwards, persecuted by both the ecclesiastical and secular authorities. Goliards (*skomorokhi*) wandered through the villages earning a few kopecks here and there, but often driven to thieving, they were ultimately rejected by the Establishment. With the loss of patronage by church and aristocracy, the Russian players were expelled from Moscow and eventually settled in the North.

After the wedding of Tsar Mikhail Fyodorovich in 1626, when the traditional church choir was replaced by Russian mummers, foreign comedians and dancers found their way to court, displacing any native performers owing to their superior expertise. But all forms of entertainment were then suppressed and old prejudices were revived. It was prohibited by the tsar and patriarch 'to dance, play games or watch them; at wedding feasts either to sing or play on instruments; or to give over one's soul to perdition in such pernicious and lawless practices as word-play, farces and magic'. The wearing of *skomorokhi* costumes for the widely practised entertainment of bear-baiting was decreed illegal.

The stage thus suffered momentary eclipse. Meanwhile Russian churchmen had made the discovery that their Jesuit opponents regarded the drama as a method of instruction. Accordingly, in order to counter Jesuitical activities inside Russia, religious seminaries were established at Kiev and other cities. A form of spiritual drama was instituted in these 'academies' which came to be known under the title of the *Academic Theatre* (*Shkol'nyy teatr*). The repertoire consisted of subjects borrowed from medieval mystery-cycles and adapted into Russian from Polish. Nevertheless, in spite of the emergence of this form of drama, it was court patronage which was finally responsible for the future growth of the Russian stage, and the pattern was set by foreigners from western Europe.

Officially a Russian court theatre was founded in 1672. Tsar Alexis wished to bring his own court into line with the more polished court life abroad where a tradition of music, dance and drama had long existed. A favourite of the tsar, the Boyar Artamon Matveyev, instructed the Russian ambassador to Sweden, von Staden, to gather recruits for the stage from abroad, but von Staden only succeeded in bringing to Moscow one trumpeter and four musicians. Sinister reports about conditions in Russia dismayed western comedians and so Matveyev was compelled to seek elsewhere. He was lucky in discovering a Lutheran minister in Moscow, Pastor Johann Gottfried Gregory, who encouraged amateur dramatics amongst the foreign merchants. On 4 June 1672 the tsar ordered Gregory to institute a comedy, to act at that comedy the story of Esther, and to construct a theatre (*khoromina*) for the same play.

Sixty children were selected from the foreign school – mostly the sons of German merchants – and these were taught the art of acting. The repertoire was mainly borrowed from Germany, and included the tragi-comedy *Esther and Ahasuerus* (possibly based on an English source), *Judith*, and a drama (modelled perhaps after Marlowe's *Tamburlaine*) written by George Huebner, Gregory's assistant. The stage of the new wooden theatre was elaborate, perspective effects were painted by the Dutch scenic artist Engels, music was provided, and the costumes were remarkably luxurious. The tsar, who occupied a central seat, was so affected by this novelty that he is said to have watched for ten hours on end without leaving his seat. The cast was suitably rewarded with titles and rich sable furs. Further recruits, this time from Russian families, were taken into the company, but Gregory found these youngsters unruly and had to bludgeon them into learning their lines. They were underpaid and underfed, but nevertheless obliged to act. By these means the court theatre swiftly flourished, efforts at ballet were attempted, and the orchestra improved.

Unfortunately the death of Pastor Gregory in 1675 caused a setback to productions. He was succeeded by Huebner, who did not get on with the tsar and was replaced by Stefan Chizhinsky, a former teacher of Latin from the Kiev theological college. Chizhinsky composed several plays and was commanded to write a comedy about David and Goliath, as well as instructing eighteen pupils of various classes in dramatic art. The theatre, however, collapsed as a court venture after the death of Alexis in 1676, and the whole playhouse and company were disbanded.

The next tsar, Fyodor, felt disinclined to continue official interest in the stage, yet the idea of a theatre had taken root amongst the leading families of Russia. Theatrical diversions were arranged at the homes of the Boyar Miloslavsky, Prince Odoyevsky, Prince Golitsyn, the Boyarina Arsen'yeva and in the apartments of Sofiya Alekseyevna.

The eighteenth century witnessed the firm beginnings of the stage in Russia. Peter the Great was anxious to found a national public theatre as part of his civilizing programme. A fresh start, however, had to be made, and once again the aid of foreigners was sought. In 1701, soon after the start of the Northern War, the tsar commanded a certain Jan Splavsky, a Hungarian puppet-master, to go to Danzig and collect a troupe of actors. Splavsky approached a leading actor of the time, Johann Christian Kunst, but he declined the invitation. Splavsky did not give up and in 1702 he succeeded in bringing Kunst to Moscow with a company of seven German actors.

Kunst, 'a leader of comedy of his Imperial Majesty', undertook to teach a number of Russians the art of acting and received an annuity of 3,000 roubles for all his troupe. Performances were first held at the house of General Lefort in the foreign quarter of Moscow, and Kunst was aided by a powerful statesman, F. A. Golovin, who occupied much the same position with regard to the theatre as had the Boyar Matveyev. But soon the troupe met with many snags: sufficient rehearsal time was never allowed and opposition was encountered. Eventually a wooden theatre was built in the Red Square, known as the *Komedial'naya khramina*. It was quite large and handsomely decorated with scarlet silk on the inside walls. Kunst never saw the *khramina* completed. After presenting only three comedies at Lefort's palace, he died in 1703. He was followed by another impresario, Otto Fürst, who drew upon the native population for new actors in his company from 1704 to 1707.

The repertoire of the *khramina* was entirely secular. On state occasions there were histories about such personages as Alexander the Great, Scipio Africanus, Tamburlaine and Don Juan, as well as occasional modern comedies like *Le Médecin malgré lui*. Natal'ya Alekseyevna, Peter's sister, also wrote Russian plays with such titles as *The Comedy of Saint Catherine* and *The Comedy of the Prophet Daniel*. Music and dancing were introduced into productions, and some singing. The dialogue, however, was half in German and half in mediocre Russian translations: each actor declaimed in the language with which he was most naturally acquainted. The result was bizarre.

By 1705 it became clear that Peter's theatrical enterprise was a failure. The Russian actors turned unreliable; excessive drinking and quarrelling back stage, coupled with gambling and physical violence, deprived the company of any artistic quality; the audience became disorderly and riots were frequent in the house. Attendance declined to such an extent that on 31 May 1706 Otto Fürst's troupe was dispersed for ever, and the *khramina* with all the properties was dismantled.

Natal'ya Alekseyevna still maintained her troupe at Preobrazhenskoye, but in 1710 she moved to St Petersburg where she had a new theatre constructed in her apartments. Plays continued to be presented there until her death in 1716. Yet another attempt at finding actors was made in 1720, but these efforts proved abortive. Nevertheless, a German troupe led by Mann established itself on the Moyka River at St Petersburg in 1723. Mann was perhaps the first of the long line of foreign impresarios who sensed the golden opportunities awaiting them in a culturally expanding empire.

Meanwhile the Academic Theatre continued to thrive. In 1702 the Moscow Slavo–Graeco–Latin Academy produced a panegyric play on the *Awesome Portrayal of the Second Coming of the Lord*, an allegory eulogizing the tsar in his struggle against Sweden. Various other plays were projected and an attempt was made by Feofan Prokopovich to found a secular theatre as opposed to the religious drama of the theological colleges. Although his efforts failed, the Academic Theatre broadened its repertoire with new genres, the introduction of comic characters, satirical comments on everyday fashions, more natural dialogue and a musical interlude. The example of the theological academies was followed by secular scholastic institutions, such as the College of Surgeons on the River Yauza at Moscow and the Moscow Navigation School. The tsar encouraged these amateur school plays.

This form of academic theatre persisted until the mid-eighteenth century in various regional cities, and a national type of folk-drama might have been evolved had conditions been more favourable. The old-fashioned style of drama, however, could hardly have competed with foreign influence and the higher artistic level required at court. The didactic element of the Academic Theatre was alien to the modern spirit of music and opera which was soon to sweep the capital, and after a last noble effort at panegyric plays for the coronation of Elizabeth and her visit to Kiev in 1744, the Russian academic drama faded from the scene.

Although the political confusion following Peter's death in 1725 caused a further standstill in the history of the theatre, hopes of reviving the stage in Russia were increased on the accession of Anne in 1730. It was in this empress's reign that opera and ballet began to expand. There had been a ballet in the capital since 1727, when a company started to give performances at the *Narodnyy Teatr* by the Green Bridge on the Nevsky Prospekt, close to where Rastrelli was to build the Stroganov Palace. On

1 January 1730 a musical comedy *Orpheus in Hades* was performed there, and later *The Destruction of Babylon*. This proved prophetic, for on 25 April 1731 the theatre crashed into the Moyka because of the erosion of its foundations.

The ballet caught the taste of the empress and several companies were thereafter invited to come from Italy in 1735 and 1736, the year that the ballet really became established when it was introduced into Italian opera productions. Two new court theatres were constructed – one in the Fir Grove and the other in the old Winter Palace fitted up in a sumptuous style. A most competent *maître de ballet* was appointed – Jean Baptiste Landet who had been at the Swedish court. He soon established a ballet school in the old Winter Palace and instructed young Russians in the art of the dance.

At the beginning of 1740 an academy was opened in St Petersburg, 'to maintain for the Court Chapel at our Imperial Court up to twelve persons selected from junior children of Little Russian origin instructed in singing'. The organizer of the new Academy of Music was a dynamic personality from Naples – Francesco Araja – who arrived in Russia in 1735. His production of *La Forza dell' amore e dell' odio* (1736) introduced the vogue for Italian *opera-seria* into Russia and a new-found sophistication into musical and balletic representations.

The baroque court theatre of the Empress Elizabeth was soon to rival the most brilliant theatres of Europe. It was her ebullient personality which sought out real qualities inherent in those who showed a propensity for creative art, music, dancing and the drama. The empress, an impresario by nature, possessed natural good taste, a flair for encouraging talent and a gift for promoting it.

In 1742 Elizabeth inaugurated a regular series of masquerades and court theatricals. A splendid opera house, designed by Rastrelli, was erected by the Yauza River in Moscow. Here an 'incomparable' *opera-seria* was staged entitled *La Clemenza di Tito*, with libretto by Metastasio and music by Adolphe Hasse. The success of this work set a high standard for future productions.

Elizabeth had succeeded in assembling an efficient production team around her. The orchestra was particularly accomplished, and the principal singers were superb. The *maître de ballet*, Landet, was responsible for serious choreography, while Antonio Rinaldi-Fusano looked after light burlesque. There was a prima-ballerina *assoluta*, Tonina Rinaldi-Fusano, and a supporting company of excellent dancers.

A small German troupe also arrived in the capital. Directed by the ex-principal of the Königsberg Theatre, Johann Peter Hilferding, it played in a small wooden theatre (accessible to the general public) on the Bol'shaya Morskaya. A more important troupe of actors, from France,

235

came to Russia in 1743. This was under the direction of M. de Sérigny and soon gained the personal favour of the empress. The repertoire consisted of works by Molière, Racine, Destouches and Corneille. Performances were given every Thursday at six o'clock.

The Italian and French companies played in the newly renovated theatre inside the Winter Palace. Here magnificent series of opera were presented regularly throughout the reign, with a great triumph in 1755, when A. P. Sumarokov composed a Russian libretto for a modern opera, *Cephalus and Procris*, with music by Araja. The artistes, for the first time, were all native Russians.

Nobody was permitted to be absent from any court theatrical productions and attendance at all masquerades and festivities was compulsory. The theatre was limited to an exclusive clientèle, and the general public was scarcely considered.

In 1749 the rococo-style opera house on the Nevsky Prospekt burned down. The empress thereupon ordered a transportable *Malyy Teatr* to be designed for setting up in the Winter Palace and a fine new stone theatre to be built in the Summer Garden to the design of Valeriani and Peresinotti, the court scene-painters.

The influence of the court theatre now extended over the daily life of the city's inhabitants. Private theatricals were inaugurated at home and an amateur stage, *lyubitel'skiy teatr*, became popular. The empress gave permission for such domestic entertainments, and private theatres grew in popularity throughout the remaining part of the century. A vogue for amateur dramatics had also infected the inmates of a fashionable new establishment, The Noble College of Land Cadets. This developed into a most august academy and played a significant part in contributing to Russian letters and the drama. The cadets began by rehearsing French plays, reading papers and reciting poetry. They also took part in Landet's corps-de-ballet. They were instructed in fortification, drawing, music, French and German, oratory and other liberal studies. The curriculum was wide and the administration admirable. The *Kadetskiy Korpus* was a model of its kind.

A. P. Sumarokov, one of the first cadets, had, after leaving, given readings of poetry at literary society meetings within the college. It was not long, therefore, before the cadets took the initiative and performed one of his plays. *Khorev*, a tragedy of Kievan Russia, was put on in 1747, the first Russian neo-classical play to be performed by Russians. Sumarokov subsequently composed several more dramas, the cadets were commanded to perform in the Winter Palace, and the empress even became enamoured of the leading boy actor in Sumarokov's play *Sinav i Truvor*.

Just about this time an amateur company of actors had started to give performances of mystery plays in a barn at Yaroslavl', under the direction of Fyodor Volkov (1729–63), a merchant's son who later became the first Russian actor of renown. Volkov was fortunate in being brought to the notice of the empress, and it was not long before he, his brother Gavrila, and members of the Yaroslavl' troupe were ordered to appear in St Petersburg. As a result of the presentation of a morality play, *A Sinner's Repentance* by Dimitri Rostovsky, in 1752 at the Winter Palace, the Volkov brothers, together with I. Dmitrevskoy (who was soon to be celebrated as the most distinguished Russian actor, the Garrick of Russia) were assigned as students to the *Kadetskiy Korpus* in order to perfect their histrionic abilities and acquire the rudiments of education.

Amateur dramatics had been officially sanctioned in 1750, but on 30 August 1756 the Government Senate was enjoined by the empress to found a proper national theatre in the capital. Actors and actresses were required to be signed on, 5,000 roubles per annum were to be assigned to the new Russian Patent Theatre, which was to be situated in the Golovkin Stone Mansion, next to the *Kadetskiy Korpus*, with Sumarokov installed as director. An official Russian theatre had at last been achieved.

From 1756 until 1759 Sumarokov encountered much opposition and many unlooked-for snags. The endowment was insufficient, and compared most unfavourably with the annual sums collected by M. de Sérigny's French players and the vast subsidy granted to the Italian impresarios. Indeed, the Russian Patent Theatre ran into so much financial trouble that on 6 January 1759 the whole enterprise passed into the control of the imperial household – the beginning of the famous tradition of the Russian Imperial Theatres.

The enthusiasm displayed by the Empress Elizabeth for all forms of entertainment naturally encouraged the more adventurous foreign impresarios to try their fortunes in St Petersburg and Moscow. To any spirited entrepreneur Russia seemed a paradise, and in the autumn of 1757 the Italian Opera-Buffa Company under Giovanni-Battista Locatelli arrived in St Petersburg, and received a contract from the empress. The company enjoyed the express privilege of playing in a charming play-house 'The Theatre by the Summer Palace', and had an instantaneous success with Locatelli's magnificent spectacle 'Il Retiro degli Dei' (described as 'a serious pastoral') in honour of the anniversary of the empress's accession. Elizabeth loved the new mode of entertainment. Productions for the court were held weekly and, when public performances took place, the empress would sometimes appear 'incognito', occupying a seat at the back of three boxes reserved for the court. Her pleasure was such that the very first year she bestowed a gift of 5,000 roubles on

Locatelli. The nobility also took to the fashion and rented boxes for an annual subscription, and each owner of a box would decorate it according to his own taste. 'The theatre', commented von Staehlin, 'was always overcrowded', and significantly he noted, 'Foreign ministers and local connoisseurs all declared of this ballet that nowhere in Europe could one encounter anything comparable and considered that it was in no way inferior to the best that either Italy or Paris could produce.'[1]

Sumarokov, director of the poorly subsidized Russian Patent Theatre on the other bank of the River Neva, viewed with ever-increasing dismay the swift success of his Italian rival. He and his star-actor, Fyodor Volkov, could hardly compete with the glitter of the novel genre of opera-buffa, grand-ballet and imperial patronage. Locatelli's fortunes, however, were soon to change. The empress granted him permission to erect a new wooden theatre in Moscow, which was inaugurated in January 1759 with a gala performance of a new opera-buffa production composed by Baldassare Galuppi, *La Calamità dei Cuori*. At first the Moscow public found the show a great success, and the winter season augured well for the future. Soon, however, because of the cold and the distance of the theatre from the social centre of the city, attendance began to decline. Locatelli was obliged to provide other attractions besides opera-buffa and turned his theatre firstly into masquerade rooms, next into an exclusive casino, and then into a superior form of masquerade. But the public was no longer interested, and they all failed. At length Locatelli attempted one last novelty – he turned for help to the bright young undergraduate actors of Moscow University.

Moscow University, founded in 1755, supported a skilful band of student actors presided over by the dean, Mikhail Kheraskov (1733–1807), who was later to become rector and a playwright of considerable importance. Performances of plays by Sumarokov together with translations from foreign tragedies and comedies were at intervals presented within the confines of the University before members of Moscow society. Notices appeared in *The Moscow News* requesting possible actresses to come for auditions at the University Registry. It was perhaps from the year 1757, when the first such announcement appeared, that ladies were finally accepted into the Russian theatre: there were some famous names – Tat'yana Troyepol'skaya, Agrafena Musina-Pushkina, Mariya and Ol'ga Ananina, all of whom continued on the stage.

It had been planned to build a permanent theatre for the University Dramatic Society, but Locatelli's arrival forestalled this development. Locatelli now proposed an amalgamation with the Moscow University Dramatic Society which was given the opportunity of performing once or

---

[1] J. von Staehlin, *Nachrichten von der Tanzkunst in Russland*, Russian trans. B. I. Zagursky in *Muzyka i balet v Rossii XVIII veka* (Leningrad, 1936), 154–6.

twice a week in Locatelli's theatre. Kheraskov became jointly responsible for the theatre, and the University thus acquired a theatre under professional direction but with university control.

Although the repertoire was most varied – operas, straight plays, comedy and tragedy, pastoral ballets – Locatelli was still unable to make ends meet. Towards the end of 1760 the final break-up was imminent. When the Empress Elizabeth died on 25 December 1761 (o.s.) and a year's mourning was imposed, no entertainment was permitted, all theatres were closed and the company was dispersed for ever. In 1762 the impresario's assets, properties and scenery passed directly into the stores of the Imperial Bursary. Catherine II awarded Locatelli 3,000 roubles in recognition of four years' work for the theatre, and for the remainder of his days he was appointed proprietor of an elegant cabaret on the outskirts of St Petersburg, which enjoyed the patronage of an exclusive clientèle.

Locatelli's theatrical venture had failed because the time was not yet ripe for a professional theatre in Moscow, although in a couple of decades the picture was to be decidedly changed. The presence of the Opera-Buffa Company in Russia had an important effect on the development of the theatre. Locatelli's production methods set a high standard for all who followed him, and never before had such a brilliant assembly of musicians, dancers, singers and stage technicians been brought into the empire.

In the autumn of 1762 Vincenzo Manfredini composed an Italian opera, *L'Olimpiade*, for the coronation of Catherine II. Francesco Gradizzi, recently appointed décor-master of the Imperial Court Theatre, was instructed to renovate the old Yauza Opera House, originally built for Elizabeth's coronation, so that the new performance could take place there. Gradizzi created many superb décors throughout the next thirty years in the field of opera and ballet for the Imperial Theatres. On his death in 1793 he was succeeded by the celebrated Pietro Gonzaga, perhaps the most remarkable scene designer of the age. It was clear from the brilliant mounting of *L'Olimpiade* that the Empress Catherine intended to sponsor a magnificent approach to theatrical production throughout her reign.

Amateur theatricals had proved very popular ever since the Empress Elizabeth had authorized them in 1750. Spectacular entertainments at the imperial court, calling for the participation of the nobility, favoured the growth of the aristocratic amateur stage, while the commonalty continued to find their amusement in traditional fairs, carnivals, and pageants, reinforced by foreign subjects and techniques.[1] The grandest event was the great masquerade entitled *Minerva Triumphant*, organized to cele-

[1] See: M. Burgess, 'Fairs and Entertainers in 18th Century Russia', *The Slavonic and East European Review*, vol. XXXVIII, no. 90 (December 1959), pp. 95–113.

brate the enthronement of Catherine II. All the leading actors, poets, musicians and designers had a hand in this show. The empress was represented as Pallas Athene, while a train of floats depicting all the frailty and falsehoods of human kind rolled down the streets of Moscow. Wisdom was thus paraded and ignorance confounded. The whole show was an unbounded success and set the tone for the next thirty years.

The subsequent course of the theatre in Moscow is a story of the rise and fall of independent impresarios seeking patents from the crown. The first of these was a Sergey Titov, an amateur playwright, who requested a patent at the end of 1765 to open a private theatre in Moscow. In this he was successful, but instead of the usual twenty-five per cent tax levied on every production by the Foundling Hospital, which had been instituted by Catherine in 1763, Titov was to make an annual contribution of 1,500 roubles towards the charity. By 1769, however, he had fallen into debt and 'the managers of masquerades and concerts in Moscow, the Italians Belmonte and Ciutti' petitioned the empress to allow them to construct a new wooden theatre and run a company. Perhaps the reason for Titov's collapse was the arrival from Vienna in 1766 of the empress's new *maître de ballet*, Gasparo Angiolini, whose glamorous entertainments must have diverted the public from Titov's troupe.

Belmonte and Ciutti obtained their patent with the help of Sumarokov and, after some complications and trouble incurred in paying the twenty-five per cent tax, began giving performances in the house of Count Roman Vorontsov, which was hired for the purpose. They were allowed to stage Sumarokov's works only with his express permission and with proper billing.

At first all seemed propitious, but the times and the taste of the public were changing. Sumarokov still believed in the worth and pre-eminence of his style of neo-classical tragedy and comedy, which was now seen to be rather old-fashioned by the more enlightened theatre-going public. The new genre of sentimental comedy had found its way to Russia after 1760 and was soon enjoying a widespread vogue. The repertoire included many examples of the style. In 1770 Belmonte and Ciutti staged a Russian translation of Beaumarchais's *Eugénie* which proved so popular that it was revived four times in succession. Sumarokov was an ardent critic of this new style; this irritated its followers, and his own new, revised production of *Sinav and Truvor* was wrecked by the intrigues of adversaries in the early months of 1770. This ended Sumarokov's career in the theatre, and when the terrible plague of Moscow in 1771 prevented further dramatic activity and both Belmonte and his wife fell victims, the theatre was closed. The actor Dmitrevskoy then considered forming a fresh company, and was followed by the director of Moscow University, Melissino, and even Sumarokov. The contract finally went to another foreigner, Melchiore Groti, who refused Sumarokov entry to the theatre. The latter took to drink, got seriously into debt, his property was sequestered, and he died in 1777 forlorn and forgotten.

In 1776 Groti took into partnership the Moscow Attorney-General, Prince Pyotr Urusov, and that same year handed over all his rights in the theatre, leaving Urusov sole proprietor of the Znamenka Theatre. The Moscow University Dramatic Society, meanwhile, was put under the direction of an eminent actor, Pyotr Plavil'shchikov (1760–1812), who was to achieve great renown in his later years. A new theatre was assembled in the University and the repertoire included operas, comedy and tragedy.

The theatre in St Petersburg was all this time being promoted by the Empress Catherine and her court. Although Peter III, to show his prejudice against all things French, had in 1762 summarily dismissed the French comedians directed by M. de Sérigny after nearly twenty years of continual and faithful service to the crown, Catherine immediately set about gathering a new French company which finally arrived in 1764. It was an opéra-comique band of players which proved a great success with the court.

There was an ancient, dilapidated theatre on Tsaritsyn Meadow which in 1770 was made over to the merchant Pochet by order of the senate. Then just five months later it was offered to a group of English players directed by a Mr Fisher. Their repertoire included many works written for the London stage, but after 1773 the company seems to have disbanded. Next to arrive on the scene was a merchant and manufacturer of German origin, Karl Knipper, who was much more ambitious than any of his predecessors. Knipper inaugurated performances in December 1777 and, having heard of the successes of the young amateurs of the Moscow Foundling Hospital, he persuaded the Tutelary Council to let them join his troupe. Adult and experienced actors were admitted to the cast, composers and musicians were enrolled and the veteran star-actor Dmitrevskoy was brought in to rehearse and train the company. The repertoire was healthy and soon proved popular. The wooden theatre on Tsaritsyn Meadow was completely rebuilt in the up-to-date form of an amphitheatre, and as the Free Knipper Theatre became the home of particularly Russian-style productions.

Russian authors were now writing comedies and light straight plays in imitation of foreign models. Examples are the sentimental comedies, comic operas, ballad operas and comedies of manners by Lukin, Veryovkin, Pashkevich, von Baumgarten, Ablesimov, Matinsky and Fonvizin, several of which received their première at the Free Knipper Theatre. Unhappily, however, Knipper ran into difficulties, and in

December 1782 his contract was withdrawn and the theatre was handed over to Dmitrevskoy. He found that corruption was too far advanced, and there was nothing for it but for the court to take it over. The whole enterprise was wound up and the Foundling Troupe was returned to Moscow.

While the Free Knipper Theatre was at its zenith in St Petersburg, a further blow struck the Moscow theatre, for in 1780 the Znamenka Theatre burned down during a performance. Prince Urusov faced utter ruin, and sold the theatre to Michael Maddox, an Englishman who had first appeared in St Petersburg during 1766–7, giving performances as an equilibrist. By 1775 he had turned up in Moscow to demonstrate 'a cabinet of mathematical and scientific instruments, curiosities and puzzles lately brought over by him from England'. He also exhibited some ingenious mechanical clocks. Such was the success of these inventions that in August 1776 Maddox was invited to form a partnership with Prince Urusov. Their first big venture was the establishment of a new pleasure centre, the Vokzal (on the lines of the Vauxhall Gardens at London), at the mansion of Count Stroganov. Under the terms of the licence Prince Urusov became sole director of all theatrical productions in Moscow for the next ten years, on condition that he erected within five years a new stone theatre. Maddox and the Russian manager started work on this new theatre in that same year, and in December 1780 the 'Grand Theatre on the Petrovka', now under Maddox's sole management, opened with a special gala performance of a new ballet entitled *The Enchanted School*, preceded by a prologue supplemented with a discourse composed by Ablesimov.

The building scheme was devised by Maddox himself and realized by the architect Rosberg. It was the largest playhouse in Russia, with stage equipment of the very latest design, and a repertoire which covered every type of dramatic composition. Moscow at long last possessed a thoroughly capable impresario. The 'Vauxhall', later extended to include a new site near Taganskaya Square, and the Petrovsky Theatre remained secure under his direction until the nineteenth century. The theatre was burnt down in 1805, and was replaced by the Bol'shoy Theatre, which in its turn was gutted in 1853. Today the restored Bol'shoy Theatre stands on the same site, with the vaults of the old Petrovsky playhouse still within its cellars.

Throughout her long reign the Empress Catherine spared no pains to make her court and the Imperial Theatres the most impressive in the world. She herself even wrote for the theatre, and some of the most celebrated names in European music and dance of the eighteenth century added their lustre to the Russian court, among them Baldassare Galuppi, Tommaso Traetta, and Giovanni Paisiello. Although music tended to predominate in court productions, since opera and ballet offered more lavish forms of entertainment than straight plays, the strength and quality of the Imperial Russian troupe were not allowed to decline, and indeed the troupe increased in number.

During the early years of Catherine's reign serious attention was also directed to the proper and intelligent organization of the Imperial Theatres. In 1765 Count Karl Sievers was succeeded as director of the Russian Theatre by Vasily Bibikov, while Ivan Yelagin, littérateur, playwright and scholar, acting counsellor of state and adviser to the sovereign, was in the following year commanded by the empress to compile a complete list of all personnel employed in the Imperial Theatres. This *Status for all personnel belonging to Theatres, chamber and ballet orchestras, likewise the amount of salaries per annum and the nature of the productions upon which actual expenditure is proposed* was an important step forward in co-ordinating the theatres in the realm. The total number of persons working for the Imperial Theatres was estimated at 231, and the sum of 138,410 roubles was assigned 'for the maintenance at our Imperial Court of the Italian, French and Russian Theatres, and likewise of the Chamber and Ballet Orchestras'.

After the retirement of Yelagin and Bibikov from their position in the directorate of the Imperial Theatres, financial difficulties convinced Catherine that a collective body would be able to conduct the theatrical economy to a more exact degree. Consequently, in 1783 one of the most embracing decrees concerning the Imperial Theatres was published setting out an entire programme of theatrical rules and conditions, modelled on and further elaborated from Yelagin's original *Status* of 1766, but now containing 44 lengthy paragraphs, assuring both the main points of future organization, and covering many details, no matter how particular, encountered by the directorate in their dealings with the stage. Perhaps the most significant decision of all was the final establishment in 1783 of a school of drama, an idea first suggested by Yelagin in 1766.

In addition to the overhaul of the organization of the Imperial Theatres, Catherine built two handsome new theatres in St Petersburg, the Hermitage Theatre on the site of Peter the Great's old Winter Palace and the Bol'shoy Kamennyy Theatre.

Towards the close of the eighteenth century the Russian public could enjoy regular visits to the theatre. In Moscow, under the direction of 'The Cardinal' (Michael Maddox), a bizarre figure moving round the city with his scarlet cloak floating out behind him, the stage continued to expand, while at St Petersburg the inauguration of the Bol'shoy Kamennyy Theatre provided a home for the best productions which the Imperial Theatres could mount. In the sphere of dramatic entertainment Russia had finally caught up with Europe and the West.

GUIDE TO FURTHER READING

REFERENCE WORKS

Teatral'naya entsiklopediya, 5 vols. plus supplement, main ed. S. S. Mokul'sky and, for later vols., P. A. Markov (Moscow, 1961–7), covers every facet of the stage and history of the drama, with excellent illustrations. Each entry is supported by a list of recent bibliographical material. No one specializing in the history of the stage can afford to neglect this admirable work. V. Vishnevsky, *Teatral'naya periodika (1774–1940)* (Moscow, 1949), contains a list of sources on theatre history.

HISTORIES

V. N. Vsevolodsky-Gerngross, *Istoriya russkogo teatra*, ed. B. V. Alpers (2 vols., Leningrad–Moscow, 1929), is an invaluable treatise on Russian theatre history which deals with every aspect of the stage. The same author's *Russkiy teatr ot istokov do serediny XVIII v.* (Moscow, 1957) and *Russkiy teatr vtoroy poloviny XVIII v.* (Moscow, 1960) are the best histories up to the end of the eighteenth century. N. V. Drizen, *Materialy k istorii russkogo teatra*, 2nd edn (Moscow, 1913), is an excellent supplement to theatre history, especially useful for the early period and the amateur stage. I. F. Petrovskaya, *Istochnikovedeniye istorii russkogo dorevolyutsionnogo dramaticheskogo teatra* (Leningrad, 1971). E. M. Beskin, *Istoriya russkogo teatra*, pt 1 (Moscow–Leningrad, 1928). Only the first part has appeared, which gives a reliable account of the development of the theatre; with attractive illustrations. E. N. Opochinin, *Russkiy teatr, yego nachalo i razvitiye* (St Petersburg, 1887). M. Slonim, *Russian Theatre from the Empire to the Soviets* (London, 1961), is the only full-length history of the Russian stage in English, but there are few details and the style is unattractive. B. V. Varneke, *History of the Russian Theatre*, trans. B. Brasol (New York, n.d.), the only history of the theatre in Russian, and particularly of the early period, to have been translated into English, is the key-work for the non-Russian specialist. E. Lo Gatto, *Storia del teatro russo* (2 vols., Florence, 1952), is a handsome work with carefully selected illustrations and useful bibliographies. N. S. Ashukin, V. N. Vsevolodsky-Gerngross and Yu. V. Sobolev, *Khrestomatiya po istorii russkogo teatra XVIII i XIX vv.* (Leningrad–Moscow, 1940), is a good anthology. S. S. Danilov, *Zapiski o teatre: Sbornik* (Leningrad–Moscow, 1958). A. I. Sobolevsky, 'Zametki po istorii dramy', *Russkiy Filologicheskiy Vestnik*, no. 1 (1889).

Studies of particular periods include: *Arkhiv direktsii imperatorskikh teatrov (1746–1801)* I (4 vols., St Petersburg, 1892), the most comprehensive collection of source material. *Istoriya russkogo teatra*, vol. 1, eds. V. V. Kallash and N. E. Efros (Moscow, 1914), contains many excellent articles and is well illustrated. On the early theatre: E. A. Stark, *Starinnyy teatr*, 2nd edn (Petrograd, 1922); A. I. Beletsky, *Starinnyy teatr v Rossii* (Moscow, 1923); *Starinnyy spektakl' v Rossii: Sbornik*, ed. V. N. Vsevolodsky-Gerngross (Leningrad, 1928), contains an important series of essays by notable scholars; *Starinnyy teatr v Rossii: Sbornik*, ed. V. P. Peretts (Petrograd, 1923), has some intriguing material; A. S. Arkhangel'sky, *Teatr dopetrovskoy Rusi* (Kazan', 1884). On the seventeenth and eighteenth centuries: S. K. Bogoyavlensky, *Moskovskiy teatr pri tsaryakh Alekseye i Petre* (Moscow, 1914); B. N. Aseyev, *Russkiy dramaticheskiy teatr XVII–XVIII vv.* (Moscow, 1958); V. N. Vsevolodsky-Gerngross, 'Teatr v Rossii pri imperatritse

GUIDE TO FURTHER READING

Anne Ioannovne i imperatore Ioanne Antonoviche', *Yezhegodnik imperatorskikh teatrov*, III, IV and VI (1913); P. O. Morozov, *Ocherki iz istorii russkoy dramy XVII–XVIII stoletiya* (St Petersburg, 1888), and *idem*, *Istoriya russkogo teatra do poloviny XVIII stoletiya* (St Petersburg, 1889), are still prime sources; I. F. Gorbunov, *Moskovskiy teatr v XVIII–XIX stoletiyakh*, in his *Sobraniye sochineniy*, ed. A. F. Koni, vol. 2 (St Petersburg, 1904), is a reliable survey with many unusual details.

Among works on particular aspects of the theatre: T. A. Dynnik, *Krepostnoy teatr* (Moscow–Leningrad, 1933), contains a thorough examination of country-house dramatics and the serf theatre, with useful tables. A. S. Famintsyn, *Skomorokhi na Rusi* (St Petersburg, 1889), is still the key work on early revels and the practice of bear-baiting. I. F. Gorbunov, *Pervyye russkiye pridvornyye komedianty*, in his *Sobraniye sochineniy*, gives an account of the first court companies. N. A. Yelizarova, *Teatry Sheremetevykh* (Moscow, 1944), is a study of the private theatres and troupes on the estates of the Sheremetev family. V. N. Vsevolodsky-Gerngross, 'Inostrannyye antreprizy Yekaterininskogo vremeni', *Bibliofil*, VI (1915), is a useful account of the activities of foreign impresarios during the reign of Catherine II. A. A. Kizevetter, *Pervyy obshchedostupnyy teatr v Rossii*, 2nd edn (Petrograd, 1917), gives a good description of the first public theatre in Russia. V. I. Rezanov, *K istorii russkoy dramy. Ekskurs v oblast' teatra iezuitov* (Nezhin, 1910), is a scholarly work dealing with the Jesuit theatre and academic drama. On theatre life: V. M. Doroshevich, *Staraya teatral'naya Moskva* (Petrograd–Moscow, 1923), is an interesting account of theatre life in Moscow. *Istoriya russkogo teatral'nogo byta*, vol. 1, ed. L. Ya. Gurevich (Moscow–Leningrad, 1939). Only the first volume has appeared, but it contains a very detailed description of life backstage and theatrical life and conditions in general. On theatrical buildings the most detailed surveys are V. N. Vsevolodsky-Gerngross, 'Teatral'nyye zdaniya v Moskve v XVII i XVIII st.', *Yezhegodnik imperatorskikh teatrov*, VII–VIII (1910), and *idem*, 'Teatral'nyye zdaniya v S.-Peterburge v XVIII st.', *ibid.*, II–III. *Idem*, *Istoriya teatral'nogo obrazovaniya v Rossii. Materialy po istorii teatra v Rossii*, vol. 1: *XVII i XVIII vv.* (St Petersburg, 1913), is the only detailed account of stage education, schools and theatrical institutions in Russia. G. Goyan, *Put' razvitiya russkogo teatra. O prepodavanii istorii russkogo teatra* (Moscow–Leningrad, 1939), a seminar on the teaching of theatre history.

M. B. Davydov, *Ocherki po istorii russkogo teatral'nogo iskusstva XVIII–nachala XX v.* (Moscow, 1974), is a profusely illustrated history of the development of Russian theatre design. On ballet, V. Krasovskaya, *Russkiy baletnyy teatr ot vozniknoveniya do serediny XIX v.* (Leningrad–Moscow, 1958), is reliable but unimaginative.

ACTORS

B. V. Alpers, *Aktyorskoye iskusstvo v Rossii*, vol. 1 (Moscow–Leningrad, 1945), is an account of the professional actor. *F. G. Volkov i russkiy teatr yego vremeni*, ed. Yu. A. Dmitriyev (Moscow, 1958), is an essential volume of documentary material on the actor. Also on Volkov: M. Kogan, *F. G. Volkov* (Moscow–Leningrad, 1938); M. A. Luchansky, *Fyodor Volkov* (Moscow, 1937). The fullest and most respectable biography of Dmitrevskoy is V. N. Vsevolodsky-Gerngross, *I. A. Dmitrevskoy* (Berlin, 1923). Ol'ga Chayanova, *Teatr Meddoksa v Moskve* (Moscow, 1927), is a well-documented and illustrated account of Michael Maddox and his activities as impresario and builder of the Petrovsky Theatre in Moscow.

PLAYS AND PLAYWRIGHTS

Rannyaya russkaya dramaturgiya (XVII – pervaya polovina XVIII v.), eds. O. A. Derzhavina, K. N. Lomunov and A. N. Robinson, is a 3-volume series of scholarly editions of the earliest examples of Russian plays, with commentaries, notes, vocabulary and bibliography. Vol. 1, *Pervyye p'yesy russkogo teatra* (Moscow, 1972), includes *Artakserksovo deystvo* and *Iyudif.* Vol. 2, *Russkaya dramaturgiya posledney chetverti XVII i nachala XVIII v.* (Moscow, 1972), includes productions staged at the Court Theatre of Tsar Alexis and the dramas written by Simeon Polotsky and Dimitri Rostovsky for the academic theatre. Vol. 3, *P'yesy stolichnykh i provintsial'nykh teatrov pervoy poloviny XVIII v.* (Moscow, 1974), contains plays produced at Moscow and St Petersburg and in the provinces.

Russkaya narodnaya drama XVII – XX vv. Teksty p'yes i opisaniya predstavleniy, ed. with introduction and commentary by P. N. Berkov (Moscow, 1953), is a collection of folk plays and articles. *Artakserksovo deystvo. Pervaya p'yesa russkogo teatra XVII v.* Edited with articles and commentary by I. M. Kudryavtseva (Moscow–Leningrad, 1957). N. S. Tikhonravov, *Russkiye dramaticheskiye proizvedeniya, 1672–1725 gg.* (St Petersburg, 1874). V. I. Rezanov, *Pamyatniki russkoy dramaticheskoy literatury* (Nezhin, 1907), contains examples of the academic drama and school plays. I. M. Badalić (Badalich) and V. D. Kuz'mina, *Pamyatniki russkoy shkol'noy dramy XVIII v. (po Zagrebskim spiskam)* (Moscow, 1968), is an interesting account and description of a school drama MS recently discovered in Zagreb.

9

THE NINETEENTH- AND EARLY TWENTIETH-CENTURY THEATRE

M. A. S. BURGESS

At the beginning of the nineteenth century St Petersburg had only govern-ment theatres. On the present Ostrovsky Square a new Maly Theatre was opened. On Palace Square there had been the New Theatre, known as the Kushlevsky after its proprietor, where the German troupe was headed by the celebrated playwright Kotzebue. It subsequently became a home for Russian companies, but was displaced in 1819 in the general re-construction of Palace Square. In January 1825 it was reopened, only to be destroyed by fire a mere three months later.

In 1806 the government undertook the organization of the Moscow Imperial Theatres on the basis of a wide integration of all available theatrical strength, including among others the troupe from the Petrovsky Theatre, the ballet company at the Foundling Hospital and the serf com-pany functioning on Stolypin's estate. Productions by the Moscow State Troupe took place in the Manège belonging to Pyotr Pashkov in the 'Pashkov Dom' on the Mokhovaya which had been converted for the purpose. In the spring of 1808 a new theatre was opened near the Arbat Gates, which became the second scenic stage and home of the Moscow State Troupe. Performances continued until August 1812 when Napoleon's army entered Moscow. Most of the actors had to fend for themselves and leave Moscow as quickly as they could, but the costumes and properties were lost together with the building itself, which became one of the earliest victims when Moscow burned. In August 1814, however, the troupe be-gan to provide a regular repertoire once more, playing till 1818 in the Apraksin mansion on the Znamenka. Later, productions were given in the 'Pashkov Dom'. About this time the present Theatre Square was rebuilt with the Bol'shoy Theatre at the centre, and from the autumn of 1824 productions were staged in the new Maly Theatre on the square next to the Bol'shoy Theatre. In 1840 the building housing the Maly Theatre was radically reconstructed, and in this form it has survived until today.

In order to strengthen the Moscow State Troupe further and also to keep an eye on the stage, in 1804 a government decree assigned to the directorate of the theatres the sole right of printing play-bills, and in 1808 it became an offence to offer parts in private theatricals to artists engaged by the state companies. In 1816, 'to avoid a dissolution, which might thereby be inflicted upon the takings of the Russian Theatre', permission was refused for the formation of a private French troupe of actors. A repressive state system of censorship had also been instituted with the first censorship law of 1804. Thus the government had begun to gain a complete monopoly of the stage in the two capitals of Moscow and St Petersburg.

At the beginning of the nineteenth century many noble families had their own troupes of serf actors and actresses. Even in the capitals there were quite a few of these private troupes, and many of them far surpassed the state troupes in acting technique and manner of presentation. But the partial disintegration of the old serf system gradually affected these private companies. Many landowners began to wind them up, although the more enterprising made serious attempts to consolidate them on commercial lines.

The serf theatre included a whole series of striking and successful artistes, but they became victims of their owners' caprice, and the emancipation of the serf artiste from dependence upon the landowner was one of the cardinal problems of reform in the theatre at the beginning of the nineteenth century.

At the end of the eighteenth century, when the official bureaucracy in the provinces was increased after the Pugachev rebellion and strong provincial towns were turned into administrative centres, *Dvoryanskiye sobraniya*, clubs and special theatres were set up. In these amateur theatricals were enacted and professional non-serf troupes gradually came into being. The economic insecurity and lack of funds in provincial town councils, however, militated against any permanent and fully consolidated theatre company. Soon the disbanded serf companies filtered into the new troupes and, as there was no set base for a theatre, such companies would travel on tour from one town to another. This was the beginning of a proper provincial repertory – for example, the well-known troupe led by Shteyn and Kalinovsky, with which from 1816 to 1822 the young M. S. Shchepkin worked and whence the actor N. Kh. Rybakov started out on his career.

The part played by the provincial theatre in Russia must not be underrated – its effect on budding playwrights and actors was enormous. A whole line of brilliant artistes made their début in the provinces. The famous St Petersburg comic actor V. F. Rykalov was a member of the Tula troupe; M. S. Vorob'yov, well known on the Moscow stage, belonged to the Ryazan' troupe; and M. S. Shchepkin, perhaps the greatest actor of them all, the grandest figure of the nineteenth-century Russian stage, owed his training to provincial repertory, thus ensuring the continued reputation of this early local repertory.

The private serf companies occasionally gave rise to the sponsoring of a fully fledged professional civic theatre. The combination of casts of serfs, qualified artistes, and guest players or actors from Moscow and St Petersburg could stimulate the local authority to promote or even subsidize a new town theatre. The city of Kazan' was to benefit from such an enterprise under the direction of Pavel Yesipov, who took over an earlier company in 1800. Official help and the opening in 1805 of the University of Kazan' helped his venture, and Yesipov erected a new theatre in what is now Freedom Square. Performances were advertised by handbills, playbills and announcements in the local paper. Admission prices were rather high: a ticket to the stalls cost as much as sixteen pounds of best-quality meat.

Of forty-four productions staged by Yesipov between 1804 and 1807 and in 1811, at least twenty were original Russian productions. Of the seven plays presented during 1804, only one was a Russian comedy, Fonvizin's *Nedorosl'*. In the winter season of 1805, of thirty productions ten were original Russian plays by Plavil'shchikov, Sumarokov, Knyazhnin, Ablesimov, Sandunov, Pisarev and Ozerov. Thus the Russian repertoire was well supported. By 1811, out of twenty plays over half were Russian. These included plays by Ozerov, Sumarokov, Il'in, Kryakovsky, Glinka, Titov, Matinsky, and a mixture of comedies of manners, opéra-comique, and ballad opera which by now was on the way to ousting the earlier repertoire of pseudo-classical tragedy.

With the threat of war, the writers of the new ballad-operas and plays preferred to emphasize patriotic themes and subjects dealing with Russian history. It was Plavil'shchikov who, during his tour with the Yesipov Company, furthered the adoption of a national Russian style of writing, rather than slavish imitation of western works. 'The theatre', he declared, 'should exist for the heart and spirit, and not just for the eyes.' He soon became a notable influence upon the choice of productions at the Kazan' Theatre. The public gave solid support and, as in the preceding century, were accustomed to hurl 'bouquets' of gold and silver coins, wrapped in paper or contained in purses, upon the stage at the end of a performance. But Kazan' itself was not quite suited to supporting a fully organized repertory. The town, although as large as Vienna, was very provincial, rather down at heel, the streets hardly paved. By 1810 the theatre was running at a loss and Yesipov was obliged to appeal for a subsidy to the governor, who informed the director of the Imperial Theatres. The request, however, went unheeded, and things went from bad to worse. By 1813 Yesipov was forced to sell parts of his private estate. In 1814 he died. The theatre struggled on for a further season, but in September 1815 a huge fire swept through the town destroying a large part of the city. Although the theatre building escaped, Kazan' remained without a theatre of its own for another thirty years.

In the eighteenth century the private or amateur stage had developed very fully and had closely followed the lines of the major productions and dramatic genres to be seen at court or in the state theatres. This type of *Blagorodnyy teatr* continued without a break into the nineteenth century. The popular theatre, or *Nizovoy narodnyy teatr*, had managed to survive the curbs imposed on private performances in the years following the Pugachev rising in 1773–4. The folk drama, which had developed years earlier, began to acquire an anti-autocratic feeling. Actors and artistes from this folk-drama often appeared at fairs in distant towns. They would perform outside in courts or bazaars or in the open fields. Puppet theatres, *balagany* and clowns all contributed to the provincial scene throughout the nineteenth century. *Balagan* (from the Persian 'balakhan' – an upper chamber or balcony) was a temporary structure erected for the purpose of theatrical, circus, or concert productions. *Balagany* existed in Russia from the middle of the eighteenth century, consisting of booths put up for displaying wares at markets and fairs. Soon special buildings were constructed from logs, planks and tarpaulins. The interior was provided with an auditorium partitioned off into first and second-class seats with an area called the *zagon* for standing room only. In front of the *balagan* a balcony projected, known as the *raus* (from German 'heraus' – outside), from which the artistes summoned the general public to performances. At the end of the eighteenth century plays from the Popular Theatre were being produced at the *balagany* (*The Comedy about Tsar Maximilian and his Recalcitrant Son Adolph*, etc.) as well as romantic, chivalrous pieces from the current repertoire. After the beginning of the nineteenth century, pantomimes incorporating Harlequin and Columbine were staged. There were magical transformations and fairy-tale scenes. The *balagany* of the Legat Brothers, the Leman Brothers, and of Berg achieved wide renown. Conjurors, muscle-men such as C. Rappeau, acrobats, gymnasts, and chanteurs like T. Barkov and G. Ivanov among many, were all engaged to perform. Choirs, dancers, puppeteers, and showmen with their marionettes entertained the public. A very popular character was called Grandad Rayoshnik who acted as *compère*. 'Old Jager Bombov' made this role his speciality in the middle of the nineteenth century; he was succeeded by the famous masters of the *balagany*, Leyfert and Malofeyev.

In St Petersburg during the year 1880 a new style of *balagan* was organized and established on Marsovo Pole. This was entitled 'Amusement and Profit'. A large part in this venture was played by A. Ya. Alekseyev-

Yakovlev who staged the works of Pushkin, Nekrasov and Ostrovsky. Alexandre Benois has also given a charming description of Leyfert's *balagan* in his *Reminiscences of the Russian Ballet*, in which he mentions his childhood visits to Yegorov's and Berg's *balagany* in St Petersburg. Many celebrated Russian artistes first began their theatrical careers on the stages of the *balagany*. The *balagany* survived into the 1930s, but efforts to revive this form of entertainment in the 1940s met with little success.

By the end of the eighteenth and the beginning of the nineteenth century the genre of sentimental drama was widespread throughout Europe. It remained an artificial convention: the countryside was idealized and youth equated with goodness. It was a pretty style, which required melodious music and charming scenes, a novelty which appealed to the eye, the ear and more especially to the heart. Russia was ripe for the acceptance of such a genre. There was a new aristocracy, and the manner suited the 'feudal' conditions of Russian society – it could be made to look as though the serfs were happy and carefree, working away on idyllic estates in the provinces.

The most influential Russian sentimental dramatist was N. I. Il'in (1777–1823). He achieved renown with his ballad-drama, *Liza, or the Triumph of Gratitude* (1802). Like other Russian writers of the sentimental school, he provided a naturalistic dialogue for his characters and tried to reveal an inner world of simple folk, each one emphasizing the depth of his spiritual experiences.

A whole series of sentimental-style playwrights followed. V. M. Fyodorov achieved the most renown at the beginning of the nineteenth century with his plays *Love and Virtue* and *Liza, or the Consequence of Pride and Seduction*, which were wildly successful. Translations from German were also well received.

Naturally these sentimental trifles required a certain acting style. A leading protagonist in this genre was V. P. Pomerantsev (died in 1809). A contemporary critic wrote: 'Every kind of part he played radiated feeling and warmth; a somewhat quavering voice lent an especial expression to his diction; uttering never a sound, just with eyes cast upwards to the sky, he could indicate so forcibly a profound grief.'

Certain of the sentimental dramas showed an awareness of the social evils of serfdom, and the genre may thus be said to have played a part in the development of Russian social life and thought. It taught the educated public to feel for the other half. Most of the early nineteenth-century comedies were aimed at upholding the theme of traditional patriarchal life and squirarchal conditions in the provinces. Yet even so a note of satire was beginning to creep in – shy and surreptitious observations of peasant life and veiled hints at a boorish aristocracy could now be detected in these Russian comedies.

251

The impresario–dramatist Prince A. A. Shakhovskoy (1777–1846) was the author of more than a hundred plays in various genres – tragedies, melodramas, vaudevilles, opera libretti. His polemical and satirical comedies of manners were particularly celebrated. In his comedy *Seigneurial Exploits, or the Country House Theatre* (1808), Shakhovskoy poked fun at the *nouveau riche*, the tycoon upstart Tranzhirin. The play was so successful that the type of upstart landowner became known as a *tranzhir*, and Shakhovskoy followed it up with *Tranzhirin's Boast or the Consequence of Seigneurial Pursuits* (1822).

In literature dealing with economic subjects at this time much space was devoted to the importance of adopting western European agricultural methods – a system which within the traditional serf system was doomed to failure. In a verse-comedy *Vain Mansions (Pustodomy)* (1819), Shakhovskoy defended the old landed gentry and their ways and poked fun at the ill-conceived 'modern' methods.

Similar themes were taken up by M. N. Zagoskin (1789–1852), more widely known as a romantic historian in the style of Sir Walter Scott. This type of play used all the current trappings of Russian satire, as well as rapier thrusts at the gallomania so widespread among the nobility which scorned everything Russian. But these plays had nothing in common with the progressive patriotism of the liberal thinkers of the eighteenth century. The underlying idea of all these works is that feudal squires ought not to meddle in new vogues and gimmicks from abroad but cleave to the old traditions. Zagoskin and Shakhovskoy also wrote polemical comedies satirizing literary fashions. The progressive members of the *Arzamas* circle, such as Griboyedov and Pushkin, were not much in favour of Shakhovskoy's efforts, and although the circle soon split up and yielded place to the new Decembrist liberal writers and thinkers, the 'nouvelle vague' was not to be resisted and Shakhovskoy's influence declined steadily.

The main themes in the comedies of N. I. Khmel'nitsky (1791–1845) deal with society life. The author is more concerned with situation than with artistic presentation of the characters. Everybody talks in an artificial, drawing-room style language. Khmel'nitsky delighted in a witty, racy style of dialogue with many 'natural' everyday expressions. In this he paved the way for Griboyedov.

A gifted diplomat and wit, Aleksandr Griboyedov (1795–1829) had been associated with the St Petersburg stage from his youth. Although he wrote and collaborated in a number of comedies, he is properly the author of a single work, being best known for his celebrated comedy of manners, *Woe from Wit (Gore ot uma)* (see pp. 133–4). It is valuable as a fine picture of the period, depicting Moscow society of about 1820 with its indulgent hospitality, foreign governesses and tutors, its façade of

French culture, its adventurism, its private serf-theatricals and ingrained prejudice against progress or reform. As a Russian comedy of manners it is intriguing, as a satirical piece it is masterly, but as a comic production for the theatre it is less successful.

The political and social situation in the early years of the nineteenth century helped to create a new style of tragedy in Russia – it may be termed political tragedy. This genre became a useful means of making known the author's views on a variety of important social topics without incurring the displeasure of the regime and of the rigid censorship. *The Free Society of the Admirers of Russian Belles-Lettres, Sciences and the Arts*, which flourished at this time, encouraged its members to write for a 'national' theatre more closely allied to real life. Members called themselves 'Okhotniki do svoyego' ('Those who cherish their own'), urging reform in the structure of plays and the need to pay more consideration to the acting profession.

The tragedies of V. A. Ozerov (1769–1816), such as *Oedipus in Athens*, *Fingal* and *Dmitry Donskoy*, enjoyed a brilliant, though short-lived success, although his *Poliksena* offended the censorship by reminding the public of Russia's foreign and overseas political misfortunes. Ozerov's political tendencies were revealed when he later tried to compose a play dealing with the times of Bühren – 'Bironovshchina' – in which he endeavored to show 'the miserable condition of the populace under a feeble and untrustworthy rule'. He wrote under the influence of the old neo-classical tragedy – that of Sumarokov and Knyazhnin – and never turned his ideas into abstractions or vague allegories. His manner is direct, short and clear, he dispenses with many archaic rules and adopts some of the ideas of the new sentimental romantic school of writing.

The success of many of the early romantic tragedies was due to the skill of the Russian tragic actors of the period. Mention should be made of A. S. Yakovlev (1773–1817) who had made his début with Dmitrevskoy in 1794. He had performed first in Sumarokov's and Knyazhnin's tragedies, and later in sentimental drama. It was in Ozerov's *Dmitry Donskoy* that he really made his name. The latter part of his career was distinguished by his playing of the role of Karl Moor in Schiller's *Die Räuber*. He endeavoured to get away from the old classical method of acting. His temperament was romantic, more concerned with character interpretation, and he was regarded as the best Russian Hamlet and Othello there had been.

Another good professional actor who took over from Yakovlev on his death was Ya. G. Bryansky (1790–1853), but he did not have Yakovlev's inspiring personality. 'Bryansky is always everywhere the same,' complained Pushkin, 'an ever smiling Fingal, Theseus, Orosmane, Jason, Dmitry – equally soulless, pompous, forced, wearisome ... Bryansky has never affected anyone in tragedy.' Pushkin also declared: 'Yakovlev is dead; Bryansky has taken his place, but he has not replaced him.'

Yakovlev was supported by a great tragic actress, Ye. S. Semyonova (1786–1849). The daughter of a serf, she was sent to a theatrical academy, where her first teacher was the celebrated Dmitrevskoy. She had a beautiful speaking voice, and could strongly touch an audience's sensitivity. She and Yakovlev were the last in the eighteenth-century tradition, the old neo-classical manner, yet at the same time they were the forerunners of a new school of acting, of new methods of interpretation, aiming at truth, naturalness and simplicity.

A new development in the history of the Russian stage was the rise in importance of the *régisseur* or producer. At the beginning of the nineteenth century the task of directing the cast of a play was undertaken by enlightened amateurs – *prosveshchonnyye teatraly* – who conducted their own private companies. In 1813–14 A. A. Shakhovskoy was organizing a youthful troupe which played at the New Theatre on Palace Square in St Petersburg. He became quite a professional entrepreneur, and contemporary theatre-goers often remarked upon his technical direction and admired his expertise. He demanded a faithful copying of recognizable personalities in his staging of comedy – *portretnost'* – yet adhered to the over-stylized precepts of neo-classical drama. The final decline of this artificial method of acting led to his demise as impresario. By refusing to acknowledge new trends in literature, he eventually found himself outdated altogether, and in 1826 went into retirement.

The *Rules and Regulations for the internal conduct of the Imperial Theatre Directorate*, issued in 1825, covered every aspect of theatre life including rehearsals and staging. For the first time the word *régisseur* is mentioned, referring to an administrative officer formerly designated as Inspector of the Troupe. The *régisseur* was to have complete authority over every facet of the production and free control of the cast. His function covered rehearsals, discipline and realization of each production. Henceforward the *régisseur* in Russia was to assume a position of central importance which has continued until the present day.

Later in the nineteenth century it became customary for the author to take a considerable part in the production. Gogol, who had very definite ideas on the interpretation of his comedies, would attend rehearsals and offer advice, make proposals about the scenery and properties. He directed a read-through of *The Government Inspector* towards the end of 1851 in the presence of Moscow theatre personnel.

The developing tradition of the actor-manager ensured a more professional attitude to theatre production in Russia, and the example set by Gogol as producer-playwright was followed by the leading authors of the day. Thus Ostrovsky always used to take part in the preparation of his works for the stage, and both Turgenev and L. Tolstoy were particular about the casting and mounting of their plays. Sukhovo-Kobylin furnished his scripts with directions for the producer.

By far the greatest actor-manager of the period was Shchepkin, first actor of the Moscow Maly Theatre, and top producer and director of the company. He strove for able direction subject to a single underlying idea, and thought a production must bear an individual stamp and reveal the resolute purposefulness of a master mind. Shchepkin had a profound effect on the younger generation of theatre directors and all who worked under him.

In the field of design the interpretation of tragedy at the beginning of the nineteenth century was guided by the expert hand of one of the most eminent decorators in the history of the theatre, Pietro Gonzaga (1751–1831), who was senior artist in the government-sponsored theatres at St Petersburg. Gonzaga followed the theoretical principles expounded in two of his own treatises: *La musique des yeux et l'optique théatrale*,[1] and *Information à mon chef ou éclaircissement convenable du décorateur théatral Pierre Gothard Gonzague sur l'exercice de sa profession*.[2] According to Gonzaga the impression of even the most accomplished actor's performance could be weakened or enhanced by the surrounding décor. He believed in the principle of fusing the visible, auditory and histrionic sides of production, so that all techniques complemented each other in the final presentation on stage. The scenery, true to nature, should be auxiliary to the grand effect and become 'music for the eyes'.

Judging from Gonzaga's sketches he had a preference for classical architectural motifs. His décors depict majestic palaces, handsome colonnades and grand flights of stairs. He was attracted by landscape subjects and in his later years was influenced by romanticism; 'mystical' or 'enigmatic' moonlight effects intrigued him. His backdrops were indeed most beautifully and sensitively executed. The atmosphere he created was idyllic.[3]

From 1812 the Russianized scene-designer Antonio Canoppi (1774–1832) contributed to the visual impact of the St Petersburg stage. Canoppi remained one of the last exponents of the classical style and maintained in his compositions the traditional feeling for architectural perspective. He went further than Gonzaga in experimenting with stage-lighting, imitating moonlight, the reflected glare from a fire and similar effects. Later he was caught by the prevailing mood of romanticism.

Gonzaga and Canoppi were not alone in the field of stage-design. The serf-theatre employed skilful artists such as A. Martynov and Kondrat'yev,

---

[1] St Petersburgh, 1800. [2] St Petersburg, 1807.
[3] See *Scenografie di Pietro Gonzaga* (Venice, 1967), which contains a bibliography and illustrations of Gonzaga's designs for the stage.

while K. Funtusov and G. Mukhin worked for Count Sheremetev's private theatres. Between 1830 and the 1850s stage scenery became more representational, reflecting the realistic trend of the 'natural school' in literature and painting. Technical problems in the theatres were also being solved successfully. The former system of side-wings set parallel to the footlights, with a backdrop making a perspective in a picture-frame, was transformed into the so-called 'pavilion' or 'box' stage setting in which a greater realism was achieved.

A. N. Ostrovsky considered realistic décor to be more appropriate to the drama. 'Décor is necessary', he said, 'not only to add lustre to the mise-en-scène, but for the more accurate representation of life in the play.' Gogol himself had an excellent eye for a truthful stage-set and made preliminary sketches of how he wished his plays to look. For *The Government Inspector* he drew a room with a tiled stove, a clock in the corner, portraits on the walls, a bird-cage and other details. Turgenev provides full stage directions on the placing of objects, windows, doors and other features on the set.

Gonzaga and Canoppi were succeeded by a most ambitious designer, A. A. Roller (1805–91), who specialized in décor for opera and ballet. He excelled in the execution of sumptuous stage-sets and beautifully painted backcloths, but the new-found realism was of little interest to him.

Quite frequently each theatre possessed a selection of scenes which served all types of production, but could be re-used over and over again. In the 1840s the Aleksandrinsky Theatre boasted a special Slavonic Room painted by the décor-master Fyodorov in which the romantic–nationalistic plays of Kukol'nik, Polevoy and Obodovsky were presented. There was also a Business Pavilion portraying a typical official's or merchant's room for plays of contemporary life. For the sake of economy such standard sets were usual. The Aleksandrinsky Theatre commissioned twenty complete sets for the opening gala designed by Gropius, the décor-master of the Royal Berlin Opera House. During the 1830s and 1840s it was rare to find a complete production designed and mounted by one designer, and even theatre critics would completely disregard the impact of the décor on the works which they saw. It was not until the 1860s and 1870s that the scenery really showed an improvement, when matters were firmly taken in hand by talented, experienced artists like M. A. Shishkov and M. I. Bocharov, A. F. Gel'tser and V. D. Polenov. But the real revival in stage-design had to wait for the end of the nineteenth century and the early years of the present century. Eminent designers such as V. Vasnetsov, K. Korovin and A. Golovin, the artists contributing to the publication of *The World of Art (Mir iskusstva)*, brought a unique conception of the stage-set to productions. Their work has become famous outside Russia. The influence of these artists, who worked for Diaghilev, has extended into many spheres of design. Established enterprises like Mamontov's private opera company, the Moscow Art Theatre, the Maly Theatre, the Aleksandrinsky, the Bol'shoy and the Mariinsky Theatres all are indebted to the imaginative décors devised by Léon Bakst, Alexandre Benois, Mstislav Dobuzhinsky, Nikolay Roerich, Yevgeny Lanseré, M. Larionov, N. Goncharova, N. N. Sapunov, S. Sudeykin and many other celebrated names.

For stage-design at its very best, at its most exotic, colourful and original, Russia at the beginning of the twentieth century was supreme. M. Louis Laloy, a French critic, wrote: 'The appearance of the Russian ballets at the dawn of the twentieth century will be recorded in the history of art as an event equal in importance to the formation of the French opera in the sixteenth century, and to that of the comic opera in the seventeenth century.' L. Réau added this postscript to his words: 'To this triumphant conquest of the West by the Russian art Léon Bakst powerfully contributed; and for this reason his name will surely remain among those of the greatest renovators of the modern decorative art.'

In order to regulate public security, the Third Department of His Majesty's Personal Office had been set up in 1826; two years later it brought into effect stringent new rules of censorship. These enforced a twofold censorship of the theatre. Permission for the publication of plays remained in the hands of the Ministry of Public Enlightenment which had been responsible for such permission since 1812, while surveillance of all dramatic works intended for presentation on the stage was transferred from the Ministry of the Interior to the Third Department.

The Third Department at first confined its attention to the theatres in the two capitals and to the larger provincial stages, and touring repertory companies managed to avoid censorship. But in 1842 all provincial troupes and their repertoires came under government supervision. Pushkin, Lermontov, Gogol and many other playwrights suffered censorship and mutilation of their work. Events in Europe, moreover, inclined the tsar to take further measures, and in 1848 a special secret committee, with the tsar at its head, was established. It had extensive powers over all forms of the creative arts, and Nicholas I personally would apply the stamp – 'Published to no effect, performance forbidden'.

As a result social ideas and liberal expression were excluded from the drama. The censorship was particularly strict on the representation of tsars (unless they had lived several centuries earlier). Priests, the establishment, the nobility, provincial squires and officialdom were all to be treated with respect.

To Pushkin the old school of neo-classical tragedy – the work of Ozerov, Zotov, Shakhovskoy, Katenin, Kyukhel'beker and even Griboyedov –

seemed out of date. Inspired by Shakespeare, he determined to write a new historical drama. *Boris Godunov* is a premeditated and experimental work – written more for literary form than for subject. 'It is inspired with a public-spirited desire to be useful to Russian literature.'[1] It is the most ambitiously formulated of Pushkin's works, and he regarded it as his *magnum opus*, preferring it to his narrative lyrics because it belonged to a higher literary genre. It had an enthusiastic reception from Pushkin's friends, but when published it was received coldly by the public and the critics. Its first performance was not until 1870 – forty-five years after it was written – and even then only sixteen scenes were acted. The play loses heavily when compared to Shakespeare – or indeed to the magnificent musical drama Musorgsky composed partly with its help. Nevertheless the tragedy was a complete novelty for Russia, for in all preceding works Pushkin had been intensely personal and lyrical. It may be that the sense of dissatisfaction which we experience at this play is a result of the intrusion of the 'sentiment' fashionable at the time.

In 1830 Pushkin completed four *Little Tragedies* – *The Covetous Knight* (*Skupoy rytsar'*), *Mozart and Salieri*, *The Stone Guest* (*Kamennyy gost'*) and *A Feast during the Plague* (*Pir vo vremya chumy*) – followed in 1832 by *Rusalka*. All these plays are notable for the further development of Pushkin's reform of Russian drama on realistic principles. Only *Mozart and Salieri* was performed in Pushkin's lifetime. *The Stone Guest* was first performed with Karatygin in the role of Don Juan. *Rusalka* made history by the appearance of M. N. Yermolova, who played sensitively and tragically the part of the miller's daughter turned water-nymph.

Gogol valued highly the classical heritage – with the proviso that the theatre should be prepared to look at old plays 'with fresh and contemporary eyes'. He advocated a system of realistic, natural acting techniques. He had formed an interest in the theatre from his childhood, and had already written a number of plays when in the autumn of 1835 Pushkin suggested to him an excellent plot with a really contemporary theme. Within a few months the first version of *The Government Inspector* (*Revizor*) was completed. It was clearly a social satire pointedly directed against the establishment and against official corruption in the provinces, but amazingly it passed the tsar's censorship. The first production took place at the Aleksandrinsky Theatre in 1836, and the play was published on the same day. The première was in fact rather unsuccessful. The wigs and ridiculous costumes were quite unsuitable, and Gogol was furious at the lack of care evident in the production and the blatant over-acting. It was this performance which started the tradition of turning *The Government Inspector* into a burlesque. It was not until Meyerhold produced it in 1926 that the distortions were eradicated.

[1] D. S. Mirsky, *Pushkin* (London, 1926), 153.

The reception of the play marked the starting point of the persecution mania which afflicted Gogol for the rest of his life. Piqued by criticism, he began to explain away his play in print. He added a kind of epilogue in which he declared that the real Government Inspector who appears so horrifyingly off-stage at the end of the last act is the 'conscience of man', and that the other characters are the passions of the human soul.

Romantic melodrama was by now playing itself out, though vaudeville was on much surer ground. Vaudeville could almost provide a half-way house between the romantic drama and the long-awaited realistic play. The plots were usually concerned with silly intrigues, yet there was a hint at realism in the approach to life. Popular vaudevilles included plays by Lensky, Koni and Nekrasov who instilled the principles of 'the natural school' into the vaudeville. With Gogol and Belinsky advocating a fresh approach to the theatre, it was not long before authors began to turn their attention to a more subtle, more perceptive style of dramaturgy.

Turgenev took up the challenge, and after some flirting with romantic drama, he turned in 1846 to the realistic school. After a number of one-act plays, he embarked on more substantial works for the stage. His first play in the new vein was *The Lodger* (*Nakhlebnik*), written in 1848. The plot deals with a lodger who is secretly in love with his host's wife. Turgenev repeats this theme in *The Bachelor* (*Kholostyak*) (1849) in which the hero, arranging the marriage of his ward, struggles in his heart of hearts with his hidden and – to him – ridiculous and hopeless love for her.

The lyrical and psychological atmosphere – which had first appeared in *Where it is too thin it breaks* (*Gde tonko, tam i rvyotsya*) – was now fully put into effect in Turgenev's comedy-drama, *A Month in the Country* (*Mesyats v derevne*), where for the first time he heralds the Chekhovian style of drama. It is his best-known theatrical work and has secured a place in the international repertoire, although its success was delayed when the censor did not permit it to be printed. Only in 1855 was it allowed to be published (with many alterations which spoiled the psychological undertones), and the play was only printed in its entirety in 1869. The 1879 production at the Aleksandrinsky Theatre was a triumph, much to the author's amazement.

Turgenev's dramatic work was a most useful apprenticeship for the composition of his novels. It taught him how to use dialogue, exits and entrances, dramatic situations and insight into character, and gave focus to his sharp observation of life as it is actually lived and to his keen realization of hidden motives.

The monopoly of the Imperial Theatres for the staging of productions was finally endorsed by the edict of 1827 which allowed private theatricals only with the permission of the theatre directorate. By the 1840s the directorate had suppressed private theatricals in general, and in 1854 it also reserved the right to regulate concerts and musical events. Only the fairs or 'gulyaniya' with their *balagany* shows were exempted from control by the directorate, although there was close police supervision. These festive occasions on public holidays at Shrovetide, Easter and Christmas were not considered a threat to the government. Jugglers, clowns and tight-rope walkers were hardly suitable media for social propaganda. Foreign companies were also unaccountable to the directorate because of the language problem and the limited audiences.

Before the reign of Nicholas I the St Petersburg theatres were governed by committee, but from 1829 the directorate was headed by a single official who wielded considerable power. Soon the Moscow theatres, which had previously been managed by a special director subject to the governor general of Moscow, were put under the supervision of the supreme director of the Imperial Theatres.

Since 1805, when the old Petrovsky Theatre had burned down, the Moscow Imperial Theatre had played in various places. In 1824 the replacement for the old Petrovsky Theatre, the new Bol'shoy Petrovsky Theatre, was completed. It was the grandest opera house in Russia and was opened to the public with a brilliant gala performance in January 1825. Near the Bol'shoy Theatre on Theatre Square the Maly Theatre was opened in October 1824.

The director of the Moscow theatres, appointed in 1823, was F. F. Kokoshkin, an amateur poet and translator of plays and also president of the *Society of the Admirers of Russian Belles-Lettres*. He was aided by M. N. Zagoskin, the dramatist and historical novelist, who followed him as director in 1831. The popular vaudeville composer, A. I. Pisarev, took an active part in the repertoire, while the eminent musician, A. N. Verstovsky, who had occupied various positions in the theatre directorate, became manager of the Moscow office of the Imperial Theatres in 1842. Although their policy was conservative, they achieved the smooth running of the Moscow theatres.

At that time the Maly Theatre company was headed by two of Russia's leading actors, M. S. Shchepkin (1788–1863) and P. S. Mochalov (1800–48), men whose creative activities were of great importance in the development and consolidation of a more realistic style on the Russian stage. Shchepkin considered art to be a civic duty – an idea carried on by many important artistes of succeeding generations and which was to become the basic tradition of the Maly Theatre. Indeed this theatre became known in Russia as 'The House of Shchepkin' (Dom Shchepkina).

In 1853 the Maly Theatre staged A. N. Ostrovsky's comedy *Don't get into another's sleigh* (*Ne v svoi sani ne sadis'*), an event which brought this dramatist into the public eye and marked the advent of a new era in the theatre's development. Ostrovsky wrote forty-eight plays, every one of which was presented at the Maly Theatre. These works depicted the life of the merchant classes, the peasantry, the morals of contemporary Russian society and the daily round in the provinces. To western audiences Ostrovsky's plays may seem too melodramatic, too mid-Victorian and sometimes even rather feeble dramatically.

Generations of actors maintained the scenic realism inculcated by Shchepkin at the Maly Theatre: the Sadovskys; Shumsky and Samarin; Fedotova and Yermolova; Lensky and Yuzhin. As the turn of the century approached people even began to call the Maly Theatre 'a second Moscow University'.

Nor did the theatrical life of St Petersburg remain static while the government-owned theatres of Moscow were being built and reorganized. The Bol'shoy Kamennyy Theatre, gutted by fire in 1811, had been judiciously rebuilt and further modified in 1818 and again in 1836. It was torn down in 1889–90 to make way for the building of the Conservatoire.

Between 1828 and 1831 a grandiose plan was drawn up by the architect K. Rossi for a remarkable ensemble of buildings with a large stone theatre in the centre. The Aleksandrinsky Theatre, inaugurated in 1832 with a splendid gala, became the official government show-house, placed under the conservative direction of the company's inspector, A. I. Khropovitsky, a strong adherent of classical methods in production. The leading actor was A. E. Martynov, a stalwart supporter of Shchepkin's theatrical reforms. Many major new works by contemporary Russian playwrights were presented, and many of Russia's most famous actors have performed there. (Today the theatre is known as the Pushkin Academic Theatre of Drama.)

Simultaneously with the construction of the Aleksandrinsky Theatre the government undertook to erect a series of other theatre buildings: the summer Kamennoostrovsky Theatre (opened in 1827), the New Theatre by the Semyonov Bridge and the Mikhaylovsky Theatre (opened in 1833, now the State Academic Maly Opera Theatre).

Between 1847 and 1849 the stone Theatre-Circus was erected by the state. It was intended for the presentation of pantomimic circus shows. By 1855, however, the circus had yielded to theatrical productions, and it was not revived until 1877.

In 1860 the famous Mariinsky Theatre (now the Kirov) was opened, the scene of many impressive productions of grand opera. Under the directors, K. N. Lyadov and E. F. Napravnik, many Russian operas had premières, among them works by Dargomyzhsky, Rimsky-Korsakov, Musorgsky, Chaykovsky (Tchaikovsky) and Taneyev, together with performances of Verdi, Wagner and other western composers.

While the government was expanding the number of theatres in St

Petersburg, calamity struck Moscow. In March 1853 the Bol'shoy Petrovsky Theatre was burned down, together with all the costumes of Catherine the Great's courtiers, the musical instruments, the valuable archives and the library. In May the government commissioned Albert K. Kavos (1800–63) to prepare plans for the rebuilding of the theatre. Work proceeded erratically, but in August 1856 the Bol'shoy Theatre was opened with a performance of Bellini's opera *I Puritani*. The new theatre was impressive and spacious, one of the largest in the world, and it has survived intact to the present day without alteration, except for the modernization and re-equipment of the dressing-rooms and stage.

In 1882 the monopoly of control over theatrical enterprises in the major cities held by the directorate of the Imperial Theatre was officially annulled by Alexander III. A series of reforms was carried out which raised the artistic standards of the performances, and competent administrators were summoned to serve on the directorate committee. In 1885 Ostrovsky, who had projected a far-reaching overhaul of the government-sponsored theatres, was appointed artistic overseer of a section of the Moscow Theatres.

The desire to raise artistic standards also prompted the directorate to invite to Russia distinguished foreign artistes and their productions. In 1885 the first successful tour of the Duke of Meiningen's company took place; it was followed five years later by a second visit. These tours were to have far-reaching effects on the presentation of drama throughout the empire. The Meiningen troupe surprised everybody by its precision, close attention to historical detail and scholarly research into period costume and setting. As yet unknown to each other, two dedicated and aspiring amateurs, Konstantin Stanislavsky (born Alekseyev, 1863–1938) and Vladimir Nemirovich-Danchenko (1858–1943), after watching the performances of the Meiningen company, had each decided to set about reforming the Russian stage.

Stanislavsky, the son of a rich industrialist, had been brought up in the ambience of the Moscow theatre. He had been attracted to the Maly Theatre, had visited foreign touring productions and was once a pupil at the dramatic school. He had also occasionally performed in comedy and operetta, and at one time hoped to be an opera singer. But his career was decided for him after he joined in theatricals at the Society of Art and Literature. After the auspicious tour of the Meiningen company in 1890, Stanislavsky resolved to devote a considerable part of the Society's budget to authentic historical costumes and to the faithful reproduction of native scenery. Soon he became a 'producer-despot', and the new regime of the all-powerful director came into being.

Nemirovich-Danchenko had also been intrigued by the amateur stage and had played in the provinces at Tiflis and Pyatigorsk. He wrote eleven plays, all of which enjoyed considerable success. In 1890 he became head of the dramatic class of the Moscow Philharmonic Institute which he hoped to reform. Seven years later, after he had failed to influence the directorate of the Moscow Imperial Theatres with his progressive ideas, Nemirovich-Danchenko wrote to Stanislavsky proposing that they should meet and discuss the future of the theatre.

The historic meeting took place on 22 June 1897 and lasted for eighteen hours. The future of the Russian theatre was then and there determined: they decided to found a national theatre which should serve a single artistic concept: 'The poet, artiste, painter, tailor, and artisan will serve one aim established by the author as the basis for the play.' In fact all facets of the production were to be subordinated to the general effect as conceived by the author himself. It was also agreed that Stanislavsky and Nemirovich-Danchenko should be co-directors of the new theatre, on the understanding that the latter should have the power of veto on the literary side and the former on the artistic aspect of production.

During the winter of 1897–8 the preparatory work was put in hand. The new theatre was to be slanted towards the lower-income brackets, the not-too-well-off intelligentsia. There were to be reduced prices for students. The repertoire would be diverse – both foreign and national plays were to be staged, while out-dated melodramas and silly pantomimes were to be avoided. This was certainly a revolutionary plan of action. New décor, an incisive style of acting to replace the ham, pseudo-classical declamation, a focus on the ensemble and team-spirit of the troupe – these were the precepts of the management.

The joint directors approached the Moscow City Council for funds, but met with a cold rebuff. Undeterred, they signed on actors from the Society of Art and Literature and pupils from the Philharmonic Institute. In June 1898 rehearsals began in Tsarskoye Selo. For the première a tragedy by A. K. Tolstoy was chosen, *The Tsar Fyodor Ioannovich*, a play still forbidden by the censorship. It was a test case. Special expeditions were organized to cull details and historical drawings from old Russian towns such as Yaroslavl' and Rostov, as well as from the Troitse-Sergiyevo monastery, in order to get the correct period perspective and to portray court life authentically. Such research was of paramount importance, and the result of this academic devotion to detail was impressive.

In October 1898 the new Moscow Art Open-Accessible Theatre (Moskovskiy khudozhestvenno-obshchedostupnyy teatr) was inaugurated. The audience was surprised at several novel features. In place of the traditional painted canvas cloth front curtain with swags and gold tassels, framing a cartouche of classical ruins or a distant romantic view of

Moscow, the stage was screened by plain cloth drapes which, instead of hanging vertically as had been the custom, now glided smoothly on tracks toward either side of the proscenium opening. Admittance after the start of the performance was no longer allowed, and attendants in their uniforms were banished from the auditorium. The prompter's central cubicle was also dispensed with. There was no entr'acte music. Nothing was left to deflect full concentration from the performance. The play was to be the thing.

Although some were to sneer at the experiment, the opening production heralded a fresh approach to historical drama. A. K. Tolstoy's *The Death of Ivan the Terrible* (*Smert' Ioanna Groznogo*), Shakespeare's *The Merchant of Venice* and *Julius Caesar*, Lev Tolstoy's *The Power of Darkness* (*Vlast' t'my*), were all staged with period authenticity. Succeeding productions were uneven, but the real worth of the Art Theatre was seen in the great presentation on 17 December 1898 (after a fearful flop at the Aleksandrinsky Theatre in 1896) of Anton Chekhov's *The Seagull*. Such was its triumph that the seagull has remained ever since the chief emblem of the Moscow Art Theatre.

The Moscow Art Theatre put on, according to the new realistic method, Chekhov's masterpieces, *Uncle Vanya* (1899), *The Three Sisters* (1901), *The Cherry Orchard* (1904), and *Ivanov* (1904), with that perception and understanding which have so endeared them to the audiences of the present day. It was a great triumph for the original conception of Stanislavsky and Nemirovich-Danchenko.

Chekhov's work for the theatre had carried on the traditions of Ibsen and Hauptmann, who dealt with the condition of the human mind. But for the gloomy grandeur of Scandinavia and the fantasy of Germany Chekhov's work had substituted the dreary monotony of Russian provincial daily life. It was from Ibsen and Hauptmann that Chekhov, and through him Maksim Gor'ky, borrowed the substance of the technique in which the action gave way to something in the nature of parallel monologues which never became dialogues, each character pursuing his own thoughts in phrases which he appeared to be addressing only to himself. The pauses, and the very silences, were as full of meaning as the actual responses. Gor'ky was so unsure of his craft that he generally designated his dramatic works simply as 'scenes', and it took the authority of a director such as Nemirovich-Danchenko to force him to call *Vassa Zheleznova* a 'play'. Always uncertain and tormented by doubts about his technique, Gor'ky reworked his dramas endlessly, and there are often two extant versions to be found.

In all events, his plays had a profound success, due perhaps less to their art than to their sense of reality. The characters expressed the state of mind of the Russian public at the turn of the century, the melancholy of the groups whose historic role was to end with the revolution of 1917, but with the added promise of a new hope. Indeed the impact of his plays, such as *Smug Citizens* (*Meshchane*) or the best-known *The Lower Depths* (*Na dne*), is more interesting than are the plays themselves.

A pleiad of celebrated actors became associated with the Moscow Art Theatre: Ivan Moskvin (1874–1946), Mariya Lilina (1866–1943), Ol'ga Knipper-Chekhova (1868–1959), Leonid Leonidov (1873–1941) were outstanding interpreters of Stanislavsky's 'system'. This system meant meticulous attention to naturalistic detail, extensive training and exhausting rehearsal for every production, with shrewd observance of gesture and subtle shading of voice. As this style developed, Stanislavsky came to insist that the actor should immerse himself more and more in the part, in the psychological state of the character. Altogether it was a vigorous, virile approach which has sometimes been misinterpreted since.

In 1906 the Moscow Art Theatre undertook its first tour abroad. It was a signal triumph. Ecstatic notices were published in the foreign press, and henceforth the fame of the theatre was to remain undiminished.

The period immediately preceding the revolution saw several further ventures into the theatre. Under the influence of the Moscow Art Theatre V. F. Komissarzhevskaya, aided by the directors N. A. Popov and N. N. Arbatov, opened a playhouse in St Petersburg in 1904 where the Stanislavsky line was followed for two seasons. Soon the principles employed by the Moscow Art Theatre were incorporated into the productions of opera. In 1911 the St Petersburg Theatre of Musical Drama was established, where naturalistic productions were staged by I. M. Lapitsky. Another attempt at naturalism was made by reviving a more ancient form of theatrical style somewhat in the manner of the mystery or pageant play.

In the spring of 1905 a theatre-studio was organized in Moscow under the direction of V. E. Meyerhold – the first academic experimental institution in the country. Although it called upon the talent of many famous artists, the venture failed. In the summer of 1906 Komissarzhevskaya embarked on another dramatic venture, with Meyerhold as the main director. The new theatre opened in November 1906 with Meyerhold's own production of Ibsen's *Hedda Gabler*, with Komissarzhevskaya in the title role. This performance distressed one section of the audience but delighted the other – especially the adherents of the symbolist movement. Unfortunately the new intellectuals were the more impoverished members of the public, so that the supporters of the theatre could not always afford the price of tickets. Matters were finally settled with Meyerhold's production of Maeterlinck's *Pelléas et Mélisande*, which was accounted 'incontrovertibly erroneous'. Meyerhold left the theatre to the management of F. F. Komissarzhevsky, N. N. Yevreinov and P. A.

Ungern, under whose direction it lasted two more seasons. As a result the *nouvelle vague* was left without its citadel and the necessary impetus and, deprived of a master, was obliged to merge with the naturalistic drama.

Finally, on the eve of war and revolution, the Moscow Chamber Theatre (Moskovsky Kamernyy Teatr) opened in 1914. The new enterprise, however, by this time lacked the spirit of novelty, so that the theatre seemed to be but a recapitulation of what had gone before. Grave financial difficulties dogged the management and nearly resulted in the collapse of the venture. Only the advent of yet another experimental style of drama rescued the theatre. Symbolism was exchanged for a far more fashionable trend – futurism – and the Moscow Chamber Theatre has survived to the present day.

GUIDE TO FURTHER READING

REFERENCE WORKS

Teatral'naya entsiklopediya, main ed. S. S. Mokul'sky and, for later vols., P. A. Markov (5 vols. plus supplement, Moscow, 1961–7), covers every facet of the stage and history of the drama, with excellent illustrations. Each entry is supported by a list of recent bibliographical material. No one specializing in the history of the stage can afford to neglect this admirable work. V. Vishnevsky, *Teatral'naya periodika (1774–1940)* (Moscow, 1949), is a bibliography of the theatre and of stage journals.

HISTORIES

V. N. Vsevolodsky-Gerngross, *Istoriya russkogo teatra*, vols. I–II (Leningrad–Moscow, 1929), is still the key work. Dealing with every aspect of stage history, it is indispensable to the scholar. S. S. Danilov, *Ocherki po istorii russkogo dramaticheskogo teatra* (Leningrad–Moscow, 1948), is an admirable account of dramatic production from earliest times until the revolution. N. N. Yevreinov, *Istoriya russkogo teatra*, introd. by C. Moody (Letchworth, n.d.), is a very general and rather loosely written survey. N. V. Drizen, *Materialy k istorii russkogo teatra*, 2nd edn (Moscow, 1913), contains interesting material, some of it new. *Russkiye klassiki i teatr*, ed. Ye. Kuznetsov (Leningrad–Moscow, 1947), is a useful collection of articles on the theatre. I. F. Petrovskaya, *Istochnikovedeniye istorii russkogo dorevolyutsionnogo dramaticheskogo teatra* (Leningrad, 1971), is a good source-book. B. V. Varneke, *Istoriya russkogo teatra XVII–XIX vv.*, 3rd edn (Moscow–Leningrad, 1939), remains a readable and informative work. A. Anikst, *Teoriya dramy v Rossii ot Pushkina do Chekhova* (Moscow, 1972). I. N. Bozheryanov, *Illyustrirovannaya istoriya russkogo teatra XIX v.*, vols. 1–2 (St Petersburg, 1903). S. P. Zhikharev, *Zapiski sovremennika. Redaktsiya, stat'yi 'S. P. Zhikharev i yego dnevniki', 'Obzor' teatral'nogo materiala v 'zapiskakh' Zhikhareva, Istochniki*, text and commentary by B. M. Eykhenbaum (Moscow–Leningrad, 1955), is an important source-book for the history of the early nineteenth-century theatre; Zhikharev was an ardent and enthusiastic theatre-goer. S. S. Danilov and M. G. Portugalova, *Russkiy dramaticheskiy teatr XIX v.*, 2 vols. (Moscow–Leningrad,

1957, 1974), provide a sensible and compact survey. I. F. Gorbunov, *Moskovskiy teatr v XVII–XIX st.*, in his *Sobraniye sochineniy*, ed. A. F. Koni, vol. 2 (St Petersburg, 1904), Yu. V. Sobolev, 'Russkiy teatr nachala XX v.', *Bol'shaya Sovetskaya Entsiklopediya* 49 (1941), 729–33, surveys the stage at the beginning of the century. V. A. Telyakovsky, *Imperatorskiye teatry i 1905 god* (Leningrad, 1926).

M. Slonim, *Russian Theatre from the Empire to the Soviets* (London, 1961), is the only full-length history of the Russian stage in English, but there are few details and the style is unattractive. B. V. Varneke, *History of the Russian Theatre*, trans. B. Brasol (New York, n.d.), is the only reliable history to have been translated into English. R. Fülöp-Miller and J. Gregor, *The Russian Theatre, its character and history, with special reference to the revolutionary period*, trans. by P. England (London, 1930), is a most handsome book, but not essential for the scholar. E. Lo Gatto, *Storia del teatro russo* (2 vols., Florence, 1952), with its carefully selected illustrations and useful bibliographies, is amongst the best.

SPECIFIC STUDIES
On private and serf theatres: T. A. Dynnik, *Krepostnoy teatr*, gen. ed. A. K. Dzhivelegov (Moscow–Leningrad, 1933), is still the most rewarding account of private troupes and serf companies. V. G. Sakhnovsky, *Krepostnoy usadebnyy teatr* (Leningrad, 1924), surveys the serf theatre on landed estates throughout Russia. N. A. Yelizarova, *Teatry Sheremetevykh* (Moscow, 1944), examines the private theatrical troupes and the serf theatre of the Sheremetev family, and is invaluable for the history of country-house dramatics. N. P. Kashin, *Teatr N. B. Yusupova* (Moscow, 1927), investigates Prince Yusupov's private and domestic theatrical troupe, and gives details of the theatre, which is still in existence and has preserved some of the original painted sets. I. Kruti, *Russkiy teatr v Kazani* (Moscow, 1958), is a useful account of the provincial theatre in Kazan' during the nineteenth century. On fairgrounds: A. V. Leyfert, *Balagany* (Petrograd, 1922), describes the colourful booths and sideshows of Russian fairgrounds, with a historical survey of their development. *Russkiye narodnyye gulyan'ya, po rasskazam A. Ya. Alekseyeva, v zapisi i obrabotke E. M. Kuznetsova* (Leningrad, 1948), is a history of the carnival and fairground, which gives an insight into Russian popular display at festival time. On the circus: E. M. Kuznetsov, *Tsirk* (Moscow–Leningrad, 1931); Yu. A. Dmitriyev, *Russkiy tsirk* (Moscow, 1953). On vaudeville: N. Shantarenkov, *Russkiy vodevil'* (Moscow, 1970), contains texts and commentary.

N. V. Drizen, *Dramaticheskaya tsenzura dvukh epokh (1825–1881)* (Moscow, 1913), is a good account of censorship. G. Goyan, *Put' razvitiya russkogo teatra* (Moscow–Leningrad, 1939), contains hints on the teaching of Russian theatre history.

On ballet: V. Krasovskaya, *Russkiy baletnyy teatr ot vozniknoveniya do serediny XIX v.* (Leningrad–Moscow, 1958), is a reliable though somewhat pedestrian account. Further volumes are: *idem, Russkiy baletnyy teatr vtoroy poloviny XIX v.* (Leningrad–Moscow, 1963); and *idem, Russkiy baletnyy teatr nachala XX v.*: vol. 1, *Khoreografy*; vol. 2, *Tantsovshchiki* (Leningrad, 1971, 1972). A. E. Johnson, *The Russian Ballet* (London, 1913), is a collector's volume, with many plates. W. A. Propert, *The Russian Ballet in Western Europe, 1909–1920*, with a chapter on the music by Sir Eugene Goossens (London and New York, 1921), is a handsome book for the enthusiast, with attractive illustrations.

On décor and designers: I. V. Ekskuzovich, *Tekhnika teatral'noy stseny v proshlom i nastoyashchem* (Leningrad, 1930). T. M. Rodina, *Russkoye teatral'noye iskusstvo v nachale XIX v.* (Moscow, 1961), is an intelligent survey. F. Ya. Syrkina, *Russkoye teatral'noye dekoratsionnoye iskusstvo vtoroy poloviny XIX v.* (Moscow, 1956), is an admirable and authoritative treatise, with well-chosen illustrations. M. Pozharskaya, *Russkoye teatral'no-dekoratsionnoye iskusstvo kontsa XIX – nachala XX v.* (Moscow, 1970). Works on designers include: E. A. Chernyshov, *Materialy k biografii V. D. Polenova* (London, 1964). A. Ya. Golovin, *Vstrechi i vpechatleniya. Pis'ma. Vospominaniya o Golovine*, compiled with commentary by A. G. Movshenson, introd. by F. Ya. Syrkina (Leningrad–Moscow, 1960), contains an admirable collection of material about Golovin. D. Kogan, *Golovin* (Moscow, 1960), is a short biography. *Idem, Konstantin Korovin. Zhizn' i tvorchestvo. Pis'ma. Dokumenty. Vospominaniya*, compiled by N. M. Molev (Moscow, 1963). *The Decorative Art of Léon Bakst*, with an appreciation by Arsène Alexandre, notes on the ballets by Jean Cocteau, trans. H. Melvill (London, 1913), is a grand edition with superb reproductions of Bakst's stage designs. *Inedited Works of Bakst* (New York, 1927) is a lavishly illustrated book, with essays by Louis Réau, Denis Roche, V. Svietlov and A. Tessier. M. G. Etkind, *Aleksandr Nikolayevich Benua (1870–1960)* (Leningrad–Moscow, 1965), is a sympathetic account of Benois' creative work, with source material and excellent plates. V. P. Knyazeva, *Nikolay Konstantinovich Rerikh (1874–1947), Zhivopis', skul'ptura, grafika* (Leningrad–Moscow, 1963). O. I. Podobedova, *Yevgeny Yevgen'yevich Lansere* (1875–1946) (Moscow, 1961). N. Morgunov and N. D. Morgunova-Rudnitskaya, *Viktor Mikhaylovich Vasnetsov. Zhizn' i tvorchestvo* (Moscow, 1962). A. Bassekhes, *Khudozhniki na stsene Mkhata* (Moscow, 1960), is an interesting description of the work of scenic artists and designers employed at the Moscow Art Theatre.

On theatres and theatre buildings: Yu. D. Khripunov, *Arkhitektura Bol'shogo Teatra*, ed. V. E. Bykov (Moscow, 1955), a detailed survey of the history, construction, destruction and rebuilding of the Bol'shoy, with instructive illustrations. *Moskovskiy Bol'shoy Teatr (1825–1925). Sbornik*, ed. A. Lunacharsky and I. Ekskuzovich (Moscow, 1925). *Moskovskiy Malyy Teatr (1824–1924). Sbornik* (Moscow, 1924). *Sto let Malomu Teatru. Sbornik* (Moscow, 1924). N. G. Zograf, *Malyy Teatr vtoroy poloviny XIX v.* (Moscow, 1960), and *Malyy Teatr v kontse XIX – nachala XX v.* (Moscow, 1966), a sound history. *Sto let: Aleksandrinskiy teatr – teatr gosdramy (1832–1932)* (Leningrad, 1932). M. Taranovskaya, *Arkhitektor K. Rossi. Zdaniye Akademicheskogo Teatra Dramy imeni A. S. Pushkina (Aleksandrinskiy) v Leningrade* (Leningrad, 1956), is a beautifully illustrated and documented volume. On the Moscow Art Theatre: N. E. Efros, *Moskovskiy Khudozhestvennyy Teatr (1898–1923)* (Moscow–Leningrad, 1924); Yu. V. Sobolev, *Moskovskiy Khudozhestvennyy Teatr. XXX let iskaniy i raboty* (Moscow, 1929); *idem, Moskovskiy Khudozhestvennyy Teatr* (Moscow–Leningrad, 1938); *Moskovskiy Khudozhestvennyy Teatr v illyustratsiyakh i dokumentakh (1898–1938)* (Moscow, 1938); *Moskovskiy Khudozhestvennyy Teatr (1898–1938)*, bibliography compiled by A. A. Aganbeyko, ed. S. N. Durylin (Moscow–Leningrad, 1939); *Théâtre Académique d'Art M. Gorky de l'URSS, Spectacles à l'Exposition Internationale de Paris*, 1937, compiled by I. Boyarsky (n.d.).

ACTORS, DIRECTORS, PRODUCERS

On Shchepkin: B. V. Alpers, *M. S. Shchepkin* (Moscow–Leningrad, 1943); S. S. Danilov, *M. S. Shchepkin (1788–1863). K 150-letiyu so dnya rozhdeniya* (Moscow–Leningrad, 1938); N. E. Efros, *M. S. Shchepkin* (Petrograd, 1920); V. A. Filippov, *M. S. Shchepkin i yego rol' v istorii russkogo teatra* (Leningrad–Moscow, 1938); A. P. Klinchin, *Velikiy russkiy artist M. S. Shchepkin* (Moscow, 1954); *idem, M. S.*

Shchepkin, Zapiski, pis'ma. Sovremenniki o M. S. Shchepkine (Moscow, 1952), an authoritative edition of Shchepkin's diaries and letters; Yu. V. Sobolev, *Shchepkin* (Moscow, 1933); D. Tal'nikov, *Sistema Shchepkina* (Moscow–Leningrad, 1939), studies Shchepkin's 'method' and innovations in acting techniques. On Yermolova: S. N. Durylin, *M. N. Yermolova* (Moscow–Leningrad, 1943); *idem, Mariya Nikolayevna Yermolova (1853–1928). Ocherki zhizni i tvorchestva* (Moscow, 1953); M. S. Luchansky, *Yermolova* (Moscow, 1938); M. N. Yermolova, *Pis'ma iz literaturnogo naslediya, vospominaniya sovremennikov*, compiled by S. N. Durylin (Moscow, 1955). On Martynov: B. N. Aseyev, *A. E. Martynov (1816–1860)* (Moscow–Leningrad, 1946); A. M. Bryansky, *A. E. Martynov* (Leningrad–Moscow, 1941). On Mochalov: Yu. A. Dmitriyev, *P. S. Mochalov (1800–1848)* (Moscow–Leningrad, 1948); Yu. V. Sobolev, *Pavel Mochalov* (Moscow, 1937). On Kachalov: S. N. Durylin, *V. I. Kachalov* (Moscow–Leningrad, 1943); V. I. Kachalov, *Sbornik statey, vospominaniy, pisem*, compiled and ed. by V. Ya. Vilenkin (Moscow, 1954); A. Talanov, *Kachalov* (Moscow, 1962). On Shusherin: A. P. Klinchin, *Ya. E. Shusherin* (Moscow, 1947). On Stanislavsky: I. Vinogradskaya, *Zhin' i tvorchestvo K. S. Stanislavskogo*, vols. 1–2: *Vserossiyskoye teatral'noye obshchestvo* (Moscow, 1971–), a 4-vol. series of which the first two vols. have appeared so far; E. Polyakova, *Stanislavsky – aktyor* (Moscow, 1972); N. Gorchakov, *Rezhissyorskiye uroki K. S. Stanislavskogo* (Moscow, 1950); Yu. S. Kalashnikov, *Esteticheskiy ideal K. S. Stanislavskogo* (Moscow, 1965); K. S. Stanislavsky, *Moya zhizn' v iskusstve*, 7th edn (Moscow–Leningrad, 1941), is a lively autobiography; *idem, Rabota aktyora nad soboy* (pts 1–2, Moscow, 1951), is an illuminating account of Stanislavsky's experiences both on and back-stage; *idem, Khudozhestvennyye zapisi (1877–1892)* (Moscow–Leningrad, 1939); *idem, An Actor Prepares*, trans. E. Reynolds Hapgood (London, 1936). On Nemirovich-Danchenko: Yu. V. Sobolev, *V. I. Nemirovich-Danchenko* (Moscow, 1929); L. Freydkina, *V. I. Nemirovich-Danchenko* (Moscow, 1945); *idem, Dni i gody V. I. Nemirovicha-Danchenko* (Moscow, 1962); V. I. Nemirovich-Danchenko, *Iz proshlogo* (Moscow, 1936), episodes from his life; *idem, Teatral'noye naslediye*: vol. 1, *Stat'i, rechi, besedy, pis'ma*; vol. 2, *Izbrannyye pis'ma* (Moscow, 1952, 1954), contains important material. On Moskvin: V. Ya. Vilenkin, *I. M. Moskvin na stsene moskovskogo khudozhestvennogo teatra* (Moscow, 1946); I. M. Moskvin, *Stat'i i materialy*, ed. I. Kruti (Moscow, 1948). On Ol'ga Knipper-Chekhova: B. I. Rostovsky, *O. L. Knipper-Chekhova* (Moscow–Leningrad, 1946); V. Ya. Vilenkin, *Ol'ga Leonardovna Knipper-Chekhova*, pt. 1: *Vospominaniya i stat'i, perepiska s A. P. Chekhovym (1902–1904)*; pt 2: *Perepiska (1896–1959). Vospominaniya ob O. L. Knipper-Chekhovoy* (Moscow, 1972). On Komissarzhevskaya: D. Tal'nikov, *V. F. Komissarzhevskaya* (Moscow–Leningrad, 1939); Yu. Rybakova, *Komissarzhevskaya* (Leningrad, 1971).

PLAYS AND PLAYWRIGHTS

N. S. Ashukin, V. N. Vsevolodsky-Gerngross and Yu. V. Sobolev, *Khrestomatiya po istorii russkogo teatra XVIII i XIX vv.* (Leningrad–Moscow, 1940). *Russkaya narodnaya drama XVII–XX vv. Teksty p'yes i opisaniya predstavleniy*, ed. with introd. and commentary by P. N. Berkov (Moscow, 1953). *Russkiye dramaturgi XVIII–XIX vv. Monograficheskiye ocherki*, 3 vols., ed. G. R. Berdnikov, B. I. Bursov, G. P. Makogonenko and B. S. Meylakh (Leningrad–Moscow, 1962). On Griboyedov: A. S. Griboyedov, *Gore ot uma. P'yesa, stat'i, kommentarii*, eds. N. Piksanov and V. A. Filippov (Moscow–Leningrad, 1946), recommended especially for the illuminating commentaries, articles and plates; *idem, Gore ot uma*, ed. N. Piksanov with A. L. Grishunin (Moscow, 1968); *idem, Gore ot uma*, in *P'yesy khudozhestvennogo repertuara i postanovka ikh na stnese*, II, 2nd edn, ed. Yu. A. Ozarovsky (St Petersburg, 1911), is a fine acting version with descriptions of costume design, properties and sets; excellent for achieving a correct feeling of the period. On Pushkin: S. N. Durylin, *Pushkin na stsene* (Moscow, 1951); B. P. Gorodetsky, *Dramaturgiya Pushkina* (Moscow–Leningrad, 1953); *idem, Tragediya A. S. Pushkina Boris Godunov. Kommentarii. Posobiye dlya uchiteley* (Leningrad, 1969); *Pushkin i teatr. Dramaticheskiye proizvedeniya, stat'i, zametki, dnevniki, pis'ma*, ed. B. P. Gorodetsky (Moscow, 1953), is a useful compendium of Pushkin's dramatic work, with commentaries and other articles. On Lermontov: *'Maskarad' Lermontova. Sbornik statey*, ed. P. I. Novitsky (Moscow–Leningrad, 1941); Golovin's sets and costume sketches are reproduced in colour, with a history of the production. On Gogol: N. K. Piksanov, *Gogol' – dramaturg* (Leningrad, 1952); Yu. Mann, *Komediya Gogolya 'Revizor'* (Moscow, 1966); N. V. Gogol, *'Revizor'. Stsenicheskaya istoriya v illyustrativnykh materialakh*, text by S. S. Danilov, introd. by N. S. Derzhavin (Moscow–Leningrad, 1936); *Gogol' i teatr*, ed. N. L. Stepanova (Moscow, 1952), is a useful compendium of Gogol's dramatic work. On Ostrovsky: U. M. Lotman, *A. N. Ostrovsky i russkaya dramaturgiya yego vremeni*, ed. B. M. Eykhenbaum (Moscow–Leningrad, 1961); *A. N. Ostrovsky (1823–1923). Sbornik*, ed. P. Kogan (Ivanovo–Voznesensk, 1923); *Ostrovsky (1823–1923) – yubileynyy sbornik*, eds. A. A. Bakhrushin, N. L. Brodsky and N. A. Popov (Moscow, 1923); A. N. Ostrovsky, *Dnevniki i pis'ma. Teatr Ostrovskogo*, ed. V. A. Filippov (Moscow–Leningrad, 1937); *A. N. Ostrovsky – dramaturg. Sbornik statey*, ed. V. A. Filippov (Moscow, 1946). On Nekrasov: V. E. Yevgen'yev-Maksimov *et al., Nekrasov i teatr* (Moscow–Leningrad, 1948). On Turgenev: *Turgenev i teatr*, ed. G. P. Berdnikov (Moscow, 1953). On Chekhov: E. D. Surkov, *Chekhov i teatr. Pis'ma, fel'yetony, sovremenniki o Chekhove dramaturge* (Moscow, 1961), Chekhov's own opinions on acting and production; T. K. Shakh-Azizova, *Chekhov i zapadno-yevropeyskaya drama yego vremeni* (Moscow, 1966); *'Chayka' v postanovke Moskovskogo khudozhestvennogo teatra. Rezhissyorskaya partitura K. S. Stanislavskogo*, ed. S. D. Balukhatov (Leningrad–Moscow, 1938), Stanislavsky's annotated acting version of *The Seagull*. On Blok: A. V. Fyodorov, *Teatr A. Bloka i dramaturgiya yego vremeni* (Leningrad, 1972); T. M. Rodina, *A. Blok i russkiy teatr nachala XX v.* (Moscow, 1972). On Gor'ky: Yu. Yuzovsky, *Dramaturgiya Gor'kogo* (pt 1, Moscow–Leningrad, 1940); M. Grigor'yev, *Gor'ky dramaturg i kritik* (Moscow, 1946); *Gor'ky i teatr. Sbornik* (Leningrad, 1933); *Gor'ky i teatr. Sbornik* (Moscow–Leningrad, 1938), two collections of articles; *'Na dne' Gor'kogo. Materialy i issledovaniya*, ed. Yu. Yuzovsky (Moscow–Leningrad, 1940).

10

THE SOVIET THEATRE

MICHAEL GLENNY

As the preceding chapter will have shown, in a sense it is true that in Russia the theatrical revolution took place twenty years before 1917. Such was the effect of the theatrical renaissance which began with the foundation of the Moscow Art Theatre in 1897 that Soviet Russia inherited from the old regime a theatre that was vital, rich in creativity and ready to take full advantage of the support and encouragement initially offered to it by the Bolshevik government. The result, in the first decade or so after 1917, was a flowering of theatrical art of a brilliance scarcely equalled in the history of any country. It was the Russian theatre's Elizabethan age, its *grand siècle*. The Soviet theatre of the 1920s and early 1930s was acknowledged throughout the world as a leader of the avant-garde, unique in boldness, scope and popularity with its audiences. At least, this was the case where production, acting and design were concerned; its weak point was – and still is – in the repertoire of plays by Soviet authors.

The Soviet theatre has always been a 'director's theatre' rather than a 'writer's theatre'. Further, it has always been expected to do more than provide mere entertainment. The power of the theatre as a medium of communication and propaganda was well understood and utilized by the Bolsheviks from the very beginning. In those days before radio and television, and before the cinema became so widespread, the theatre and the press were the only true mass media, and of these two the theatre had one immense advantage over the printed word – it was instantly comprehensible to the illiterate (in 1917 illiteracy was still widespread in Russia, in towns and especially in the countryside). Lenin's first government had only been in power for a few days when, in November 1917, all theatres in Russia were placed at least nominally under the aegis of the Department of the Arts of the People's Commissariat of Education (*Narkompros*). Six weeks later theatre administration was given its own special Department (*Teatral'noye otdeleniye*) of the Commissariat. The speed with which the first Bolshevik government enacted this theatre legislation is a sign of the importance which it ascribed to the theatre. On 26 August 1919 the Council of People's Commissars (*Sovnarkom*) issued its celebrated decree

271

nationalizing all theatres (or at least the theatres in those regions where the Bolshevik writ ran). The policy expressed in this document was the work of A. V. Lunacharsky, first Soviet Commissar for Education, married to an actress and himself a playwright and dramatic critic, to whom the overall control of the theatre had been entrusted. Lunacharsky did a very great deal for the Soviet theatre in the first decade of its existence; he was at once both its critic and its champion; although often in disagreement with the more extreme forms of avant-garde theatre (Lunacharsky the revolutionary was in theatrical matters a conservative), he nevertheless stoutly defended its right to be experimental and non-conformist. Without his beneficent patronage the Soviet theatre would never have reached such heights of achievement and would be poorer and less effective to this day.

Under Lunacharsky's enthusiastic direction the years 1918–21 were a brief spell of utopian extravagance. Actors were granted considerable privileges. In a time of famine and privation they were given the highest ration scale, security of employment, and generous fixed salaries instead of fees haggled over for each new engagement. Maximum working hours were laid down, beyond which overtime had to be paid. Naturally, in the disturbed conditions of the civil war, many of these directives remained on paper and were not fully observed, yet the theatre flourished and theatre people on the whole survived 'War Communism' in better shape than most other Russians. Such was the attraction of the theatre in those hard times that in 1920 in the RSFSR alone there were 428,000 people registered as in full-time employment in the theatre or studying at theatrical schools. Suddenly, too, the theatre became accessible to a vast though unsophisticated new public. The huge audiences were achieved by very simple means: most theatre tickets were simply given away free. The box office vanished and theatres were filled nightly from stalls to gallery, no matter what the play. Thanks to a carefully channelled distribution of tickets (they were issued largely via trades unions, party cells and welfare organizations) the old middle-class audience was literally elbowed out by the working class and peasantry, who poured into the theatres to gape in touching wonder at the marvellous world beyond the footlights to which the revolution had suddenly admitted them. Not all the actors, though, welcomed their new patrons – 'their lordships the proletariat', as Isaak Babel' called them in his play *Mariya*, which describes this period. They talked, jeered, stamped, coughed and spat; they were so unfamiliar with the elementary conventions of the theatre that they would leap on stage to defend an actress threatened by the villain or would excitedly intervene in the dialogue by shouting an answer to some purely rhetorical question.

In those early years the Soviet theatre not only flung open its doors to admit the masses; the theatre itself went out into the squares and fields to carry revolutionary propaganda directly to the people in the form of 'mass-spectacles'. These were vast open-air political charades with actors numbered in hundreds and spectators in tens of thousands at a time, shows designed to put across a crude, rhetorical, biased, but effective message. A famous example of this genre was Mayakovsky's *Misteriya-Buff*, a sort of farcical revolutionary morality play, first performed in Petrograd in November 1918. The 'mass-spectacles' grew bigger and bigger, increasingly ambitious and more and more unwieldy, culminating in Yevreinov's *The Storming of the Winter Palace*, produced in Petrograd on 7 November 1920, the third anniversary of the revolution. This was a vast pageant-play, in which the event was re-enacted on its actual site. At the climax the guns of the cruiser *Aurora* boomed out a repeat of her historic salvo and, as a huge red flag was hoisted to the apex of a cone of searchlights, the 100,000-strong audience sang the *Internationale*.

But this period did not last long. When Lenin adopted the New Economic Policy in 1921, there was a brisk and sobering change in the Soviet government's attitude to the theatre. Subsidies were withdrawn, a third of the theatres passed back into private ownership, and in all theatres tickets cost money again. The immediate result was a fall in average theatre attendance from 100 per cent to between 20 and 25 per cent. The vastly expensive 'mass-spectacles' were stopped. Apart from the former Imperial Theatres (newly designated 'academic' theatres), which simply became state enterprises and remained subsidized, the rest of the theatre had to regain its traditional audience and pay its way. With its international reputation the Moscow Art Theatre went off on an extended foreign tour in 1922 to raise funds. After two years abroad Stanislavsky and his company returned rich in foreign currency but poorer in actors: several leading members of the troupe had stayed in the West, including such actors as Akim Tamirov who was to have a distinguished subsequent career in Hollywood.

Despite his great and deserved fame as a trainer and director of actors, Stanislavsky by the 1920s had ceased to be in any sense a theatrical innovator. Although he and Nemirovich-Danchenko continued to run the Moscow Art Theatre until their deaths (Stanislavsky died in 1938, Nemirovich-Danchenko in 1943), their theatre simply went on purveying the same kind of subtle, refined naturalism which Stanislavsky had perfected well before 1917. Their repertoire leaned heavily on the classics of Russian dramatic realism – Gogol, Ostrovsky, Turgenev, Chekhov and Gor'ky – and remained intellectually rooted in the nineteenth century.

The real pacemakers in the Soviet theatre of the twenties were the directors who rejected realism for expressionism – Vakhtangov, Tairov and the greatest of them all, Meyerhold. To group three such individualists

273

together is to risk oversimplification. It is unlikely that they would even have accepted the common label 'expressionist', but it is a convenient piece of shorthand to describe what they shared in their approach to the theatre. Briefly, they objected to realism as inappropriate to the stage. They considered that the theatre should not be a kind of voyeur's device for peeping through keyholes into a painstaking (though conventionalized) reproduction of the surface phenomena of other people's lives; instead the function of theatre, as an art-form whose power lay in its capacity to select, suppress, emphasize and abstract, was to express a poetic or 'theatrical' reality which 'realism' could never express because its prosaic, photographic methods served only to anaesthetize an audience's imagination. Expressionism, by contrast, strove to make the audience into participants in the artistic process, by abandoning the stultifying pretences of 'realism' (whose 'reality' was in any case a fake) and by-passing the threshold of conventional visual perception to appeal directly to the emotions in the language of the subconscious, i.e. in symbols and images. These would then evoke a response in the spectator's imagination; the circuit would be complete and the voltage of artistic creation would flow – like alternating current, in both directions at once – between performer and audience.

On the Soviet stage today there is scarcely a trace to be found of expressionism, of the verve, the innovation and the excitement which Vakhtangov, Tairov and Meyerhold produced during that golden first Soviet decade. Their reputations among today's Soviet theatrical 'establishment' stands in almost exactly reverse ratio to the real magnitude of their achievements, though more enlightened opinion tends to reject the current official view, and a slow reassessment of them is under way. The greatest respect, even if it is largely lip-service, is paid to Vakhtangov. The theatre which he took over in 1921 and ran as the Third Studio of the Moscow Art Theatre was renamed the Vakhtangov Theatre in 1926 and has retained the title ever since. There is also a Vakhtangov Museum. In fact his work during the Soviet period was relatively short, owing to his untimely death in 1922 at the age of thirty-nine. He left behind a small but quite brilliant repertoire of productions whose influence is still traceable in the western theatre to this day; Brecht for instance owed much of his sense of controlled spontaneity and handling of groups and crowds to Vakhtangov's methods. The productions included Maeterlinck's *Le Miracle de St Antoine*, Strindberg's *Erik XIV*, and Gozzi's *Princess Turandot* (the original of Puccini's opera). This, his last and probably his most perfect work, was two years in preparation. Virtually from scratch he chose and schooled a company of young trainee actors who emerged at the première (Vakhtangov was too ill to attend) as skilled professionals.

The production of *Princess Turandot* was a unique fusion of fantasy and realism – indeed Vakhtangov, although not inclined to theorize, described his method as 'fantastic realism'. The fantasy lay in his use of scenery and stage convention. The sets and costumes by Nivinsky were deliberately and artfully sketchy, in order merely to suggest location and character in a humorous, throwaway fashion, without imposing too many visual preconceptions on the audience. Much of the make-up, gestures and movement were consciously adapted from the Italian *commedia dell'arte*; to bring out the play's stylistic origin as a piece of *chinoiserie* the stagehands changed the scenery in full view of the audience, as they do in the Chinese theatre. Before curtain-up four masked buffoons announced the play, the company paraded on the fore-stage in evening dress, introduced themselves, made themselves up and donned the few elaborately casual scraps which served as costumes. After this calculated glimpse of the mechanism of theatrical illusion the actors moved gaily into the action of the play, the audience's reactions a-tingle. The realistic element lay in Vakhtangov's revelation of the human psychological truth behind the fairy-tale grotesquerie of Gozzi's story.

The winning gaiety and infectious élan of this production, all concealing a theatrical substructure of great artifice and iron directorial control, had the most invigorating effect on the frozen, underfed and war-weary Moscow audience of the day. The production has been several times revived and remains one of the brightest masterpieces of the early Soviet theatre, remembered universally with love and affection. It is as a teacher of genius, able both to inspire profound devotion in his pupils and to draw from them undreamt-of resources of skill and talent, that Vakhtangov is perhaps best remembered. Among the very many stars who learned their trade under him, N. M. Gorchakov went on to become a senior director at the Moscow Art Theatre, Yelizaveta Alekseyeva crowned a distinguished career by becoming a professor of dramatic art, and Yury Zavadsky has achieved fame as artistic director of the great Mossovet Theatre in Moscow. Another of Vakhtangov's creations, the Jewish Habima Theatre, exists to this day in Tel Aviv, where his own remarkable production of Rappoport's *The Dybbuk* is still in the repertoire and where the company is headed by several actors who received their stage training from Vakhtangov himself.

In contrast to Vakhtangov, Alexander Tairov's career in the Soviet theatre was long; yet although his achievements were considerable they are now almost forgotten. When the revolution occurred Tairov had already been master of his own theatre, the *Kamernyy* or Chamber Theatre of Moscow, for three years and by a miracle of self-preservation he remained there, except for a break of a few years, until shortly before his death in 1950. Tairov's most remarkable gift lay in his training and handling of actors, whom he coached and drilled into being masters of every trade – singing, acrobatics, ballet, fencing, gymnastics and sport as well as the conventional skills of mime, impersonation, elocution and movement – before he regarded them as ready to perform in his ideal of 'total', or as he called it, 'synthetic' theatre. For Tairov the actor *was* the theatre, and the rest of the paraphernalia, such as scenery, lighting, costume and music, were accessories whose function was to emphasize the centrality of the actor on the stage. In this Tairov's aim was often in direct opposition to that of Meyerhold, who tended to see actors as another category of stage machinery and often an intractable and disobedient sort of machinery – he once even declared that in the ideal theatre he would do away with actors altogether! It was Tairov's concern for the actor as the ultimate creative stage artist that led him to adopt his most notable innovation in production technique and one which was widely copied, adapted or modified throughout the world. This was the form of stage décor called constructivism, an art most closely connected with the names of Vladimir Tatlin and Naum Gabo. As a part of the upsurge of extreme 'modernist' movements in art that exploded in Russia in the 1920s, constructivism was a development of abstract cubism; it was also an attempt to negate the art of the past and to break through into an art which used the materials and visual language of the industrial age – wire, glass, sheet metal, tubes and girders. Tatlin called it, in fact, 'the new machine art'. Constructivism was essentially architectonic: it gave rhythm and significance to space and mass by outlining and defining spatial relationships. Tairov used it not for its scenic application but for the very opposite reason – because by providing a series of visually neutral platforms in space at a number of levels it increased the actor's mobility and his dominance of the stage. By his virtuosity the actor would then supply all that the audience needed in visual stimulus and scenic illusion. Meyerhold, too, quickly adopted constructivism and carried it to further lengths, but Tairov always knew better than Meyerhold how and when to modify the mechanics of his stagecraft into more widely acceptable forms; and it was his skill in appearing to comply with party directives on the content of his plays while maintaining an originality and vitality of form that enabled him to keep his job for so long. He was responsible for introducing many leading Western playwrights into the Russian theatre in the 1920s and 1930s, including Brecht, Bernard Shaw and Eugene O'Neill. In official eyes Tairov's enthusiasm for foreign plays, even by 'progressive' dramatists, was thought excessive and he was ordered, along with other producers, to stage more Soviet plays. They provided mostly unpromising material for him, but he made an excellent version of Vsevolod Vishnevsky's civil war play *An Optimistic Tragedy* which had its première at the Chamber Theatre in 1933. After that Tairov's theatre, although hampered in repertoire and cramped in style, remained throughout Stalin's rule as the last rearguard of the great days of Soviet expressionism.

Vsevolod Meyerhold was by contrast a much more complex and intractable character. His urge to negate the reigning orthodoxy and assert the latest invention of his fertile mind was so powerful that he was frequently in the position of dismissing his own innovations of a few years before as outdated rubbish. There is scarcely a facet of what is today still regarded as 'avant-garde' theatre – symbolism, absurdity, alienation, mime, stylized clowning, abstract sets – which was not tried, developed and then rejected by Meyerhold. Underlying his frequent changes of course in pursuit of the ultimate in non-realistic theatre was his use of the two complementary techniques of constructivism and 'bio-mechanics'. His constructivist sets were generally even more stark than those of Tairov. In his production of Ostrovsky's *The Forest*, for instance, a nineteenth-century classic generally staged with painstaking naturalism, Meyerhold stripped the stage bare of everything except a ramp, a platform and a few upright supports. The layout was altered only slightly for each act, the linking feature being the three gigantic letters 'ЛЕС' which dominated the set throughout the play. By the violent overthrow of all the canons of realism, the acting as well as the stage design was intended to shock the audience out of the conventional interpretation of Ostrovsky, and to stress the elements of conflict between individuals and classes by means of stylized mimetic characterization and rhythmic movement. Since this demanded strict, metronomic, directorial control and great precision on the part of the performers, to train his actors to the required pitch of flexible obedience Meyerhold developed the system known as bio-mechanics. This impressively technological-sounding expression really meant, once the mystique is removed, that Meyerhold's actors had to learn the physical and acrobatic skills of the circus, music hall and pantomime as well as the more cerebral techniques of 'straight' acting. They were then fit to execute Meyerhold's complex and rigidly timed directorial 'scores', which plotted the movements of every character and aimed at giving the actor's body an expressive validity equal to that of speech.

In the spare, forceful near-abstraction of his stage images Meyerhold stood in very close sympathy with the futurist movement in art and literature, and above all with Mayakovsky. In addition to his early *Misteriya-Buff*, Meyerhold also created the first productions of Mayakovsky's satirical comedies, *The Bed-bug* in 1929 with incidental music by Shostakovich, and *The Bath-house* in 1930, which Meyerhold later came to regard as perhaps his best work. But undoubtedly his most ambitious production, employing every Meyerholdian device, was his version of Gogol's *The Government Inspector* which had its première in

December 1926. He took great liberties with Gogol's text, inserting dramatized passages from the *Petersburg Tales*, *Dead Souls* and other works, completely recasting the structure of the original play until it became a synthesized 'Gogoliana' in fifteen episodes. The interpretation of the play as a comedy was too insipid for Meyerhold; in his eyes Gogol could only be played as tragedy or farce. He therefore devised *The Government Inspector* as a hybrid which a critic dubbed '*tragediya-buff*'. The production was dominated by a Khlestakov who far transcended Gogol's original in complexity and sinister power. The effect on the audiences of Meyerhold's Gogol – as of nearly all his productions – was one of stupefaction, furious enthusiasm, or violent antipathy.

Meyerhold's compulsive drive to shock and excite, to explore to infinity the plastic, visual and dynamic resources of the theatre was a principal cause of the prestige and admiration which the Soviet theatre enjoyed throughout the relatively libertarian decade of the 1920s. But as Stalin gained supreme power, Meyerhold's exuberant, disturbing, non-realistic expressionism fell more and more into disfavour. In his views on the theatre, as on all the other arts, Stalin was a conservative and a philistine; quite apart from the ideological content of plays, over which he ensured strict control, he was incapable of tolerating artistic expression in forms that went beyond his own limited powers of appreciation. From the early 1930s until the mid-1950s, notwithstanding a slight revival during the war years, the theatre in Soviet Russia was progressively reduced to a state of palsied banality. Because Moscow Art Theatre realism was Stalin's notion of what plays should be like, Stanislavsky became the sole arbiter of theatrical art in the USSR; as a result the Stanislavsky System came to be imposed as the only officially approved school of acting, and naturalism as the general style for all productions. Although within its limits this set a high standard of professional competence, its ultimate effect was uniformity and a stifling of creative experiment. It produced twenty years of what Soviet theatre people now refer to as the era of 'grey realism'. It also involved the condemnation and persecution of such vital innovators as Meyerhold who, although protected by Stanislavsky as long as the latter was alive, was arrested in 1939 for his uncompromising rejection of Stalinist conformity and died in a labour camp – a tragic and disgraceful end to the career of the man with a real claim to being the most original theatrical genius of this century.

Even before it felt the deadening hand of Stalin, however, the Soviet theatre experienced constant difficulty over a problem which its great directors could do relatively little to solve – the supply of new plays. For nearly ten years after the revolution the theatre had to rely on the classics and on foreign plays for the bulk of its repertoire. Lunacharsky himself wrote several plays on historical revolutionary themes, such as his drama

Oliver Cromwell (1920), but they were somewhat fustian pieces which have since lapsed into deserved oblivion. Perhaps the first truly Soviet play of more than academic interest was written by Lidiya Seyfullina, whose *Virinea* (1925), about the impact of the revolution on Siberian villagers, has sufficient virtue to merit occasional revival today. The Moscow Art Theatre came under frequent and heavy attack for its failure to perform new plays. For a time this situation was resolved by its discovery of Mikhail Bulgakov and the production in 1926 of *The Days of the Turbins*. Despite a few years of official disfavour this play, which is remarkable in describing with sympathy and insight a group of 'Whites' during the civil war, has enjoyed constant popularity in the USSR and is in the Soviet repertoire to this day. Bulgakov then wrote a comedy each for the Vakhtangov Theatre and for Tairov's Chamber Theatre – entitled respectively *Zoë's Apartment* and *The Purple Island* – and a new play for the Moscow Art Theatre called *Flight*, in some sense a sequel to *The Turbins*. But because they did not conform to the crude political stereotypes demanded by RAPP, the left-wing Association of Proletarian Writers, Bulgakov's plays were violently attacked and he became one of the first playwrights to suffer the effects of *Glavrepertkom*, the organ of theatrical censorship created in 1929; all his plays were proscribed and *Flight* was banned while still in rehearsal. In 1930, after a personal appeal to Stalin, Bulgakov was given a job as 'resident playwright' under Stanislavsky at the Moscow Art Theatre. There he dramatized Gogol's *Dead Souls* (1932), and this too remains a standby of their repertoire; but only one more of his plays, *Molière* (1936), was produced in Bulgakov's lifetime (he died in 1940) and that, although a remarkable play, was withdrawn after only seven performances for being too obvious an attack on Stalin's cultural dictatorship. Most of Bulgakov's eleven published plays, including *Flight, Don Quixote, Pushkin* and *Molière*, have been performed since 1957, and he is belatedly receiving his due recognition as an outstanding Soviet playwright.

As with Bulgakov, it was the civil war which provided the subject-matter for many of the writers who constituted the first crop of strictly 'Soviet' Russian playwrights; many of these plays have worn quite well, treating as they do of simple, relatively clear-cut heroic themes – although even these were not free of the ideological booby-traps which were to plague all Soviet playwrights throughout Stalin's rule. One of the successful authors in the civil war genre was Vsevolod Vishnevsky (d. 1951). His *First Cavalry Army* (1930) is a documentary play in vigorous, epic style which was regarded as highly significant for its concentration on mass psychology in place of the theatre's traditional preoccupation with the individual. Considerably subtler, and still played today, was Vishnevsky's *Optimistic Tragedy* (1933) which relates how the self-sacrifice of a woman commissar inspires an anarchic gang of revolutionary sailors to act as a disciplined, effective body. However, Vishnevsky's stock has fallen badly since he truckled to Stalin in 1949 and introduced blatant distortions of historical fact into his last play, *Unforgettable 1919*. Others who have written well-made civil war plays are Vsevolod Ivanov, whose *Armoured Train 14–69*, commissioned by Stanislavsky for the tenth anniversary of the revolution, and *Blockade* (1929) still run in Soviet playhouses; Leonid Leonov, who in 1927 dramatized his own novel *The Badgers*; and K. A. Trenyov, whose *Lyubov' Yarovaya* (1926) portrayed the human conflict within a woman whose loyalties are divided between opposing sides in the civil war. Although a sound and often moving play, it too was rewritten by its author at Stalin's prompting in 1936; since 1956, however, the undoctored version has returned to the stage. Lavrenyov was yet another to join the sad ranks of playwrights who rewrote their work to please Stalin; his reputation has not recovered from the distortions he inflicted on *The Break-up* (1927), a play about the sailors of the Baltic Fleet, also originally commissioned for the tenth anniversary of the revolution.

Another theme which preoccupied Soviet playwrights in the late 1920s and early 1930s was the impact of the revolution and Soviet rule on their own social group, the still essentially middle-class intelligentsia. Authors who tackled this subject were Aleksandr Afinogenov (d. 1941) and Yury Olesha (d. 1960). Afinogenov's two best plays were *The Eccentric* (1929) and *Fear* (1931), both very telling studies in the struggle of the intellectual to come to terms with the new society. During the mid-1930s, however, Afinogenov ruined his talent by writing a succession of lifeless plays to the order of the party bureaucrats, although his patriotic drama *Mashen'ka* (1941) enjoyed a huge vogue with wartime Soviet audiences. Even more tragic was the case of Yury Olesha, who wrote his best work on similar themes of the educated individual's conflict with and ultimate acceptance of Soviet reality; his *Conspiracy of Feelings* (1929) and *A List of Benefits* (1931) are plays of great subtlety and charm which had sadly brief stage careers before being suppressed. Olesha himself reacted to the prevailing climate by relapsing into sterility as a writer and died an alcoholic, having produced nothing since 1934 except for a stage adaptation of Dostoyevsky's *The Idiot* in 1958. Two more of the great might-have-beens of Soviet dramatic literature were Yevgeny Zamyatin (d. 1937) and Isaak Babel' (d. 1941). Both made their reputations as writers in other fields, Zamyatin as a satirical novelist and critic, Babel' as a short-story writer. Zamyatin had one huge success, *The Flea*, a delightful pantomimic comedy based on Leskov, which ran from 1925 until 1930, when he went into voluntary exile. Besides this he wrote two historical dramas, *The Fires of San Domingo* about the Spanish

Inquisition, and *Attila*; it is not difficult to see why subjects like these were never staged in Stalin's Russia. It is, however, a great loss for the Soviet stage that the persistent official antipathy to Zamyatin has barred production of his satirical comedy on racial prejudice, *The African Guest*. Babel' also had one play produced before the forces of Stalinism closed around him; this was *Sunset*, which had a successful run at the Moscow Art Theatre in 1928. Based on his short-story cycles of life in the ghetto of pre-revolutionary Odessa, it is the wry account of how a Jewish father is elbowed out of his position of family dominance by his sons. Babel''s next play, although published in a very small edition in 1935, was banned while in simultaneous rehearsal at the Vakhtangov Theatre and the State Jewish Theatre under the great director Solomon Mikhoels (d. 1948). This is *Mariya*, set in Petrograd in 1920, which aims to portray the dissolution of a whole order of society – the pre-revolutionary intellectuals – by a technique of deceptive simplicity which conceals great dramatic expertise. After completing *Mariya* Babel' realized that in writing plays he had discovered his true vocation; he wrote another piece, *The Chekist*, but it was seized and presumably destroyed by the NKVD when he was arrested in 1939 and consigned to his death in a labour camp.

Some writers proved that it was possible to continue writing plays under Stalin and survive; but it was usually achieved at the expense of artistic integrity and their works are only performed, with dwindling audiences, in theatres whose main concern is to stage the quota of Soviet plays (a minimum of two out of every six plays in the repertoire) required of them by official directive. One such author was Gor'ky, whose two plays of the Soviet period, *Yegor Bulichov and Others* (1932) and *Dostigayev and Others* (1933), were no more than tired restatements of his critiques of pre-revolutionary society. Perhaps the most typical and prolific conformist playwright of the Stalinist period was N. Pogodin, who wrote thirteen plays between 1929 and 1958 and who could be relied upon to churn out every two or three years an efficient if generally lifeless piece on the approved topic of the day. Another method of survival was to write plays for children. Here the acknowledged Soviet master was Yevgeny Shvarts (Schwarz) (d. 1958), who nevertheless succeeded with astonishing skill in also writing thoroughly adult parable-plays within fairy-tale form, generally adapting his stories from Hans Andersen. His first satire of this kind was *The Naked King* (1933); despite its implicit attack on Nazism its wit was rightly construed by Stalin's censors as being equally mordant at the expense of Soviet Communism, and neither this play nor Shvarts's other two, *The Shadow* (1940) and *The Dragon* (1943), could be staged (apart from brief wartime productions) until Nikolay Akimov (d. 1968) ran a highly successful Shvarts season at his Comedy Theatre in Leningrad in 1962. Another interesting case of artistic longevity is Aleksey Arbuzov, who today enjoys almost as much success in the West, with plays like *The Promise*, as he does in the Soviet Union. Arbuzov's formula for survival has been to concentrate on plays dealing with personal relations, whilst skirting commitment to larger issues. Mention should also be made of Valentin Katayev, one of the few Soviet playwrights capable of writing sustained, unforced comedy. His best piece of this kind is *Squaring the Circle* (1928), a hilarious satire on the manners and morals of the NEP period; in 1932 he made a skilful stage version of his novel *Time Forward!* Like Shvarts, Katayev wrote well for children, and his novella about the adventures of two little boys in 1905, *The Lone White Sail*, was adapted for stage and film.

The nadir of the Soviet theatre, both in dramatic content and physical extent, was the period between the end of World War II and Stalin's death. Artistically it was throttled by Zhdanov's infamous 'theses' on art and literature propounded in 1946: by 1953 the total number of theatres open in the USSR had been reduced to 250, a figure slightly lower than the total number in tsarist Russia in 1913 (in 1941 there had been 960). The grim atmosphere of fear, uncertainty and cowardice stifled any attempt at creative originality. Authors were cowed into writing feeble plays which were no more than hortatory lantern-lectures to illustrate the latest twist in the zig-zagging party line. All plays had to have 'positive' heroes, and soon it became impossible to make them positive enough: the truly 'positive' hero was never permitted a shadow of doubt or a flicker of humour. Matters reached the depth of absurdity when one of the most compliant Stalinist playwrights, Nikolay Virta, propounded the theory of 'lack of conflict'. According to this, the only possible basis of drama for a Soviet play was the struggle between the 'good' and the 'better'. The resulting plays were so abysmal that even the party was forced to disown them. By 1953 the once-great Soviet theatre presented the sorry spectacle of empty houses, frustrated producers, troupes of ageing actors and the universal sameness of ossified, sub-Stanislavskian naturalism.

In the 'interregnum' between Stalin and Khrushchev the simmering discontent in the theatre broke out in disjointed efforts to enliven the Soviet repertoire and inject a few tentative new ideas into stage production. The first swallow of this premature summer was Leonid Zorin's *The Visitors* (1954). A mediocre piece, it nevertheless contained one shocking idea – that Soviet society had produced a repulsive neo-bourgeoisie, a caste of privileged bureaucrats cocooned in power and utterly remote from the people in whose ostensible name they governed. In the uneasy political atmosphere of the time this otherwise poor play was banned after two performances. As in the other arts, the real 'thaw' came after the Twentieth Party Congress in 1956. The speed and vigour with which the theatre revived were extremely impressive, and the change in the political climate coincided with the appointment of two of the most vigorous and adventurous directors of the contemporary Soviet stage – Georgy Tovstonogov at the Gor'ky Theatre in Leningrad and Oleg Yefremov at Moscow's Contemporary Theatre. Tovstonogov has specialized in revitalizing the classics, in encouraging contemporary playwrights such as Viktor Rozov, and in trying to break down Soviet prejudice against such foreign imports as Brecht. It is an interesting and rather puzzling fact that Soviet audiences have, in general, shown a marked distaste for Brecht, despite his impeccably communist beliefs and his genius as playwright and producer. Tovstonogov has also produced a very successful play by one of the most promising of the younger Soviet playwrights, Eduard Radzinsky. This is a bitter-sweet love story, called *104 Pages about Love*, ending in the heroine's tragic death, which has proved one of the longest-running plays in the Soviet Union since the war. This alone is evidence of the advance that has been made since the dreary 'boy-meets-tractor' drama of the 1930s.

Yefremov, who has had something of a reputation as an *enfant terrible* in the post-1956 theatre, produced the first Soviet version of John Osborne's *Look Back in Anger*. Besides Aksyonov's comedy *Always on Sale*, an extremely bold satire on Soviet society, perhaps Yefremov's most striking work at the Contemporary Theatre has been the trilogy of *The Decembrists*, *The People's Will* and *The Bolsheviks*, produced for the fiftieth anniversary of the Soviet Union in 1967. Yefremov's success has been such that in 1970 he stepped into Stanislavsky's shoes as artistic director of the Moscow Art Theatre. The Taganka Theatre under Yury Lyubimov has been responsible for the Soviet theatre's nearest approach to genuinely avant-garde stage production, of which some of the most remarkable examples have been a dramatized rendering of Voznesensky's poetic cycle *Anti-Worlds*, a stage version of John Reed's reportage on the Russian revolution, *Ten Days that Shook the World*, and a vigorous if flawed attempt to give life to Yesenin's dramatic fragment *Pugachev*.

Under directors such as these the modern Soviet theatre is gradually recovering from the almost mortal blow dealt it by Stalin; but cultural policy is notoriously likely to change and no over-confident predictions should be made. All the real innovation and advance in the theatre is now being made outside the USSR, much of it in Eastern Europe, and the Soviet theatre is still slow to accept new ideas. To achieve, therefore, even a semblance of its former stature it must be granted a period of real intellectual and artistic freedom, when the undoubted Russian theatrical genius may be able to astonish the world again.

GUIDE TO FURTHER READING

REFERENCE WORKS

Teatral'naya entsiklopediya, vols. 1–5, ed. S. S. Mokul'sky *et al.* (Moscow, 1961–7), one of the best general reference books on the theatre in any language. Worldwide in scope and includes ballet, opera etc.

GENERAL HISTORIES

Istoriya sovetskogo dramaticheskogo teatra, ed. A. Anastas'yev *et al.* (Moscow, 1966–9): vol. 1, 1917–20; vol. 2, 1921–5; vol. 3, 1926–32; vol. 4, 1933–41; vol. 5, 1941–53, includes the theatrical history of the non-Russian nationalities; stodgy but comprehensive. *Theater in a Changing Europe*, ed. T. H. Dickinson (New York, 1938): part IIA: 'The Theater of Soviet Russia', by Joseph Gregor; part IIB: 'The Development of Soviet Drama', by Henry W. Dana, a well-informed, detailed history of the Soviet theatre and dramatic literature from 1917 to the mid-1930s, valuable for placing the Soviet theatre in a European context. J. Macleod, *The New Soviet Theatre* (London, 1943), an enthusiastic but uncritical account by a British observer. Marc Slonim, *Russian Theatre from the Empire to the Soviets* (London, 1961), relates the history of the Russian theatre from its origins to the mid-1950s.

CONTEMPORARY SURVEYS

Faubion Bowers, *Entertainment in Russia* (New York, 1959), a brisk but informative round-up of Soviet theatre, ballet etc. in the mid-1950s. R. Fülöp-Miller and J. Gregor, *The Russian Theatre* (London, 1930), a review of the Soviet theatre in the 1920s by a sympathetic German observer. V. Shershenevich, 'Das revolutionäre Theater', ch. in *Das heutige Russland* (Berlin, 1923), 61–72, propagandist account of the Russian theatre immediately after the revolution; useful account of Bolshevik policy on the theatre. E. I. Zamyatin, 'Le théâtre russe contemporain', *Cahiers du monde russe et soviétique*, V (Paris, 1964), 479–501.

PRODUCERS/DIRECTORS: MEMOIRS, STUDIES, THEORY

Meyerhold on Theatre, ed. E. Braun (London, 1969), a selection of Meyerhold's most important writings on theory and method, with a critical commentary. A. Gladkov, 'Meyerkhol'd govorit', in *Novy Mir*, no. 8 (Moscow, 1961), 213–35, a collection by his amanuensis of Meyerhold's observations, aperçus and reminiscences of the theatre. *Le théâtre théâtral*, ed. Nina Gourfinkel (Paris, 1963), another selection of Meyerhold's writings, complementary to Braun cited above. N. Gorchakov, *The Vakhtangov School of Stage Art* (Moscow, n.d.), a detailed account of Vakhtangov's directional method by a former pupil. V. N. Nemirovich-Danchenko, *My life in the Russian Theatre* (New York, 1936), memoirs of the celebrated co-founder of the Moscow Art Theatre. A. M. Ripellino, *Il trucco e l'anima: i maestri della regia nel teatro russo del novecento* (Turin, 1965), the only thorough study of the work of the great Soviet directors of the 1920s. K. S. Stanislavsky, *Moya zhizn' v iskusstve* (Moscow, 1962), Stanislavsky's theatrical autobiography; this edition contains a useful introduction by A. D. Volkova. *Idem, An Actor Prepares* (New York, n.d.), the classic textbook of Stanislavsky's 'Method'. The English translation is cited as the Russian edition is extremely rare,

GUIDE TO FURTHER READING

G. A. Tovstonogov, *O professii rezhissyora* (Moscow, 1965), the theory and practice of a leading modern Soviet director.

ON PLAYS AND PLAYWRIGHTS

A. O. Boguslavsky and V. A. Diev, *Russkaya sovetskaya dramaturgiya*, vols. 1–3 (Moscow, 1965), a biased but quite informative work on Soviet dramatic literature from 1936 to 1945. A. M. Ripellino, *Majakovskij e il teatro russo d'avanguardia* (Turin, 1959), a study of the theatre and playwrights of the 1920s, in particular of the collaboration between Mayakovsky and Meyerhold. S. E. Roberts, *Soviet Historical Drama* (The Hague, 1965). Ye. I. Polyakova, *Teatr i dramuturg* (Moscow, 1959), a general survey of Soviet playwriting.

INDEX

INDEX

Babel', Isaak, 191, 193, 196, 208, 280–1; *The Chekist*, 281; *Mariya*, 272, 281; *Red Cavalry*, 191; *Sunset*, 281
Bagritsky, Eduard, 187, 193
Bakst, L. S., 52, 257
balagany, 250–1, 260
Baldwin I, King of Jerusalem, 74
Bal'mont, Konstantin, 165
Baltic languages, 2, 13, 29
Balto-Slavonic, 2, 11, 29
Baratynsky (Boratynsky), Yevgeny, 141, 164
Barkov, T., 250
Barlaam and Josaphat, 60
baroque, 111–18, 121–2
Barthélemy, J.-J., 120
Basil of Caeserea, St, 58
Batu, Tatar ruler, 81, 98
Batyushkov, Konstantin, 134, 135
Baudelaire, C., 149, 164
Baumgarten, von, 241
Beaumarchais, P.-A. de: *Eugénie*, 240
Belinsky, Visarion, 120, 146–7, 151, 259
Bellini, V.: *I Puritani*, 262
Belmonte, theatre manager, 240
Belorussian, Bielorussian, Byelo-russian, *see* White Russian
Belov, Vasily, 201
Bely, Andrey, 167–8, 185, 189, 192; *Kotik Letayev*, 168; *Petersburg*, 168
Benois, Alexandre, 52, 251, 257
Berg, producer, 250, 251
Berggol'ts, Ol'ga, 207
Bergson, Henri, 195
Bestuzhev-Marlinsky, Aleksandr, 143
Bibikov, Vasily, 243
Bilibin, I. Ya., 52
biography: secular, 81–2, 93; ecclesiastical, *see* hagiography
'bio-mechanics', 277
birch-bark texts, 3–4, 35, 44–5, 46
Bitov, Andrey, 201
Blok, Aleksandr, 147, 164, 166, 167–8, 172, 206; and the October Revolution, 185, 189–90; *Retribution*, 210; *The Twelve*, 167, 189
Boccaccio, G.: *Decameron*, 101
Bocharov, M. I., 256
Bogdanovich, Ippolit, 127; *Dushen'ka*, 127
Bogomilism, 59–60
Bol'shoy Theatre, 242, 247, 257, 260
Bol'shoy Kamennyy Theatre, 243, 261
Bol'shoy Petrovsky Theatre, 260, 262
Book of Chronicles, The, 100

Book of the Holy Men, The, 59
Book of Ranks of the Tsars' Genealogy, 98
Boratynsky, Yevgeny, *see* Baratynsky
Boris, St, son of Vladimir I, 65–7
Boris Godunov, Tsar, 99–100
Boyan, bard, 79
Brecht, Berthold, 274, 276, 283
Brezhnev, L. I., 199
Brodsky, Iosif, 206
Bryansky, Ya. G., 253–4
Bryusov, Valery, 164, 165, 170, 185; *The Altar of Victory*, 165; *The Fiery Angel*, 165; *The Scales*, 165
Bukharin, N. I., 188, 193
Bulgakov, Mikhail, 191, 207–8, 279; *Black Snow*, 207–8; *The Days of the Turbins*, 279; *Don Quixote*, 179; *Flight*, 279; *The Master and Margarita*, 207, 209; *Molière*, 279; *The Purple Island*, 279; *Pushkin*, 279; *Zoë's Apartment*, 279
Bulgaria, 13, 22; influence on Russian literature, 29, 35, 42, 56–7, 59–60, 62, 91; translated literature from, 57, 61, 92
Bulgarian language, 1, 29, 35, 43
Bulgarin, Faddey, 143
Bunin, Ivan, 169, 190; *The Gentleman from San Francisco*, 169
Bürger, G. A., 134
Burgi, R., 116
Burtsov, Vasily Fyodorovich, 49
Bykov, Vasil', 202
byliny, 75–9, 81
Byron, Lord, 135, 137, 138, 142, 143
Byzantium: biography, 68–9, 81–2; 'Byzantine heritage', 79, 95; influence on Russian literature, 56–7, 58–61, 64–5, 71–2; Russian attacks on, 42; writing, 45

Canoppi, Antonio, 255–6
Cantacuzene, Kassandra, 114
Catherine II, Empress, 116, 118, 120, 121, 123–6, 239–43, 262
censorship, 50–3, 125; Soviet, 188, 193, 203, 209–11, 271–2, 279; state, of theatre, 248, 253, 257–60, 263; *see also* Stalin, J. V.
Cephalus and Procris, 236
Chaadayev, Pyotr, 146
chapbooks and broadsheets, 51
Chasovnik (Book of Hours), 48
Chaykovsky (Tchaikovsky), P. I., 261
Chekhonin, S. V., 53
Chekhov, Anton, 143, 147–8, 161–3,

INDEX

169, 259, 264, 273; language of, 162; *The Cherry Orchard*, 163, 264; *The Duel*, 162; *Ivanov*, 264; *My Life*, 162; *The Seagull*, 163, 264; *The Steppe*, 162; *The Three Sisters*, 163, 264; *Uncle Vanya*, 163, 264
Chernyshevsky, Nikolay, 151; *What is to be Done?*, 151
Chet'i Minei, 59, 98, 112
Chizhinsky, Stefan, 232
Choeroboscus, George, 58
Christianity, and development of medieval Russian literature, 29, 41, 42, 56, 57–9, 63–4, 65–9, 71–2
chronicles, 60–1, 69–71, 80, 90–2, 97–8; of Constantine Manasses, 91–2; of George the Monk (Hamartolos), 61, 70, 90, 93; of John Malalas, 61, 70; of John Zonaras, 91–2; Lvov Chronicles, 98; Moscow Chronicles, 92, 98; Novgorod Chronicles, 17, 97; of the Principality of Tver', 91, 94; Pskov Chronicles, 97; *see also* Primary Chronicle
Chukovskaya, Lidiya, 211
Chukovsky, Korney, 210
Chulkov, Mikhail, 124, 126–7; *Peresmeshnik*, 126; *Prigozhaya povarikha*, 126–7
Church Slavonic, 4, 8, 9, 10, 13, 16–17, 19–23, 24, 25, 27, 28, 35, 36–8, 41, 66, 71, 122, 133, 136; function in the Russian literary language, 66, 71, 113, 122, 129, 138
Ciutti, theatre manager, 240
Clement Smolyatich, 65
Cohen, J. M., 112
cokan'je, 34
Colonne, Guido delle, 95, 100
Comedy about Tsar Maximilian and his recalcitrant son Adolph, The, 250
Common Slavonic, 1–3, 4–8, 11–12, 13–14, 16–18, 20, 22–3, 25–7
Congresses, Communist Party: Twentieth (1956), 198, 200, 283; Twenty-third (1966), 202
Congresses of Writers: First (1934), 196; Third (1959), 198
Constantine VII Porphyrogenitus, Emperor, 5
Constantine IX Monomachus, Emperor, 72
constructivism, 187, 195, 276–7
Contemporary Theatre, Moscow, 283
Corneille, Pierre, 119, 236
Cosmas Indicopleustes, 60

Cyril, Bishop of Turov, 65
Cyril, St: influence on medieval literature, 56–7, 58, 59; liturgical language of, 29; and written language, 41–3
Cyril of Scythopolis, 68
Cyrillic, *see* alphabet

Daniel, Abbot, 74–5
Daniel, Prince of Galicia, 82
Daniel the Prisoner, 'Supplication of', 79–80
Daniel', Yuly (Nikolay Arzhak), 211; *Atonement*, 211; *This is Moscow Speaking*, 211
Daniil, Metropolitan, 97, 98
Dargomyzhshky, 261
Dashkov, Princess, Ye. R., 126
Davydov, Denis, 135
De administrando imperio, 5
Decembrists, 51, 252
Defoe, Daniel, 127
Del'vig, Baron Anton, 116, 140, 143
Derzhavin, Gavriil, 121–2, 133, 141; *Ode on the Occasion . . .*, 121; *Ode to Felitsa . . .*, 121
Destouches, Philippe, 236
Destruction of Babylon, The, 235
Diaghilev, S., 257
dialects, 9–10, 25, 32–5
Digenis Akritas, 60
Dimitri Donskoy, Prince, 92–3
Dimitri Tolmach (Gerasimov), 97
Dimitri Tuptalo, St, of Rostov, 112–13, 237
Dispute between Life and Death, The, 95
Dmitrevskoy, I., 237, 240–2, 253–4
Dmitriyev, Ivan, 127
Dobrolyubov, N. A., 151
Dobrynya Nikitich, 76
Dobuzhinsky, Mstislav, 257
Domostroy, 12, 36, 98
Dorosh, Yefim, 201
Dostoyevsky, Fyodor, 142, 144, 148, 153, 157–9, 161, 165, 191; language, 159; new techniques in novel, 157–8; philosophy of, 157–9; *The Brothers Karamazov*, 159; *Crime and Punishment*, 159; *The Double*, 158; *The Idiot*, 159, 280; *The Landlady*, 158; *Notes from the House of the Dead*, 158; *Notes from the Underground*, 158–9; *Poor Folk*, 158; *The Possessed*, 159; *Mr Prokharchin*, 158; *A Raw Youth*, 159; *White Nights*, 158

289

INDEX

Dubov, Nikolay, 201
Dudintsev, Vladimir: *Not by Bread Alone*, 198, 200
dukhovnyye stikhi, 60
Dutch influence on Russian language, 31

East Slavonic, 1–2, 4–7, 9, 13, 21, 37–8; writing, 42–3, 47
egofuturism, 173
Ehrenburg, Il'ya, 190, 194, 202; *Julio Jurenito*, 190; *Second Day*, 194, 200; *The Thaw*, 198, 200
Elizabeth, Empress, 115, 118, 123, 234–9
Emin, Fyodor, 124, 126; *History of Russia*, 126; *Letters of Ernest and Doravra*, 126
Enchanted School, The, 242
Engels (scenic artist), 232
English influence: on literature, 123; on theatre, 119, 241, 242–3
Epiphany Premudry, 91
Epistle of Spiridon-Savva, 95
Epistle to Ivan Vasil'yevich, 96
Esther and Ahasuerus, 232
Euchologion, 58
Eulogy of Prince Boris Aleksandrovich, The, 94
expressionism, 273–5, 276–8

fables, 119, 127–8
Fadeyev, Aleksandr, 191–2, 195, 196; *Rout*, 192
Falconet, E., 125
Favorsky, V. A., 53
Fedin, Konstantin, 186, 197
Fedotova, G. N., 261
Fellini, Federico, 202
'fellow-travellers', 189–90, 192, 194–5, 202
Fénelon, François de, 116
Feodor, Bishop of Tver', 91
Fet, Afanasy, 152
Feuerbach, Ludwig, 147
Fichte, J. G., 147
Fielding, Henry, 123
Filofey of Pskov, monk, 96
Firdousi, Persian poet, 100
Fisher, Mr, 241
Flaubert, Gustave, 149
Fofanov, Konstantin, 164
Foma, monk, 94
Fonvizin, Denis, 119–21, 241; *The Brigadier*, 120; *An Epistle to My Servants...*, 120; *On the Freedom of the French Aristocracy*, 120; *An*

Honest People's Friend, 120; *Joseph*, 120; *Korion*, 119; *Lisitsa-Koznodey*, 120; *The Loves of Charita and Polydore*, 120; *Nedorosl'*, 120, 249; *The Nobility of Commerce...*, 120; *A Panegyric Upon Marcus Aurelius*, 120; *Sydney*, 120
formalism, 186–7, 195, 196, 205
Foundling Hospital, Moscow, 240–2, 247
Frederick II, King of Prussia, 121
Free Knipper Theatre, 241–2
Free Society of the Admirers of Russian Belles-Letters, Sciences and the Arts, The, 253
Freemasonry, 123, 124
French influence: on language, 31, 136, 138; on literature, 115, 116, 118, 119, 120, 136–7, 141, 150, 164–6, 171; on theatre, 119, 120, 236–7, 241; impact of French Revolution, 124
Funtusov, K., 246
Fürst, Otto, 233–4
futurism, 171–3, 185, 187–8, 206, 266, 277
Fyodor, Tsar, 233
Fyodorov, décor-master, 256
Fyodorov, V. M., 251; *Liza, or the Consequence of Pride and Seduction*, 251; *Love and Virtue*, 251

Gabo, Naum, 187, 276
Galician and Volhynian Chronicle, 82
Galich, Aleksandr, 207
Galuppi, Baldassare, 242; *La Calamità dei Cuori*, 238
Garshin, Vsevolod, 161; *Attalea Princeps*, 161; *Four Days*, 161; *Nadezhda Nikolayevna*, 161; *What Never Was*, 161
Gastev, Aleksey, 189
Gel'tser, A. F., 256
Genghis Khan, 79–80
Gerasimov, Mikhail, 189
German influence: on Russian language, 30, 31–2; on literature, 95, 101, 251; on theatre, 119, 232, 234–5, 241
Gippius, Zinaida, 166
Gladilin, Anatoly, 201
Glagolitic, *see* alphabet
Gleb, St, son of Vladimir I, 65–7
Glinka, S. N., 249
Gnedich, N. I., 116
Gnyozdovo inscription, 41–2

290

INDEX

Mel'nikov, Pavel (Andrey Pechersky), 150; *In the Woods*, 150; *On the Mountains*, 150
Menshutin, A., 211
Mercator, Nicholas, 95
Merezhovsky, Dmitry, 165, 190; *Leonardo da Vinci*, 165
Merzlyakov, A. F., 119
Methodius, St, 56–7, 58, 59
Mey, L., 151
Meyerhold, V. E., 189, 190, 196, 258, 265–6, 273–4, 276, 277–8
Mikhail, of the Klopsky Monastery, 97
Mikhail Aleksandrovich, Prince of Tver', 94
Mikhail Romanov, Tsar, 231
Mikhail Yaroslavich, Prince of Tver', 90
Mikhaylovsky Theatre, St Petersburg, 261
Mikhoels, Solomon, 281
Miloslavsky, I. M., 233
Minerva Triumphant, 239–40
Mir iskusstva school, 52–3, 256
Misyur' Munekhin, M. G., 96
Mitrokhin, D. I., 53
Mnemosyne, 143
Mochalov, P. S., 260
Molière, 133, 236; *Le Médecin malgré lui*, 233
Monastery of the Caves, Kiev, 66–70, 74
Mongol conquest: influence on language, 30, 38; influence on literature, 82, 90; literature concerning, 80–1
Moore, Thomas, 135
Mordvinian language, 11
Morits, Yunna, 206
Moscow: dialect of, 9, 10, 27, 34–5, printing, 48–50, writing, 46–7; literature of, 63, 92–102
Moscow Art Theatre, 163, 257, 263–5, 271, 273–5, 278–9, 281, 283
Moscow Chamber Theatre, 266, 275–6, 279
Moscow Imperial Theatre, 260
Moscow Messenger, 143
Moscow News, 238
Moscow Printing House, 49
Moscow State Troupe, 247
Moscow Telegraph, 143
Moscow the Third Rome, theory of, 96
Moscow University, 122, 124, 238–9, 240–1
Moskvin, Ivan, 265

Mossovet Theatre, Moscow, 275
Mozhayev, B., 201
Mstislav, son of Vladimir Monomakh, 73
Mstislavets, Pyotr Timofeyev, 48
Mstislavova gramota (c. 1130), 35
Mukhin, G., 256
Müller, Ludolf, 66
Murav'yov, M. N., 119
Murom, 98, 100
Musina-Pushkina, Agrafena, 238
Musorgsky, M. P., 258, 261

Nadson, Semyon, 164
Nagibin, Yury, 201, 211
Napravnik, E. F., 261
Narezhny, Vasily, 143
Narodnyy Teatr, 234–5
Naryshkin, S., 121
nasal vowels, 4–5
Natal'ya Alekseyevna, sister of Peter I, 233–4
naturalism, 150, 156–7, 161, 168–9, 264–6, 273
Nekrasov, Nikolay, 151, 199, 251, 259; *Who Lives Well in Russia?*, 151
Nekrasov, Viktor, 201
Nemirovich-Danchenko, Vladimir, 207, 262–3, 264, 273
neo-classicism, 118–19, 134, 136, 140, 255
Nestor, monk, 66–8, 70
Nestor Iskander, 95
New Tale of the Most Glorious Russian Tsardom, 100
New Theatre, St Petersburg, 247, 254, 261
newspapers, 50–2
Nichevoki, 187
Nicholas I, Emperor, 51, 191, 257, 260
Nietzsche, Friedrich, 170, 171
Nikol'sky, N. K., 69
Nikonian Illustrated Compilation, 98
Nil Sorsky, 96
Nivinsky, I. I., 275
Norse influence on Russian language, 7, 29–30
novel: early forms, 100, 126–7, 139–40; historical, 143, 165; new techniques, 157–8; picaresque, adventure, 143, 207; psychological, 142–3, 153–6, 158, 163; Soviet, 192–3, 197
Novikov, Nikolay, 51, 122–4, 128; *Ancient Russian Library*, 123; *The Drone*, 122, 124; *Historical Dictionary*, 122; *The Medley*, 124; *Morning Light*, 123; *Moscow Gazette*, 123;

294

INDEX

South Slavonic languages, 1, 7;
writing, 45
Southey, Robert, 135
Spiridon-Savva, Epistle of, 95
Splavsky, Jan, 233
Staden, von, Russian ambassador,
232
Staehlin, J. von, 238
Stalin, J. V., 185, 189–91, 194–9, 200–
4, 205, 207, 208–9, 211; and theatre,
277, 278, 279–83; *see also* censor-
ship; literature, Soviet Russian
Stanislavsky, Konstantin, 163, 207,
262–4, 273, 279, 280, 283; 'system',
208, 265, 278–9
State Academic Maly Opera Theatre,
261
State Jewish Theatre, 281
Stefan, St, of Perm', 91
Stefan Lazarević, Despot of Serbia, 92
Stefan of Novgorod, 91
Stefanit and Ikhnilat, 92
Steiner, Rudolf, 168
Sterne, Laurence, 123, 125, 128, 143
Stoglav, 98
Story of Mamay's Battle, 92–3
Strindberg, A.: *Erik XIV*, 274
Sudeykin, S., 257
Sukhovo-Kobylin, Aleksandr, 152,
255
Sumarokov, Aleksandr, 118–19, 122,
127, 143, 236–8, 240–1, 249, 253;
Alcestis, 118; *Artistona*, 118;
Cephalus and Procris, 118; *Hamlet*,
118; *Khorev*, 118, 236; *The
Miracles*, 118; *Semira*, 118; *Sinav
and Truvor*, 118, 236, 240; *Treso-
tinius*, 118; *The Vain Squabble*, 118;
Yaropolk and Demiza, 118
'Supplication of Daniel the Prisoner',
79–80
Surkov, Aleksey, 197
Suvorin, A. S., 52
Svyatopolk, Prince of Kiev, 65
Svyatoslav II, Prince of Kiev, 58, 59
Svyatoslav III, Prince of Kiev, 78
Swift, Jonathan, 123
Sylvester, priest, 98
symbolism, 147, 163–70, 98, 185, 206,
265–6, 277
Symeon, Tsar of Bulgaria, 57
Synaxarion, 59
Syomin, Vitaly, 201
Sytin, I. P., 52

Taganka Theatre, 283
Tairov, A. Ya., 273–4, 275–6, 277, 279

*Tale of the Attack of Stefan Batory
on Pskov*, 99
*Tale of the Battle of the Grand Prince
Dimitri Donskoy*, 93
Tale of the Battle on the River Kalka,
80–1
Tale of Dracula, 95
Tale of Father Terenty's Vision, 99
Tale of Frol Skobeyev, 100
Tale of Grief and Ill-Luck, 100
Tale of the Indian Kingdom, 91
*Tale of Karp Sutulov and his Very
Wise Wife*, 100–1
*Tale of the Life and Demise of the
Grand Prince Dimitri Ivanovich,
Tsar of Russia*, 93
Tale of Merkury, 98
*Tale of the Most Glorious Russian
Tsardom*, 100
Tale of the Origin of Tobacco, 100
*Tale and Passion and Eulogy of the
Holy Martyrs Boris and Gleb*, 66–7
Tale of Prince Dovmont, 91
Tale of the Princes of Vladimir,
95
Tale of Pyotr and Fevroniya, 98
Tale of the Ruin of the Russian Land,
82
Tale of the Ruin of Ryazan', 81
Tale of Savva Grudtsyn, 100
Tale of Shakhansha's Twelve Dreams,
91
Tale of Shchil, 97
Tale of Shevkal, 90
Tale of 1606, 99
Tale of Solomoniya the Possessed, 100
Tale of the Taking of Constantinople,
95
*Tale of the Taking of Moscow by
Tokhtamysh*, 93
*Tale of the Taking of Pskov by the
Grand Prince Vasily III*, 97
Tale of Temir Aksak, 93–4
Tale of the White Cowl, 97
Tale of Yersh Yershovich, 101
Tale of Yeruslan Lazarevich, The,
100
Tales of Troy, 92, 95
Tallemant, Paul, 116
Tamirov, Akim, 273
Taneyev, S. I., 261
Tarasy, *Vision of*, 97
Tarkovsky, Arseny, 207
Tasso, T., 135
Tatar invasion, 80–1
Tatishchev, V. N., 114
Tatlin, Vladimir, 276

298

INDEX

Vasily, Bishop of Novgorod, 91
Vasily, icon-painter, 99
Vasily, I, Grand Prince, 94
Vasily III, Grand Prince, 95, 96
Vasily IV (Shuysky), Tsar, 99
Vasnetsov, V., 256
Vassian (Prince Patrikeyev), 96–7
Vel'tman, Aleksandr, 143
Venevitinov, Dmitry, 141
Verdi, G., 261
Veresayev, V. V., 185
Verlaine, Paul, 166
Vershigora, Pyotr: *People with a Clear Conscience*, 197
Verstovsky, A. N., 260
Veryovkin, M. I., 241
Vinokurov, Yevgeny, 206
Virgil: *Aenid*, 118
Virta, Nikolay, 282
Vishnevsky, Vsevolod: *First Cavalry Army*, 279; *An Optimistic Tragedy*, 276, 279–80; *Unforgettable 1919*, 280
Vitus, St, 59
Vladimir I, Prince of Kiev, 42, 65, 75; conversion of, 35, 41–2, 56, 64–5, 70; and development of literature, 57, 70
Vladimir Monomakh, Prince of Kiev, 71–4, 75, 82; *Instruction*, 71, 72–3
Vladimir Polychron, 92, 93
Vladimov, Georgy, 201
Vokzal, 242
Volkov, Fyodor, 237, 238
Volkov, Gavrila, 237
Voloshin, Maksimilian, 171
Voltaire, 119, 127, 137–8, 147; *Alzire*, 119; *Henriade*, 127
Vorob'yov, M. S., 248
Voronsky, Aleksandr, 194–5
Vorontsov, Count Roman, 240
Voynovich, Vladimir, 201, 202
Voznesensky, Andrey, 205–6, 209; *Anti-Worlds*, 283
Vsevolod, prince, 72–3
Vsevolozhsky, N. S., 51
Vsyakaya vsyachina, see *Variety Titbits*
vyaz', 45–7, 48
Vyazemsky, Prince Pyotr, 121, 134, 140

Wagner, R., 261
Wenceslas, St, Duke of Bohemia, 59, 66

'West Russian', 2, 38
West Slavonic languages, 1, 6–7
'Westerners', 146, 200
Wetstein, Heinrich, 49
White Russian, 1–2, 9–11, 21, 25, 27, 34, 38, 63
Worth, Gerta H., 31

Xenia, mother of Prince Mikhail Yaroslavich, 90

Yakovlev, A. S., 253–4
Yaroslav, Prince of Kiev, 57, 63–4, 70, 72
Yashin, Aleksandr, 198, 200–1
Yavorsky, Stefan, Metropolitan, 112–13
Yazykov, Nikolay, 140
Yefremov, Oleg, 283
Yegorov, V. Ye., 251
Yelagin, Ivan, 243
Yermolay Erazm, 99
Yermolova, M. N., 258, 261
Yesenin, Sergey, 171, 187, 189–90, 193, 205; *Pugachev*, 283
Yesipov, Pavel, 249
Yevreinov, N. N., 265; *The Storming of the Winter Palace*, 273
Yevtushenko, Yevgeny, 205–6, 212
Yulianiya Lazarevskaya, 100
Yury, Prince of Moscow, 90
Yuzhin, A. I., 261

Zabolotsky, Nikolay, 193–4, 208
Zadonshchina, 93
Zagoskin, Mikhail, 143, 252, 260
Zalygin, S., 201
Zamyatin, Yevgeny, 186, 195–6, 208, 280–1; *The African Guest*, 281; *Attila*, 281; *The Fires of San Domingo*, 280–1; *The Flea*, 280; *We*, 195
Zavadsky, Yury, 275
Zhdanov, A. A., 197, 282
Zhemchuzhnikov, Aleksey, *and* Zhemchuzhnikov, Vladimir 'Koz'ma Prutkov'), 152, 164
Zhukovsky, V. A., 116, 134, 142
Zlatostruy (sermons of John Chrysostom), 58
Znamenka Theatre, 241, 242
Zorin, Leonid: *The Visitors*, 282
Zoshchenko, Mikhail, 186, 191, 208
Zosima of Solovki, 97
Zotov, P. M., 257

300